THE ECONOMICS OF COMPUTERS

Costs, Benefits, Policies, and Strategies

C. C. GOTLIEB

University of Toronto, Canada

PRENTICE-HALL, INC., Englewood Cliffs, New Jersey 07632

Library of Congress Cataloging in Publication Data

Gotlieb, C. C. (date)
  The economics of computers.

  Bibliography: p.
  Includes index.
  1. Automation. 2. Computers. 3. Automation—
Cost effectiveness. 4. Computers—Cost effectiveness.
I. Title.
HC79.A9G67 1984   658.5′14   84-26375
ISBN 0-13-224452-7

Editorial/production supervision: *Lynn Frankel*
Cover design: *20/20 Services Inc.*
Manufacturing buyer: *Gordon Osbourne*

Printed in the United States of America

10 9 8 7 6 5 4 3 2 1

ISBN 0-13-224452-7 01

Prentice-Hall International, Inc., *London*
Prentice-Hall of Australia Pty. Limited, *Sydney*
Editora Prentice-Hall do Brasil, Ltda., *Rio de Janeiro*
Prentice-Hall Canada Inc., *Toronto*
Prentice-Hall Hispanoamericana, S.A., *Mexico*
Prentice-Hall of India Private Limited, *New Delhi*
Prentice-Hall of Japan, Inc., *Tokyo*
Prentice-Hall of Southeast Asia Pte. Ltd., *Singapore*
Whitehall Books Limited, *Wellington, New Zealand*

To Phyllis

Contents

PART IV NATIONAL POLICIES FOR COMPUTERS AND COMMUNICATIONS 273

Preface

The computer industry, or in its wider form, the computer/communications industry, is one of the great driving engines of current world economy. Yet courses on computer technology, information technology, or the economics of computers (as distinct from the theory of computing, and applications of computers) are practically nonexistent either in computer science or management science university programs. This in spite of the fact that the first book called *The Economics of Computers* was written by Sharpe in 1969, and subsequently there appeared *The Economics of Informatics,* edited by Freelink (1975), and *The Economics of Information Processing,* edited by Goldberg and Lorin (1982). One main reason for the lack of formal courses is that there is no well-defined body of material which can be packaged as a single offering. The earlier books are out of date or, written in the form of a collection of articles by different authors, are not coherent enough to serve as a textbook. The present work attempts to overcome these shortcomings.

There are good reasons why texts for a course on the economics of computers, or the economics of information technology, have been slow to emerge. The scope of the subject is enormous. The economics of computers as seen by a user is very different from the economics seen by a hardware manufacturer or the computer sector of the national economy. My way of dealing with this diversity has been to divide the book into four distinct but interrelated sections, each written from a different viewpoint. Another aspect of the subject's range is that there is both a theoretical side, grounded in general economic theory, and a practical side, of interest to users and practitioners. The literature on economic theory as applied to computers is sparse (although there is a *very* wide body of writing on the related subject of telecommunications); the literature of a descriptive, qualitative nature about the pragmatics of computer economics is overwhelming. In different places (e.g., Chapter 5 and Section 9.3) I have attempted to identify what theoretical basis there is, and generally have sought to emphasize the quantitative aspects of the subject. Still another difficulty arises from the extremely rapid pace of technological development and of structural change in the industry. This has meant that no sooner is a description of some part of the industry put to paper than it becomes out of date. But the process of growth has been going on over thirty years, and it becomes increasingly urgent to apply perspective and to discern patterns of change. The economics of computers, like any branch of economics, is accompanied by a bewildering array of statistics, tables, and charts which are constantly appearing in trade journals, government periodicals, consultants' reports, and the everyday press. From these often inconsistent figures it is necessary to derive meaningful information about trends. In this respect I must acknowledge my debt to Montgomery Phister for his remarkable work, *Data Processing Technology and Economics*. To say that it is a mine of information is an understatement. There are data on almost every conceivable aspect of computer technology, and many of the tables and charts are accompanied by highly illuminating explanations. Phister's work has made the present text easier to write, and its availability is a great help in designing the problems and exercises that should accompany a course on the economics of computers.

One practice regarding data that involve currency needs justification. It is usual in monographs to express all currencies in the same unit, most frequently the U.S. dollar. Also, in tables very often amounts are adjusted for inflation and given in constant dollars for some year. In Part IV there are considerable data in the form of currencies, and I have chosen to leave these exactly as given in the source from which the data were taken. This has sometimes meant that even in the same paragraph some figures are given in U.S. dollars and others in pound sterling, or in Japanese yen. During recent years especially, currency fluctuations have been relatively large, and to do a proper conversion it would be necessary to know not only the year in which the original source appeared, but also the month, information which is usually not available. Converting to a common currency would not improve the accuracy of the data. Usually, figures are quoted for several years and the quantity of principal interest is the growth rate, which, of course, is independent of exchange rates.

The present work has developed out of notes prepared while teaching the course over a period of five years at the University of Toronto and one semester at the University of California, Berkeley. In all cases the students have been in their senior years, drawn from a variety of backgrounds, principally management science, computer science, and engineering. But since the text is intended as an introduction for a student body which has a wide diversity of backgrounds, some elementary material, such as that on determining the throughput of a computer, or evaluating the costs and benefits of a project, has been included. Prerequisites for the course have included courses on computer organization and programming (although the exercises do not require programs to be written) as well as a general course on economics. Because of the absence of texts, good library backup services in the form of collected articles have been essential, and books like Phister's, and subscription services of the type provided by Auerbach and Datapro, are important sources of technical data needed for problems.

I would like to thank students, colleagues, and others who have helped in the preparation of the manuscript. Stephen Richardson, Randy Packham, Siobhan Baker, Teoh Teik Lin, Vincent Fung, have pointed out errors and Jeffrey Watts provided helpful comments. Discussions with Professor William Kahan at U.C. Berkeley on some of the numerical procedures have been useful. Much of the last section of the book is based on earlier work done in collaboration with Dr. Zavis Zeman. Discussions with Mark Hepworth and Dr. Peter Robinson of the Department of Communications, Ottawa, about transborder data flows, have been rewarding, as have been those with Hudson Janisch and Darrell Parsons about telecommunication policy. I am indebted to Uriel Domb for the data in Table 8.3, and to John Bennett who, through his papers and correspondence, has raised many interesting questions. The response of Dr. M. Melkanoff and UCLA to preliminary versions of the manuscript has been an important encouragement. Stephanie Johnston has been a constant help in the library searches, which have extended over years. Vicky Shum added Unix to her repertoire of text-processing languages to cope with the variety of equations and tables in the manuscript. Finally, to my dear wife Phyllis, go special thanks for encouraging me to keep writing during the many occasions when I seemed to be running in place on a fast-moving escalator.

CALVIN GOTLIEB

Part I

THE SERVICE CENTER

This first section is concerned with management's attempt to obtain the most value for money spent on computing. Only certain important aspects are treated. Management problems in drawing up contracts with vendors and customers, in guaranteeing security of access to files or to the installation site, or in training personnel are not considered here, even though such activities are also important. The problems that are considered have been selected because they are of historical interest, and for them there is a significant body of literature indicating how quantitative measures can be applied to answer recurring questions.

1

Computer
Performance

To be sure that a computer is being used efficiently, it is necessary to assess its actual and potential performance. Such assessments are needed when:

- Comparing systems so as to make a choice
- Installing a new system to determine whether it lives up to expectations
- Changing or tuning a system to determine whether it is operating at greatest capacity
- Prices are being established to ensure that rates will be competitive and yet guarantee cost recovery

Important as it is to evaluate computer performance, it is surprisingly difficult to do so, to the point where computing as a professional activity has been criticized because the lack of standards for measuring systems undermines the ability to establish norms for professional competence. The difficulty is that there are so many aspects to performance. Some of these aspects (e.g., cost, throughput capacity, response time, and reliability) are easily expressed in quantitative terms; others (e.g., the quantity and quality of the hardware and software facilities available, the compatibility with current and future systems, and the ease of operation) are difficult to gauge. Any attempt to describe overall performance by a single number, or even a small set of numbers, is necessarily based on arbitrary assumptions about the relative importance of the various aspects. We shall concentrate here on some of the more obvious features: speed, cost, system throughput, and response time. Simple as these are, it is still not easy to come up with accepted measures on which to base comparisons. To take an example, when comparing the cost of computer systems, one somehow has to compare "equivalent" systems—which is not easy to do in view of the numerous ways in which different components can be combined to assemble a configuration. What is usually done is to suggest some "standard" configuration of a manufacturer's model, and the whole range of models might be classified into three groups, designated as "small," "medium-sized," and "large." These are vague groupings, but to complicate things further they do not remain constant as new systems develop. The large systems of one generation become the medium-sized or even the small systems of a later generation, as the central processing unit (CPU) speed and memory capacity increase. Thus, although the price of a particular computer is definite, the cost of a *system* is not well defined.

Attempts to rate computer systems by calculating a figure of merit (FOM), based primarily on the operating speed of selected components, go back to the early 1960s. As computers grew more complex it was recognized that these first rating schemes were too simple. More complicated measures were proposed, but even these proved inadequate as time sharing, multiprocessing, and virtual memories evolved. Three techniques are commonly used to evaluate system performance:

1. Calculate a single FOM from component ratings.
2. Adopt a standard work load, variously referred to as a kernel, a synthetic job stream, or a benchmark, and determine a performance measure by observing how the system behaves with this work load.
3. Construct a model of the system, using simulation, analytical tools, or measurements taken on the system, and describe the performance in terms of the behavior of this model.

The second technique is used widely in providing system specifications for contract bidding. Increasingly, the third technique is gaining acceptance as the most useful way of describing performance, especially if one of the principal goals is to predict how job throughput will change when the system is altered. The first technique is recognized as being simplistic, but it is still used to express very basic measures for the operating speed of machines. So in spite of the changes that have taken place in ideas on how computer performance should be expressed and measured, it is useful to start by seeing how the simple ratings were first computed.

1.1 FIGURES OF MERIT

For the early commercial computers of the 1950s the CPU was the most expensive component. CPU speed was the critical factor in determining the time taken to solve a problem and the cost of computation. Hence the first measures for computer performance were based on the execution times required to do arithmetic operations. Usually, a weighted time was calculated, the weighting factors being determined from observations on the relative frequencies of instruction-type occurrences in certain classes of problems. Table 1.1 shows two sets of weights suggested by Arbuckle (1966) and Smith (1968). Other weighting sets have been proposed by Raichelson and Collins,* Solomon (1966), Knight (1968), and Gibson.†

Given the times required to execute the instructions of Table 1.1 on any particular computer, it is easy enough to calculate an FOM for the machine. But this figure takes no account of factors such as memory access time, word size, or input/output speeds, and a more complex FOM was sought to take these variations into account. The most ambitious attempt to define an FOM derived

TABLE 1.1 INSTRUCTIONAL WEIGHTS FOR COMPUTING FIGURE OF MERIT

Instruction Type	Weight	
	Arbuckle[a]	Smith[b]
Data transfer	0.285	0.193
Add/subtract		
Fixed		0.104
Floating	0.095	0.075
Multiply		
Fixed		0.006
Floating	0.056	0.061
Divide		
Fixed		
Floating	0.020	
Logic		0.047
Branch		
Conditional	0.132	0.096
Unconditional		0.085
Index	0.225	0.334
Miscellaneous	0.187	
Total	1.000	1.001

[a]R. A. Arbuckle, "Computer Analysis and Thruput Evaluation," *Comput. Autom.,* 15, no. 1 (January 1966), 12–15. These are for a "scientific" mix of problems using floating-point arithmetic.

[b]J. M. Smith, "A Review and Comparison of Certain Methods of Computer Performance Evaluation," *Comput. Bull.,* May 1968, 13–18.

*E. Raichelson and G. Collins, "A Method for Comparing the Internal Operating Speeds of Computers," *Commun. ACM,* 7, no. 5 (May 1964), 309–10.

†J. C. Gibson, "The Gibson Mix," *IBM Tech. Rep. TR00.2043,* June 1970.

from component ratings available from the manufacturer was that of Knight (1966). He used a formula for the *performance index, I,* of the form

$$I = \frac{10^6 \times \text{memory factor}}{\text{processor factor}}$$

where

$$\text{memory factor} = \left[\frac{(L - 7)T(\text{WF})}{(36 - 7)(32,000)} \right]^i \qquad (1.1)$$

where L = word length, bits
   T = number of words in high-speed memory
   WF = word factor (1 for a fixed-word-length machine, 2 for variable-word-length machines)
   i = 0.5 for scientific machines, 0.333 for commercial machines

and

$$\text{processor factor} = t_c + t_{\text{I/O}}$$

where t_c = time, μsec, to execute 1 million instructions, with assigned weights for the instruction types
   $t_{\text{I/O}}$ = nonoverlapped time, μsec, to execute 1 million input/output operations

Knight's equation is given in full in Table 1.2, together with a sample calculation.* Complex as this equation is, there are serious objections to it. For one, factors such as 7 and 0.333 are arbitrary, with no theoretical basis. Even more serious, the index is really meant for systems with magnetic tape I/O; the more the machine architecture differs from such systems—which happens when multiprocessing, time sharing, and virtual memories are present—the less valid is the equation. Even by 1970 Knight recognized that the index was not an adequate measure of machine power, and since then the trend has been to accept much simpler measures for individual basic components, such as processors, channels, memory units, and I/O devices, rather than attempting to compute an overall FOM (see Knight, 1976).

For the CPU a very simple figure, such as

$$t_{\text{CPU}} = 0.95t_{\text{add}} + 0.05t_{\text{mult}}$$

where t_{add} and t_{mult} are the times for addition and multiplication, respectively, including the fetch times for the instructions, can be taken, and the result

*Other sample calculations are given in Phister (1979, p. 359).

TABLE 1.2 KNIGHT'S PERFORMANCE INDEX

	Value for IBM 370/135 commercial
Performance index, $I = \dfrac{10^6 \times \text{memory factor}}{\text{processor factor}}$	171,330
Memory factor $= \left[\dfrac{(L-7)\ T\,(\text{WF})}{(36-7)(32,000)}\right]^i$	0.875
L = word length (bits)	8
T = total number of words in memory	311,296

WF = word factor
  = 1 for fixed-word-length system
  = 2 for variable-word-length system
	2

i = memory weighting coefficient
  = 0.5 for scientific computation
  = 0.333 for commercial computation
	0.333

Processor factor $= t_c + t_{i/o}$ (sec)	5.107
t_c = CPU time per million operations $= (C_1 A_{Fi} + C_2 A_{Fl} + C_3 M + C_4 D + C_5 L)$	3.03
A_{Fi} = fixed-point addition time (μsec)	4.2
A_{Fl} = floating point addition time (μsec)	
M = multiplication time (μsec)	25.5
D = division time (μsec)	
L = logic operation time (μsec)	2.3
C_i = weighting factors representing the percentages of various operations	

	Scientific Computation	Commercial Computation	
C_1	0.10	0.25	0.25
C_2	0.10	0	0
C_3	0.06	0.01	0.01
C_4	0.02	0	0
C_5	0.72	0.74	0.74
Add to C_1 if CPU has no index registers or indirect addressing	0.25	0.20	

$t_{i/o}$ = nonoverlapped I/O time per million operations
  $= P_c$(primary I/O system time)
  $+ (1 - P_c)$ (secondary I/O system time)
			2.077

P_c = fraction of the I/O characters handled by the primary I/O system			0.9

TABLE 1.2 (Continued)

	Value for IBM 370/135 commercial	
	Mag Tape	Unit Record
I/O system time—primary or secondary $$= (OL)(R)\left[\frac{W_i B}{K_i} + \frac{W_o B}{K_o} + N(S + H) \right]$$	1.694	5.522
where (OL, R, W_i, W_o, K_i, K_o, N, S, and H depend on whether the primary or secondary I/O time is being calculated		
OL = overlap factor—the fraction of I/O time not overlapped with the CPU		
= 1.0 for system with no overlap		
= 0.85 if system permits read or write with compute		
= 0.70 if system permits read, write, and compute		
= 0.60 if system permits multiple read, write, and compute		
= 0.55 if system permits multiple read, write, and compute with program interrupt	0.55	0.55
R = 1 + the fraction the useful I/O time that is required for nonoverlapped rewind time	1.1	1.0
W_i = number of input words per million internal operations entering on the I/O system	100,000	10,000
W_o = number of output words per million internal operations leaving on the I/O system	100,000	10,000
B = number of I/O characters per word	1	1
K_i = input transfer rate (char./sec)	80,000	1600
K_o = output transfer rate (char./sec)	80,000	2640
N = number of times separate records are read or written per million operations		
S = I/O system start time not overlapped with computation	.006	0
H = I/O system stop time not overlapped with computation	0.009	0

Values for W_i, W_o, N	Scientific Computation	Commercial Computation		
$W_i = W_o$				
Magnetic tape	20,000	100,000		
Other I/O	2,000	10,000		
N	4	20		20

expressed in millions of instructions per second (MIPS).* Thus, for the CDC 6600 the add time is 0.333 μsec, the multiplication time is 1.0 μsec, and the fetch time or *memory cycle* is 1.0 μsec, so that it is a 0.7-MIPS machine. Other simple but useful measures are the *cycle time,* expressed in μsec or nsec (nanoseconds = 10^{-9} sec), and the *bits per cycle* = word length in bits per cycle time. For comparing very fast computers, Turn (1974) suggests a slightly different measure, taking into account the fact that such systems usually have interleaved memories which make it possible to access several operands simultaneously. Turn's equation is

$$\text{MIPS} = \frac{10^6}{t_{\text{CPU}}}$$

where $t_{\text{CPU}} = 0.7t_{\text{add}} + 0.3t_{\text{mult}} + 2k_m t_{\text{memory cycle}}$ and $0 < k_m \le 1$ is the memory overlap factor, equal to 1 if there is no memory overlap (in this equation the fetch times are included in the memory cycle factor). As an example, for the UNIVAC 1110 computer, introduced in 1972, $t_{\text{add}} = 0.3$ μsec, $t_{\text{mult}} = 1.5$ μsec, $t_{\text{memory cycle}} = 0.48$ μsec, and $k_m = \frac{1}{4}$, so that $t_{\text{CPU}} = 0.90$ μsec, and it is a 1.1-MIPS machine. The supercomputers of the 1980s are rated in MFLOPS (mega-FLOPS, or millions of floating-point operations per second). In 1983 the fastest operational computers ran at 100 MFLOPS, with Cray Research and Nippon Electric Company announcing machines expected to reach or exceed 1000 MFLOPS.†

Data on calculating FOMs for systems, including such aspects as configurations available, memory and peripheral speeds, and physical characteristics, have appeared regularly in several publications, notably the Auerbach reports, those of Datapro, and the GML *Computer Characteristic Review.* The most comprehensive compilation of historical data on component ratings, as well as on other system features to be described in the next two sections, is in Phister (1979). Limited as FOMs are, they are still useful for providing a crude indication of the "raw" computing power, that is, the execution capacity, without taking into account speedup that might be achieved from parallel operations, or slowdown resulting from device contention and software limitations. They have also been used as the basis for studying how performance depends on price, and how performance has improved with changes in computer technology.

---

*Sometimes t_{CPU} is calculated *without* taking the instruction fetch times into consideration, but the form given is more realistic and will be used in this book.

†Such speeds are nominal only and can be attained only for short bursts. In practice, the system is highly processor bound (Section 2.1) and there is no way of feeding data fast enough to sustain the computation rate. See F. G. Withington, "Winners and Losers in the Fifth Generation," *Datamation,* 29, no. 12 (December 1983), 193–209.

1.2 PERFORMANCE AND PRICE

It is a general economic law, going back to the time of Adam Smith, that in a manufacturing process the unit cost of making a product decreases as the number being produced increases. This is illustrated in Fig. 1.1, where the cost for manufacturing a single unit of the IBM 370/168 CPU is shown as a function of the number of units made. The economies arising out of large production runs are a natural consequence of the fact that to initiate production, significant investments are needed for research, development, administration, and setting up the production line. As more units are made these costs can be apportioned over a larger batch. Eventually, the unit cost approaches the marginal value, determined by the cost of labor and materials. Economy of scale does not apply without qualification; for example, a barbershop is a labor-intensive activity, and there are no savings to be had by going into large-scale production of

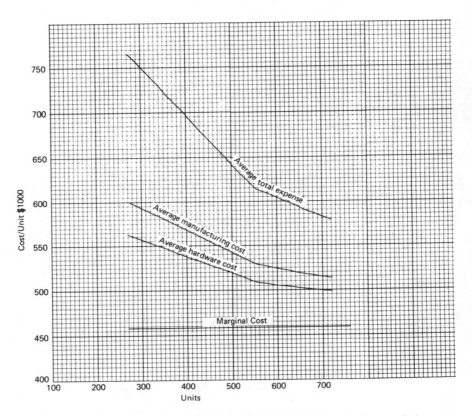

Figure 1.1 Cost Curves for the IBM 370/168 CPU [Reprinted with permission from G. W. Brock, *The United States Computer Industry: A Study of Market Power,* Copyright 1974, Ballinger Publishing Company, Cambridge, Mass. Originally from Source: IBM, "Poughkeepsie SDD Cost Engineering, Estimate No. C-460-DF, Pisces (A)," July 14, 1972 (Telex vs. IBM, Plaintiff's Exhibit 213).]

haircuts. Also, as production volume grows, the costs of administering the large supportive organization may go up very rapidly, so that eventually the unit cost may start to increase again.* When there is a minimum in the cost–production curve it tends to be rather shallow, but as a first approximation we may expect economy of scale to hold (i.e., the unit cost to decrease with production volume), initially at least.

Applied to *using* computers (rather than manufacturing them) economy of scale means that it should be cheaper to run a computing job on a large computer than on a small one, assuming, of course, that the large computing system has sufficient load for the economies to become apparent. Even though large computing systems are more expensive than small ones, this means that it should cost less to run a job on a large system than on a small one. A specific form of this relation, suggested by H. J. R. Grosch, came to be known as *Grosch's law*. If E is the effectiveness of a computing system (measured in units yet to be determined) and C the cost, Grosch's law states that

$$E = kC^2 \qquad (1.2)$$

where k is a constant. A justification for this law can be made if one is prepared to make some rather simplistic assumptions about effectiveness. Thus, if one assumes that $E \propto$ MIPS $\times$ memory size, and further that memory size $\propto C$ and MIPS $\propto C$, then the law follows.

More generally, one might write

$$E = k_1 C^{k_2} \qquad (1.3)$$

where k_1 and k_2 are constants. If $E \propto 1/T$, where T is the time to do something, and logarithms (to base 10) are taken in both sides of Equation 1.3, then log $C = a - $ b log T, where a and b are constants and the value of b determines when there are economies of scale. In particular,

If $b > 1$, there are diseconomies of scale; that is, it costs more to run a job on a large system than it does on a small one.

If $b = 1$, there is neither gain nor penalty to be had on going to a larger system; this is expressed by saying that there are returns to scale.

If $1 > b > \frac{1}{2}$, there are economies of scale, but not as large as those indicated by Grosch's law.

If $b = \frac{1}{2}$, Grosch's law, as stated, holds.

If $b < \frac{1}{2}$, there are economies of scale greater than those suggested by Grosch's law.

---

*The number of possible pairwise interactions between n people goes up as n^2, so that the factor by which administrative costs increase can be greater than linear.

Solomon (1966) tested Grosch's law on a series of IBM 360 computers (models 30, 40, 50, 65, 75) by fitting regression curves to the cost versus the time required to carry out three kernel programs (i.e., relatively short routines regarded as being important because they were often called upon). For matrix multiplication, Solomon found

$$\log C = 15.41 - 0.4935 \log T$$

For a square-root routine: $\log C = 13.263 - 0.4783 \log T$

For a field-scan routine: $\log C = 15.901 - 0.6817 \log T$

The closeness of the slope to $-\frac{1}{2}$ in the first two cases is noteworthy, but a doubt immediately arises as to whether this reflects IBM's pricing policy rather than any natural law.

Knight (1966, 1968) tested the relationship between price and performance over a much larger range of manufacturers. He expressed his results in the form

$$\ln \overline{C} = a - b \ln I + B_1 S_1 + B_2 S_2 + B_3 S_3 + B_4 S_4$$

where $\overline{C}$ is the number of seconds of computer operation purchased per dollar, I is the computer index (commercial or scientific) as computed by Equation 1.1, $S_i = 1$ if the year is $(1962 + i)$, 0 otherwise, and $B_1 \cdots B_4$ are fitted constants. Since $\overline{C} = 1/C$ and $I \propto 1/T$, a slope of $\frac{1}{2}$ again means that Grosch's law is followed.

Figure 1.2 shows the four regression lines Knight obtained for 1963–1966 using his commercial index. The results for these years are summarized in the following table:

	a (Base for 1962)	b	B_1 (1963)	B_2 (1964)	B_3 (1965)	B_4 (1966)
Commercial	7.441	0.404	0.385	0.723	1.186	1.550
Scientific	6.823	0.322	0.272	0.415	0.828	0.988

Note that $b < \frac{1}{2}$, indicating economies of scale greater than those suggested by Grosch's law, although, as is usually the case, the increase is not as large for commercial calculations as it is for scientific.

From these observations it is possible to calculate a quantity that can be interpreted as the increase of performance due to technological improvement of computers with time. Thus for scientific calculations,

$$\ln \overline{C} = 6.823 - 0.322 \ln I \text{ in } 1962$$

$$\ln \overline{C} = 6.823 - 0.322 \ln I + 0.988 \text{ in } 1966$$

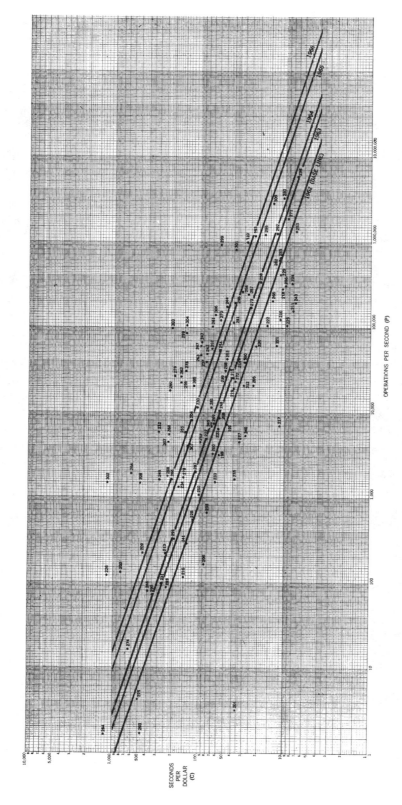

Figure 1.2 Regression calculation for Knight's commercial index (From K. E. Knight, "Evolving Computer Performance 1963–1967," *Datamation*, 14, no. 1 (January 1968), 31–35, with permission.)

13

At constant cost

$$0.322 (\ln I_{1966} - \ln I_{1962}) = 0.988$$

where $I_{1966}/I_{1962} = e^{3.068} = 21.5$. Therefore, the *improvement factor per year* = $21.5^{¼} = 2.15$, corresponding to an average increase of 115% per year over the 4-year period. Using the commercial index, the increase factor is 2.6 or 160% per year, even greater. It need hardly be said that these are remarkably high. If an attempt is made to calculate the factors over a longer span of years, as already noted, basic changes in machine architecture limit the applicability of the equation for calculating I. But as will be seen in Chapter 8, from similar calculations based on the performance of individual components rather than the computer as a whole, it can be argued that comparable improvements have been sustained for over 20 years, and there is reason to believe that they will continue to hold well into the 1980s.

The main reason that it is so difficult to use a single FOM for different computers which have appeared over a long time span is that regularly there have been significant breakthroughs in technology resulting in systems that differ qualitatively from their predecessors. The sense of this is captured by designating successive "generations" of computers, which roughly have the characteristics shown in Table 1.3. A key feature of the change in generations is increased bit rate and memory capacity from one to the next, so that the "maxi" computers of one generation tend to become the "midi" of the next and the "micro" of the generation after that. But it will be seen in Chapter 8 that the changes in technology, particularly in the last 10 years, have come much more continuously than is suggested by Table 1.3, and that progress in components, memories, and architecture has gone on independently in each, so that the distinction between generations becomes increasingly blurred.

Cale et al. (1979) give up altogether on attempting to use instruction execution time as any measure of computer power or effectiveness. They note that Control Data, because of concurrent operations in the 12-word instruction stacks in the Cyber 76, 175, and 176 series, state that instruction timings are poor indicators of overall performance; and that Burroughs even refuses to divulge instruction timings for the B6807, maintaining that because of the unconventional architecture, timing comparisons would be meaningless. They do, however, go about finding a relationship between cost and memory capacity, using data published by Datapro for several hundred computers appearing between 1970 and 1976. The memory capacity is measured in kilobytes of main storage and megabytes of DASD (direct-access storage device); further, they introduce another factor which depends on whether the system is a standardized general-purpose system (GPS) or a small business system (SBS). Thus their regression plot is of the form

$$\begin{aligned}
\ln \text{cost} = B_0 &+ B_1 \ln \text{memory} + B_2 \ln \text{DASD} \\
&+ B_3 Y_{72/73} + B_4 Y_{74/75} + B_5 Y_{75/76} + B_6 \text{SBS}
\end{aligned} \tag{1.4}$$

TABLE 1.3 COMPUTER GENERATIONS

| Gener-ation | Approximate Time Interval | ALU Technology | Memory | | Architecture |
			Primary	Secondary	
First	1946–1956	Vacuum tube (10 kops)	Mercury delay lines, cathode ray tubes	Magnetic drums	Von Neumann (i.e., sequential logic)
Second	1957–1964	Transistor boards (200 kops)	Magnetic cores	Magnetic tapes, magnetic disks	I/O channels, time sharing
Third	1964–1978	Small- to medium-scale integration (5 MIPS)	Semiconductors, overlapped segments	Virtual memories	Multiprogramming, multiprocessing
Fourth	1978–	Medium- to very large scale integration (50 MIPS)	Semiconductors	Optical disks, diskettes, hierarchies	Distributed systems, networks
Fifth	1990 projected	Ultra-large-scale integration (1000 MFLOPS)	Data bases representing human knowledge with inferential capabilities		Parallel processing, speech input, human-like capabilities

where $Y_{72/73} = 1$ if the year of introduction is 1972 or 1973, and 0 otherwise; and similarly for the other Y's, and SBS $= 1$ for a small business system and 0 for a general-purpose system.*

    Two-year groupings are taken to give more consistent results. The factors as found are shown in Table 1.4. From the variances of the observations the statistical significances of the various terms can be estimated, and B_6 turns out to be highly significant. This suggests that instead of determining a single equation for both general-purpose and small business systems, separate equations should be fitted for each. The coefficients for the separate equations are also shown in Table 1.4. As an illustration, for a system with 100 kilobytes in main memory and 100 megabytes of DASD, introduced in 1974 or 1975, the computed costs are as follows:

	GPS	SBS
Cost using combined equations	$313,400	$104,300
Cost using separate equations	327,600	98,200

*For a modified regression form and criticisms of the results derived from Equation 1.4, see J. C. Winteron and I. H. Mann III, "Technical Correspondence on Price/Performance in U.S. Computer Systems," *Commun. ACM,* 24 (September 1981), 606–7.

TABLE 1.4 COEFFICIENTS IN FITTING COST VERSUS MEMORY CAPACITIES

| Variable | Symbol | Coefficient[a] | | |
		GPS	SBS	Single Equation for GPS and SBS
Constant	B_0	10.2	9.3	10.3
In memory	B_1	0.42	0.46	0.5
In DASD	B_2	0.24	0.11	0.12
$Y_{72/73}$	B_3	− 0.4	− 0.14	− 0.3
$Y_{74/75}$	B_4	− 0.54	− 0.43	− 0.5
$Y_{76/77}$	B_5	− 0.83	− 0.54	− 0.71
SBS effect	B_6			− 1.1

[a]GPS, General-purpose systems; SBS, small business systems.

Source: E. G. Cale, L. L. Gremillon, and J. L. McKenney, *Commun. ACM,* 22, no. 4 (April 1979), 225–33.

These can be compared with costs of $253,000 and $100,000 for actual GPS and SBS systems (the IBM S/3 model 10 and the Computer Horizon Distribution System).

Equation 1.4 simply expresses a statistical relationship between cost and memory capacities, valid with qualifications, for computers appearing between 1970 and 1976. It can be regarded as a cost predictor, and be used to estimate a technological improvement factor, but one which has to be interpreted as being applicable for memories rather than systems as a whole. Thus for GPS systems

$$\ln C = 10.2 + 0.42 \ln M + 0.24 \ln \text{DASD} \qquad \text{in 1970–1971}$$

$$\ln C = 10.2 + 0.42 \ln M + 0.24 \ln \text{DASD} - 0.83 \qquad \text{in 1976–1977}$$

For constant memory size,

$$\ln \frac{C_{1970-71}}{C_{1976-77}} = 0.83$$

where $C_{1970-71}/C_{1976-77} = 2.293$ and the advantage factor *in cost* is $2.293^{1/6} = 1.148$ (i.e., about 15% per year). Observe that this is considerably less than the improvement in *effectiveness* previously estimated for 1962–1966. The factor as computed here depends on reliability of B_5, and an examination of the statistics for B_2 to B_5, as seen in the tables of Cale et al., shows that only limited confidence can be attached to the results. But it also has to be pointed out that this 15% reduction is what the customer saw. The technological improvement was certainly greater, the difference being reflected in increased profits for the computer industry, increases that were recognizably high in the period under study.

A question that has to be asked is why there is such a significant price differential between GPS and SBS systems, since the memory capacities are comparable for the two. Moreover, the late 1970s marked the appearance of personal microcomputers (PCs) whose memories were soon expanded, and the price ratio of an SBS to a PC is comparable with that of a GPS to an SBS. Some of the difference stems from the fact that GPS systems have faster CPUs, but much of it has to be justified in the better software and support services available for GPS computers. These last are hard to quantify and, moreover, as SBS systems mature, more software is developed for them, so that the distinctions become blurred. In the same way, as more packaged software was developed for PCs, they began to look like SBSs. This confirms the general conclusion, already noted, that the relationship between performance and price (or between memory and price) is too complicated to be expressed in terms of single factors, and any such expression will not be applicable to the full range of computers appearing over a long time interval. One has to consider a small class of similar equipment to obtain meaningful results.

The price difference between GPS and SBS systems is an indicator of a trend that has continued even more strongly into the 1980s: a decreasing economy of scale for hardware costs. This shows up even for IBM's pricing for the 3000 series of computers compared with the 4300 series* (see Problem 4). The decreasing advantage of size has important implications in the centralization versus decentralization argument (Chapter 4), and in the growth of the mainframe sector of the computer industry (Section 9.2).

1.3 WORK LOADS

In the light of the difficulties in computing a figure of merit from system components, it is natural to try to estimate performance by observing how the system behaves when a standard work load is submitted to it. The work load can be constituted by choosing tasks thought to be representative of those that the system will be called upon to do; it may consist of complete jobs, or of job segments. A collection of actual jobs will be called a *benchmark;* a work load consisting of programs constructed to test the system under a variety of conditions will be called *synthetic;* and a small segment of a work load will be called a *kernel.* In order to rate the system the work load will usually be executed (i.e., actually run on the system under test); but for prospective systems, and even in other situations, the work load may be run on a simulated computer, or the execution time may be calculated from the work-load program and known timing data. From the very beginnings of computers synthetic jobs have been designed to exercise hardware components, carry out maintenance, and test software; but here our interest is in the *performance* as measured by such

---

*But it must be noted that when hardware plus software costs are considered, economies of scale still show up for the larger IBM system.

observations as execution time and response time, rather than just verifying that the system can operate properly.

1.3.1 Kernels and Synthetic Jobs

A simple example of a kernel is the GAMM measure, often quoted by manufacturers, especially in Europe, to indicate the speed of machines for scientific calculations (see Wichmann and DuCroz, 1979). This kernel contains five program loops:

1. Addition of two vectors of order 30
2. Element-by-element multiplication of two vectors of order 30
3. Evaluation of a polynomial of order 10 by Horner's method
4. Selection of the maximum component of a vector of order 10
5. Computation of a square root by Newton's method, using five iterations

If the times are these for $T_1 \cdots T_5$, the GAMM figure of merit is a weighted mean, given by

$$GAMM = \frac{T_1/30 + T_2/60 + T_3/20 + T_4/20 + T_5/15}{5}$$

This can also be written as

$$GAMM = \frac{t_1 + t_2/2 + t_3/2 + t_4/2 + t_5/3}{5}$$

where t_i are the inner loop timings for the operations ($i = 1 \cdots 5$) ignoring initialization and termination effects.

On current machines the GAMM value comes out in microseconds, an interval that is difficult to measure with most built-in timers, so a driving program is needed to repeat each loop a large number of times. Aside from this minor difficulty, the reservation about accepting GAMM as an FOM is obvious. There is no assurance that these five simple tasks for doing small problems in elementary numerical analysis are representative of what the system will really have to do. At best, GAMM is a highly arbitrary measure scarcely if at all better than an FOM based on weighting the execution time for individual instructions.*

A much more ambitious effort in assessing computer performance by means of synthetic programs is to be found in the series of tables and charts which appeared regularly for many years in Auerbach publications.† For each

---

*Another example of a synthetic program constructed from kernels is described in W. Buchholz, "A Synthetic Job for Measuring System Performance," *IBM Syst. J.,* 8, no. 4 (1969), 309–18.

†These were referred to as benchmarks, but the programs were not actually executed. Instead, they were coded using information available from the manufacturer's instruction manuals, and the running time calculated. Thus in our terminology they are better described as synthetic jobs.

system being reported on, standard configurations were carefully defined (there were often 10 or more, starting with small card-driven systems and going up to systems with large memories and high-speed I/O devices) and rental prices given. There were five programs:

1. A file processing problem in which a master file (usually on magnetic tape) was updated by transactions presorted into master file sequence. The time for processing and printing a report was calculated as a function of the activity factor (A), the fraction of transactions needing to be updated.
2. A file processing problem in which the master file was on a random-access device (usually a disk) and the transactions presented in random sequence for updating. The arrival rate was such as to keep the CPU busy.
3. A sorting problem involving 80-character records each having an eight-digit key.
4. A matrix inversion problem.
5. Mathematical calculations involving evaluation of a polynomial of degree five (P1), divisions (P2), and taking square roots (P3).

At first, problems of different sizes were studied. For example, the results of program 1 were shown as graphs in which A varied from 0 to 1; the sorting times were plotted against the number of records in the file, and the matrix inversion times were plotted against the order of the matrix. Details on these synthetic programs are given in Hillegass (1966) and Gosden and Sisson (1962). It was soon realized that the dependence on problem size was readily computable from the algorithms, and later results were compressed by limiting the range of the problems, for example, to three activity factors (0, 0.1, and 1), to a file of 10,000 records to be sorted, and to matrices of order 10 and 40.

Parameters specifying the Auerbach standard configuration are displayed in Table 1.5, and a typical performance chart showing the times required by various configurations of systems in the Honeywell 8200 series to process a master file is shown in Fig. 1.3. Such charts were presented for hundreds of computers in reports appearing between 1960 and 1970. Detailed as the reports are, questions remain about how faithfully they reflect overall performance.

- For the file processing problems the times are essentially determined by a peripheral device (e.g., the speed of a card reader, a magnetic tape drive, or disk memory) and elementary calculations using record format and device speed produce results equivalent to those given (see Section 2.1).
- For more complicated programs, such as sorting or matrix inversion, the execution time is only one aspect of performance. In practice, sorting large files is almost always done using a sort generator, and the *quality* of the package (options available, ability to take advantage of partially sorted data, editing features, etc.) are at least as important as the speed. Similarly,

TABLE 1.5 AUERBACH CONFIGURATIONS

Specification	Unit	I, Card	II, Tape	III, Tape	IIIR, RAM	IV, Tape	IVR, RAM	V	VIIA	VIIB Paired Main	VIIB Paired Sat.	VIIIA	VIIIB Paired Main	VIIIB Paired Sat.	VIIIR	IX	X	XI
Internal memory																		
One-address instruction	k	1	1	2	2	4	4	2	12	8	.5	24	16	1	24	2	4	4
Characters of data	kby	4	4	8	8	16	16	8	48	32	2	96	64	4	96	16	32	32
Random-access storage—characters of data	Mby	0	0	0	5	0	20	20	0	0	0	0	0	0	100	0	0	0
Magnetic tape																		
Units		0	4	6	1	12	4	6	10	8	2	20	16	4	4	0	0	4
Nominal speed	kbps	—	15	30	30	60	60	30	60	60	30	120	120	60	120	—	—	15
Simultaneous transfers		—	0	1	1	2	2	1	2	2	0	5	4	1	4	—	—	0
Printer speed	klpm	1	0.5	0.5	0.5	1	1	0.5	0.5	—	0.5	1	—	1	1	0.005	0.005	0.1
Card reader speed	kcpm	1	0.5	0.5	0.5	1	1	0.5	0.5	0.1	0.5	1	0.1	1	1	0.010	0.2	0.5
Card punch speed	kcpm	0.2	0.1	0.1	0.1	0.2	0.2	0.1	0.1	—	0.1	2	—	0.2	0.2	0.010	0.1	0.2
Other features																		
Floating-point arithmetic		No	No	No	No	No	No	No	Yes	Yes	No	Yes	Yes	No	Yes	No	Yes	Yes
Index registers		1	0	3	1	10	10	3	6	6	0	10	10	3	10	0	1	1

Source: M. Phister, Jr., *Data Processing Technologies and Economics*, 2nd ed. Santa Fe, N. Mex: Santa Monica/Bedford, Mass.: Digital Press, with permission.

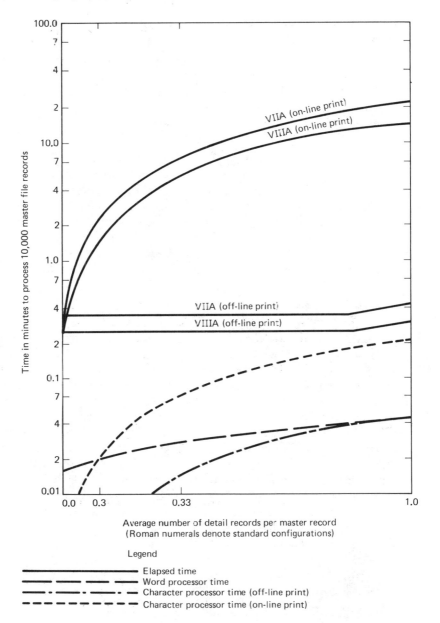

Figure 1.3   Time to Process a File (From Auerbach, *Computer Technology Reports* (Pennsauken, N.J.: Auerbach).) Copyright 1967, with permission.

for matrix inversion the precision attained and the ability to deal with ill-conditioned matrices are just as important as the execution speed.

- It cannot be expected that the programs written for these synthetic jobs will take advantage of special features so often available on particular computers. Thus a package program provided by a manufacturer or a software house can conceivably perform significantly better than the synthetic program used in the Auerbach reports.

The overall conclusion is that although the comparisons based on these synthetic problems undoubtedly provide some indication of computer performance, it is impossible to be certain that these results really indicate how an actual or prospective system will perform on a particular work load. It is noteworthy that, as time progressed, the Auerbach reports devoted less space and emphasis to such tables. Nevertheless, as pointed out in Oliver et al. (1974), synthetic programs do provide useful comparisons of different systems when it is necessary to rate them with some degree of objectivity.*

1.3.2 Benchmarks

Benchmarks are usually elaborate programs, often constructed by assembling a collection of kernels which are run under a variety of conditions to obtain comprehensive statistics. Three examples will illustrate them.

Table 1.6 shows a benchmark mix consisting of 15 kernel segments, written in either ALGOL, COBOL, or FORTRAN; when these are executed (in sequential mode) the processing, I/O, and elapsed times are recorded, as well as the memory used.

Heller (1976) described the use of a benchmark to compare costs of executing programs in university computing centers, using systems of different manufacturers. There are nine kernel programs written in FORTRAN (Table 1.7), and each program could be run using three different compilers: a standard version, an optimizing compiler designed to minimize execution, and an in-core student compiler with good diagnostics but with no special attention given to producing an efficient program. In addition to gathering statistics on the individual kernels, two different mixes, A and B (Table 1.8), were defined. These were regarded as being representative of the actual work load at two universities, with B corresponding to an environment where research (as compared to instruction) is more important. Since costs were the objects of special interest, the prices for running the benchmarks at different universities were observed; Table 1.9 shows statistics on these costs. These results are interesting in the light of pricing policies of computer services in university computing centers (see Section 3.2).

The final example shows that benchmarking is just as popular for

---

*For a more detailed discussion of synthetic work loads, see Ferrari (1978, Chap. 5).

TABLE 1.6 BENCHMARK MIX

Name	Type[a]	Serial Times			Memory Words			Description
		Proc.	I/O	Elapsed	Save	Overlay	Total	
BRUNIO	A	181	627	940	921	64	985	Channel-bound (tape) program
DIFFEQ	F	319	10	333	1,005	1,374	2,379	Differential equations
TIDY	F	258	30	271	3,473	11,460	15,189	FORTRAN source deck editor
SNOBOL3	A	107	18	115	2,827	13,610	16,437	SNOBOL3 interpreter: symbolic differential
FDLSR	F	464	91	474	1,989	16,883	18,872	Crystallographic application
DETAB65	C	26	23	36	1,677	3,958	3,635	DETAB-65 preprocessor
BMDO5R	F	150	20	158	1,093	13,575	14,668	Least-squares polynomial regression
CROS-REF	C	64	28	70	4,890	762	5,652	COBOL cross-reference generator
BMDO2T	F	163	23	177	1,236	13,517	14,753	Time-series analysis
GUMTER	F	200	21	208	1,204	19,290	20,494	Induction motor rotor response
SYMAP	F	110	17	118	1,376	14,148	16,024	Symbolic map program
FAC-TORA	A	58	13	61	1,288	6,027	7,315	Factor analysis (30 × 30)
MATRIX	A	167	9	168	1,070	10,534	11,604	Matrix inversion (40 × 40, 100 × 100)
RTLOC	F	304	11	308	1,080	5,476	6,556	Root-locus computation and protting
TES-TRAN	F	148	14	154	1,057	3,398	4,455	Tests of random sequences

[a]A, ALGOL; C, COBOL; F, FORTRAN.

Source: A. Batson and F. Brundage, ACM SIGOPS Workshop on System Performance Evaluation, Harvard University, Cambridge, Mass., April 5–7, 1971.

microcomputers as it is for the larger systems. Table 1.10 lists a benchmark comparison of five personal computers all running BASIC programs. The first two (the Victor 9000 and IBM PC) use the Z8088 processor running at 5 MHz and 4.77 MHz, respectively. Although they are 16-bit machines the arithmetic is basically 8-bit; the others contain the 4-MHz Z80 8-bit processors.

Benchmarks are widely regarded as the best overall indicators of performance, for when they are run information is obtained about software, diagnostics, and system robustness. It is for these reasons, and also because they provide objective measures as bases for decision making, that benchmarks are especially common where equipment is needed by a group in the public sector (e.g., for a defense application or for a municipal department). In such situations it is usual to have manufacturers submit formal competitive bids and demonstrate the suitability of their equipment by furnishing benchmark statistics. However,

TABLE 1.7 BENCHMARK PROGRAMS

Name	Description
TRIVIAL	Does almost nothing, to highlight job overhead and minimum charges
CRUNCHER	A loop containing the four arithmetic operators is executed 1M times
MATMUL1	Two 60 × 60 matrices are multiplied 50 times
MATMUL2	Two 221 × 221 matrices are multiplied once
CTOD	Card-to-disk; 2k data cards are read and 10k card images are written sequentially onto disk
DSKRD	Disk-read; the sequential file created by CTOD is accessed and summarized
PUREIO	50k binary card images are written to disk
ARMWHIP	Writes and reads a 20M-character random-access file nonsequentially
ARMGLIDE	Writes and reads a 20M-character random-access file sequentially

Source: P. Heller, "Benchmarking the Price of Computing," *Comput. Netw.,* 1 (1976), 27–32, with permission.

TABLE 1.8 WORK-LOAD MIXES

	Number of jobs in:	
Job Name and Compiler Type	Mix A	Mix B
TRIVIAL—student	50.00	21.43
TRIVIAL—standard	14.58	4.17
TRIVIAL—optimizing	9.45	0.00
CRUNCHER—student	0.96	0.80
CRUNCHER—standard	0.38	20.55
MATMUL1—standard	0.61	1.21
MATMUL1—optimizing	1.15	0.57
MATMUL2—standard	0.00	0.00
CTOD—standard	0.90	0.30
DSKRD—standard	3.49	4.37
PUREIO—standard	0.58	0.58
ARMWHIP—standard	0.20	0.02
ARMGLIDE—standard	0.20	0.02

Source: P. Heller, "Benchmarking the Price of Computing," *Comput. Netw.,* 1 (1976), 27–32, with permission.

Brock (1974) provides a convincing example of how excessive dependence can be placed on benchmark trials. In 1971, the U.S. Department of Defense invited bids for a replacement of its Worldwide Military Command and Control System. Initially, 80 installations were to be installed, with the prospect of many more later; the order was therefore one of considerable importance. Brock reports that the cost to the three finalists for preparing and running the benchmark programs was in the range of $3 million to $6 million dollars *each*. Only one company was awarded the contract, but one must assume that all the bidders eventually had to distribute the costs for such efforts over the prices for their other products. To make matters worse, in spite of the winner having

TABLE 1.9 (a) FORTRAN BENCHMARKS, INTERNAL PRICE STATISTICS

Compiler type	TRIVIAL Student	TRIVIAL Standard	TRIVIAL Optimizing	CRUNCHER Student	CRUNCHER Standard	MATMUL Standard	MATMUL Optimizing
Number of installations with successful run[a]	17	25	18	13	26	24	20
Mean price($)	0.21	0.55	0.73	7.57	2.99	20.17	13.93
Highest price($)	0.91	1.51	1.90	18.42	10.76	54.19	57.57
Lowest price($)	0.00	0.00	0.17	0.00	0.67	3.18	2.05
Highest/lowest			11.18		16.06	17.04	28.08

Compiler type	MATMUL2 Standard	CTOD Standard	DSKRD Standard	PUREIO Standard	ARMWHIP Standard	ARMGLIDE Standard
Number of installations with successful run[a]	9	24	23	25	20	19
Mean price($)	73.79	7.37	2.85	17.40	84.13	70.64
Highest price($)	414.95	18.04	8.16	59.10	405.46	231.22
Lowest price($)	10.58	3.54	0.93	3.21	10.14	5.04
Highest/lowest	39.29	5.10	8.33	18.41	39.99	45.88

(b) Work-Load Mix Prices

Price Basis	Work-Load Price For: Mix A	Mix B
Lowest price	$ 60.10	$ 45.22
Mean price	144.82	137.00
Highest price	338.96	376.64
Highest/lowest	5.64	8.33

[a] $N = 26$ installations.

Source: P. Heller, "Benchmarking the Price of Computing," *Comput. Netw.,* 1 (1976), 27–32, with permission.

presumably fulfilled the benchmark requirements, when installed, the system was regarded as being unsatisfactory, and in 1980 a great deal of controversy was generated when another replacement of the system was sought.

1.4 SIMULATION AND MEASUREMENTS

As noted in the introduction to this chapter, simulation is one of the techniques that can be used to evaluate system performance. In this section we consider

TABLE 1.10 BENCHMARK COMPARISON OF PERSONAL COMPUTERS

Benchmark for BASIC	Times (sec) for the:				
	Victor 9000 (16 bit)	IBM PC (16 bit)	Applesoft (8 bit)	Z80[a] (8 bit)	TRS-80 model II (8 bit)
Empty do-loop	7.7	6.43	6.66	5.81	7.98
Division	21.8	23.8	29.0	24.9	19.4
Subroutine jump	16.9	12.4	13.9	9.4	17.1
MID$ (substring)	24.6	23.0	32.3	18.6	24.8
Prime-number program	197.0	190.0	241.0	151.0	189.0
Disk-write program—64-Kbyte file	50.3	32.0	175.0	n.a.	246.0
Disk-read program—64-Kbyte file	21.3	22.9	217.0	n.a.	96.0

[a]n.a., not applicable.

Source: Data from *Byte,* November 1982, 246.

simulations based on using general simulation languages, such as SIMSCRIPT or GPSS, to describe a configuration and its work load, or on special software developed to simulate computers, but which in effect works like a general simulation language. In Chapter 2, analytical computer models designed to yield results on performance are examined. Both simulation models and analytical models have parameters whose values have to be known to calibrate the models and to make calculations possible. In practice, these values have to be determined from observations and measurements taken on the system, and this section also describes how such measurements are taken and interpreted.

1.4.1 Simulations of Computer Systems

Among the most useful applications of computers are simulations of systems which are too complex to admit precise mathematical formulation. Computer simulations are found in many disciplines, for example, chemistry, physics, biology, environmental studies, and operations research. Given the complexity of large-scale computers, with their many interconnected components and changing work loads, it is natural enough to think of simulating computer behavior. For simulation purposes a computer system has the same structure as other systems. There is:

- A set of interconnected components each of which has a functional purpose—in this case the processors, channels, I/O devices, and so on
- A set of inputs from the environment in which the system operates, in this case the job work load
- A controlling function that allows parameters characterizing the components to be varied or the interconnections to be altered

• A set of goals or criteria according to which the system performance is evaluated—in this case cost, throughput, and response time.

The computer literature abounds with descriptions of device and system simulations, as well as complete books on the methodology for constructing simulators and at interpreting the results.* Here we limit ourselves to a brief description of two commercial simulation packages, SCERT (Systems and Computers Evaluation and Review Technique) and CASE (Computer-Aided System Evaluation), both of which have been marketed widely and used extensively for comprehensive evaluation of computer systems.†

The two products are similar in that each has:

• An internal library containing cost and performance specifications and a parametric description of the hardware and software of all major components of a great number of vendors. These libraries are updated regularly on a monthly or quarterly basis.
• A method of specifying the data, file descriptions, equipment configuration, and software of the system to be investigated.
• An elaborate reporting system for presenting results according to the operational mode of interest (real-time, multiprogrammed, time-shared, sequential, etc.). These reports provide details on performance, usage statistics, management summaries, and so on.

SCERT proceeds in five phases as shown in Fig. 1.4. (The CASE flow diagram is very similar.)

Phase I: The run description is hardware dependent. It provides a mathematical model of each run, based on the file description and costing information.

Phase II: Configuration assembler is where the library of vendor hardware and software is called on to produce a report detailing the configuration appropriate to the run needed.

Phases III and IV: The simulation is actually carried out here, usually assuming a multiprogramming mode.

Phase V: Report generation; presents and displays the results.

---

*See, for example, Ferrari (1978), Svobodova (1976), Drummond (1973), and Teichroew and Lubin (1966).

†SCERT, released in 1962, is a product of COMPRESS, a division of Comtem; for a description, see Cornalba and Goosens (1970). CASE, first delivered in 1969, is a product of Tesdata Systems Corp.

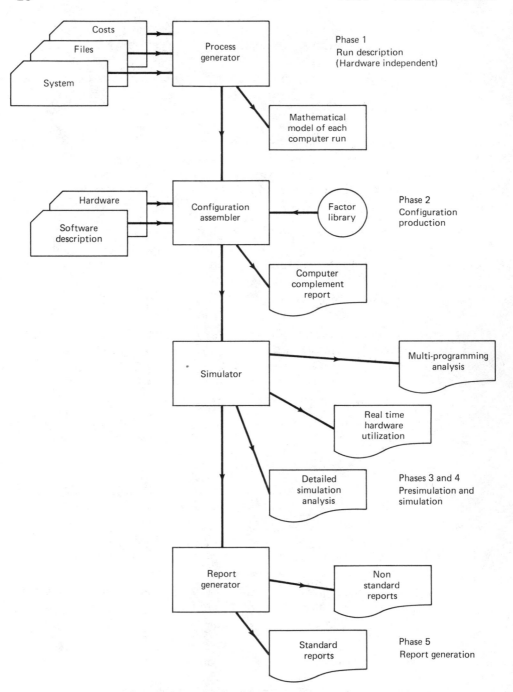

Figure 1.4 Compress SCERT (Systems and Computers Evaluation and Review Technique) (From F. L. Cornalba and A. Goosens, "The Simulation Program SCERT and SCERT a Tool for Product Planning," *IAG J.,* 3, no. 2 (August 1970), 151–78.

Because SCERT and CASE are fairly complex, the distributors provide personnel who install and use the packages. Simulations of proposed systems can be costly, running into the tens of thousands of dollars, but they are much less expensive than benchmark evaluations. Provided that the work load is specified carefully, it is claimed that the results of simulations will typically be within 10% of those that would be observed with the actual system under investigation, but it is safe to state that the packages are most useful for comparing the performance of two similar configurations, in one of which some proposed upgrade is being considered.

1.4.2 Measurements

Simulations and models both need information about critical quantities relating to the configuration and work load to be useful. Basic configuration quantities are resource utilizations (CPU, I/O devices, channels) and device service times. Basic work-load parameters are arrival rates and distributions, and statistics for demands on resources. Beyond these basics a great deal of additional detail is of interest, such as queue lengths at each device, overlap device usage, the number of paging faults per second, and observations of system response time under standard conditions. These are needed to calibrate or validate the model before it is used to predict results for new conditions.

Measurements and observations can be taken using either (or both) hardware and software. Once again there is a considerable body of literature on measurement tools and an increasing variety of products available from commercial sources.

In hardware monitors the fundamental devices are simply "and" gates, which record the occurrence of two simultaneous events; and "or" gates, which detect when either of two specified events has transpired. By combining gates with counters and attaching observation probes at suitable points, it is possible to record a great deal of information while a program is being executed. As an example, Fig. 1.5 shows how it is possible to detect when the CPU is executing instructions which are within a specified region of memory bounded by an upper address, U, and a lower address, L. Since the storage region occupied by the operating system is known, such a configuration makes it possible to observe when the CPU is under control of the operation system and, by complementation, when it is under control of the user program. Similar measurements can be obtained by using software programs, which in effect are interpreters interrupting execution to record events in counter registers. Software monitors have the usual disadvantages of interpreters in that they incur overhead, typically 2 to 5% of the run time. On the other hand, they are more flexible than hardware monitors, because certain kinds of information not easily detected by using hardware (e.g., queue lengths) can be observed by software. Table 1.11 compares the two kinds of monitors.

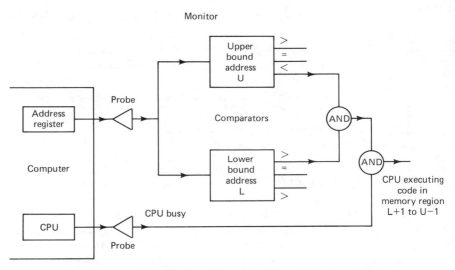

Figure 1.5 Detecting Regional Execution Using A Hardware Monitor

Monitoring is an important aspect of computer performance evaluation, and mini-industries have grown up around both hardware and software monitors. Additional information is available in the published proceedings of the many conferences which have been held on performance evaluation, and in *Performance Evaluation Review,* the quarterly published by SICMETRICS, the

TABLE 1.11 PERFORMANCE MONITORS

	Hardware	Software
Component		
Probe	Physically attached to a device, register, etc.; triggered by event	A program interrupt which records that a certain device or program has been activated
Control	Connection matrix which governs sequencing and synchronization of probes; combines events by logical operations (and, or, not, etc.)	The monitor program governing process flow
Analyzer	Interprets data from probes as meaningful processes	
Output	Records and displays analyzer data—tables, histograms, charts, etc.	
Advantages	Can be applied continuously; requires no overhead; many simultaneous measurements possible	More flexible—can be used to monitor quantities not available to hardware monitor (e.g., queue lengths)
Disadvantages	Limited applicability—some quantities not easily measured; requires calibration, cables, perhaps an engineer	Requires overhead for time and storage—typically 3–5% of running time; sampling rate must not be too high

Special Interest Group on Measurement and Evaluation of the Association for Computing Machinery.

PROBLEMS

1. Using the data in Phister (1979) for computers that appeared in the years 1961, 1963, and 1965, plot regression lines of the form

    $$\ln C = a_0 + a_1 \ln \text{FOM} + B_1 Y_{1963} + B_2 Y_{1965}$$

    where FOM is a figure of merit and $Y_{1963} = 1$ only for 1963 and $Y_{1965} = 1$ only for 1965:
    (1) Calculated using Knight's Index for commercial machines
    (2) Calculated from $\dfrac{\text{word length (bits)}}{\text{memory cycle time } (\mu\text{sec})}$

    From these regression lines estimate the technological rate of improvement in 1962 (for the interval 1961–1963) and 1964 (for the interval 1963–1965). How do the indices compare for the two FOMs? Suggest reasons for the difference.

2. Use the reference data given in Auerbach's *Business Minicomputers* to estimate the cost for a computer configuration as close as possible to the following:

    - High-speed memory: 48 Kbytes
    - DASD memory: 5 Mbytes
    - Line printer: 200 lpm
    - Disk file: 500 Kbytes
    - Console printer or display unit: 1000 characters

    Do this for each of the following systems:
    (a) Burroughs B80
    (b) Data General CS/40
    (c) Honeywell Series 60 Level 62
    (d) ICL System Ten 220
    (e) IBM System 34
    (f) NCR 8000 series
    (g) UNIVAC BC/7 series
    Where a component does not exactly fit the specification, take the one nearest to the one desired. Compute the cost for each configuration using the estimator given by Equation 1.4. Rate the systems using computed cost/actual cost as a figure of merit.

3. Microcomputers such as the Commodore Superpet, the Apple IIe, the Radio Shack TRS-80, or the IBM Personal Computer are relatively simple systems, very much like those for which Knight's Index was first computed. Obtain the characteristics of these computers and calculate Knight's performance index for them. (Most of these machines use programs for even basic arithmetic operations, so it is necessary to choose an operating

system and language in making the comparisons. For data see the manufacturer's specifications, or issues of *Byte,* and make "reasonable" assumptions for parameters whose values are not given.) Using Knight index/cost as an FOM (assume that rental cost = purchase price/70), compare the microcomputers with representative computers that appeared in the period 1960–1980.

4. The table shows costs and performance indexes (Knight's and those of the International Data Corporation) for four IBM computers.
   (a) Are the indexes (reasonably) consistent with each other?
   (b) Is it reasonable to fit a straight line of the form log $C = a + b$ log Index?
   (c) If such a line is fitted, do the results support Grosch's law, or are there significant economies or diseconomies of scale? What does this suggest about IBM's pricing policy for the 4300 series relative to the 3000 series?

IBM Model	C (thousands of dollars/month)	Index IDC	Index Knight's
3031	61.0	54	2317
3032	114	124	6921
4331	7.3	11	562
4341	18.9	37	2141

BIBLIOGRAPHY

AUERBACH, *Computer Technology Reports.* Pennsauken, N.J.: Auerbach.

BROCK, G. W., *The United States Computer Industry: A Study of Market Power.* Cambridge, Mass.: Ballinger, 1974.

CALE, E. G., L. L. GREMILLON, and J. L. MCKENNEY, "Price Performance Patterns of U.S. Computer Systems," *Commun. ACM,* 22, no. 4 (April 1979), 225–33.

CORNALBA, F. L., and A. GOOSENS, "The Simulation Program SCERT and SCERT a Tool for Product Planning," *IAG J.,* 3, no. 2 (August 1970), 151–78.

Datapro 70, Datapro Research Corp., Delran, N.J.

DRUMMOND, M. E., *Evaluation and Measurement Techniques for Digital Computer Systems.* Englewood Cliffs, N.J.: Prentice-Hall, 1973.

FEDOROWICZ, J., "Comments on Price/Performance Patterns of U.S. Computer Systems," *Commun. ACM,* 24 (September 1981), 585–86.

FERRARI, D., *Computer Systems Performance Evaluation.* Englewood Cliffs, N.J.: Prentice-Hall, 1978.

GAVER, D. P., "Probability Models for Multiprogramming Computer Systems," *J. ACM,* 14, no. 3 (July 1967), 423–38.

GML *Computer Characteristics Review.* Lexington, Mass.: GML Computer.

GOSDEN, J. A., and R. L. SISSON, "Standardized Comparisons of Computer Performance," *Information Processing 62* (Proc. IFIP Congress 62). Amsterdam: North Holland. pp. 57–61.

HELLER, P., "Benchmarking the Price of Computers," *Comput. Netw.,* 1 (1976), 27–32.

HILLEGASS, J. R., "Standardized Benchmark Problems Measure Computer Performance," *Comput. Autom.,* 15, no. 1 (January 1966), 16–19.

KLEINROCK, L., *Queueing Systems,* Vol. 1: *Theory.* New York: Wiley, 1975.

KNIGHT, K. E., "Changes in Computer Performance," *Datamation,* 12, no. 9 (September 1966), 40–58.

———, "Evolving Computer Performance 1963–1967," *Datamation,* 14, no. 1 (January 1968), 31–35.

———, "Performance of Computers," in *Encyclopaedia of Computer Science,* ed. A. Ralston. Princeton, N.J.: Petrocelli/Charter, 1976, pp. 1065–78.

MAJOR, J. B., "Processor, I/O Path and DASD Configuration Capacity." *IBM Syst. J.,* 20, no. 1 (1981), 63–85.

OLIVER, P., J. BAIRD et al., "An Experiment in the Use of Synthetic Programs for System Benchmarks," in *AFIPS Conf. Proc.,* Vol. 43 (NCC), 1974, pp. 431–38.

Performance Evaluation Review, published quarterly by SIGMETRICS, Special Interest Group on Measurement and Evaluation, Association for Computing Machinery.

PHISTER, M., Jr., *Data Processing Technology and Economics,* 2nd ed. Santa Fe, N. Mex.: Santa Monica/Bedford, Mass.: Digital Press, 1979.

SOLOMON, M. B., "Economics of Scale and the IBM System/360," *Commun. ACM,* 9 (1966), 435–40.

SVOBODOVA, L., *Computer Performance Measurement and Evaluation Methods.* New York: Elsevier, 1976.

TEICHROEW, D., and J. F. LUBIN, "Computer Simulation: Discussion of the Technique and Comparison of Languages," *Commun. ACM,* 9, no. 10 (October 1966), 723–41.

TURN, R., *Computers in the 1980s.* New York: Columbia University Press, 1974.

WICHMANN, B. A., and J. DU CROZ, "A Program to Calculate the GAMM Measure," *Comput. J.,* 22, no. 4 (1979), 317–22.

2

Throughput, Response Time, and Capacity Planning

A truly satisfactory way of evaluating a computer system would be to rate, in quantitative terms, its capacity (i.e., its ability to do information processing) similar to the way an engine is rated by its ability to do mechanical work. Information theory does provide a measure of the amount of information present in a string of characters; complexity theory, a branch of the theory of algorithms, addresses the question of finding the least number of operations required to carry out mathematical processes such as finding the median of a set of numbers, sorting a file, or traversing a list structure. But these subjects are a long way from being able to suggest quantitative measures for the operating capacity of a computer system, taking into account all that is done by both hardware and software. In attempting to arrive at such measures we are reduced to modeling the system under study, usually by simplifying it considerably, and making some highly arbitrary assumptions about the nature of the work load being processed. With such restrictions it becomes difficult to be certain that the ratings which result genuinely reflect information-processing capability. But there are situations where the calculations can be of considerable use, for example, when we suspect that there is some bottleneck in the computing system and would like to estimate how much upgrading a particular component would improve performance. In this case a model can be constructed to emphasize the differences between the actual and the proposed systems, and a reasonable degree of confidence can be attached to the calculations on the *change* of performance and throughput.

In this chapter two models for calculating throughput are presented. The first depends on the notion of system balance, that is, the relative importance of the I/O processors and the central processing unit. The basic ideas go back very early in the development of computers, but we shall use the concise terminologies and notation of Gaver (1967) and Phister (1979). The second model derives from the notion of a computer as a queueing system or, rather, an interconnected network of queueing systems. Here again there is a considerable body of work (see especially Kleinrock, 1975), but we shall use a very simple approach due to Buzen and Denning (1977). In both cases only the beginning and elementary sections of the theories are presented, but even this is enough to perform some useful and interesting calculations about system throughput.

2.1 SYSTEM BALANCE

In both models the various computer components (input and output devices, channels, high-speed memory, CPU) are regarded as *resources*. Jobs enter the system from an input device, call upon different resources, and eventually leave via an output device. The system as a whole will be used efficiently if the various resources can be kept busy simultaneously. Of special interest is the utilization of expensive resources such as the CPU and I/O channels.

The most general system we shall consider is a multiprogrammed one, in which there are many inputs, outputs, and channels [as illustrated in Fig. 2.1(a)].* Note that in this model magnetic tapes and disk drives are regarded as I/O devices. (The diagram suggests that any I/O device can be connected to any channel, but in practice each channel will have a particular cluster of devices associated with it.) The notation we need can be derived from a simple buffered system with only one input and one output device [Fig. 2.1(b)], and we shall also consider the even simpler unbuffered system of Fig. 2.1(c).

The following parameters characterize jobs:

$$D_I = \text{number of characters of input data}$$

$$D_o = \text{number of characters of output data}$$

$$D = D_I + D_0 = \text{total number of I/O } \textit{data} \text{ characters}$$

$$kD = \text{number of I/O characters for both program and}$$
$$\text{data; } (k-1)D \text{ is the program size}$$

$$s = \text{average number of computer operations required}$$
$$\text{per I/O character}$$

It follows that the total number of computer operations per job $= sD$, a relation that can be regarded as plausible in many situations but which may not be true generally.

---

*More generally, we could consider multiprocessor systems with several CPUs and hierarchies of memory.

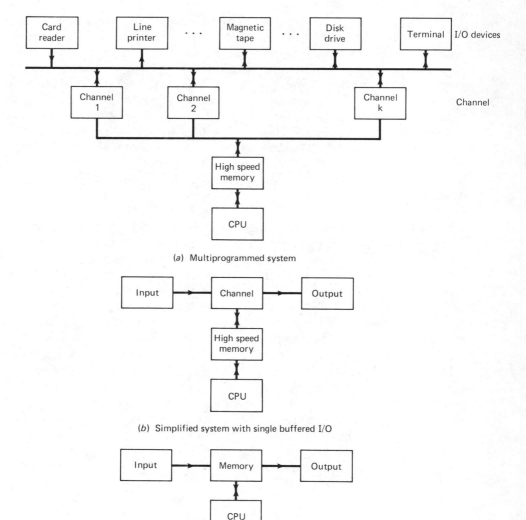

(a) Multiprogrammed system

(b) Simplified system with single buffered I/O

(c) Basic unbuffered system

Figure 2.1   Computer System Models

To characterize the computer system we define:

C' = processor speed, operations per second; in our examples
we shall usually take $1/C' = 0.95t_{add} + 0.05t_{mult}$

D' = I/O speed, characters per second (cps)

From these definitions it follows that

1. t_{CPU}, the processor time for a job $= sD/C'$
2. $t_{I/O}$, the I/O time for a job $= kD/D'$

It is useful to define two other parameters, s_c (the critical value of s) and r. s_c is the value of s such that $t_{CPU} = t_{I/O}$, so that

$$s_c = \frac{kC'}{D'} \tag{2.1}$$

$$r = \frac{t_{CPU}}{t_{I/O}} = \frac{sD/C'}{kD/D'} = \frac{sD'}{kC'} = \frac{s}{s_c} \tag{2.2}$$

Finally, the system throughput, X, in cps, is defined by*

$$X = \frac{\text{number of data I/O characters}}{\text{total system time required}} \tag{2.3}$$

Consider now the simple unbuffered system of Fig. 2.1(c). For this

$$X_{\text{unbuffered}} = \frac{D}{kD/D' + sD/C'} = \frac{D'/k}{1 + s/s_c} \tag{2.4}$$

For the buffered system of Fig. 2.1(b)

$$X_{\text{buffered}} = \frac{D}{\max\left(k\dfrac{D}{D'}, s\dfrac{D}{C'}\right)} = \frac{D'/k}{\max(1, s/s_c)} \tag{2.5}$$

The well-known concepts of I/O-bound and processor-bound systems suggest themselves immediately from Equations 2.4 and 2.5. For an I/O-*bound* system, $t_{I/O} > t_{CPU}$ and $k/D' > s/C'$. If $t_{I/O} \gg t_{CPU}$, then

$$X_{\text{unbuffered}} \approx X_{\text{buffered}} \approx \frac{D'}{k}$$

For a *processor-bound* system, $t_{CPU} \gg t_{I/O}$ and $s/C' > k/D'$. If $t_{CPU} \gg t_{I/O}$,

$$X_{\text{unbuffered}} \approx X_{\text{buffered}} \approx \frac{C'}{s}$$

---

*Note that in Equation 2.3 we have accepted a definition which seems reasonable but which may not always reflect the real ability to process jobs. Thus in this definition we are neglecting times that the system must remain idle due to operator action, maintenance, malfunctions, and other possibly important limitations on system throughput. It might be desirable to define throughput in terms of *jobs per second* rather than *characters per second*, but this would require the notion of a standard job.

For a perfectly *balanced* system $t_{I/O} = t_{CPU}$, $s = s_c$, and

$$X_{\text{buffered}} = 2X_{\text{unbuffered}} = \frac{D'}{k} = \frac{C'}{s}$$

It is helpful to display the results in graphical form and, in doing so, to represent the variables in dimensionless form. Let

$$X^r = X^{\text{reduced}} = \frac{kX}{D'}$$

and

$$s^r = s^{\text{reduced}} = \frac{s}{s_c}$$

Equation 2.4 becomes

$$X^r_{\text{unbuffered}} = \frac{1}{1 + s^r}$$

and Equation 2.5 becomes

$$X^r_{\text{buffered}} = \frac{1}{\max{(1, s^r)}}$$

These are shown in Fig. 2.2(*a*). On a logarithmic scale X^r_{buffered} simply becomes two straight lines, as shown in Fig. 2.2(*b*).

An idea of the magnitudes of the quantities in an actual situation may be had by considering the IBM 370/165. Using data given in Phister (1979, p. 344) for this system and adding an instruction fetch time of 0.08 μsec to the instruction execution time, $t_{\text{add}} = 0.24$ μsec, $t_{\text{mult}} = 0.78$ μsec, so that the weighted instruction time $= 0.95 \times 0.24 + 0.05 \times 0.78 = 0.2678$ μsec, where

$$C' = \frac{10^6}{0.2678} = 3734 \text{ kops} \quad \text{(thousands of operations per second)}$$

To determine D' it is necessary to select an I/O device, obtain the data on its performance, and make some assumptions about the record format. Moreover, for any peripheral it is necessary to distinguish between the maximum or nominal data transfer rate and the effective transfer rate, which is less than the nominal because of overhead due to format characters, latency time, and so on.

In general, for a peripheral

$$D'_{\text{effective}} = \frac{B}{t_{\text{acc}} + (B + f)/D'_{\text{max}}} \tag{2.6}$$

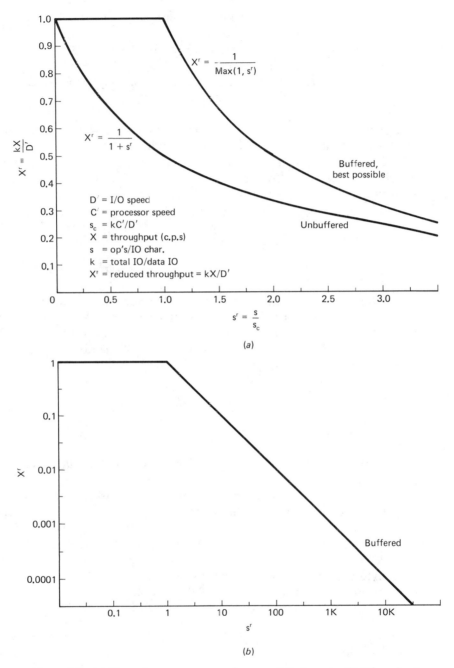

Figure 2.2   (a) Throughput versus operations per I/O character (b) Throughput versus operations per I/O character (logarithmic scales)

where D'_{max} = maximum or nominal data transfer rate, cps
B = block size, bytes
f = format bytes required by the device
t_{acc} = access time, sec
= average seek time + average latency time, for a drum or disk
= start time + stop time, for tapes

For example, suppose that the I/O device is an IBM 3420 model 3 tape drive and the block size is 1200 characters. For this device (Phister, 1979, p. 377) D'_{max} = 120 kcps, and f the interblock gap = 0.6 in., corresponding, at a recording density of 1600 b/in., to 960 characters. Also, the start time = 6 msec and the stop time = 4 msec, so that t_{acc} = 10 msec. Thus

$$D'_{effective} = \frac{1200}{0.01 + (1200 + 960)/120,000} = \frac{1200 \times 120,000}{3360}$$

$$= 42.8 \text{ kcps}   \text{(thousands of characters per second)}$$

What are reasonable values for k and s? Data in the literature seem to indicate very wide variations from one application to another. We shall take $k = 10$. For s, Phister (1979, p. 556) quotes a rule of thumb, suggested by Amdahl, to the effect that a balanced system needs two bytes of memory and 1 bit per second I/O for each instruction per second. This implies that $s = 8$; we take $s = 10$ for our example. Then

$$\frac{k}{D'} = \frac{1}{4.28 \times 10^3} \quad \text{and} \quad \frac{1}{C'} = \frac{1}{3.7 \times 10^6}$$

so that this system is very much I/O bound, and the data throughput rate is $D'/k = 4280$ cps.

It is no surprise that a single channel devoted to one magnetic tape drive is not an adequate I/O for the IBM 370/65. From the very beginnings of computers CPU speeds have exceeded I/O rates and it has been necessary to look for high-speed I/O devices to achieve system balance. Suppose that an IBM 2305-1 fixed-head file were used for I/O. Assume a block size of one-half track = 7068 bytes; 415 bytes are required for format, D'_{max} = 2827 kcps and the average latency time is 2.5 msec (Phister, 1979, p. 372).

$$D'_{effective} = \frac{7068}{.0025 + 7483/2,827,000} = 1373 \text{ kcps}$$

Now $k/D' = 1/(1.37 \times 10^5)$ and the data transfer rate is considerably higher, at 137 kcps, but with this as the only I/O device the system is *still* I/O bound. To achieve balance, multiple devices, using several channels, are needed.

Before examining how the results just derived have to be modified for the more complex multiprogrammed systems of Fig. 2.1(a), it is instructive to consider the utilization of the resources in the buffered and unbuffered systems. This can be done with the help of a timing diagram, for three types of systems, as shown in Fig. 2.3. For illustrative purposes it is assumed that for every job i, the input time t_I^i, the processing time t_P^i, and output time t_O^i are all equal. In each of the three cases the efficiencies (i.e., utilization ratios U) are shown for the I/O and CPU resources, as well as the system throughputs. To calculate these

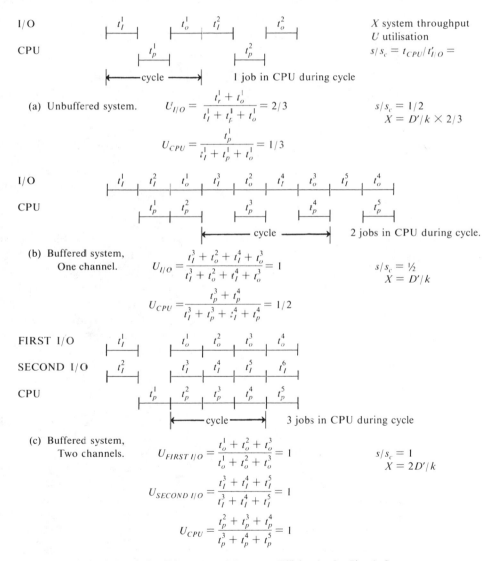

Figure 2.3 Timing Diagrams and Resource Efficiencies for Simple Systems

quantities it is necessary to identify a periodic interval, after which conditions are repeated. It will be observed that as I/O devices are added to bring the system into better balance and increase throughput, the number of different jobs handled by the CPU during one period increases. In effect, the CPU must be multiprogrammed so as to switch from one job to another; to improve balance and obtain maximum resource utilization, it is necessary to increase the multiprogramming level when the number of channels is increased.

Gaver (1967) examined not only the effect of increasing the number of I/O channels, I, and the multiprogramming level, J, but also the effects of variablity in the CPU and I/O times for jobs. The latter was done by assuming that jobs obeyed various distribution patterns (hyperexponential, gamma, exponential, constant). For each pattern the CPU utilization

$$U_{\text{CPU}} = \frac{\text{expected CPU busy period}}{\text{expected CPU busy period} + \text{expected CPU idle period}}$$

(2.7)

was calculated for a number of values of I and J. With one channel we had

$$r = \frac{t_{\text{CPU}}}{t_{\text{I/O}}} = \frac{s}{s_c}$$

(Equation 2.2), but with I channels $s/s_c = rI$. The differences in CPU efficiency due to the different job distributions turn out to be appreciable only when the multiprogramming level is fairly high. Table 2.1 shows representative excerpts from Gaver's table for the hyperexponential distribution with $\sigma^2 = 8$, the situation where there is the greatest variation from the case of uniform job distribution. Besides tabulating U_{CPU} in Table 2.1, the reduced throughput is shown. Recall that $X' = X(k/D')$, where X is the data throughput rate. The effective CPU rate is $U_{\text{CPU}}C'$, so that the data throughput rate is $U_{\text{CPU}} C'/s$:

$$X' = \frac{U_{\text{CPU}}C'}{s} \times \frac{k}{D'} = \frac{U}{Ir} \qquad \text{on substituting} \qquad \frac{s}{s_c} = \frac{sD'}{kC'} = Ir$$

To illustrate the effect of increasing the multiprogramming level, some of the data of Table 2.1 are plotted in Fig. 2.4 so as to compare the throughputs with those for the unbuffered and (best case) buffered systems. Some observations help to make the results more understandable.

1. Increasing the multiprogramming level, other parameters remaining constant, increases CPU efficiency and throughput. However, even at high levels U_{CPU} is appreciably less than 1 unless the number of channels is high and s/s_c is small. For example, with $J = 10$ and $I = 7$, $U_{\text{CPU}} = 0.81$ when $r = 0.2$.

TABLE 2.1 CPU UTILIZATION, U_{CPU}, AND REDUCED THROUGHPUT, X', FOR MULTIPROGRAMMED SYSTEMS[a]

Multiprogramming Level J	$r = 0.1$						$r = 0.2$						$r = 0.5$			
	$I = 3$		$I = 5$		$I = 7$		$I = 3$		$I = 5$		$I = 7$		$I = 3$		$I = 5$	
	U_{CPU}	X'	U_{CPU}	X'	U_{CPU}	X'	U_{CPU}	X'	U_{CPU}	X'	U_{CPU}	X'	U_{CPU}	X'	U_{CPU}	X'
1	0.091	0.303	0.091	0.182	0.091	0.130	0.167	0.276	0.167	0.167	0.167	0.119	0.333	0.222	0.335	0.133
2	0.177	0.667	0.177	0.354	0.177	0.253	0.310	0.517	0.310	0.310	0.310	0.221	0.548	0.365	0.548	0.219
3	0.258	0.860	0.258	0.516	0.256	0.369	0.432	0.720	0.432	0.432	0.432	0.309	0.692	0.461	0.692	0.277
4			0.334	0.668	0.334	0.477	0.464	0.773	0.536	0.536	0.536	0.383	0.738	0.492	0.789	0.316
5			0.405	0.810	0.405	0.579	0.479	0.798	0.624	0.624	0.624	0.446	0.764	0.509	0.857	0.313
6					0.471	0.673	0.496	0.830	0.657	0.657	0.697	0.498	0.790	0.527	0.866	0.354
7					0.532	0.760	0.513	0.855	0.667	0.667	0.754	0.541	0.815	0.542	0.901	0.360
8							0.526	0.877	0.690	0.690	0.765	0.561	0.832	0.555	0.916	0.367
9							0.537	0.895	0.710	0.710	0.791	0.565	0.849	0.586	0.931	0.372
10							0.546	0.910	0.728	0.728	0.812	0.580	0.864	0.576	0.943	0.377

[a] $r = t_{CPU}/t_{I/O}$; $X' = U_{CPU}/Ir =$ throughput$/(D/k)$; $s/s_c = Ir$; hyperexponential distribution for processing times, $\sigma^2 = 0.8$.

[b] U_{CPU} from D. P. Gaver, "Probability Models for Multiprogramming Computer Systems," *J. ACM*, 14, no. 3 (July 1967), 423–38; see also Phister (1979, 434–35).

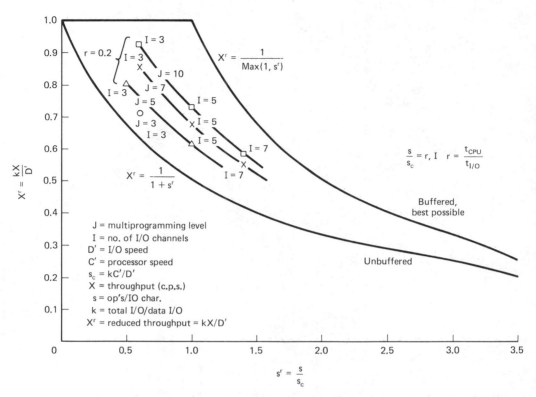

Figure 2.4   Effect on throughput of increasing the multiprogramming level and number of I/O channels

2. Increasing the number of channels increases CPU efficiency, at least to the point where the number of channels becomes equal to the multiprogramming level ($I = J$), after which extra channels cannot be utilized. Throughput as a fraction of the maximum I/O rate decreases, but throughput in cps increases since the maximum I/O rate is proportional to the number of channels.

3. When the system is highly processor bound (s/s_c is large), multiprogramming makes the CPU efficient, but throughput efficiency is small, because it takes many channels to make the multiprogramming effective.

4. The model makes no allowance for the overhead introduced by multiprogramming. When the CPU is engaged in switching from one program to the next it is said to be in the *supervisor* state as opposed to the *idle* state when it is not busy, and the *problem* state when it is working on a user's service request. Although it is not always clear which activities should be charged to the supervisor and which to the user, by definition the CPU is said to be in the supervisor state when it is executing instructions resident

in that part of the memory devoted to the operating system. As will be seen in the next section, time spent in the supervisor state is by no means negligible, and in consequence high levels of multiprogramming (greater than six) do not seem to be common in practice. The effect tends to lower CPU efficiency for systems with a high throughput rate.

2.2. QUEUEING MODELS

In the discussion of system balance in Section 2.1 the focus was on device utilization. It was assumed that whenever an I/O device that accepts jobs from the outside completed service on one job, another job was available for input. The I/O peripherals would always be busy when the system was I/O bound, in which case the CPU would sometimes be idle. This means that there are queues associated with I/O devices for I/O-bound systems, and queues associated with the CPU for processor-bound systems, but these queues did not appear explicitly in the model. In order to be able to say something about the response times of system, (i.e., the time it takes for a job to receive services from all the devices it needs), it is necessary to bring device queues into the model explicitly. For time-sharing systems, response time is the factor that really determines throughput capacity. For interactive systems it is natural to measure throughput rate as the number of transactions completed per second, and the dependence on response time is obvious. Models in which there are queues associated with each device, and jobs flow through the system, possibly waiting in a queue, receive service, and then move on to the next device, are called *queued network models*. The theory of such models has been developed extensively, and the mathematics can be complex, but even when it is simplified by making some basic assumptions it is possible to derive quite useful results about throughput and response times of basic interactive systems.

2.2.1 A Single Queue

To appreciate what happens when queues are present, it is helpful to consider a very simple model consisting of a single device (a processor) and its queue (Fig. 2.5). Jobs arrive requiring service; if the processor is busy they are queued; when they receive service they leave. Queues are characterized by:

- The number of servers (in Fig. 2.5 there is only one)
- The arrival-rate distribution for incoming jobs
- The service-time distribution
- The service discipline

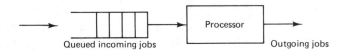

Figure 2.5   A single server queue

There are various aspects and possibilities for this last. The service may be first-come-first-served (FCFS) or may be determined by priorities associated with the job. It may be independent of the service requirements or dependent on them (e.g., short jobs get served first). Given assumptions about the queue, it is possible to derive, mathematically or by simulation, results about the expected response time and queue length.

The simplest case, mathematically, is a single FCFS queue, in which the arrival rate is governed by a Poisson distribution with the average number of arrivals per second equal to λ, and the service time is governed by an exponential distribution with an average service time of $1/\mu$s.* Such a queue is called M/M/1. A two-server queue with exponential arrival rate and general service time distribution is specified as M/G/2. For an M/M/1 queue it is easy to show that

$$E(n), \text{ the expected length of the queue} = \rho/1 - \rho$$

$$E(r), \text{ the expected response time} = 1/(\mu - \lambda)$$

where

$$\rho = \frac{\lambda}{\mu} = \frac{\text{arrivals rate}}{\text{service rate}} \text{ (a dimensionless number)}$$

$E(n)$ is plotted in Fig. 2.6 and it will be noted that as $\rho \to 1 (\lambda \to \mu)$ the queue length and response time both become infinite. If the queue is full and there are always jobs to be processed, the throughput is the maximum (μ jobs/sec), but this maximum is associated with an infinite response time.

In queueing networks with more complicated service time and arrival distributions, the relationship between throughput and response time is of course more complex. But as will be seen, in such systems there is often a bottleneck device, the effect of which is to make the system look like a simple queue, with the same inverse relationship between throughput and service time. Note that from the service center's point of view, long queues mean a maximum throughput; from the user's point of view long queues mean long response time

---

*Explicitly, probability of k arrivals in t seconds $= (\lambda t)^k e^{-\lambda t}/k!$, and probability of service time between t and $t + dt = \mu e^{-\mu t} dt$.

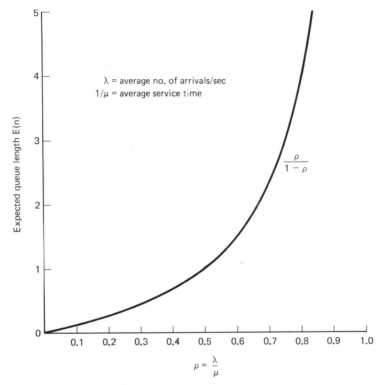

Figure 2.6   Expected length of m/m/1 queue

and poor service, and somehow these differing points of view have to be reconciled and reflected in the pricing policy.

2.2.2 Queued Networks

Consider now a more complicated queueing network, with several devices (CPU, disks, channels, terminals) as shown in Fig. 2.7. Each resource is a queueing device, with characteristic service times and discipline. For theoretical purposes it is desirable to consider a *closed* system in which the number of jobs is constant, so that for every job departure there is a job arrival (as opposed to an open system where jobs come and go at different rates). The behavior of such systems is complex, especially if the number of jobs in the system, J, is high, but adopting an approach of Buzen and Denning (1978) which they call "operational analysis," attention can be focused on parameters which describe the *average* behavior during some period of observation, T, rather than on statistical distributions. This greatly simplifies the analysis, but still allows useful conclusions to be drawn.

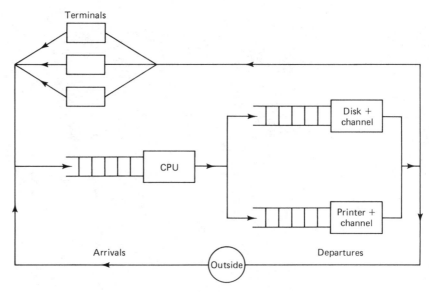

Figure 2.7 A queueing network

For each device D_i $(i = 1 \cdots K)$ during time T, let

A_i = number of arrivals

B_i = total busy time (i.e., time for which there are jobs in the queue or a job receiving service)

n_i = length of the queue (a time-dependent variable) and $\bar{n}_i$ be the average length

After receiving service at D_i, a job moves to D_j, and the job flow is characterized by

C_{ij} = number of job requests for service at D_j, immediately after completing service at D_i

With the system closed, the outside may be regarded as device 0, so that

A_{0j} = number of job whose *first* service request is for D_j

C_{i0} = number of job whose *last* service request is for D_i

$$\text{number of arrivals} = \sum_{j=1}^{K} A_{0j} \equiv A_0$$

$$\text{number of departures} = \sum_{i=1}^{K} C_{i0} \equiv C_0$$

Since the system is closed, $A_0 = C_0$. The system throughput $= C_0/T \equiv X_0$. We further define

$$C_i = \sum_{j=0}^{K} C_{ij} = \text{number of completions at } D_i$$

$$U_i = B_i/T = \text{utilization of } D_i$$

$$X_i = C_i/T = \text{output rate of requests from } D_i$$

$$q_{ij} = \text{fraction of jobs proceeding to } D_j \text{ on completing service at } D_i$$

$$= C_{ij}/C_i; \text{ in particular}$$

$$S_i = \text{mean service time between requests at } D_i = B_i/C_i$$

It follows that

$$U_i = \frac{B_i}{T} = \frac{B_i}{C_i}\frac{C_i}{T} = S_i X_i$$

$$X_0 = \frac{\sum_{i=1}^{K} C_{i0}}{T} = \sum_{i=1}^{K} \frac{q_{i0} C_i}{T} = \sum_{i=1}^{K} q_{i0} X_i$$

Also let

$$W_i = \text{total number of jobs queued at } D_i \text{ during } T \text{ (this}$$
$$\text{is the area for interval } T \text{ of the curve showing the}$$
$$\text{number of jobs versus time for the device)}$$

$$R_i = \text{average waiting time at } D_i \text{ for requests} = W_i/C_i$$

Then

$$\bar{n}_i = \frac{W_i}{T} = \frac{R_i C_i}{T} = R_i X_i \tag{2.8}$$

Equation 2.8, which relates the service time to the average queue length, is a very general one; it holds over a very wide class of distributions and service disciplines and is known as *Little's law*.

As seen in the preceding section, for a single-server queue, when the arrival and service distribution are known it is possible to calculate the queue length and response time. For queued networks with general distributions the calculations are much more difficult and depend on certain assumptions regarding the job flow. If these assumptions are not true, it is of course possible to measure the device parameters and then calculate what would happen if different demands are made on the resources, or the configuration changed in some way.

In order to derive additional results, a rather strong assumption is made at this time—to the effect that *at each device* (not just for the system as whole), the number of outputs equals the number of inputs. With this assumption of job flow balance for each device,

$$C_j = A_j = \sum_{i=0}^{K} C_{ij} \qquad j = 0 \cdots K$$

Dividing by T and substituting $q_{ij} = C_{ij}/C_i$ and $X_j = C_j/T$, we have

$$X_j = \sum_{i=0}^{K} X_i q_{ij} \qquad j = 0 \cdots K$$

The job flow balance equations may be rewritten by dividing each side by X_o and defining $X_i/X_o \equiv V_i$, the *visit ratio* for D_i. Then

$$V_o = 1$$

$$V_j = q_{oj} + \sum_{i=1}^{K} V_i q_{ij} \tag{2.9}$$

Given the q_{ij} characterizing the configuration, Equation 2.9 is a system of $K + 1$ independent equations for the $K + 1$ quantities $V_o \cdots V_K$. This system can always be found for a connected network and solved for the V's. For our examples the visit ratios will be given directly instead of the q's, on the assumption that these are observed from measurements taken on the system.

Finally, we would like to obtain the *system response time* and this can be defined as $R \equiv \bar{N}/X_o$, where $\bar{N} = \bar{n}_1 + \bar{n}_2 + \cdots + \bar{n}_k$. Now from Little's law, $\bar{n}_i = X_i R_i$ for each device, so that

$$R = \frac{\bar{n}_1 + \cdots \bar{n}_n}{X_o}$$

$$= \frac{X_1 R_1 + \cdots X_K R_K}{X_o} \tag{2.10}$$

$$= \sum_{i=1}^{K} V_i R_i$$

Equation 2.10 can be used to compute the response time for an interactive system. Consider the pure time-sharing system (i.e., no batch service) with M terminals as shown in Fig. 2.8. In this system every job is either queued at a device or waiting at a terminal because of the users' "think" time, assumed to be Z seconds on the average. The mean total service time for a job is $(Z + R)$, where R is now the response time of the rest of the system. Assuming that X_o is the number of jobs completed per second, when job flows are balanced, by Little's law

$$(R + Z)X_o = \overline{N} = M$$

since *all* jobs are either being served or in the think state. Therefore,

$$R = \frac{M}{X_o} - Z \qquad (2.11)$$

Two examples will illustrate the use of formulas that have been derived.

Example 2.1

In the system shown in Fig. 2.8, suppose that $M = 30$ and Z equals 15 sec. Measurements taken at the disk show that it is visited, on the average, 18 times by each job, that the disk utilization is 60%, and that the mean service time is 25 msec. Thus $U_2 = 0.6$, $V_2 = 18$, and $S_2 = 25$ msec. What is the system response time?

The system response time, $R = (M/X_o) - Z$. On the right-hand side of this equation X_o is not known. But

$$X_o = \frac{X_2}{V_2} \qquad \text{and} \qquad X_2 = \frac{U_2}{S_2} = \frac{0.6}{0.025} = 24 \text{ jobs/sec}$$

Working backward, $X_o = 24/18 = 1.33$ jobs/sec and $R = 30/1.33 - 15 = 7.5$ sec.

Example 2.2

Consider now a mixed system similar to that shown in Fig. 2.7, but where there is both batch and interactive services, so that the output has two components, the batch job X_o^B and interactive job X_o^I. Observations show that:

M, number of terminals $= 30$

Z, think time $= 18$ sec

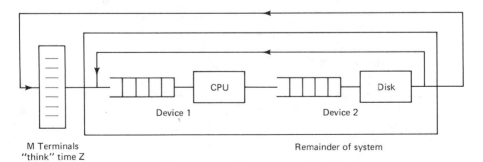

Figure 2.8   A simple time-sharing system

R^I, interactive response time $= 6$ sec

S_2, average disk service time $= 50$ msec

U_2, disk utilization $= 80\%$, and that on the average, each interactive job generates eight disk requests, (V_2^I), and each batch job generates six requests (V_2^B)

What is the batch throughput rate?

We have $X_o^B = X_2^B / V_2^B$. To determine X_2^B

$$X_2^B + X_2^I = X_2 = \frac{U_2}{S_2}$$

where X_2^I is not known. But $X_2^I = V_2^I X_o^I$ and $X_o^I = M/(Z + R^I)$. Working backward, we have

$$X_o^I = \frac{30}{18 + 6} = 1.25 \text{ jobs/sec}$$

$$X_2^I = 1.25 \times 8 = 10 \text{ jobs/sec}$$

$$X_2^B = \frac{0.8}{0.05} - 10 = 16 - 10 = 6$$

$$X_o^B = \frac{6}{6} = 1.0 \text{ job/sec}$$

If the batch throughput is doubled, what happens to the interactive response time?

Assuming that the visit ratios are unchanged, $R^I = (M/X_o^I) - Z$. To determine X_o^I we have

$$X_o^I = \frac{X_2^I}{V_{2I}} \quad \text{and} \quad X_2^I + X_2^B = X_2 = \frac{U_2}{S_2}$$

where $X_2^B = V_2^B X_o^B = 6 \times 2 = 12$. But we need U_2 to find X_2^I, and this is unknown. Suppose that we have a best use condition such that the disk is driven at maximum capacity and $U_2^B = 1$. Then $X_2^I = (1/0.05) - 12 = 8$ jobs/sec, $X_o^I = 8/8 = 1$ job/sec, and $R^I = (30/1) - 18 = 12$ sec. Thus the interactive response time is at least 12 sec and will be greater than this if the disk does not work at maximum capacity.

2.2.3 Bottleneck Analysis

Of particular importance is the performance when the number of jobs is large, and some device is used so heavily that it impedes the flow through the system. If device b restricts the flow, it is called a *bottleneck*. Since $U_i = X_i S_i = V_i S_i X_o$, for the bottleneck,

$$V_b S_b = \max_i \{V_1 S_1 \cdots V_K S_K\}$$

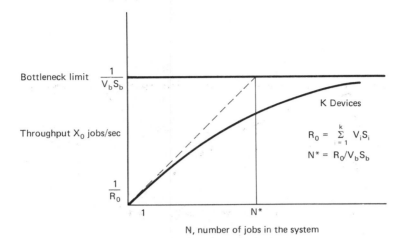

Figure 2.9   Throughput versus number of jobs

where there are K devices. For N large, $U_b = 1$, $X_b = 1/S_b$, and $X_o = 1/V_bS_b$. Let us define $R_o = V_1S_1 + \cdots V_KS_K =$ sum of service times at the various devices. R_o is the smallest possible response time; it will be achieved only if there is no queueing, but it will certainly be observed with $N = 1$. We are now able to sketch the throughput behavior as N, the number of jobs in the system, increases (see Fig. 2.9). For $N = 1$, $X_o = 1/R_o$ jobs/sec; for N large, $X_o \rightarrow 1/V_bS_b$ jobs/sec. Thus the throughput starts with a slope of $1/R_o$ and approaches $1/V_bS_b$ as shown. When $N = K$ the throughput is bounded by K/R_o, and $1/V_bS_b$. As long as there is no queueing in the system, the throughput $= K/R_o$. Thus

$$\frac{K}{R_o} \leq \frac{1}{V_bS_b} \qquad \text{and} \qquad K \leq \frac{R_o}{V_bS_b} = \frac{V_1S_1 + \cdots V_KS_K}{V_bS_b}$$

Let N^* be defined as the saturation point,

$$N^* = \frac{V_1S_1 + \cdots V_KS_K}{V_bS_b}$$

For $N > N^*$ there must be queueing. N^* is determined by the intersection of the line with slope $1/R_o$ and the horizontal line at height $1/V_bS_b$. Generally, there is queueing for $N < N^*$.

A similar diagram can be drawn for the response time in an interactive system (see Fig. 2.10). With M terminals $R = M/X_o - Z$. For $M = 1$, $R = R_o$ the minimum possible response time. Since $X_o \leq 1/V_bS_b$,

$$R \geq MV_iS_i - Z \qquad i = 1 \cdots K$$
$$\geq MV_bS_b - Z$$

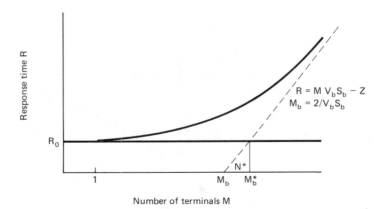

Figure 2.10   Response time of an interactive system

As M gets large, $R \rightarrow MV_bS_b - Z$. Thus the response curve is asymptotic to the straight line $R = MV_bS_b - Z$. The asymptote intersects $R = 0$ at $M = Z/V_bS_b$; call this M_b. It intersects $R = R_o$ where

$$M = \frac{R_o + Z}{V_bS_b} = \frac{R_o}{V_bS_b} + \frac{Z}{V_bS_b} = N* + M_b$$

where, as before, $N*$ is the saturation point; call this value M_b^*. Then $M_b^* = N*$ $+ M_b$. When there are more than M_b^* terminals, queueing is bound to occur.

Example 2.3

For a central server time-sharing system based on a DEC 11-45 (Fig. 2.8) with 25 terminals on-line it is observed that the CPU utilization is 30%, the average system service time is 0.03 sec, on the average a job visits the system eight times, and the response time is 5 sec. What will happen to the response time if the DEC 11-45 is replaced by a DEC 11-40?

At present

$$X_o = \frac{X_1}{V_1} = \frac{X_1 S_1}{V_1 S_1} = \frac{U_1}{V_1 S_1} = \frac{0.3}{8 \times 0.03} = 1.25 \text{ jobs/sec}$$

Think time

$$Z = \frac{M}{X_o} - R = \frac{25}{1.25} - 5 = 15 \text{ sec}$$

For the DEC 11-45, $t_+ = 1.21$ μsec, $t_\times = 71$ μsec, and

$$C' = \frac{1}{0.95 \times 1.21 + 0.05 \times 71} = \frac{10^6}{5.8} = 172.4 \text{ kops}$$

For the DEC 11-40, $t_+ = 2.84$ μsec, $t_\times = 174$ μsec, and

$$C' = \frac{1}{0.95 \times 2.84 + 0.05 \times 174} = \frac{10^6}{11.4} = 87.7 \text{ kops}$$

Therefore, reduction in CPU speed $= 87.7/172.4 = 0.51$. Installing the slower CPU cannot increase throughput. But the throughput will not be reduced below $0.51 X_o$, because if the CPU were the bottleneck, it would be reduced by just this amount, and if some other device (e.g., the disk) were the bottleneck, the effect would be less. Then for the DEC 11-40, $X_o' = U_1'/V_1' S_1'$, and since $U_1' \geq U_1$, $S_1' \leq S_1/0.51$, $V_1' = V_1$, then $X_o' \geq (0.3 \times 0.51)/(8 \times 0.03) = 0.638$ job/sec. Then $R' \leq 25/0.638 - 15 = 39.2 - 15 = 24.2$ sec. Thus if the CPU is the bottleneck, the response time could rise to 24.2 sec; if the disk or some other device turns out to be the bottleneck, the response time will be less. The savings are considerable ($750 per month for the DEC 11-40 versus $200 per month for the DEC 11-45), but a rise to 24.2 sec would be an unacceptably high increase in response time.

Although the equations just developed allow us to determine some useful results on throughput and response time, the theory as presented is inadequate for determining more detailed behavior. For example, the system response time, $R = \Sigma_{i=1}^K \bar{n}_i$, cannot be computed for batch jobs because there is no way to estimate the average queue lengths, $\bar{n}_i$.

At any instant we can regard the system as being specified by its *state vector* $(n_1, n_2, \ldots, n_K)$, where n_i is the length of the queue at device i, and $\sum_{i=1}^K n_i = N$, the total number of jobs in the system (i.e., the multiprogramming level). The problem is to determine the state vector at any time (or at least its steady-state value) given the initial job level and the transitions which can take place as jobs move from one device to another. In general, solving the system of equations for the state transitions require lengthy, iterative calculations, but if certain simplifying assumptions are made, the computations become manageable. An example of one such assumption is that of device homogeneity, which assumes that the output rate of a device is determined completely by its own queue length; an even stronger assumption is that of homogeneous service times, which asserts that the service time for the device i is always equal to a constant, S_i, for all queue lengths. With appropriate assumptions, analytical solutions for the state equations can be found, but even if only restricted assumptions hold, there are now a number of standard computer packages, which, given a system configuration and parameters specifying the job load, compute the state vector after the job flows have settled down. From this all quantities of interest can be determined. A typical such program is BEST/1 (Buzen et al., 1978). Table 2.2(a) shows the work-load description for obtaining a system profile with BEST/1 and Table 2.2(b) shows the system throughput CPU utilization and the average response times for the different devices. More detailed reports on such factors as queue-length distribution, waiting-time profiles, and memory use are also available. With tools such as these

TABLE 2.2 WORK-LOAD SPECIFICATIONS AND RESULTS PRODUCED IN A QUEUEING SYSTEM SIMULATOR

(a) Workload Descriptions

----WORKLOAD 1----DESCRIPTORS----
PP   BATCH PROCESSING
3.8   AVERAGE MPL
----WORKLOAD 2----DESCRIPTORS----
TP   DATA BASE TRANS
4.0   MAXIMUM MPL
4000.0 TRANSACTIONS/HR
----WORKLOAD 3----DESCRIPTORS----
TS   TIME SHARING USERS
6.0   MAXIMUM MPL
30.0 NO. OF TERMINALS
25.0 THINK TIME (SECS)
----WORKLOAD 4----DESCRIPTORS----
TP   DATA BASE UPDATE
800.0 TRANSACTIONS/HR
1.0   PRIORITY
1.0   DOMAIN NUMBER

SERVER	WORKLOAD 1	WORKLOAD 2	WORKLOAD 3	WORKLOAD 4
1 CPU-370/168	13000.0	205.0	320.0	425.0
2 DRUM 1	1099.0	83.0	92.0	115.0
3 DRUM 2	1940.0	147.0	175.0	235.0
4 TAPE	395.0	0.0	0.0	0.0
5 TAPE	496.0	0.0	0.0	0.0
6 2314	747.0	0.0	0.0	0.0
7 2314	204.0	0.0	0.0	0.0
8 3330 SYSTEM PACK	4642.0	13.0	80.0	13.0
9 3330/ASPQ	12461.0	0.0	0.0	0.0
10 3330/ASPQ	12462.0	0.0	0.0	0.0
11 3330 SCRATCH	2474.0	64.0	42.0	240.0
12 3330 SCRATCH	2474.0	62.0	46.0	230.0
13 3330 SWAP AND USER	3034.0	150.0	100.0	350.0
14 3330 SWAP AND USER	3035.0	150.0	100.0	350.0
15 3330 MODI USER PACK	1073.0	27.0	200.0	75.0
16 3330 MODI USER PACK	1073.0	29.0	0.0	85.0
17 3330 MODII USER PACK	1717.0	49.0	0.0	165.0
18 3330 MODII USER PACK	1727.0	52.0	0.0	176.0

(b) Principal Results

WORKLOAD	RESPONSE TIME	THROUGHPUT	%CPU
1 BATCH PROCESSING	133.98 SEC	102. PER HOUR	36.9%
2 DATA BASE TRANS	3.17 SEC	4000. PER HOUR	22.8%
3 TIME SHARING USERS	3.31 SEC	3815. PER HOUR	33.9%
		TOTAL CPU UTILIZATION = 93.6%	

RESPONSE TIME PROFILE
BY WORKLOAD (msec)

SERVER	1	2	3
0 MEMORY	0.0	838.1	221.5
1 CPU-370/168	65680.5	1159.7	1873.0
2 DRUM 1	1410.7	107.0	119.4
3 DRUM 2	3244.4	242.0	292.4
4 TAPE	397.4	0.0	0.0
5 TAPE	500.2	0.0	0.0
6 2314	757.8	0.0	0.0
7 2314	204.3	0.0	0.0
8 3330 SYSTEM PACK	5865.2	17.1	105.6
9 3330/ASPQ	17053.1	0.0	0.0
10 3330/ASPQ	17054.9	0.0	0.0
11 3330 SCRATCH	3005.0	79.5	52.3
12 3330 SCRATCH	3012.5	77.2	57.4
13 3330 SWAP AND USER	4675.4	231.8	156.4
14 3330 SWAP AND USER	4677.1	231.8	156.4
15 3330 MODI USER PACK	1477.6	37.3	277.6
16 3330 MODI USER PACK	1137.1	31.4	0.0
17 3330 MODII USER PACK	1909.1	55.4	0.0
18 3330 MODII USER PACK	1916.5	59.0	0.0
TOTAL RESPONSE TIME	133978.6	3167.1	3312.1

Source: J. R. Buzen et al., "BEST/1—Design of a Tool for Computer System Capacity Planning," *Proc. 1978 AFIPS Natl. Comput. Conf.*, Vol. 47, 1978, p. 447, with permission.

it is now practical to model systems in ways that lead to quite trustworthy results on system behavior, throughput, and response times. The results are particularly useful for exploring alternative configurations and the behavior of the system under varying work loads. For a comprehensive treatment of the method, see Lazowska et al. (1983).

Although the calculations may not be simple, system and work-load specification, and interpretation of the results *are* fairly simple, and to a large extent it can now be said that computer performance *is* well understood and can be effectively evaluated. With this understanding it is possible to design balanced systems (i.e., those where there are no bottlenecks) so that performance, as measured in transactions per second per dollar, is optimized. But for actual transaction processing systems such as travel reservation systems or on-line banking systems, the transactions will originate at terminals remote from the central data processor. This means that communication devices and their queues have to be included in the list of resources, and the costs of communication lines have to be included with component costs. Another resource that has to be considered explicitly in a transaction-oriented system is virtual memory, for which there are parameters such as the page fault rate (i.e., the rate at which a reference to memory causes a new page, not already present, to be read from disk) and the average I/O service time for a page fault. The overall system becomes even more complex, and the total system design problem correspondingly harder. There is some discussion of communication costs in Section 8.3, but the total design or analysis of a system which includes communications components is well beyond the scope of this book. A model that is based on average values for memory and communication devices, much like the one we have presented here for a system where these devices are not brought in explicitly, is described in Deitch (1982).

PROBLEMS

1. (a) Calculate C', the processing rate in kops/sec, for the IBM 370/168-3, and $D'_{effective}$ the *effective* I/O rate in kcps for the following peripherals:
   (i)   3420-8 tape drives
   (ii) 3330-II moving-head file
   (iii) 2305-1 head per track (a fixed-head file)
   (b) Suppose that the multiprogramming level, J, is 3, $r = 0.2$, and there are three channels: for a tape control unit, a moving-head file, and a fixed-head file. Calculate the maximum throughput.

2. A company is currently using an IBM 370/165 system which rents for $66,000 per month. One of the main uses is for sorting on tape, which is done with eight IBM 3420 model 3 drives (and controller). It is considering replacing the drives by an IBM 3420 model 8. For the sort it has been found that

$$s, \text{ computer operation per I/O character} = 20$$

$$k = \frac{\text{total number of I/O characters}}{\text{total data I/O characters}} = 10$$

block size = 1200 characters

Calculate X_1 and X_2, the throughput rates in cps with the model 3 and model 8 drives, assuming that the best achievable rate is attained in each case. What fraction of the time must the system be used on sorting if this application alone is to justify the increased cost? [See Phister (1979) for the data on computer cost and speed; assume that for the high-performance drive the block size would be 2400 characters.]

3. For the M/M/1 queue where the probability of k arrivals in t seconds $= (\lambda t)^k e^{-\lambda t}/k!$ and the probability of service time between t and $t + dt = \mu e^{-\mu t}\, dt$, show that:

   (a) The average number of arrivals/sec $= \lambda$.
   (b) The average service time $= 1/\mu$ sec.

4. Measurements on a time-shared computer system with 40 terminals show that it is disk bound. During the busiest hour, when all terminals are in service, it is observed that, on the average, the think time is 30 sec and the response time is 1 sec.

   (a) What will the response time be if 10 more terminals are added, all of them used?
   (b) If the charging rate is $16.00 per CPU minute and 0.06 per connect minute when there are 40 terminals, what should the CPU rate be when there are 50 terminals, assuming that users are to pay the same for their job submissions?

   What objections are there to allowing the number of terminals to be increased and the prices to be readjusted in this way?

5. Measurements taken on the interactive system shown in Fig. 2.7 yield the following:

	CPU	Disk	Drum
Average service time (sec)	0.05	0.08	0.04
Visit ratio	20	11	8

The average think time at a terminal is observed to be 20 sec.

   (a) Sketch the curve showing response time as a function of the number of terminals. What is the saturation point? Is an 8-sec response time possible when 30 users are logged on? Explain.
   (b) When 25 users are logged on, the response time is observed to be 8 sec. Assuming that the users are charged $3.00 per hour for connect time and $24.00 per minute for CPU time, calculate:
      (i) The average cost for a user job.
      (ii) The earnings per month for the service center. (Assume that the center operates for 165 hours per month, with 25 users always present.)
   (c) The center acquires a new CPU rated to be twice as fast. The new charging rate is $3.00 per hour connect time and $40.00 per minute for CPU, and the center allows the number of users logged on to increase so that the response time is still 8 sec. Calculate:
      (i) The average cost for a user job.
      (ii) The earnings per month for the center with the new system. (Assume that there are always the maximum number of users logged on.)

6. The supervisor of a system used for both batch and interactive jobs is taking measurements to determine how many interactive terminals are in use and makes the following observations:

(1) For the disk the batch throughput rate is 8 jobs/sec, the average service time is 35 msec, and the utilization is 70% (for both batch and interactive jobs).
(2) The average interactive response time is 4 sec.

From experience the supervisor knows that for interactive jobs the think time is 16 sec, on the average, and that 10 disk requests are generated. How many interactive terminals are signed on?

BIBLIOGRAPHY

Buzen, J. R., et al., "BEST/1—Design of a Tool for Computer System Capacity Planning," *Proc. 1978 AFIPS Natl. Comput. Conf.,* Vol. 47, 1978, p. 447.

Deitch, M., "Analytic Queueing Model for CICS Capacity Planning," *IBM Syst. J.,* 21, no. 4 (1982), 454–70.

Denning, P. J., and J. P. Buzen, "The Operational Analysis of Queueing Network Models," *Comput. Rev.,* 10, no. 3 (September 1979), 228–61.

Gaver, D. P., "Probability Models for Multiprogramming Computer Systems," *J. ACM,* 14, no. 3 (July 1967), 423–38.

Kleinrock, L., *Queueing Systems,* Vol. 1: *Theory.* New York: Wiley, 1975.

Lazowska, E. D., J. Zahorjan, G. S. Graham, and K. C. Sevcik, *Quantitative System Performance.* Englewood Cliffs, N.J.: Prentice-Hall, 1983.

Phister, M. Jr., *Data Processing Technology and Economics,* 2nd ed. Santa Fe, N. Mex.: Santa Monica/Bedford, Mass.: Digital Press, 1979.

3

System Financing
and Cost Recovery

Equipment needed to run an enterprise can be purchased or rented. The choice depends on such factors as available capital, expected lifetime of the equipment, and the tax position of the firm. In the computer industry, perhaps more than in any other, both options are widely used, together with intermediate alternatives. Some way of recovering the cost of equipment and service is needed, and again there is a wide divergence in the methods adopted to recover the costs. These two problems, financing the acquisition of systems and recovering the costs for providing service, are examined in this chapter.

3.1 FINANCING OPTIONS

Renting computer equipment rather than buying it has been a common practice in the computer industry, dating back to the time when IBM made its accounting machines available only on a rental basis. After a consent decree between the U.S. Department of Justice and IBM, reached in 1956 following an antitrust suit, IBM began to sell its equipment, but even then rental continued to be popular with customers. The fact that a large number of computers are rented has profound implications for the computer industry, and some of these are examined in Chapter 10, but here we are concerned with the practice from the point of view of the customer. There are several reasons why companies may prefer rental to purchase. During the early days of computers companies were often uncertain whether acquiring a computer would be profitable, or how long the system being considered would suffice. All through the history of computers the rate of technological improvement has been extremely high, and in such a situation it may be better to avoid long-term commitments. A rapid rate of improvement means a rapid rate of obsolescence, and this has tended to make the cost difference between purchase and rental appreciable. The difference has left room for leasing companies, which buy computers from manufacturers and lease them to users for contracted periods significantly less than the expected life of the system. The leasing companies count on being able to find a new customer for a system no longer wanted by the original leaser. The tax positions of the lessor (the leasing company) and the lessee (the user) also play a role. Leasing increases the range of options open to a computer center, and it becomes more important than ever to carry out a careful financial analysis.

The lease–purchase choice is an important topic in accounting, and a thorough analysis is beyond the scope of this book. For such a treatment, see Ferrara et al. (1979). However, it is possible to provide a simplified calculation, and this can be done in two ways which differ, although they are essentially similar in that both depend on calculating discounted amounts for the various cost items, such as purchase price, rental and maintenance payments, and insurance. The first method is based on determining for the computer a *break-even* point, that is, the number of months the system must be retained so that the total cost of rental is equal to the total cost of purchase. It is very approximate in that tax calculations are ignored. In the second method detailed tables are calculated for the cash flow needed each year, the sum of the discounted cash flows over L, the lifetime of the computer, determines the cost for the alternative being considered. Taxes can be taken into consideration.

3.1.1 Estimating the Break-Even Point

Let

$C =$ cost for buying the computer outright

$R =$ monthly cost for rental, including maintenance

$M =$ monthly cost for maintenance only

$i =$ effective monthly rate of interest.*

$v =$ present value of $1 1 month hence $= 1/1 + i$

L is determined by noting that the present value of an immediate payment of C, plus L maintenance payments of M, starting immediately, equals the present value of L rental payments of R starting immediately.† Figure 3.1 shows the

*If the annual rate is I, $(1 + i)^{12} = 1 + I$, and to a first approximation $i = I/12$.

†In doing so, tax considerations are ignored; these will be treated in the second method. Also, when equipment is purchased there is often a warranty period, perhaps as long as 3 months, during which maintenance does not have to be paid, but we do not take this into account. Nor do we take into account the fact that rental and service contracts are for fixed periods and are subject to escalation. For all these reasons the result is only an approximation for L.

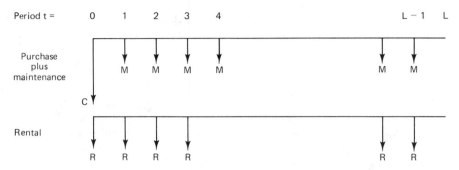

Figure 3.1   Payment schedule for break-even analysis, Purchase vs Rental

payment schedule diagramatically. Thus

$$C + M + Mv + \cdots Mv^{L-1} = R + Rv + \cdots Rv^{L-1}$$

It is not difficult to solve this equation explicitly for L.

$$C = (R - M)(1 + v + \cdots v^{L-1})$$

and using the formula for the sum of a geometric series, we have

$$\frac{C}{R - M} = \frac{1 - v^L}{1 - v} \tag{3.1}$$

where

$$v^L = 1 - \frac{C}{R - M}(1 - v)$$

Therefore,

$$L \times \ln v = \ln \left[1 - \frac{C(1 - v)}{R - M}\right]$$

and since $1 - v = i/(1 + i)$,

$$L = \frac{-\ln \left(1 - \frac{C}{R - M}\frac{i}{1 + i}\right)}{\ln (1 + i)} \tag{3.2}$$

Instead of using this "exact" solution it is easier to see what is happening by obtaining an approximate solution. From Equation 3.1

$$\frac{C}{R-M}\frac{i}{1+i} = 1 - v^L = 1 - (1+i)^{-L} \approx iL\left[1 - \frac{i(L+1)}{2}\right]$$

For $i = 0$, $C/(R-M) = L$ and $C/L = R - M$. This means that ignoring the cost of money, the difference between rental and maintenance is the capital cost, amortized over the L periods. As a next approximation,

$$\frac{C}{R-M} \approx L\left(1 - \frac{iL}{2}\right)$$

$$\frac{R-M}{C} \approx \frac{1}{L} + \frac{i}{2} \qquad (3.3)$$

$$R - M \approx \frac{C}{L} + \frac{iC}{2}$$

In other words, the difference between rental and maintenance has to be corrected by the simple interest on the average capital cost, namely on $C/2$.

To illustrate, suppose that $C = 48R$, $M = 1/4R$, and $i = 1\%$ per month = 0.01. If L_1 is a first approximation to L, $48R/L_1 = R - 1/4R$ and $L_1 = 4 \times 48/3 = 64$ months. As a next approximation, $R - 1/4R = 48R/L + 0.1 \times 24R$ and $L_2 = 48/0.51 = 94$ months. The exact solution is

$$L = -\frac{\ln\left(1 - 64 \times \frac{0.01}{1.01}\right)}{\ln 1.01} = \frac{1.00420}{0.009950} = 101 \text{ months}$$

3.1.2 Discounted Cash Flow Calculations

The second method of analyzing financing alternatives is to apply the conventional technique of determining the periodic cash flows for each of the alternatives being considered, and to base the choice on a comparison of the net present values of the alternatives (we shall encounter this technique again in Chapter 6). Before the calculation is started, it is assumed that the lifetime of the computer has been determined from previous experience of how long the system can be expected to stay in service. At any payment period the cash flow will be the net result of negative components, corresponding to payments for purchase, rental, maintenance, insurance, and so on, and positive components, corresponding to tax or other credits. If, at the end of the lifetime, the system has some residual value, V, for which it can be sold, and the user owns the machine, there will be a final positive cash flow, V.

The method will be illustrated by calculating the cash flow tables for acquiring a system by four alternative modes: purchase, rental, and two forms of leasing. Leasing options come in different varieties, but there are two basic kinds: *financial* and *operating*. A financial lease is very much like a loan of capital to the lessee. Title to the equipment remains with the lessor until the end of the term, after which it reverts to the lessee, perhaps on an option basis upon payment of a residual amount (e.g., 10% of the purchase price). The lessee is obliged to continue payments for the full term of the lease. One of the main attractions of leasing is that an investment tax credit (up to 10% of the purchase value) can be claimed by the lessee. The lessee has to meet certain conditions for this to be allowed by the tax department (it must not be *exactly* equivalent to a loan), and for this reason costs such as insurance and property tax are usually borne by the lessee in financial leases. An operating lease is more like a rental contract, and the payment is often computed as a percentage of the rental cost. Title remains with the lessor, even at the end of the lease, and after a year or two the obligation of the lessee to continue leasing may be terminated on short notice.

The four modes of financing presented here are by no means the only ones. There are other kinds of leases which, in effect, are mixtures of financial and operating, and forms of rental contracts that make them look more like purchases (it is not uncommon for, say, 20% of the first 2 years' rental to be applicable against subsequent purchase). We shall base our selection on the net present values of the alternatives, but there can be other underlying factors to be taken into account. For example, the investment tax credit will be of no immediate use to a company in a loss position, and it may be advantageous to work out a lease whereby the lessor can claim it. Purchase and financial leases, as opposed to rentals and operating leases, show as long-term commitments on a company's books, and for accounting and borrowing purposes the latter options may be preferable, even though their costs, as determined by net present values, tend to be higher. Possibilities of trade-in and up-grade are also relevant; these may be available if the lessor is the equipment manufacturer but are not offered if the lessor is a third party. Legal factors, such as those discussed by Auer and Harris (1981) in *Computer Contract Negotiations,* are also important.

Table 3.1 shows the cash flows for the four types of financing for the system under consideration, an IBM 370/145, which is assumed to have a lifetime of 6 years. In the table credits or savings are shown bracketed. Since rental and maintenance are paid monthly, properly there should be 72 periods over the lifetime, but for clarity of presentation these payments have been aggregated into annual sums. This aggregation introduces an error, since discounting a single payment at the end of a year to the beginning of the project produces a different result than discounting 12 payments of one-twelfth the amount. To reduce this error the table has been calculated as if all payments (and credits) were made at the middle of a year rather than at the end (or beginning). Thus, with an assumed annual interest rate of 16%, the monthly interest rate is $(1.16)^{1/12} = 1.012445$.

TABLE 3.1 CASH FLOW ANALYSIS (DOLLARS) FOR DIFFERENT MODES OF EQUIPMENT ACQUISITION[a]

(a) Purchase: $P = \$1,131,835$

$$\text{NPV} = \sum_j \text{PV} = \$668,353$$

	Year, j						
	0	1	2	3	4	5	6
Depreciation, D_j	0	323,381	269,485	215,588	161,691	107,794	53,897
Depreciated value, $V_j = V_{j-1} - D_j$	1,131,835	808,454	538,969	323,381	161,691	53,897	0
Insurance and property tax, $T_j = .012V_{j-1}$	—	13,582	9,701	6,468	3,881	1,940	647
Maintenance, M_j	—	28,296	28,296	28,296	28,296	28,296	28,296
Pretax cash flow, $PC_j = T_j + M_j$	1,131,835	41,876	37,997	34,764	32,177	30,236	29,943
Tax savings, $TS_j = (PC_j + D_j) \times 0.5$	(113,184) investment tax credit	(182,629)	(153,741)	(125,176)	(96,934)	(69,015)	(42,920)
After-tax cash flow, $AC_j = PC_j - TS_j$	1,018,651	(140,753)	(115,744)	(90,412)	(64,757)	(38,779)	(13,977)
Discount factor, $F_j = 1/(1.16)^{j-0.5}$	1.000000	.928477	.800411	.690009	.594836	.512789	.442060
Present value of cash flow $PV_j = AC_j \times F_j$	1,018,651	(130,686)	(92,643)	(62,385)	(38,520)	(19,885)	(6,179)

(b) Rental: $R = \$25,141/\text{month}$

$$\text{NPV} = \$598,645$$

	Year, j						
	0	1	2	3	4	5	6
Rental, R_j	—	301,692	301,692	301,692	301,692	301,692	301,692
Tax savings, $TS_j = 0.5R_j$	—	150,846	150,846	150,846	150,846	150,846	150,846
After-tax cash flow, $AC_j = 0.5R_j$	—	150,846	150,846	150,846	150,846	150,846	150,846
Present value, $PV_j = AC_j \times F_j$	—	140,057	120,739	104,085	89,729	71,352	66,683

(c) Financial Lease: Leasing payment, G = \$275,736
Purchase price = initial value of equipment, V = \$1,131,835
NPV = \$511,268

	Year, j						
	0	1	2	3	4	5	6
Leasing payment, G_j	—	275,736	275,736	275,736	275,736	275,736	275,736
Interest, $I_j = .016V_{j-1}$	—	181,094	165,951	148,385	128,009	104,373	76,955
Equipment value, $V_j = V_{j-1} - (G_j - I_j)$	1,131,835	1,037,193	927,408	800,057	652,330	480,967	282,186
Insurance and property tax, $T_j = .012V_{j-1}$	—	13,582	12,446	11,129	9,601	7,828	5,772
Maintenance, M_j	—	28,296	28,296	28,296	28,296	28,296	28,296
Pretax cash flow, $PC_j - G_j + T_j + M_j$	—	317,614	316,478	315,161	313,633	311,860	309,804
After-tax cash flow, $AC_j = 0.5PC_j$	(113,184) investment tax credit	158,807	158,239	157,581	156,816	155,930	154,902
Present value, $PV_j = AC_j \times F_j$	(113,184)	147,449	126,656	108,732	93,280	79,859	68,476

(d) Operating Lease: NPV = \$408,982

	Year, j						
	0	1	2	3	4	5	6
Leasing payment, $G_j = 301,692(0.915 - 0.015j)$	—	271,522	266,907	262,472	257,946	253,421	248,896
After-tax cash flow, $AC_j = 0.5G_j$	(113,184) investment tax credit	135,761	133,499	131,236	128,973	126,711	124,448
Present value, $PV_j = AC_j \times F_j$	(113,184)	126,051	106,854	90,554	76,718	64,976	55,013

[a]Interest rate, I = 16% per year.

The discount factor for payments made in the first year is therefore $1/(1.012445)^6 = 0.928477$.

The basic data for the example are the same as that in an article by Szatrowski (1976), but there are differences in the calculations as presented here. [See also Kearney and Mitutenovich (1976) for a discussion of alternative financing and an example.] The following notes will explain the calculations in detail.

Purchase.   The total price for outright purchase is \$1,131,853. Title passes to the purchaser and an investment tax credit of 10% is available immediately. Insurance and maintenance are paid by the purchaser. The company is assumed to be paying taxes at the 50% level, so that half of the expenditures, including depreciation allowance, appear as (bracketed) tax savings.

Depreciation allowance is calculated by the *sum-of-the-years'-digits method*. According to this method, since the equipment has a lifetime of 6 years, the sum of the years is $1 + 2 + 3 + 4 + 5 + 6 = 21$. In the first year a depreciation of $6/21$ of the purchase price, P, is taken; in the jth year the depreciation, D_j, is

$$D_j = P \times \frac{L - j + 1}{\sum_{i=1}^{L} i}$$

where L is the lifetime in years. This is one of three depreciation schemes commonly allowed by tax departments. The other two are straight-line depreciation (a fixed fraction of the original price is depreciated each year) or declining balance (a fixed fraction of remaining amount is claimed each year).

The pretax cash flow is the money actually expended (i.e., the purchase price immediately) and the sum of insurance and maintenance in later years. The tax savings is the 10% investment tax credit immediately, and half the sum of depreciation and pretax cash flow later. After-tax cash flow is 90% of the purchase price in year 0, and for following years it is the tax savings reduced by the actual expenditures for maintenance and insurance. Applying the discount factor, the present value of the cash flow is calculated for each year. The net present value (NPV) is the sum over all years, and it comes to \$668,353.

Rental.   The rental is constant each year, and the after-tax cash flow is equal to half the rental. Applying the discount factor we obtain the present value for each year, and summing for the 6 years the NPV for this alternative is \$598,645.

For the given values of C, R, M, and i, using Equation 3.1 (which makes no allowance for taxes) the break-even point comes to 80.1 months. Thus it is not surprising that over a period of 6 years rental turns out to be less costly than purchase.

Financial lease.   It is assumed that G, the constant annual payment for a financial lease, is \$275,736. Regarding the lease as a loan for the original price of the equipment, the loan is amortized by reducing the principal by G less the interest, thus determining an equipment value at each year. The insurance and property tax (1.2% of the equipment value) are paid by the lessee, who also pays maintenance and claims the 10% investment tax credit. The pretax cash flow is the sum of the leasing payment, insurance, and maintenance. NPV, calculated as the sum of the after-tax cash flow, is \$511,268.

It is to be expected that the NPV here will be less than that for purchase, because in the latter case the depreciated value of the equipment at the end of the 6 years is zero, whereas in the financial lease there is still an unamortized equipment value of \$282,186 after 6 years. Title to this remains with the lessor, so that the lessee experiences a saving.

Operating lease.   It is assumed that the leasing payment is the only cost borne by the lessee. The leasing charge starts at 90% of the rental charged by the manufacturer and is reduced by 1.5% of the rental each year. Thus not only are the annual charges less than those for rental, but there is a 10% investment credit savings, so that the NPV is least for this option.* It comes to \$406,982.

In this example an operating lease turns out to the least cost, but depending on the time for which the equipment is retained, the interest rate, and other parameters, one of the other options might be best. In general, if the equipment is held long enough, purchase is preferable to rental. Also, leases are designed to be more attractive than the straight purchase or rental contracts offered by the manufacturer, but the relative values of C, M, and R (all set by the manufacturer) strongly determine how much opportunity there will be for leasing alternatives.

This last-mentioned point means that leasing companies are very vulnerable to actions taken by the manufacturer. There is another factor that makes them even more vulnerable—the time interval between release of new systems. If this is short, clients with operating leases will turn in their machines in favor of the new equipment, and the leasing company that purchased the machine will not be able to find a customer for it. In the late 1970s this happened with IBM equipment, with disastrous results for many leasing companies. Also, a manufacturer needing capital might well price a model so as to make purchase more attractive than rental to users.

3.2 PRICING OF SERVICES

When a computer is dedicated to one application or used by a small community of users, each doing similar work, there are no strong reasons for keeping track

---

*Since title to the system remains with the lessor, who also assumes the obligation of insurance and maintenance payments, it could be a moot point whether investment tax credit can be claimed by the lessee.

of how much each user is spending, or how much each job costs. But for a general-purpose system, available to a large number of users with conflicting demands, it becomes necessary to allocate usage, carry out some kind of accounting, and perhaps institute some kind of a pricing policy. There are two principal reasons why prices are charged for a commodity or service—to recover cost (including, perhaps, profit) and to encourage better use of scarce resources. A policy designed to achieve one of these goals may do so at the expense of the other. For example, prices may be set at the marginal cost of production in order to recover costs, a policy that is best under certain circumstances. But this may result in underutilized resources, and to achieve the second goal a decision may be taken to *bill* users according to some quite different scheme. The pricing/billing algorithm is further complicated because there are many different kinds of computer services, or to use the economist's terminology, the product is highly differentiated. In such a situation it should be expected that different policies will be adopted for the different products.

There is one other reason why pricing of computer services presents some special problems, and this is because even when prices are set and bills rendered, there is often no real transfer of funds arising out of the transaction. A customer at a commercial service bureau pays for the computer services received; a municipal department will almost certainly *not* pay for services received from a centrally operated computer center, although some accounting entries may be recorded as a result of such use. At a university there may be no direct transfer of funds for instructional use of computers, but for research use it may be that charges are calculated and levied very much as would be done at a commercial bureau. Although, almost invariably, the operating system computes a cost for every job executed, and informs the person submitting the job of this cost, there is a very wide variation in practice of just how much money is transferred as a result of the jobs being run. It is quite common for there to be a debit for the cost of the job against a "computer account" held by the user, and a credit to an account of the computer center. But if these debits and credits do not initiate a real movement of corresponding amounts from one budget to another, the payments are said to be in "computer dollars," "funny money," or "soft money," as opposed to "hard money." The feature of computer dollar accounts is that the holder has few choices about how the money can be used. Usually, it must be spent at a designated, in-house computer center. When an account is exhausted there may or may not be additional funds available before the start of the next budgeting cycle, but *unspent* funds will certainly revert to the computer center or the administration. Why is there so much variation in practices for payment of computer services? It is this question we attempt to answer in this section. Although there is a strong case to be made that every computer center ought to be run as a *cost center,* in which there is a pricing structure intended to recover fully all capital and operating costs incurred by the center, there are arguments based on history, accounting practices, and operational efficiency which made it difficult, and not necessarily best, to run a center in this way. In a commercial environment, where maximizing profit is the goal, the service will be run as a *profit center*. In this case the prices may be set according to the market or perceived value to the user, and can bear little relation to costs, as long as the overall objective of maximizing profit is met.

3.2.1 Pros and Cons of Charge-Out

A system in which there is a transfer of real dollars, not just computer dollars, from one budget to another as a result of computer use will be called a *charge-out* scheme. The mark of a charge-out policy is that the account holder has a choice about how computer funds are spent. It may be that they have to be spent for computing services, but they do *not* have to be spent at the in-house computer center. The user may be allowed to purchase services or software outside, and he or she may be allowed to acquire hardware; in the extreme case the funds may be almost completely convertible and be used either for services or for staff, or for purposes other than computing.*

The arguments for and against a charge-out policy have been made frequently. See Nielsen (1968), Singer et al. (1968), Smidt (1968), Gotlieb (1973), and Bernard and Emery (1977). The pro arguments are easily summarized. Charge-out:

- Is a proven way of allocating expensive service resources.
- Encourages users to make comparisons with other ways of achieving the same results (i.e., to carry out cost-benefit analyses) and leads to the efficient use of resources. There are many situations where extra time spent on analysis and planning result in more efficient programs, requiring much less running time. If the user can spend allotted funds only on machine time, there is no incentive to examine alternatives.
- Promotes efficient service by controlling demand and by making comparisons with other centers possible.
- Decentralizes control by distributing the decision whether to use the service or acquire extra resources over the group of users.

In many organizations the computer center is one of the most difficult units the administration has to manage. Computing is a constantly growing activity,

---

*In most budgeting systems a manager has line items or compartments, each corresponding to some function, and usually administrative approval is needed to effect a transfer from one compartment to another. Approval is almost always needed for transfers to salary because such transfers have long-term implications. In a charge-out system there will be a line item for computing, and at least some transfers can be made at the discretion of the manager. Also, when the manager submits the budget, since the *total* is often of major significance, the amount allocated for computing will directly affect other items in the budget. In systems that are not charge-out, the connection between computer dollars and other budgetary items is not direct.

and there are recurrent periods when the capacity is inadequate and the service is seen to be intolerable. Administrators are continually being forced to decide whether the request of the director to upgrade the facility is reasonable, or whether a dissatisfied user should be given authority to acquire a separate, additional facility. Is too much capacity being acquired too soon? Are the planned services those the users really want? Is the center being run efficiently? It is difficult to judge how well these questions are being answered if the case is being made by just one person, the director of the computing center. If there are competing interests, with several existing or proposed computer centers, the difficulties are compounded. Having a charge-out policy in effect makes the computer center a cost center, and this tends to take the decision out of the hands of the administrator or the computer center's director and puts it in the hands of the computer users. The issue is closely tied to that of centralization/decentralization, a subject that will be examined at greater length in Chapter 4.

All of the above makes a powerful case for charge-out, but there are also arguments against charge-out, some easily countered, and others which must be accepted.

- Implementing a charge-out system entails overhead costs that do not contribute directly to more efficient computing. Even if the operating system already computes a cost (this has been estimated as adding about 5% to running time), there are additional costs due to billing and account management.
- Giving users freedom to spend their money elsewhere creates uncertainties in the computer center's budget, making it more difficult to plan wisely. Departments in government or educational institutions must work within their prescribed budgets. Usually, there is no mechanism to carry over a deficit or a profit from one year to the next. A cost center is not consistent with the way budgeting and expenditure are done in most publicly run organizations.
- Charging schemes are often complex, and users have difficulty in understanding them. They must be accompanied by educational programs.
- Existence of charge-out may create barriers to innovation. The budgeting cycle is long, often annual, and a prospective user might be inhibited from an imaginative application because no funds were planned for an unanticipated application. This is especially true for new users who have had little experience in what might be done with computers (e.g., faculty in the humanities or social sciences in a university, compared with faculty in science or engineering). In essence this is the other side to the argument that charge-out controls demand.
- Charge-out can result in underutilized resources, as happens when a system stands idle because a user, who has a job to be done, has no funds available.*

*But recall that reserve capacity is needed to ensure good response time.

- Computing is recognized as an essential capability, necessarily available if one is to do one's work well. Similar resources (e.g., access to a library) are free. Why should there be a charge for access to the computing resource?*
- Charge-out encourages large users, sooner or later, to attempt to set up their local centers. The result may be fragmented services and redundant resources. This is another aspect of the centralization/decentralization argument to be discussed later.

With these conflicting arguments it is no surprise that in many organizations charge-out is regarded as a controversial policy and that there is such a wide variety of practice in how computer use is billed. In a comprehensive study, Drury and Bates (1979) examine both the theoretical basis for charge-out and current practices. They classify charge-out systems into two major groups which correspond to the two principal goals noted at the beginning of this section: *cost recovery* and *resource allocation*. Both techniques lie in a class of problems which has proved to be particularly difficult in accounting theory, that of transfer pricing, and of the two, resource allocation has a somewhat better theoretical justification. The theory is based on an analogy which compares the providers and users of computer services with two profit centers, the selling division and buying division. With appropriate assumptions the general economic condition by which profits are maximized when marginal revenue is equal to marginal cost holds, and this results in an optimal transfer price for the service provided. But a real data processing environment is far more complicated than the model—it is much more dynamic (i.e., time varying), there are more than one supplier and more than one user of a service, and there is no economic measure for the information which a computer department supplies in addition to data processing capabilities (see Chapter 5). Thus the resource allocation schemes cannot really be used to determine transfer prices, and in practice the prices are based on cost recovery, although in determining the costs there is often some measure of resource consumption. In the survey portion of their study Drury and Bates found that a majority of the firms had charge-out policies in place for both operations and systems programming,† but that there was considerable variation in the charge-out systems, and it is useful to look at these before suggesting an overall approach.

3.2.2 Computing Pricing Methods

Table 3.2 lists six principal methods of billing, along with comments on their application. It is obvious that for a large system with many users and a variety of

---

*A partial answer to this is that no one person is capable of preempting the whole library. It *is* possible that one user can make unreasonable demands that would preempt the whole computer system.

†The Drury and Bates study is based on the replies from 95 Canadian firms, but they provide evidence that the sample is representative of North American firms. Also their basic observations are consistent with those of earlier surveys in the United States. See E.D.P. Analyzer, "Charging for Computer Services," vol. 12, 1974; and *1978 CRV Survey* (Conoga Park, Calif.: Informatics, Inc., 1978).

TABLE 3.2 METHODS OF BILLING FOR COMPUTER SERVICES

Method	Description	Comments
Overhead distribution	The cost of running the computer center is charged against the users according to some predetermined formula—e.g., pro-rated according to previous usage	A non-charge-out scheme; no incentive for careful use
Flat rate	Fixed charge per run	Does not allow center to control use (e.g., discourages usage during peaks); simple and useful for small jobs where calculation of cost is relatively expensive
Differential pricing	Different rates for different priority classes—priorities may depend on time of run, volume of service, class of user, etc.	Priorities can be difficult to assign
Resource consumption	Measurements made of CPU use, connect time, I/O use, etc.; rates set for each resource	Can be complicated; needs complex accounting program; user education needed; most common
Transaction volume	Rate computed for each transaction type	Related to resource consumption but not simply (consumption may be greater at high volumes)
Subscription	Fixed rate for an amount of service up to some prescribed level; additional costs thereafter	Cost of service may depend on time when delivery is taken; another pricing algorithm needed for additional service

operational modes, a combination of methods may be appropriate. In many ways a large center is like a public utility such as a telephone company or a power corporation, where mixed charging schemes are common. Thus the telephone company has a monthly charge for local calls plus a schedule for long-distance charges based on distance and time of call (differential pricing). Questions regarding rates that come up for utilities also come up for computer centers. Some examples follow.

Should users of one type of service subsidize users of another? For telephones it is a matter of regulatory policy that home users should not subsidize business users. This has important implications, not the least of which is putting into place a complicated accounting system to calculate how much it costs to provide service for different classes of users. A computer center might have users at several sites, some of them situated close to the computers and others connected by public or private communication channels. It is a policy question whether all users are charged according to the same rate schedule, or the remote users alone pay for the costs of the extra resources they need.

What is the impact of price elasticity on services? It is conceivable that a computer center might wish to encourage use of a new service by setting the price low initially. Some services, such as advisory services, may be provided free, because they educate users and promote widespread use of the system, both goals thought to be highly desirable.

How much encouragement should be given for load balancing and for use of the system when it might otherwise not be occupied? Should overnight and weekend users be allowed to run at lower costs—possibly just over the marginal rate? One argument in favor of such practice is that it encourages use of a resource that might otherwise be idle. On the other hand, using up reserve capacity provides justification for enlarging the system—a justification that might not be there if users had to pay the "real" cost of their use.

3.2.3 Dedicated and General-Purpose Computers

When a computer is run as a cost center and a charge-out system is in place it is important to decide exactly which costs are to be recovered through charge-out. The cost center approach is to decide that *all* costs are to be recovered; these would include direct costs such as salaries of operators and programmers, and indirect costs such as those for space, utilities, and capital equipment replacement. But whether all equipment costs should be included can be debated.* For some kind of computer installations the hardware replacement cost is an extraordinary item; it is not part of the normal budgetary process but met through a special capital acquisition. Yet in other installations the equipment is rented; the rental payments are part of the regular operating budget, and there is a stronger case for recovery through charge-out.

Probably the most important factor in determining whether equipment costs are part of the normal operating budget or are regarded as special is whether the computer is being run as a general-purpose facility or is a dedicated system. In much of what has been said so far there has been an implicit assumption that the computer facility is being operated as a service center (i.e., a general-purpose system). Such systems are characterized by the presence of very many users, each of whom requires only a small part of the resources. Often there is no one who uses more than 2 or 3%, given a sufficiently long period, say a week. But from their very beginnings minicomputers, and now microcomputers, have been used differently. These are often dedicated to a single application (e.g., controlling a manufacturing process, capturing data in a scientific experiment, or monitoring a patient in a hospital) and often there are a relatively small number of users of the computer. In an office, a word processor is a dedicated

*These generally run between 35 and 45% of all costs (see Table 6.4).

system, as is a personal workstation.* Similarly, a small business computer, devoted to one or two specialized applications, is a dedicated system.

A dedicated system running on a mini- or microcomputer may cost in the range of $10,000 to $100,000, an amount much less, of course, than that of a general-purpose computer. Also, the software costs for a dedicated system may be much less, since the whole range of system software needed to support a large user base is not required.† Not only are the hardware and software costs for dedicated systems an order of magnitude less than those of a general-purpose system, there are other factors which may make it preferable not to attempt to recover these costs through charges levied to users. Very often the equipment is paid for by a special grant, or its cost is included as part of the capital cost of the larger project for which the computer is being used (e.g., a manufacturing process or a hospital unit). The user of a general-purpose system may want a language processor or software package very similar to that available elsewhere. The pricing system should reflect this situation—it should be competitive and it should allow the user to go elsewhere (i.e., be based on hard money). The user of a dedicated system is likely, on the other hand, to require a very special service, developed on the local facility, and to be much less interested in even looking at other alternatives. If the system is small enough, it may be regarded as equipment needed to do the job, like the telephone or a desk calculator. Thus for a dedicated system a partial charge-out, where only certain operating costs are recovered, may be appropriate, or even no charging system whatever. For a general-purpose computing system, however, the arguments given previously for charge-out are likely to be valid. In the remainder of this chapter it is assumed that this is the type of facility being considered.

3.2.4 Calculation of Prices for a General-Purpose Computer Facility

With this background it is possible to outline the steps for establishing a rate structure for a multipurpose computer facility.

1. Identify the different services for which rates are to be set. There might, for example, be an on-line time-sharing service, an overnight batch service, and a word-processing service. In a university environment there might be a high-speed batch stream (processing short jobs, under a variety of languages in batch mode, but with fast turnaround). Educational services (courses, advice on programming) may or may not be a chargeable item.

2. Determine the total budget for the center for the period under consideration (quarterly, semiannually, or annually). Here decisions have to be made on

---

*Although word processing can also be done on a time-shared basis through a large general-purpose computer.

†Recall the difference in costs between small business systems and general-purpose business systems in Section 1.2.

the extent to which the computer facility is to operate as an independent cost center. How are equipment costs to be handled? If all equipment is rented, the answer is easy, but for purchased or leased equipment a lifetime has to be established and an amortization schedule of costs set up. In general, there are three types of costs:

(a) *Capital*—for which amortization schedules are needed

(b) *One-time*—site preparation, installation of security measures, purchase of software, and so on

(c) *Recurring*—salaries, rental, maintenance, communication costs, utilities, supplies, training, travel, and so on

If the computing center is an in-house service for a larger organization, it will also be necessary to determine how much overhead it shall pay for services it draws upon (e.g., purchasing and administration). These costs are described in greater detail in Table 6.3.

3. Apportion the budgeted costs to the chargeable services. This will require data about the resource consumption of each service, gathered from measurements taken on the system, summary statistics on volume use, and time sheets of employees, such as system programmers who support several services.

Project the costs and service demands for the next period and determine the amounts to be recovered from each type of service. [Note that each service will require a loading factor to allow for costs that cannot be charged directly to users (e.g., those arising out of maintenance, malfunctions, and idle time).]

4. Using an appropriate charging scheme, determine a detailed rate structure for each individual service. As already noted, this will vary from service to service. For a high-speed job stream (HSJS) in a university, where resource consumption by each job is low, it might be best to charge a flat rate per job; for word processing a charging scheme based on CPU use, connect time, and number of lines printed might be set; in an environment where many large files are kept on-line, it would be desirable to charge for storage residency.

The process is shown diagramatically in Fig. 3.2.* It will be illustrated by a

TABLE 3.3 HARDWARE COSTS FOR YORK–RYERSON COMPUTING CENTRE

	IBM 370/158		DEC 10 Time-Sharing System	Total
	Cost	Fraction		
CPU	$390,600	0.45		
DASD and tapes	303,800	0.35		
Communications	86,000	0.10		
High-speed memory	86,800	0.10		
Total	$868,000	1.00	$296,000	$1,164,000

*This is similar to the process suggested in *Charging for Computer Services* by Bernard and Emery (1977, Fig. 4.2). Here, however, we have emphasized the definition of service classes, as well as an identification of resource types as proposed by Bernard and Emery.

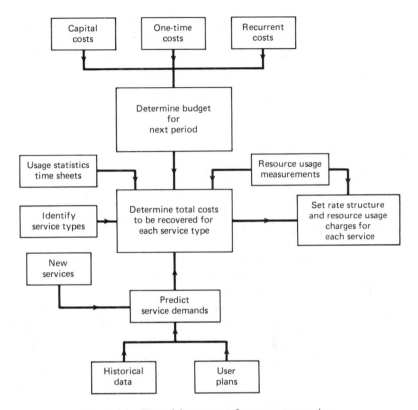

Figure 3.2   The pricing process for computer services

simple example based on 1977 data from the York–Ryerson Computing Centre, a facility then operated jointly by York University and the Ryerson Institute of Technology in Toronto. At the time, the facility consisted of two computers, an IBM 370/158 and a DEC 10, for which the annual hardware costs were as shown in Table 3.3. The total budget for the center, including salaries, space costs, and supplies, was $1,906,000.* Assuming that other costs are proportional to hardware, the total cost for all services provided on the IBM 370/158 = $868,000 × 1,906,000/1,164,000 = $1,421,300, and the total cost for services provided on the DEC 10 = $296,000 × 1,906,000/1,164,000 = $484,700.

The identifiable services were a time-sharing service (TS) provided on the DEC 10, and a group of four services on the IBM 370/158. The latter were designated as OS batch, HSJS, Storage (on- and off-line), and Taskmaster (this consisted of several systems used by the two university administrations). From

---

*The fraction of budget devoted to hardware is unusually large here. Generally, educational computing facilities have smaller salary budgets than do computing centers in government and industry, because many of the users are faculty and students who are not on the center's payroll. A survey on budget expenditures is shown in Table 6.4.

TABLE 3.4 RESOURCE CONSUMPTION BY SERVICE FOR THE IBM 370/158

Resource	Fraction of Hardware Cost	OS Batch Fraction Consumed Cost		HSJS Fraction Consumed Cost		Taskmaster Consumed Cost		Storage Consumed Cost	
				Service					
CPU	0.45	0.89	0.40	0.09	0.04	0.02	0.01		
DASD and tape	0.35	0.55	0.19	0.05	0.02			0.40	0.14
Communications	0.10	0.70	0.07	0.05	0.01	0.25	0.02		
Memory	0.10	0.70	0.07	0.05	0.01	0.25	0.02		
Total			0.73		0.08		0.05		0.14

measurements taken with hardware and software monitors, a breakdown of resources consumed by each service was determined, and this is shown in Table 3.4.

From these data the following target incomes are generated:

OS batch: 73% of $1,421,300 = $1,037,500 annually or $86,400 per month
HSJS: 8% of $1,421,300 = $113,700 annually or $9475 per month
Taskmaster: 5% of the $1,421,300 = $71,000 annually or $5900 per month
Storage charges: 14% of $1,421,300 = $199,000 annually or $16,600 per month
TS: 100% of $484,700 = $484,700 annually or $40,400 per month
    Total: $158,775 per month

Using projected demands for the chargeable items within each service, and adjusting the existing rates for these items, a rate structure as shown in Table 3.5 was drawn up, to yield projected revenues slightly higher than those required by the budget.

3.2.5 Additional Considerations

Even for the simple situation just presented the pricing algorithm is rather complicated, and users have to be educated in the way to submit jobs so as to minimize costs. Besides meeting the requirements of recovering costs and encouraging efficient use of resources, the pricing algorithm should have other features if it is to be seen as fair. Users should be able to budget *their* costs, and this means that there should not be frequent changes in the algorithm. For the same reason, a job submitted at different times should not incur different charges. Recall, however, that in a multiprogramming environment the residency time of a job will depend on how heavily the system is loaded, and some

TABLE 3.5 RATE STRUCTURE FOR SERVICES ON THE
YORK-RYERSON COMPUTING CENTRE

Service	Volume Estimate	Rate	Revenue
OS batch	26,100 jobs	$ 0.25 per job	$ 6,500
	170 CPU hours	260.00 per hour	44,200
	190 I/O hours	60.00 per hour	11,400
	300 Spool hours	60.00 per hour	18,000
	43,200 Kbyte hours	0.15 per hour	6,500
	10,000 mounts	1.00 per mount	10,000
		Subtotal	$ 96,600
HSJS	47,000 jobs	$ 0.15 per job	S 7,000
	17 CPU hours	260.00 per hour	4,400
		Subtotal	S 11,400
Taskmaster	York copy	$3000.00	$ 3,000
	Ryerson copy	3000.00	3,000
		Subtotal	$ 6,000
On-line DASD	8 spindles	$2100.00 per spindle	$ 16,800
Interactive	6,000 connect hours	$3.00 per hour	$ 18,000
	1,500 Kword hours	5.00 per hour	7,500
	12,000 log-ins	0.25 per log-in	4,000
	6,000,000 disk blocks	0.0005 per block	3,000
	400 tape drive hours	3.00 per hour	1,200
		Subtotal	$ 33,700
		Total projected monthly revenue	$164,500

variation in running the same job at different times must be expected. In practice, price fluctuations of a few percent are acceptable.

Much more complex pricing schemes than the one described above have been proposed, especially on time-sharing systems where there are several job classes, each class forming a queue which is processed according to its priority. In general, a utility function can be associated with response time, since results of a submission are of diminishing value the longer it takes to get them back.* If queue sizes and prices are displayed, one can imagine a market where the cost of processing a job depends on the queue priority and response time, and users effectively bid for a position to gain a short response time. Interesting as such

*For further discussion of this utility function and the trade-offs between time sharing and batch, see Section 6.2.2.

possibilities are, users prefer stability and consistency. According to the surveys mentioned earlier, most charge-out systems in business environments are relatively simple. Nevertheless, complicated pricing schemes have been adopted. Stefferud* describes an algorithm at the Triangle University Computing Center, North Carolina, where departments subscribe to a given amount of service each day, and where users within a department can have different priorities. A department that allows most of its users to operate with high priority will find that its daily allotment is rapidly depleted, and that its users will have to wait until other subscribers receive their entitlement. Kleinjen and van Ruben† also describe a charge-out scheme suitable for a university environment, in which users subscribe for fixed amounts of computing capability. Luderer‡ describes an approach used at the Bell Telephone Laboratories based on defining a service-invariant computing work unit which is priced differently according to grade of service. Time sharing and batch are considered to be different grades of service, for which factors derived from work loads and costs can be calculated. A user is then in a better position to judge the cost of moving from one service to another.

Any charge-out system has to be backed up by a considerable body of accounting routines. Besides the programs generally built into the operating system for assigning authorization and controlling access and for measuring resource consumption, there have to be packages for billing and accounts payable, mechanisms for dealing with mistakes and errors, and routines for gathering statistics over a long term and analyzing them, so that the effects of changes in pricing can be projected.

In summary, the importance of the role played by pricing in determining not only the market value of computations to users, but also how a system is used, has to be emphasized. This is true both for general-purpose computing facilities, and for special computer services such as those provided by the Prestel¶ videotex system or a bibliographic utility such as UTLAS§ (University of Toronto Library Automation Systems). With Prestel, in addition to telephone charges, subscribers pay for each page displayed (although the page charge may be borne by the information provider who is marketing some product). This

---

*E. Stefferud, Sigmetrics Technical Meeting on Pricing Computer Services, *Performance Evaluation Review*, 5C, no. 1 (1976), 31–70.

†J. P. C. Kleinjen and A. J. van Ruben, "Principles of Computer Charging in a University-Type Organization," *Commun. ACM*, 26, no. 11 (November 1983), 926–32.

‡G. W. Luderer, "Charging Problems in Mixed-Time Sharing/Batch Systems: Cross Subsidization and Invariant Work Units," Sigmetrics Technical Meeting on Pricing Computer Services, *Performance Evaluation Review*, 5C, no. 1 (1976), 89–93.

¶Videotex offers access in the home to computerized data bases using a TV receiver and a keyboard connected to the system by telephone. For a description of the British Prestel, see Wolfe (1980).

§Bibliographic utilities offer a variety of on-line services to librarians, the most important being the ability to consult a very large catalog file. For a description, see Mathews (1979).

method is justified by the need to have a simple algorithm, comprehensible to a very large public. With UTLAS there is a complicated algorithm in which there are fixed-cost components, connect-time charges, costs dependent on the number of entries accessed, and so on. In all cases users have to be taught how to approach the system efficiently, and the pricing policy is a fine instrument which can direct them into modes which will balance loads and make efficient use of resources. For this reason pricing is just as important in government, educational, or institutional computing situations as it is in commercial or business environments, where it is used in the majority of cases. As a final note, Drury and Bates (1979) carry out a statistical analysis to determine what type of computing situation is likely to be associated with the presence of charge-out. They find that a firm which is growing quickly, is decentralizing, and which is adding diverse new applications is most likely to use charge-out. In Chapters 8 and 9 it will be seen just how fast the computer industry has grown, and in the next chapter it will be seen that there is a major long-term trend toward decentralizing computer hardware. So it is not surprising that there is also a trend toward an increasing use of charge-out systems.

PROBLEMS

1. An organization is considering two options for acquiring a small computer.

   (1) Purchase, at a cost of $75,000 with monthly maintenance and insurance of $588
   (2) Rental, at a monthly cost of $2160

   It expects to use the computer for 5 years, after which it is estimated that the resale value would be $15,000. Which option is preferable if:
   (a) The organization is nonprofit and borrows money at a 14% annual rate to finance the purchase?
   (b) The organization is a small company that pays income taxes at the rate of 25% and has an internal rate of return of 18% per year?
   Monthly payments may be approximated by a single annual payment made in the middle of the year. For the company, depreciation (calculated on a straight-line basis at the end of the year) is taken over 5 years. Assume a 10% investment tax credit.

2. A company is considering two alternatives for financing a computer:

   (1) Purchase for cost C, with monthly maintenance M
   (2) Rental, with monthly charge R (rental and maintenance are paid in advance)

   After the computer is not needed it will have a residual value V.
   (a) If i is the monthly interest rate, develop an *exact* expression for L, the length of time the computer should be retained for the alternatives to be equivalent.

(b) Assuming that $i \ll 1$ show [either using (a) or proceeding independently] that

$$R - M = \frac{C - V}{L} + i\,\frac{C + V}{2}$$

Give a simple interpretation of this result.

3. Recompute the purchase and rental examples of Table 3.1(a) and (b) using annual interest rates of 12, 14, 18, and 20%. Plot $NPV_{purchase}$ and NPV_{rental} versus interest rate, i. At what values of i would you estimate that these curves intersect? Explain why $NPV_{purchase}$ is an increasing function of i, while NPV_{rental} is a decreasing function.

4. A computer can be purchased at a cost of $1,034,000 or rented for $22,000 per month. If the computer is purchased during the first year, 90% of the amount paid for rental can be applied against the purchase price; during the second year 75% of the amount paid for rental can be applied against the purchase price; during the third year and thereafter, 50% of rentals can be applied against the cost until the total purchase credit = 70% of the original price. Calculate a table of the value of cost to convert at month j, for $j = 0, 6, 12, 18, 24, \ldots$ months, assuming an annual discount rate of 16% and present-value cost = accumulated rental cost (discounted) + purchase price on conversion (discounted). When is the present-value cost least? Is this a reasonable way to determine the best alternative? Explain.   (Kearney and Mitutenovich, 1976)

5. A computer system can be purchased for cost C, with maintenance M, or rented for R. An increase in the interest rate, Δi, is accompanied by an inflationary increase Δf such that $C\,\Delta f$, $M\,\Delta f$, and $R\,\Delta f$ are increases in the cost, maintenance, and rental, respectively. Derive an (approximate) expression for the corresponding change, $\Delta L/L$, where L is the period for which there is break-even rental and purchase. Explain why, to a first approximation, this is independent of Δf, other than through the influence of Δi.

BIBLIOGRAPHY

AUER, J., and C. E. HARRIS, *Computer Contract Negotiations.* New York: Van Nostrand Reinhold, 1981.

BERNARD, D., and J. C. EMERY, *Charging for Computer Service: Principles and Guidelines.* Princeton, N.J.: Petrocelli Books, 1977.

DRURY, D. H., and J. E. BATES, *Data Processing Charge Back Systems: Theory and Practice.* The Society of Management Accountants of Canada, Hamilton, Ontario 1979.

FERRARA, W. L., J. B. THIES, and M. W. DIRSMITH, *The Lease-Purchase Decision.* New York: National Association of Accountants/The Society of Management Accountants of Canada, Hamilton, Ontario 1979.

GOTLIEB, C. C., "Pricing Mechanisms," in *Advanced Course of Software Engineering,* ed. F. L. Bauer. New York: Springer-Verlag, 1973, pp. 492–502.

KEARNEY, J. M., and J. S. MITUTENOVICH, "A Guide to Successful Computer System Selection," *Management Reference Series 4.* Data Processing Management Association, Park Ridge, Illinois 1976.

MATHEWS, J. R., *The Four Online Bibliographic Utilities.* Library Technology Reports, November–December 1979, pp. 665–841.

NIELSEN, N. R., "Flexible Pricing: An Approach to the Allocation of Computer Resources," *FJCC 1968,* AFIPS, Part 1, pp. 521–31.

SINGER, N. M., H. CANTOR, and A. MOORE, "Prices and the Allocation of Computer Time," *FJCC 1968,* AFIPS Part 1, 493–512.

SMIDT, S., "The Use of Hard and Soft Money Budgets and Prices to Limit Demand for Centralized Computer Facility," *FJCC 1968,* AFIPS, Part 1, pp. 499–509.

STREETER, D. N., "Cost-Benefit Evaluation of Scientific Computing Services," *IBM Syst. J.,* 11, no. 3 (1972), 219–33.

SZATROWSKI, T., "Rent, Lease or Buy," *Datamation,* 22, no. 2 (February 1976), 59–68.

WOLFE, R., *Videotex.* London: Heyden, 1980.

4

Centralized, Decentralized, and Distributed Systems

The debate about how much control of a system ought to be exercised at a central locus, and how much should be delegated to managers at other sites, goes far beyond computers and information systems. It is a recurrent theme in government and business—indeed, in every type of extended political, social, and industrial organization. The basic arguments are clear on both sides. A centralized system makes global planning possible, and this results in better overall use of resources because of greater harmony between the system's constituent parts, decreased redundancy, and a well-defined chain of command. On the other hand, in a decentralized system decisions are made closer to the point at which they have to be implemented and with the help of those most directly affected. This means that the decisions are more likely to address the real problems, and are more likely to have the human support needed to make them effective. It may be noted that the arguments in favor of centralization are mainly economic, whereas those in favor of decentralization are mainly political and social, but this distinction does little to settle the debate. The approach in this chapter is essentially that of Chapter 6, where costs and benefits of various alternatives relating to using computers are discussed. Here the issue is how *computing facilities* ought to be managed, so it is one aspect of the management of computer resources, the topic being considered in this section of the book. The discussion will serve as a useful introduction to the arguments of Chapter 6.

With computer systems the centralization/decentralization debate becomes especially complicated because there are different aspects that need careful distinction. To start with, it has not always been clear what is being centralized or decentralized. There are several, almost independent properties of a system which have to be considered. Two are readily identified: the control or management, and the degree to which the components are geographically concentrated or distributed. Moreover, for each aspect it is hardly sufficient to describe the system as just being centralized or decentralized. There is a very wide range in both management arrangements and component interconnections, in fact almost a continuum for each, and there is no accepted means of attaching a simple numerical measure of centralization to a management structure, or a measure of concentration to a geographical configuration. This difficulty in assigning numerical values means that quantitative studies of the centralization/decentralization issue are rare. Although the subject can be explored, it is not possible so far to apply the cost-benefit comparisons in a way that will allow one to conclude exactly what balance between centralized and decentralized systems will achieve the optimum (i.e., least expensive) results in a particular situation. The difficulties are compounded because whatever cost estimates *can* be made are subject to continuous revision due to the rapid rate of technological developments in the computer and communication industries.

We start by attempting to identify those features of a system which can be centralized or decentralized, using examples and approaches taken by other authors to illustrate the possibilities. This is followed by a tabular array in which the advantages and disadvantages of centralized and decentralized modes are elaborated. Although a general approach to treating the subject quantitatively is suggested, this approach has not been tried in a variety of real situations. In the last section there is a brief summary and an examination of trends.

4.1. A CLASSIFICATION OF SYSTEMS

Before attempting to assess the relative merits of centralization and decentralization it is necessary to be more precise about what is meant by the terms. What is being centralized or decentralized? In a political or sociological context the concept of interest is power, defined as the ability to get someone else to do your bidding. In our computer context, power may be identified with management control, particularly over the management of information processing. This means authority to define a system, to allocate resources among its components, to approve the feasibility of designs, and to exercise responsibility over implementation, operation, and maintenance. Perhaps the clearest way in which management control can be recognized is through the budget-making process. This will be discussed at greater length later in this section, but for now we can assume that system management is a well-defined authority which can be exercised at a single site or shared among several persons or groups.

But management control is not the only facet of centralization and decentralization. The phrase *distributed system* is in one sense analogous to a decentralized system and yet it has another connotation—that of geography. Most writers on centralization and decentralization distinguish the placement of the components (i.e., hardware and software) of a system from the activity of exercising management control. It turns out that many writers identify a *third* feature of a system—an aspect in addition to both management and to hardware location. Lucas (1982) discusses management of information services, equipment, and information; Lorin (1980) specifies system management, system components, and system development skills; King (1978) describes control, technology, and user–provider interface; Norton (1972) talks of management, hardware, and software development. We shall follow these authors in specifying *three* system features which can be centralized or decentralized, and to help distinguish the three we shall use slightly different terminology for each. The three are:

1. *Management,* which can be *centralized* or *decentralized*
2. *Hardware* (including software), which can be spatially *concentrated* or *distributed*
3. *Application development skills,* which can be *localized* or *dispersed*

Assuming that the three features are independent of one another, we can draw a three-dimensional space wherein a system may reside and classify systems according to where they are located in this space (Fig. 4.1). In fact, the three system aspects are *not* completely independent—for instance, dispersion of

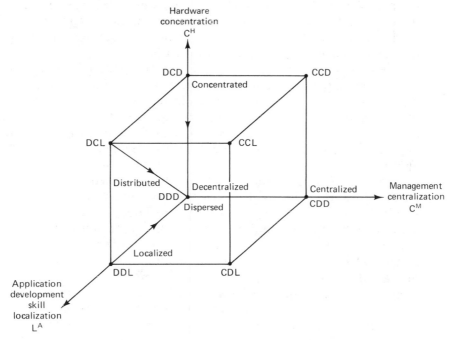

Figure 4.1 The space of system possibilities

application development skills implies, to some degree, a decentralization of management control over information processing. But the three are *almost* independent, and it is possible to describe or conceive of systems in which each aspect is either close to the origin of Fig. 4.1 or distant from it along one axis, regardless of the other two aspects, resulting altogether in eight basic system types.

A CDL system has centralized management, distributed hardware, and localized application development skills. This is the type of system to be found in a supermarket chain where there are point-of-sales terminals connected to a minicomputer in each branch store, but where much (but not all) of the computer power, and almost all of the knowledge about hardware and software, resides at the head office where management is located. Such a system is illustrated in Fig. 4.2(*a*), where differently shaped boxes are associated with each of the three system aspects.

A multistation key-edit system, used to record data from key-entry terminals into a computer equipped with a large magnetic disk store and a set of programs for data manipulation [Fig. 4.2(*b*)], provides an example of a CCL system. Such a system would probably be located within one building, perhaps even in one room, and all authority and most skills are vested in operators and managers other than data-entry personnel.

International time-sharing services such as the APL service provided by I.P. Sharp, or Tymshare by Tymnet, illustrate CDD systems [Fig. 4.2(*c*)]. Here the hardware and the user skills are very widely dispersed geographically, but there is a tight central control over system design matters such as the kind of hardware that may be connected, the languages that are accommodated, communication devices, protocols, and interfaces.

Figure 4.2(*d*) illustrates a CCD system. This could be found in a small, one-site manufacturing company, where a single computer is shared by the different departments within the organization and used for a variety of applications: production control and scheduling, inventory management, accounts receivable and payable, payroll calculations, and budget preparation. The application development skills are dispersed among the operating departments, although all happen to be located in one physical site.

A system of computers in which each is operated wholly independently, in its own location, with its own management, and servicing its own user community is the extreme version of system type DDD—decentralized management, distributed hardware, and decentralized application skills. It may be questioned whether such a configuration really meets the criteria of belonging to a single system, where the components are generally regarded as having to interact with one another; perhaps the term *cluster* is more appropriate. Where there is interconnection between the constituents, there must be some agreement regarding communication protocols and interfaces. Such agreement might be derived from an overall management structure, or it could be based on standards promulgated by the International Standards Organization (ISO), which are

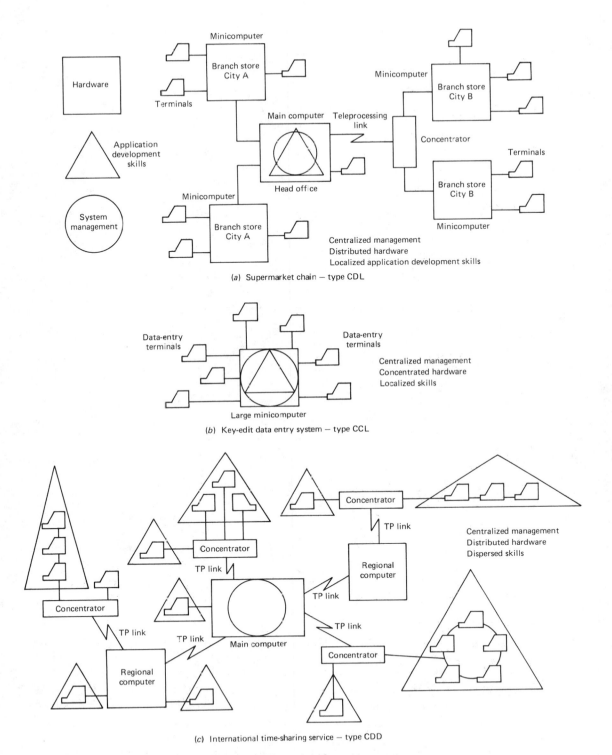

Hardware

Application development skills

System management

Minicomputer

Branch store City A

Terminals

Main computer

Teleprocessing link

Head office

Minicomputer

Branch store City B

Concentrator

Branch store City B

Terminals

Minicomputer

Minicomputer

Branch store City A

Centralized management
Distributed hardware
Localized application development skills

(a) Supermarket chain — type CDL

Data-entry terminals

Data-entry terminals

Centralized management
Concentrated hardware
Localized skills

Large minicomputer

(b) Key-edit data entry system — type CCL

Concentrator

TP link

TP link

Concentrator

TP link

Regional computer

Concentrator

TP link

Regional computer

Main computer

TP link

TP link

Concentrator

Centralized management
Distributed hardware
Dispersed skills

(c) International time-sharing service — type CDD

Figure 4.2 Examples of system types

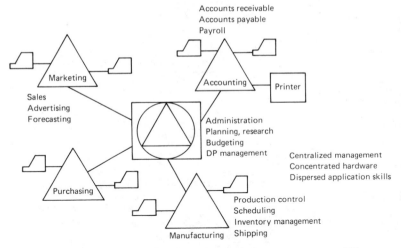

(d) DP installation for a small, one-site manufacturing company — type CCD

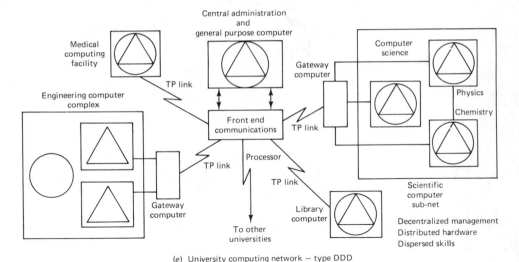

(e) University computing network — type DDD

Figure 4.2 Continued

gaining general acceptance as the recognized modes for intercommunication between systems with different architecture. We have here a network [Fig. 4.2(e)]. DDD systems are computer networks, although it should be noted that the global time-sharing system of Fig. 4.2(c) is also a network. The computers in a network often have, or interface with, "front-end communications processors" or "gateway" computers, where many of the networking functions are carried out. The variety in networks is enormous.

It appears to be very difficult to find examples of systems that correspond to points DDL, DCL, and DCD in Fig. 4.1. Note that in all of these there is decentralized management control, but there is also concentration of hardware or localization of skills. It may well be that such points are unstable. Management control implies authority to spend money and acquire resources, and it is not unreasonable to expect that where such authority is present, sooner or later a decision will be taken to purchase hardware or hire people. In effect, systems that were located at DCD, DCL, or DDL would tend to migrate toward DDD.

The categorization of systems just presented is useful in that given the configuration and functional description of a system, it is not difficult to say which of the eight modes, corresponding to the corners of the cube of Fig. 4.1, the system most closely resembles. But there is no agreement on how to calculate *exactly* where in the space of Fig. 4.1 a given system lies—what its three coordinates are. The *neighborhood* of a coordinate can be recognized by comparing the structure (management, hardware configuration, or skill dispersion) with a few basic structures in graph theory which are clearly associated with either a centralized or decentralized mode. Thus the star of Fig. 4.3(a) is strongly centralized [see Fig. 4.2(b)]. On the other hand, the complete graph of Fig. 4.3(b), in which every node is connected to every other node (and all nodes are alike), is the most completely decentralized. This idea that every node is a peer among equals is the key one in decentralized structures. Figure 4.3(c) and (d) shows two other peer groups frequently seen in computer architecture; processors connected by a common bus are usually found where parallelism is needed, and the loop or ring is a standard way of connecting terminals. The tree or hierarchy of Fig. 4.3(e) is partially decentralized; the greater the depth of the tree, the greater the degree of decentralization.

It is interesting to consider what might be taken as a numerical measure of centralization/decentralization in order to determine position along an axis of Fig. 4.1. With respect to hardware, Lorin (1980) suggests that for each component in the system the computer power might be determined, from which the system hardware coordinate could be calculated. In Chapter 1 we saw some of the problems encountered in trying to estimate computer power. The problems are not made simpler by the fact that there is an enormous range in the power of a single chip; as a consequence even a terminal may be "dumb," that is, have a

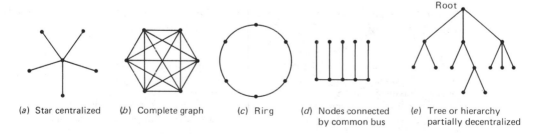

(a) Star centralized   (b) Complete graph   (c) Ring   (d) Nodes connected by common bus   (e) Tree or hierarchy partially decentralized

Figure 4.3 Graphs corresponding to centralized and decentralized structures

very limited range of capabilities, or "smart," that is, be able to carry out many of the operations relating to code interpretation, error checking, and protocol analysis usually performed by the communications processor. Still it is conceivable that computer power could serve as a hardware measure. Another possibility is to associate with each node a cost or budget expended. There are several attractive features to this. A given component or collection of components has a well-defined cost. Also, for management purposes, the budget (salary and other items) associated with a group of people is generally well defined. Budgeting responsibility is well recognized as an indicator of management control and decision-making authority (see, e.g., Barnet and Miller, 1973). Further, it is not difficult to assign costs other than hardware to either management functions or application development. Thus there is a dollar figure associated with each of hardware, management, and application, and all three of the coordinates would be measurable.* Suppose that in the system illustrated in Fig. 4.2(d), a_i is the (nonhardware) budget expended in department i for carrying out its application, where $i = 1 \cdots N$, corresponding to marketing, accounting, purchasing, marketing . . . administration. Let $A = \Sigma_{i=1}^{N} a_i$ and $\overline{A} = A/N$. Then a measure of the localization of application development is given by

$$L^A = \frac{1}{A^2} \sum_{i=1}^{N} (a_i - \overline{A})^2 \tag{4.1}$$

Note that for $a_i = \overline{A}$, all i, then $L^A = 0$ (i.e., there is no localization). Also, for $a_i = 0, i = 1, \ldots, N-1, a_N = A$, then $L^A = 1 - 1/N$ (i.e., the localization gets closer and closer to 1 as there are more nodes in the system). In a similar way, using corresponding budgets for hardware, h_i, and management m_i, it is possible to define measures for management centralization C^H and hardware concentration C^M. In effect, these definitions normalize the measures so that Fig. 4.1 represents a unit cube. An *overall* measure for centralization, C, can then be defined by

$$C^2 = (C^M)^2 + (C^H)^2 + (L^A)^2 \tag{4.2}$$

C is simply interpreted as the distance between the point that represents the system and the origin, in Fig. 4.1. Further, we can define

---

*It is not common for the salaries of the users (i.e., those possessing application skills) to appear in the budget of a computer center. But these costs are becoming dominant (see Section 6.2.2), and it is reasonable to assume that they can be identified and estimated. Also, the hardware cost is the cost of *operating* the hardware and should include costs for software, supplies, power, salaries of operators, and so on—in fact all costs other than those associated with management and developing or running applications.

$D^M = 1 - C^M$, as a measure of decentralization of management

$D^H = 1 - C^H$, as a measure of hardware distribution

$D^A = 1 - L^A$, as a measure of application skill dispersion

Then $D^2 = (D^M)^2 + (D^H)^2 + (D^A)^2$ is a measure of *overall* decentralization, and D is the distance between the point representing the system and CCL in Fig. 4.1.

There are occasions when it is desirable to consider centralization or decentralization of management separately, but to regard hardware and application skills as two facets of the application of computer technology. For such cases it is possible to define a measure for technology centralization, C^T, where

$$(C^T)^2 = (C^H)^2 + (L^A)^2$$

Two additional points can be made about the measures. If there were strong reasons to believe that C^M, C^H, and L^A were not of equal importance, it would be possible to define C^2 as a weighted sum of the three, but it is not easy to see how these weighting factors could be assigned, except in a subjective way. Second, budgets change from year to year, so that a given system does not occupy a point statically. It is interesting to speculate whether systems show *systematic* motion.

4.2. COMPARATIVE ADVANTAGES AND DISADVANTAGES

With this classification of systems according to the degree of centralization, the next question is how we are to judge the merits of each type. A review of the literature reveals that most of the discussion can be captured under two headings, each with subcategories.

1. *Cost:* Since budgeted amounts on computer expenditures are being proposed for measures of management control, hardware, and application development skills (the independent variables), cost as an observed (or dependent variable) must pertain to something else. We take it to be the cost of providing some designated type and level of service. In his 1978 study King examines the services provided to various municipal departments—police, finance, planning. In an educational institution the service types would be those provided by the computer center: for example, administrative computing (probably subdivided further into payroll, marks accounting, planning, etc.), instructional computing (again categorized by mode), and research computing. In a comparative study of other environments, like categories of service would have to be identified and the costs compared.

2. *Effectiveness:* This pertains to both the quality of service and the extent to which the possible user community avails itself of the offerings—in other words, how well and how widely the technology is being disseminated. Quality of service itself has at least two aspects—quality as compared to that available in a recognizably well run installation (or as compared to best practice) and quality as perceived by the user. It need hardly be said that the two can be different.

With this framework we can examine the arguments for and against centralizing or decentralizing information-processing facilities and the evidence in support of them. This is done in Tables 4.1 and 4.2 in a format that will be used frequently throughout this book. Strictly, there ought to be a separate table for each of the *three* variables. But hardware location and development of application skills can both be viewed as aspects of *operations,* as distinct from management, and it is convenient to group the arguments for these two aspects together. Besides, there is a general acceptance that application development skills, which are the results of education and training, ought to be as widespread as possible, and there are really no issues about the desirability of achieving this. There is some redundancy in the format of the tables, because an advantage for one course of action can, at the same time, be regarded as a negation of the counterargument. However, this redundancy is useful as a reminder that different writers have supported their views with varying evidence and that sometimes even contradictory views can be taken on the same evidence. Elaborations on the points in the tables, and references to articles where evidence regarding the points is to be found, are given in the following notes.*

Notes 1 to 3

This is essentially the argument based on Grosch's law, as discussed in Section 1.2, with evidence presented by Solomon (1966), Knight (1968), and Phister (1979). In his 1978 report on municipal governments King studies management control, technology, and user–provider interaction as related to cost, extent of use, and satisfaction. Of the nine possible relationships, the only two unequivocally supported by his data are that increasing centralization of control is accompanied by reduced use of computing, and that increasing concentration of technology is accompanied by lower costs for computing. It is important to realize that the statistical technique that establishes relationship does not prove causality, but causality can sometimes be inferred. Thus the results show that concentration of technology is accompanied by significant reductions in cost, but that there is no significant correlation between concentrated technology and *use* of computers and only a weak (negative) correlation between cost and centralization of control. Thus one can infer that the reduction in cost is due to the concentrated technology. Even though centralization of control is accompanied by less use, there is no evidence that concentration of technology goes with less use.

*A very extensive bibliography, with indications as to whether the writer is primarily addressing problems of management control or of operations, is given in King (1978).

TABLE 4.1 ARGUMENTS FOR AND AGAINST DISTRIBUTION OF HARDWARE AND DISPERSION OF APPLICATION DEVELOPMENT SKILLS IN INFORMATION PROCESSING

Approach	For	Note	Against	Note
Concentration localization	More effective use of equipment resources because of economies of scale	1	Hardware costs are already a small fraction of computer costs and they will become less and less important; they ought not to count in the debate	4
	Staffing problems are reduced	5	Communication costs are increased	14
	Better continuity assured through larger staffing	6	Greater system vulnerability	15
	Standards in files, programs, documentation security; easier to maintain	17		
Decentralization dispersion	Service can better match local needs	7	Equipment and staff redundancies are greater	2
	Better and more prompt accessibility	8	Small centers are affected more severely by high load levels and fluctuations in load	3
	Hardware upgrades easier because they can be made incrementally as needed	9	Incompatibilities in programs, data hardware more likely to occur	18
	Overhead factors of large operating systems are eliminated	10		
	Simpler installation problems	11		
	Greater user acceptability; large systems often have many dissatisfied users	12		
	Develops local abilities and hence draws on a more widely dispersed talent pool	13		
	Better security because of reduced access, better system reliability	16		

Streeter (1972) attempts a quantitative assessment taking into account economies of scale in hardware, communication costs, possibilities of service interruption, and queueing factors arising out of subdivided systems. But his models of economy of scale, communication costs, and reliability are very simple, and it is difficult to accept his quantitative conclusion about the optimum number of installations.

TABLE 4.2 ARGUMENTS FOR AND AGAINST CENTRALIZATION OF CONTROL
IN INFORMATION PROCESSING

Approach	For	Note	Against	Note
Centralization	Better manageability	19	Structures are rigid—less amenable to criticism and correction of faults	24
	Better ability to adopt to outside changes	20	Directors of centralized facilities are not subject to effective control because often senior management does not understand computers; the directors tend to overexpand their systems—a poor policy because rapidly decreasing costs of hardware make it expensive to acquire more capacity than is needed currently	28
Decentralization	This mode is more consistent with the decentralized approach to management—one which is said to be favored in many organizations and is more likely to motivate people to perform well	25	Overlapping jurisdictions difficult to manage	21
	Decisions are closer to the user and hence more likely to address real needs	26	Decentralized information systems can be fragmented and thereby be less useful	22
	Fewer political and priority conflicts—small systems have fewer users, and conflicts less likely to arise	27	Networks are not fully understood yet and are the objects of much research; prudence dictates a "go slow" approach	23

Note 4

This is the argument, advanced very strongly now, that the introduction of chips and large-scale integration (LSI) have made hardware costs negligible, so that Grosch's law, if it ever held, is no longer true.

Notes 5 and 6

Shortage of qualified personnel, especially at the senior levels, has long been a phenomenon in information processing. The argument here is that the larger staffs associated with large-scale systems offer better opportunities for scheduling, so that fewer people are needed. Total salary costs, as related to hardware costs, are less, even though *individual* salaries may be greater because of greater responsibilities. This allows large systems to attract more highly qualified people, something likely to happen anyway because these systems are more interesting to computer professionals. In a survey conducted in 1974, Solomon presents evidence that the fraction of costs spent on personnel goes down with the size of the operation [see Table 4.3(*a*)], and this is supported by later surveys undertaken by *Datamation* magazine [Table 4.3(*b*)].

Notes 7 to 13

These are the basic reasons favoring decentralized operations. Supporting them are the facts that small systems are more manageable (9 to 11) leading to a generally accepted belief that small systems are more acceptable to users (12 and 13, i.e., "small is beautiful"). It is worth noting that in King's study there was no conclusive evidence either in support of the hypothesis that users are more satisfied with centralized systems, or in support of its converse. He found that in the environment of municipal government some departments (e.g., police) tended to favor centralized systems, while others (e.g., planning) would prefer decentralized ones; this ambiguity held for both centralization of operations and control. King speculated that experience with computers might be one factor influencing the preference (sophisticated users prefer their own equipment), and possession of the computer as a demonstrable sign of power might be another. A study by D'Oliveira (1977) groups decentralizing forces into three categories—functional, economic, and psychological—and argues that functional and psychological factors, 7 to 12, have the greatest force.

Note 14

Communication costs are considered in some detail in Section 8.3, although as noted at the end of Chapter 2, in a proper design the computer and communication systems must be treated together. It is generally conceded that communication costs are higher for centralized systems, but Lorin (1979, 1980) notes that carrier tariffs are often complicated and expected savings do not always materialize. Also, the need for interaction between users in a network of computers will increase the amount of communication necessary.

Notes 15 and 16

The conventional argument is that a centralized system is less reliable and more vulnerable. There are more people about, increasing risks, and when the system goes down the penalties are much higher. But Lorin (1979) notes that the CPU is one of the most reliable components of a computing system, and replicating it does little to reduce risk. On the other hand, replication of storage is not only expensive, but it can lead to problems of data integrity. Further, reliability and security depend heavily on factors other than the possibility of the system going down (e.g., controlled access to data and operations, encryption practices, backup facilities, etc.), and these are more likely to be found in a large installation.

TABLE 4.3

(a) Economies of scale in computer salary costs

				Range of Monthly EDP Rentals				
	$1–3k	$3–6k	$6–12k	$12–25k	$25–50k	$50–75k	$75–150k	$150–300k
Number of companies surveyed	201	437	590	462	277	104	75	30
Number of employees	1902	5811	13,444	17,950	19,402	11,120	11,375	6,273
Average salary for computer personnel	155	156	160	167	173	178	184	174
Average salary × number of employees	$1466	$2075	$3646	$6488	$12,117	$19,028	$27,905	$36,383
Dollars/week/company per k of rental	978	462	405	351	324	304	248	162

Source: Data from M. B. Solomon, "Economies of Scale and Computer Personnel," *Datamation*, 16, no. 3 (March 1970), 107–11.

(b) Personnel costs in relation to installation size

	Percent of Budget Devoted to Personnel in Installation of Size:					
Item	To $25k/Year	$25k to $100k	$100k to $250k	$250k to $500k	$500k to $1M	Over $1M
Salaries and fringe benefits	50.92	52.13	54.91	48.73	52.03	38.87
Training	0.23	0.28	0.37	0.40	0.49	0.25
Conferences	0.10	0.30	0.39	0.28	0.24	0.19
Other (travel, etc.)	1.57	0.08	0.17	0.19	0.34	0.12
Total personnel budget	52.82	52.79	55.84	49.60	53.10	39.43

Source: R. A. McLaughlin, "A Survey of 1974 d.p. Budgets," *Datamation*, 20, no. 2 (February 1974), 52–56. With permission.

Notes 17 and 18

These points illustrate the generally held opinion that in small installations it is very difficult to get computer analysts, data managers, programmers, and operating personnel to conform to standards that are consistent with good professional practices. In fact, the administrative costs of establishing these practices and disseminating information about them are high for small organizations, and their very presence makes the computing environment more constrained and less attractive, so that these points reinforce observations made earlier.

With a few exceptions, the arguments in Table 4.1 are primarily economic. The points made in Table 4.2, on the other hand, are really political and the two sets there reflect opposing philosophies.

Notes 19 to 23

Governments, organizations, and individuals which are basically centralist in their approach emphasize the need for clear lines of authority, the ability to act decisively, and the importance of having decisions implemented promptly. They are wary of distributing control and power, for the consequences can be unpredictable. Information systems are not only objects of control—they are generally recognized to be *instruments* of control. Thus those who have a centralist philosophy will argue for a centralized, or in practice, a hierarchical mode of computer management, and they will regard such an organization as best suited for effecting the system of governance they favor.

Notes 24 to 28

The point here is that concentration of power not only deprives the majority of the opportunity of controlling their own actions, but centralized systems are worse because they are less open, less responsive to criticism, and in the long run less feasible economically because they are more prone to major strategic blunders.

When the opposing arguments are presented as they have been in these tables, it should be clear why the debate on centralization of computer power has been going on for so long, and why it is so hard to resolve.

4.3. TRENDS

Historically, going back to the time when computers were regarded as giant brains, and a concentration of funds and expertise was needed to acquire and use them, a centralized mode was necessary. Subsequent developments have made it possible to implement decentralized and distributed processing. These developments include the emergence of new technologies for data communications, dramatic reductions in the cost of computer operations accompanied by corresponding decreases in error rates, size, and power consumption, and the dissemination of knowledge about all aspects of computers. The question of interest here is whether these developments are resulting in greater or less centralization in the use of computing facilities.

In part, the statistics on the growth of the computer industry provide an answer. These will be discussed in Chapter 9, but the general trends are well known. For 30 years the number and dollar value of computers installed has been increasing at a steady high rate, and the resulting spread of computers into every sector of the economy must be viewed as a decentralization process. A more detailed look at the types of equipment being installed confirms that computer processing is being spread over wider and wider geographic regions, corresponding to a more widespread distribution of hardware facilities. The largest growth is in two hardware groups: (1) keyboard and point-of-sale terminals, showing that more and more data entry is taking place at point of origin rather than at the computer site, and (2) microcomputers and small business systems (as opposed to general-purpose systems), showing that there is a preference for installing small computers in many locations over larger systems in a few. This trend to distributing computer power culminates in the personal computer or workstation, where the capability is given to an individual. But in the light of the distinction drawn earlier it will be realized that these statistics on hardware expenditures support the evidence for increasing distribution of *operations* only. They say nothing about the *management control* of computing, which is related to making such decisions as allocating budget for computing purposes.

It is important to understand that computers are themselves seen to be key instruments for decision making and control in general. Computers are used for control of production and inventory, for controlling machine tools, and for hundreds of other specialized purposes. As will be emphasized in later chapters, the management of information is seen to be the central function of computers, and this management is vital in controlling an organization. If management holds a centralist philosophy, a computerized network can be viewed as the ideal means for collecting data at distributed nodes, relaying them to the decision center, and promulgating the decisions back to nodes. It is for this reason, in part, that governments with centrally planned economies pay so much attention to computerized systems. These possibilities of having data flow in one direction of a hierarchy, and decisions in the other, lie at the root of much of the concern about transborder data flows (see Section 11.2.2). But it is also true that a distributed computer network is potentially the most effective means of coordinating a highly *decentralized* organization so that the global system acts efficiently. The point being emphasized here is that increase in distributed computer *operations* says nothing about whether decision making about computers is becoming more or less decentralized. In this respect the technology is neutral; it can be used to reinforce either a centralist or decentralized management style. To know which style is actually gaining ground would require an investigation that is beyond the scope of this book, but one of the principal findings in a survey conducted in *Fortune* was that large companies were switching to distributed processing precisely to maintain centralized control over remote branches operating as profit centers (Scannell, 1981).

In summary, as computing grows there are increases in the numbers of both centralized and distributed systems. Distribution of computer operations, as measured by a proliferation of sites where expenditures are made on computing, is especially on the increase. The growth rate for distributed systems is significantly greater than the growth rate of large centralized systems (see Figs. 9.3 and 9.4). But neither the distribution of computer power, nor the dissemination of knowledge about using computers, are proof that management is choosing to decentralize control of decisions about computing. Perhaps the best evidence that management is reluctant to give up control over computing is the attitude taken to the proliferation of microcomputers, which are being acquired by individuals for use at home and in the workplace, sometimes at their own expense. There is a definite approval of the trend, but at the same time there are moves to make these personalized devices part of the corporate system. To maintain control, there may be incentives or even directives to the effect that particular brands of microcomputers, compatible with the company system, be acquired. At the same time the capabilities of company networks are extended to bring personal computers into the system and training programs on the use of microcomputers are instituted.* It is interesting to observe the directions, but the very existence of the concern shows that the debate about centralization and decentralization of computing resources is an ongoing one.

PROBLEMS

1. Assign each of the following systems into one of the eight categories described in Section 4.2.
   (a) A local area network based on Xerox Star workstations which are placed in managers' offices throughout the various functional divisions of an organization (marketing, accounting, research, etc.)
   (b) The SITA international network for airline reservations (for a description, see Schwarz, 1977, Chap. 2)
   (c) ARPANET (for a description, see Schwarz, 1977, Chap. 2)
   (d) A bibliographic utility such as OCLC or UTLAS [for descriptions, see Mathews (1979)]
   Justify your assignment in each case.

2. A computer system containing three nodes has annual expenditures (thousands of dollars) for management, hardware, and applications as follows:

**Managing Microcomputers: A Guide for Financial Policymakers* (New York: National Association of Accountants, 1984).

| | Node | | |
Expenditure Type	I	II	III
Management	60	15	15
Hardware	150	30	45
Applications	90	120	180

Calculate C/C_{max} for this system, where C_{max} is the maximum centralization possible for the system.

3. Budgetary changes are made in a system with N nodes such that the budgets of all nodes but one are increased (or decreased) by the same fraction, and the budget of the remaining node is adjusted so that the *total* budget remains constant. Thus

$$da_i = fa_i \quad i = 1 \cdots N - 1$$

$$da_N = -f \sum_{i=1}^{N=1} a_i$$

Show that the change in L, the localization index, is given by

$$dL = 2f\left(L - \frac{a_N}{A} + \frac{1}{n}\right)$$

Verify that this has the expected behavior for:
(a) A highly localized system (a_i very small, $i = 1 \cdots N - 1$, $a_N \approx A$).
(b) A highly dispersed system ($a_i \approx A/N$, $i = 1 \cdots N$).

BIBLIOGRAPHY

BARNET, R. J., and R. E. MILLER, *Global Reach: The Power of the Multinational Corporations.* New York: Simon and Schuster, 1974, p. 43.

CHANDLER, A. D., JR., *Strategy and Structure: Chapters in the History of the American Industrial Enterprise.* Cambridge, Mass.: MIT Press, 1962, pp. 194, 277.

DAVENPORT, R. A., "Design of Distributed Data Base Systems," *Comput. J.,* 24, no. 1 (February 1981), 31–41.

D'OLIVEIRA, C. R., "Analysis of Computer Decentralization," *MIT/LCS TM-90, NTIS* AD-A045 526.

JAMES, E. B., "Microelectronics: The Impact on Computer Centres," *Comput. J.,* 24, no. 1 (February 1981), 9–13.

KING, J. L., *Centralization vs. Decentralization of Computing: An Empirical Analysis in City Governments.* Public Policy Research Organization, University of California, Irvine, WP-78-78, 1978.

————, "Organizational Cost Consideration in Centralized vs. Decentralized Computing Operations," in *The Economics of Information Processing,* Vol. 2, ed. R. Goldberg and H. Lorin. New York: Wiley, 1982.

LORIN, H., "Distributed Processing: An Assessment," *IBM Syst. J.,* 18, no. 4 (1979), 582–603.

————, *Aspects of Distributed Systems.* New York: Wiley, 1980.

————, "Distributed Data Processing: How to Fail," *Datamation* (February 1981), 60–64B.

LUCAS, H. C., "Alternative Structures for the Management of Information Processing," in *The Economics of Information Processing,* Vol. 2, ed. R. Goldberg and H. Lorin. New York: Wiley, 1982.

MATHEWS, J. R., *The Four Online Bibliographic Utilities.* Library Technology Reports, November–December 1979, pp. 665–841.

NORTON, D. P., "Information Systems Centralization: The Issues," Harvard Business School Paper 9-172-286, 1972.

PHISTER, M., JR., *Data Processing Technology and Economics,* 2nd ed. Santa Fe, N. Mex.: Santa Monica/Bedford, Mass.: Digital Press, 1979.

REYNOLDS, C., "Issues in Centralization," *Datamation,* 23, no. 3 (March 1977), 91–100.

SCANNELL, T., "Fortune Survey Finds No Loss of Corporate Control in Move to DDP," *Comput. World,* no. 23 (March 1981), 10–11.

SCHWARZ, M., *Computer Communications Network Design and Analysis.* Englewood Cliffs, N.J.: Prentice-Hall, 1977.

STREETER, D. N., "Cost-Benefit Evaluation of Scientific Computing Services," *IBM Syst. J.,* 11, no. 3 (1972), 219–33.

Part II

THE USER

The point of view taken in this section is that of the computer user. Admittedly, the term is somewhat ambiguous. A computer manufacturer sees the director of a computer center as a user, and the director of a computer center sees a programmer as a user, but neither of these is what is meant by user here. Perhaps the term "end user" is most appropriate, and this is intended to mean the person or organization responsible for running an application on a computer system.

The yardstick to be adopted for deciding whether an application is to be run, or choosing among alternatives, is an accounting of the costs and benefits for each possibility. This is not meant to suggest that in practice a cost/benefit comparison is the only factor that influences choice, that it is the principal one in all cases, or even that it should be. It is well known that considerations of prestige, or the desire to maintain (or change) the balance of power between competing interests, play an important, sometimes decisive, role in the choice of a system or its location. There are occasions when social factors such as those relating to employment must come into the picture. The approach of this book is economic, as opposed to political or sociological, but some of these other factors will also be discussed.

Where economic considerations are accepted as the principal ones governing user choice about information processing, we might think that there would be little difficulty in justifying the benefits of having more and better information. But the justification turns out to be surprisingly difficult to establish, and it is to this problem that we turn first.

5

Data, Information, and Knowledge

Information can certainly be valuable. Doctors, lawyers, and accountants make their living by dispensing it. Newspapers sell it, and market analysts who have information useful for predictions will make themselves and their clients rich. The lawsuit instituted in 1982 by the U.S. Federal Bureau of Investigation against officials of Hitachi for attempting to purchase details about the design of IBM computers is a reminder that in a commercial environment information about a competitor's plans can have a very high value. Hitachi representatives paid hundreds of thousands of dollars so that they would be in a better position to anticipate the products that IBM would be releasing.* Much of this suggests that in certain regards information is like property in that it can be owned and sold. But information is obviously different than tangible commodities. Arrow (1962) points out that information differs from privately supplied goods in three important respects:

1. Since producers cannot normally charge for further use, the returns on information once disseminated are not fully appropriable.
2. Since further users are able to employ or transmit information at lower cost than the original supplier, information is subject to increasing returns in use.
3. Information is not infinitely divisible, a property usually assumed to hold for goods.

*Later dropped by the FBI, but taken up in different form by IBM, See R. Sharpe, "The Consequences of Keeping Abreast of IBM," *Computing J.,* August 1982, 16.

It may also be noted that in many situations the value of information tends to decline with time much faster than does that of its material counterparts. In neoclassical economic theory decision making is supposed to take place in the light of full information about all the alternatives, information that is produced and disseminated without cost. Clearly, this last assumption does not hold. As Samuelson notes, one consequence of its truth would be zero costs for advertising. Trying to determine the value of information, or even to define what information is, turns out to be a formidable undertaking. It is only since the 1940s that scientists have addressed the task of measuring information, and even more recently that economists have recognized that information, in addition to capital and labor, is a primary resource which must be taken into account when determining the values of goods and services, and that it is not sufficient to regard it as a production cost.

Computers are often defined as information processors. To make an analogy with manufacturing, we might think that "raw" data are fed into a computer, which processes and organizes the data, resulting in a product of greater value. Value has been added to the original data, so that now it is something different—information—and is worth more. Beyond information there is knowledge. Knowledge depends on the availability of data and information, but it has a more general meaning that is difficult to capture. A wider context or frame of reference than the problem of immediate concern is implied. Whereas information is in some respects like private property, which can be possessed by an individual, knowledge is more like a resource that is in the public domain. This suggests that quite different criteria might be necessary in assessing the worth of information and knowledge. If the value-added concept of information processing is accepted, we ought to be able to attach numbers to the increase in the worth of information that comes about by processing data. But the truth is that such numbers turn out to be highly elusive, in part because for many information-related activities there is no real market, so that it is impossible to determine either market or shadow prices for the products. If computer users do not feel that they will benefit from having information, presumably they will not produce and disseminate it. This is the approach that we shall take in this chapter, but before looking at the possible benefits, it is useful to identify and categorize attributes of data and information.

5.1. ATTRIBUTES OF DATA, INFORMATION, AND INFORMATION SYSTEMS

As soon as we think of particular forms of data, for example, observations in a scientific experiment, numbers specifying a bank transaction, or attitudes recorded in an opinion survey, certain attributes come to mind. There is *accuracy* and *precision*. The first reflects whether the data correctly represent what they are supposed to represent; the second indicates the "fineness" of recording or measurement scale. Thus 3.14 and 3.14159 are both accurate approximations to π; the second is more precise. In aggregation, detail is suppressed and precision is decreased. When dealing with the large amounts of data present in a data base, the concept of accuracy is broadened to *completeness, consistency,* and *integrity.* Completeness recognizes that there may be missing values. Consistency means that when the same attribute value of an entity is stored in two different places, the values agree; also that inferences that can be drawn from the value of an attribute are consistent with those that are captured by different attribute values elsewhere in the data base. Integrity is a security property of the data collection as a whole—whether access is controlled so that accuracy and consistency can be maintained and errors arising out of system malfunction can be corrected. The term *quality* is sometimes used to mean the same thing.

We shall define data as *encoded representations of the attributes of an entity.* The presence of the word "encoding" is a reminder that the same data can exist in different forms. The properties enumerated in the preceding paragraph refer to the representation. The entity has the attributes, and the values presumably exist whether they are recorded as data or not (i.e., independently of an observer). Information, on the other hand, is definitely associated with an observer who interprets the data and attaches meaning to it. We define information as *data used for decision making.* We talk about the *relevance* of information and its *timeliness,* terms that imply the existence of goals, purpose, and function. Relevance is a subjective judgment as to whether the information is related to some goal in mind, and little more can be said about it.* Timeliness also refers to a purpose in mind, but time provides a scale, and the concept can be examined in greater depth. Knowledge is *information for which the decision making is deferred* to some possibly distant time in the future. It is an *investment* in information. The definitions of data, information, and knowledge just given are useful in that they could in certain circumstances be used for legal purposes, as might arise in the theft of a document.† Note that the difference between data and information depends on intent, something which the law handles with difficulty but which must nevertheless be considered at times. In the case of knowledge, if the

---

*It is usual to calculate or estimate quantities, based on relevance, which rate the usefulness of the answers to a query in an information retrieval system. In response to a query let

N_{tr} = total number of relevant documents in the system
N_{rr} = number of retrieved documents which are relevant to the query
N_t = number of total documents retrieved

Then the *recall* for the query = N_{rr}/N_{tr}, and the *precision* = N_{rr}/N_t. When these quantities are averaged over a large number of queries, they may be used to characterize the retrieval system.

†It is tempting to extend the trio data, information, and knowledge. *Experience* might be regarded as the decision *not* to use available data, and *wisdom* might be defined as the accumulated knowledge acquired by an individual from information and experience.

decision making is deferred long enough, or there is only a small probability that it will be made, the value of the information becomes very small, but it may still happen that many people will need the information. This makes it reasonable to treat knowledge as a public good and have it stored in libraries at public expense. Like other public goods (air and water) it is plentiful and the marginal value is essentially zero.*

Information systems are devices designed to aid decision making. Decisions are traditionally classed into three types, distinguished by the time horizons associated with them: *operational, tactical,* and *strategic.* Operational decisions are taken about day-to-day events; they are valid for relatively short time intervals and are made by junior management. Strategic decisions are made irregularly; they are in force for relatively long times and they are made by senior management. Tactical decisions are intermediate in time span to operational and strategic. Table 5.1 elaborates on these properties and gives some illustrations.

Information systems are also characterized by the mode for providing the information. The most common is a *status reporting* system in which management reports are produced periodically. A *query* system produces information (possibly in the form of reports) in response to a query by the user. In a *report-by-exception* system reports are produced for management decision only when some designated set of events occurs. In the light of the computer's ability to generate mountains of unread reports, there is a marked preference, in middle and senior management, for query and report-by-exception systems.

Although some attributes of data and information are qualitative, others can be expressed quantitatively. The precision of measurement can be described by the number of digits used to represent it. Also by defining t_1 as the time when information is received, t_2 as the time when the decision for which the information is being acquired is made, and Δ as the interval over which the decision holds (so that the next decision is made at $t_2 + \Delta$), we can define, τ, the timeliness of information.

$$\tau = \frac{t_2 - t_1}{\Delta}$$

Thus the information is useful only if $\tau < 1$.†

The most basic quantitative aspect of data is the measure of the *quantity of data.* Data are always represented in terms of some set of character symbols. Let N_S be the size of the character set (i.e., the number of characters in it) and d be

---

*Machlup (1979), who was the first to write on knowledge and the information economy (see Section 11.1), rejects the notion that actions taken as a result of knowledge ought to be regarded as part of the information and taken into consideration when evaluating it. The approach taken here *is* consistent with that of Marschak (see the next section), also a recognized authority on the subject. In this respect Machlup's use of the term *information* corresponds more closely to data as defined above.

†For a more detailed discussion of timeliness, see Kleijnen (1980, Chap. 6).

TABLE 5.1 TYPES OF MANAGEMENT DECISIONS

Property	Type of Decision		
	Operational	Tactical	Strategic
Purpose	Immediate action To develop tactics	Short-term planning To help determine strategy	Long-term planning
Time Duration Periodicity	Short-term—hours to months Frequent	Intermediate term—days to years Regular	Long-term—years to decades Rare—often precipitated by events rather than the clock
Requirements Source Accuracy Format	Data Internally generated Details required Accuracy important Highly structured	Information Aggregation desirable—reports, summaries, etc.	Knowledge Much comes from outside the organization May be aggregated Inaccuracies tolerated Often unstructured, qualitative
Responsibility	Junior management	Middle management	Senior management Board of directors
Associated systems	Transaction processing systems	Decision support systems	
Examples	Determining labor needs assignments and timetables Production schedules Inventories	Budgeting Labor negotiations Plant location Marketing Production	Mergers Entry into a new market Research projects

the number of symbols or digits used to represent the datum, D. Each symbol in the character set can be encoded in binary form (in many ways, actually) using $\log_2 N_s$ bits. Therefore, the number of bits needed to represent $D = d \log_2 N_s$. This leads at once to the natural units for data rates, bits per second, and, further, to a measure of the bandwidth of a communication channel. But it is important to note that the number of bits in a data collection says nothing about accuracy or relevance. It is a measure of quantity, not quality. Still, data flows and data rates of communication channels have been used to estimate information flows in order to project how society is becoming increasingly dependent on information exchanges. The media for such exchange takes many forms: newspapers, banking transactions, stock market quotations, and so on. Table 5.2 is taken from an article of Tomita (1975), which is an ambitious attempt to

TABLE 5.2 VOLUME OF INFORMATION FLOW CLASSIFIED BY CATEGORY OF MEDIA

Category of Media	Year	Supply (bit)	Consumption (bit)	Average Flow Distance (km)	Standard Supply Distance (bit-km)	Effective Consumption Distance (bit-km)	Annual Circulation Cost (yen)	Standard Supply Unit Cost (yen)	Effective Consumption Unit Cost (yen)
Broadcast group	1960	0.6670×10^{20}	2.5632×10^{-16}	56.9	3.8973×10^{21}	1.4593×10^{18}	3.9383×10^{10}	1.011×10^{-11}	2.699×10^{-3}
	1965	1.1807	5.2812	49.5	6.3862	2.6119	7.8998	1.237	3.025
	1970	1.8397	7.1262	49.9	9.4380	3.5589	10.8883	1.154	3.059
	1972	1.9969	7.1650	50.5	10.2279	3.6155	11.9480	1.168	3.305
Print communication group	1960	5.4862×10^{17}	2.7036×10^{15}	70.2	3.8548×10^{19}	1.8966×10^{17}	1.0350×10^{11}	2.685×10^{-9}	0.546×10^{-6}
	1965	6.6846	2.8448	68.9	4.6169	1.9612	1.3370	2.896	0.682
	1970	8.1503	2.8988	67.7	5.5305	1.9616	1.8021	3.258	0.919
	1972	8.8207	2.9193	67.2	5.9416	1.9607	2.0461	3.444	1.044
Facility communication group	1960	4.5536×10^{18}	3.6776×10^{16}	1.95	2.0504×10^{19}	0.7165×10^{17}	0.4171×10^{12}	2.034×10^{-8}	0.582×10^{-5}
	1965	4.3841	3.6043	2.47	2.3003	0.8896	0.7290	3.169	0.819
	1970	4.1680	3.2906	3.09	3.3063	1.0169	1.3209	3.995	1.299
	1972	4.2153	3.1638	3.20	4.1965	1.0115	1.6690	3.977	1.650
Record communication group	1960	2.5301×10^{16}	1.6289×10^{15}	40.6	1.0272×10^{18}	6.6132×10^{16}	0.2846×10^{11}	2.771×10^{-8}	0.430×10^{-6}
	1965	3.5758	1.7431	40.6	1.4518	7.0769	0.6460	4.450	0.913
	1970	5.8391	2.3600	40.6	2.3707	9.5817	1.4944	6.304	1.506
	1972	5.4149	2.6298	40.6	2.2008	10.6768	2.5713	17.683	2.409
Total of all mass communication media	1960	0.7183×10^{20}	6.6741×10^{16}	26.8	3.9573×10^{21}	1.7867×10^{18}	0.5885×10^{12}	1.487×10^{-10}	3.294×10^{-7}
	1965	1.2316	9.3443	31.8	6.4569	2.9678	1.0063	1.559	3.391
	1970	1.8901	10.9427	36.1	9.5290	3.9526	1.7595	1.847	4.452
	1972	2.0485	10.8836	35.0	10.3315	4.0195	2.2503	2.178	6.583

Source: Reproduced with the permission of the International Telecommunication Union (ITU), Geneva, Switzerland, from T. Tomita, "The Volume of Information Flow and the Quantum Evaluation of Media" in *ITU Telecommun. J.*, 42, no. 6 (1975), 339–49.

document the rate of growth of data dissemination and personal "consumption" of these data as a function of time. Tomita writes about information (we prefer the term *data*), and attaches values to the quantities, based on the cost of circulation. We return to this question of information and its dissemination in Section 11.1.

Claude Shannon's classic work on information theory extends measurement of quantity of data to quantity of *information*. Shannon's measurement of information about an event is based on the "surprise" imparted when the event is known to have occurred. Thus, if we look out the window and observe that it is raining and at the same time are listening to a weather report which states that rain is expected, the report conveys no information. In mathematical terms, let p_i be the probability of occurrence of event e_i, one of a possible set, $i = 1 \cdots N$, which can occur ($\Sigma_{i=1}^{N} p_i = 1$). The information associated with e_1 is defined to be $-p_i \log p_i$ (note that it is always positive), and the information associated with a whole set of events, H, is given by

$$ H = -\sum_{i=1}^{N} p_i \log_2 p_i $$

H is analogous to entropy in thermodynamics, and there are several aspects of this definition that make it consistent with an intuitive notion of information content. Thus the information conveyed when a particular event is known to have occurred is greatest when p is least (i.e., there is greatest surprise when the most unlikely event occurs), and the total information content of a set is least when all events are equally probable. Further, it is easy to show that the information content of two independent (unconnected) events is the sum of the information contents of the separate events, a desirable property. Information theory is a subject in its own right and is of great importance in communication theory. Yet it does little to help us in our task of trying to develop concepts of the change in information resulting from submitting data to an information processor. The processor *can* be looked on as a communication channel which may be *lossless* (i.e., does not change the information content of the data being transmitted) or *noisy* (it reduces the information content because of aggregation or errors). But in the Shannon measure of information there is no notion of relevance to a task at hand. This removal of subjective judgment is, from the point of view of communication theory, just what makes the Shannon definition of information content so useful. It allows the topic to be treated at an objective, scientific level. But from an economic point of view, where we would like to develop the notion of the *value* of information, a market concept enters, and the market is, in essence, an averaged *subjective* judgment. In seeking to attach a value to information we must be prepared to deal with subjective judgments expressed in the form of markets, expectations, and prices.

5.2. *THE VALUE OF INFORMATION*

When a customer buys something, he or she *expects* it to be worth the price, and in looking for the value of information perhaps the framework needed is that of *probabilistic* cost/benefit analysis. But it is useful to start by looking at actual costs and prices.

From a purchaser's point of view, price is a measure of the utility of a product. Following Sharpe (1969), classical economic theory establishes a simple relationship among cost of production, price, and market elasticity. Let R be the revenue derived from selling a quantity, Q, of a product for unit price P.

$$R = P \times Q$$

The *marginal revenue,* R_M, is the slope of the curve of revenue versus Q.

$$R_M \equiv \frac{dR}{dQ} = P + Q\frac{dP}{dQ}$$

The *elasticity* of the market is the sensitivity of the sales to price—more precisely, the ratio of the (relative) change in sales to (relative) change in price:

$$e \equiv \frac{dQ/Q}{dP/P}$$

The elasticity is always negative, and the demand is inelastic when $-1 < e < 0$ and elastic when $-\infty < e < -1$. We then have

$$R_M = \left(1 + \frac{Q}{P}\frac{dP}{dQ}\right)P = \left(1 + \frac{dP/Q}{dQ/Q}\right)P = \left(1 + \frac{1}{e}\right)P$$

If the market is perfectly elastic, $e = -\infty$, and $R_M = P$ (i.e., the price is the marginal revenue). More generally, price may be regarded as an imperfect measure of the marginal cost of production.

Where there is a genuine market for information or information services, it is not unreasonable to regard price as a measure of the value (utility) of the information.* Such a situation prevails when a manufacturer is trying to decide whether it is worthwhile to conduct a market survey, to estimate what level of production he or she should undertake, or when a researcher is deciding whether to conduct a literature search using a commercial data base searching service such as ORBIT or DIALOG. However, a manager who receives a report on

---

*But recall the objection to accepting price as a measure of the performance of a computer system (Section 1.1). The problem there was that we would like to compare different systems, and use performance/price as a figure of merit.

some activity in the company in which the interest is only peripheral is definitely *not* in a market situation. This point is emphasized by the observation that not only does the value of the information level off as the quantity delivered increases (as is characteristic of the traditional utility function), but it may well be that more is *less* valuable, as the well-known phenomenon of information overload comes into play (see Ackoff, 1967). Not only is there a point of diminishing returns (decreasing slope), but there is also one of *negative* returns (the elasticity is positive), as shown in Fig. 5.1. Knowledge, especially, is provided mainly through such institutions as libraries and schools, and traditionally, these do not operate in a market environment.

Confining ourselves for the moment to situations where there *is* a market, there is a branch of economics which bears on the topic at hand, namely, information economics as developed by Marschak and expounded especially in the book *Economic Theory of Teams* (Marschak and Radner, 1972). Information economics, in turn, depends on probabilities and on Bayesian decision theory; the whole subject is a sophisticated discipline, formulated in mathematical terms, but a simple numerical example will serve to illustrate both the main ideas behind the method and the limitations from our point of view. The goal in the example is to calculate the value of an information system given in the form of a market survey which yields data on the state of the market for a product being sold.

Suppose that a company manufacturing a product, say widgets, does not know whether the demand for its product will be large (a firm market) or small (a soft market). From past experience the company knows that it can sell 10 widgets in a firm market, but only 4 in a soft market. It also has only three levels

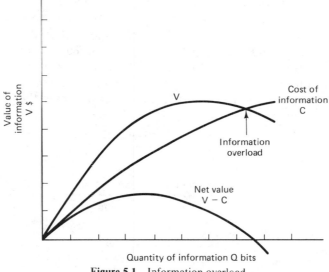

Figure 5.1   Information overload

of production capability, high (10 widgets), medium (8 widgets), and low (4 widgets). Moreover, a widget costs 3 units to make and sells at a price of 4; thus for each widget sold there is a profit of 1, and for each one not sold there is a loss of 3. The question is: How many should be produced?

The benefit matrix, *B,* showing the profit for the various combinations of actions (i.e., production level selected) and market states is shown in Table 5.3. *B* is an $a \times s$ matrix where there are a actions and s states.

If the market state is known, that production level is selected which will maximize the benefits; the level should be 10 for a market known to be firm, and 4 for a market known to be soft. If the market is not known but there are estimates for the probabilities for each state, the production decision should maximize the *expected* benefits, taking all possibilities into consideration. Suppose that there is probability of 0.6 that the market will be firm and 0.4 that it will be soft. The expected benefits for the three courses of action can be calculated by multiplying *B* by the state probability vector,

$$p = \begin{pmatrix} 0.6 \\ 0.4 \end{pmatrix}$$

to obtain

$$B \times p = \begin{pmatrix} 0.4 \\ 1.6 \\ 4 \end{pmatrix}$$

The action to be taken is that which maximizes the expected benefit; therefore, choose the low production level for an expected benefit of 4.

It is not difficult to place bounds on the value of any information system in this situation. The greatest possible benefit is 10 and the least -14, so that $10 - (-14) = 24$ is certainly an upper bound. But by making the rational choice of the lowest production level, as just determined, there is an expected benefit of 4, so a better upper bound to the value of an information system is $10 - 4 = 6$.

Suppose now that the information system is one that yields *predicted states* rather than actual states, but there are uncertainties in the predicted values. These

TABLE 5.3 BENEFITS MATRIX[a]

	Market State	
Production Level	Firm = 10	Soft = 4
High = 10	10	-14
Medium = 8	8	-8
Low = 4	4	4

[a]$B = 4 \times$ market state $-3 \times$ production level.

uncertainties are expressed in the form of a matrix, U, with elements $U_{i/j}$, where $U_{i/j}$ is the probability that the predicted state will be i, given that the actual state is j. In our example let

$$U = \begin{pmatrix} p \text{ (pred. firm|actual firm)} & p \text{ (pred. firm|actual soft)} \\ p \text{ (pred. soft|actual firm)} & p \text{ (pred. soft|actual soft)} \end{pmatrix} = \begin{pmatrix} 0.8 & 0.2 \\ 0.2 & 0.8 \end{pmatrix}$$

Actions will now be taken on the basis of predictions, and again we wish to calculate the expected benefits for the different courses of action. For this we need to know the matrix

$$\overline{U} = \begin{pmatrix} p \text{ (actual firm|pred. firm)} & p \text{ (actual firm|pred. soft)} \\ p \text{ (actual soft|pred. firm)} & p \text{ (actual soft|pred. soft)} \end{pmatrix}$$

since the product matrix $B\,\overline{U}$ will be an $a \times s$ matrix whose two columns correspond to the benefits accruing from a firm prediction and the benefits accruing from a soft prediction. To compute the elements of $\overline{U}$, from the definition of conditional probability it follows that

$$p(a|b) = \frac{p(a \cap b)}{p(b)} \quad \text{and} \quad p(b|a) = \frac{p(b \cap a)}{p(a)}$$

so that $p(a|b)p(b) = p(b|a)p(a)$. Therefore,

$$p \text{ (actual firm|pred. firm)} = p \text{ (pred. firm|actual firm)} \times \frac{p \text{ (actual firm)}}{p \text{ (pred. firm)}}$$

Further,

$$p \text{ (pred. firm)} = p \text{ (pred. firm|actual firm)} \times p \text{ (actual firm)}$$
$$+ p \text{ (pred. firm|actual soft)} \times p \text{ (actual soft)}$$

Using the values for $p(\text{actual firm}) = 0.6$, $p(\text{actual soft}) = 0.4$ and for the components of U,

$$p \text{ (pred. firm)} = 8.0 \times 0.6 + 0.2 \times 0.4 = 0.56$$

and similarly

$$p \text{ (pred. soft)} = 0.2 \times 0.6 + 0.8 \times 0.4 = 0.44$$

Then p(actual firm|pred. firm) $= 0.8 \times 0.6/0.56 = 6/7$. Computing the other terms of $\overline{U}$ in a similar way, we get

$$\overline{U} = \begin{pmatrix} 6/7 & 3/11 \\ 1/7 & 8/11 \end{pmatrix}$$

Then

$$B \times \overline{U} = \begin{pmatrix} 10 & -14 \\ 8 & -8 \\ 4 & 4 \end{pmatrix} \begin{pmatrix} 6/7 & 1/7 \\ 1/7 & 6/7 \end{pmatrix} = \begin{pmatrix} 46/7 & -82/11 \\ 40/7 & -40/11 \\ 4 & 4 \end{pmatrix}$$

The first column gives the benefit for the three courses of action when the prediction is for a firm market. To obtain the maximum benefit of 46/7 a high production level should be undertaken. To obtain the maximum benefit of 4 when a soft prediction arises, the low production level should be chosen. But it was just calculated that the probability of a firm prediction is 0.56 and the probability of a soft prediction is 0.44. Then the *expected benefits* are $46/7 \times 0.56 + 4 \times 0.44 = 5.44$. The value of the information system characterized by U is the expected benefits, taking advantage of U, less the expected benefits when rational action, without knowledge of U, is chosen, namely, $5.44 - 4 = 1.44$.*

It is easy to verify that for an information system U' characterized by

$$U' = \begin{pmatrix} 1/2 & 1/2 \\ 1/2 & 1/2 \end{pmatrix} \quad \text{then} \quad \overline{U}' = \begin{pmatrix} 0.6 & 0.4 \\ 0.4 & 0.6 \end{pmatrix} \quad \text{and} \quad E \text{ (benefits)} = 4$$

the same as was obtained without any information system. For this system the probability that the actual market is firm is just the same when the prediction is for a firm market, as it is without the prediction. Such a system provides no additional information and it is not surprising that it has a value of zero.

The computation of the value of an information system in this way is convincing, and information economics which can be viewed as a branch of decision theory in the presence of uncertainty is elegant and satisfying. But the limitations are obvious. To carry out the calculations a great deal must be known about past performance and probabilities of the market. It is very rare that such probabilities can be estimated with any degree of confidence. For the really important decisions, the strategic ones of Table 5.1, almost no numerical estimates of probability can be derived, and it is impossible to begin calculating

---

*For a slightly different method of arriving at the same result, see Neave and Wiginton (1979). The expression derived there includes a decision matrix, D, which is chosen so as to yield the maximum expected benefits, and it allows for the possibility that the number of predicted states will be different than the number of actual states.

the value of information along the lines just described. Even in situations which are much more highly structured, and which resemble the problem outlined (e.g., deciding whether to subscribe to an investment counseling service), it is extremely difficult to carry out the calculations. The amounts of data are very large, the probabilities are hard to estimate, and they are time dependent. In a very few areas of decision making (e.g., inventory management) the problem is sufficiently well defined and the data collection methods are good enough that one might think of accumulating historical records, estimating probabilities, and applying decision theory. But where the information is in the form of tables and reports resulting from computer processing, information economics cannot be used. Sometimes, highly pragmatic rules have been proposed for evaluating information. For example, Weiser (1971) derives a figure of merit for management reports calculated as the weighted sum of three attributes: (1) U, a use factor (indicating whether the report is to be used for an immediate decision, is a reply to a query, or is a status description); (2) F, a function factor (depending whether the report is for control, planning, or coordination); and (3) R, a recipient factor (depending on the rank of the recipient). Numerical values for U, F, and R, as well as for the weighting factors, are determined from a survey of well-informed persons. The approach is interesting, and perhaps useful, but highly subjective. Others have attempted to evaluate the information in special situations [e.g., when supplying accounting reports or engineering estimates (Ostwald, 1974)]. Perhaps the most systematic scheme for bringing in subjectively determined weights for the value of different benefits occurring from the use of an information resource is that described by Hawgood (1977) for optimizing library services. But it is necessary to admit that any general theory based on expected value of benefits, capable of being applied in a practical way to evaluate the outputs of information processors, still seems to be very remote.

Yet if we are to have any objective, quantitative way of knowing whether acquiring information or setting up an information-processing system is worthwhile, it is impossible to avoid the problem of estimating the value of the activity. Since really satisfactory ways of calculating the value of information or the benefits of information processing are not available, by default, the calculations are carried out on the basis of a simplifying assumption, one that is usually credible but difficult to prove. The assumption derives from the concept of the *productivity* of the information user. In an industrial environment productivity is a well-defined term—it is measured by the units of production per person-hour of labor input. In a research or managerial environment it is much less clear how productivity should be measured, but it is reasonable to argue that the products of research or the efforts of managers are eventually translated into dollars earned by the enterprise. It is then assumed that more or better information will increase the productivity of the researcher or manager. The problem of evaluating information thus becomes the problem of determining what productivity increase should be attributed to processing the information or having the information-processing capability at one's disposal. This is the approach to the value information most often adopted, and it will be the one taken in Chapter 6. Estimating productivity increases for individual tasks presents no little challenge. In most cases the estimates are based on subjective judgments, although there are reports based on statistics accumulated from actual cases which quote increases that can be expected when computers are used for a variety of on-line applications (see COPICS, 1979). The most serious objections to productivity estimates is that they are usually based on too narrow a view of the objectives. In a discussion of productivity assessment in an office environment, Bair (1982) identifies four levels of performance: equipment, throughput, organizational, and institutional. The second level, throughput, pertains to the productivity of the individual, while the third and fourth levels pertain to the overall performance of the organization or company, and the performance of the particular organization within its industrial and societal context. Productivity measurements usually focus on the second level, and in doing so concentrate on what might be termed *efficiency*, whereas they should address themselves to the high levels that concern *effectiveness* (i.e., the degree to which progress toward stated goals is being achieved). Whatever the methodology of estimating, calculations of the value of information based on productivity increases are approximations at best.

We conclude with some additional comments about the economics of information, following on those made earlier in this chapter. Flowerden and Whitehead (1975) list reasons why it is so difficult to measure the benefits of scientific and technical information:

- When applying information we are often simultaneously engaged in activities other than maximizing a particular benefit. There is what economists call *joint consumption*, and this brings with it the problem of cost allocation.
- Information is largely an investment good, although it has consumption features.
- The benefits and costs of obtaining information are not fully borne by the consumers and producers because there is a social good in a well-informed public. Thus there is *joint production*, and again the problem of cost allocation.

When we realize that products of computers have a much wider range than scientific and technical reports, it is easily appreciated that determining the value of information in general is a formidable problem.

But economists have come to place increasing importance on the role of information in production processes. As noted by Lamberton (1976), more and more attention is being paid to the economics of information and the value of information in economic journals and meetings. Although there are several collected volumes of writings (see Lamberton, 1971, and King et al., 1983), quantitative theories are just beginning to emerge. Newman (1976) is certainly right in his insistence that such a theory must take into account both market sources for information and institutional sources, and that information can bring about important changes in the institutional structure of the economy. Given these as facts, he suggests a framework for information and institutional structures such that demand for, and supply of, market-supplied information depends on *both* the price of the market-supplied information and the institutional structure of the economy. Further, the supply of institutional information depends on the institutional structure of the economy. From such a framework one can begin to see how a dynamic model might be constructed to explain the activities of market-driven information systems, and of institutional systems such as libraries, and eventually yield credible estimates of the volume and worth of the products for each. To be credible, the model would also have to be consistent with input-output, Leontieff models, which are the accepted way to portray national economic activity. The most promising recent theory for bringing information-related activities into a macroeconomic model of production is that of Jonscher (1983). This follows on earlier work of Porat and others on the so-called *information economy,* a subject that is discussed in Section 11.1. Jonscher derives estimates for the value which the aggregated information sector adds to the aggregated goods production sector, together with estimates of the productivities in the sectors. For now, however, our interest is focused at the microeconomic level (i.e., on decisions taken by companies and individuals about specific tasks).

PROBLEMS

1. Look up the terms *data, information,* and *knowledge* in a dictionary or in the *IFIP-ICC Vocabulary* (1966). Do the definitions support the view of information processing as an activity that adds value to data (e.g., by organizing, selecting, and attaching meaning to it)?

2. In the example of Section 5.2, suppose that an information system with perfect knowledge is available, such that

$$U = \begin{pmatrix} 1 & 0 \\ 0 & 1 \end{pmatrix}$$

What is the value of this system? Show that the value of a system which is always wrong, $\left[\text{i.e., with } U = \begin{pmatrix} 0 & 1 \\ 1 & 0 \end{pmatrix} \right]$ is the same. Why should this be so?

3. In response to a request for proposal (RFP) on a software project, a company may take three actions:

   (1) Bid without building a prototype, $B/\bar{P}$

(2) Bid, first building a prototype, B/P

(3) Not bid

The possible outcomes are to win the contract, W, or lose, L. The production function is $M = 2.54I^{1.05}$ ($I =$ thousands of instructions, $M =$ person-months of effort) and the cost $C = M \times S$, where $S =$ average salary/month. Profit $= PM \times C$, where $PM =$ profit margin. The cost of preparing a bid $= f_B \times C$, where f_B is a bidding factor when there is no prototype and is increased by the cost of the prototype when one is built. From experience the company knows the probability of winning the bid without a prototype $(p/\overline{P})$ and winning with a prototype (p/P). Hence it knows the matrix

Probability matrix P			
Action Outcome	$B/\overline{P}$	B/P	N
Win	$p/\overline{P}$	p/P	0
Lose	$1 - p/\overline{P}$	$1 - p/P$	1

(a) Derive the expected benefits matrix, $E(B)$. (This is a 3×3 matrix for which only the diagonal terms are meaningful.)

(b) Show that a bid without prototype is worth making only if

$$\frac{p}{\overline{P}} \geq \frac{f_B}{PM}$$

(c) What is the best course of action for $PM = 0.25$, $p/\overline{P} = 0.3$, $p/P = 0.5$, $I_{\text{main program}} = 50k$, $I_{\text{prototype}} = 10k$, $S = \$20,000$ per month, and $f_B = 0.06$.

4. Libraries are both repositories of knowledge and sources of information for specific needs. Under what conditions should information be provided at zero (or very low) cost to the user, and when is it reasonable to expect the user to pay? When there are charges for information, what are some of the common pricing methods? How do computers affect the balance between knowledge as a public and a private good? (See King et al., 1983.)

BIBLIOGRAPHY

ACKOFF, P. L., "Management Misinformation Systems," *Manag. Sci.,* 14, no. 4 (December 1967), B147–56.

ARROW, K. J., "Economic Welfare and the Allocation of Resources for Invention," in National Bureau of Economic Research, *The Rate and Direction of Inventive Activity: Economic and Social Factors.* Princeton, N.J.: Princeton University Press, 1962, pp. 609–25.

BAIR, J. H., "Productivity Assessment of Office Information Systems Technology," in *Emerging Office Systems,* ed. R. L. Landau, J. H. Bair, and J. H. Sregman. Norwood, N.J.: Ablex, 1982.

COPICS Benefit Opportunities Workbook. San Jose, Calif.: IBM Manufacturing Industry Education, 1979.

FLOWERDEN, A. D. J., and C. M. E. WHITEHEAD, "Problems in Measuring the Benefits of Scientific and Technical Information," in *The Economics of Informatics,* ed. A. B. Frielink. Amsterdam: North-Holland, 1975, pp. 119–27.

HAWGOOD J., "Participation Assessment of Library Benefits," *Drexel Library Q.,* 13, no. 3 (1977), 68–83.

IFIP-ICC Vocabulary. Amsterdam: North-Holland, 1966.

JONSCHER, C., "Information Resources and Economic Productivity," *Inf. Econ. Policy,* 1 (1983), pp. 13–35.

KING, D. W., N. K. RODERER, and H. A. OLSEN, eds., *Papers in the Economics of Information.* White Plains, N.Y.: Knowledge Industry Publications, 1983.

KLEIJNEN, J. P. C., *Computers and Profits: Quantifying Financial Benefits of Information.* Reading, Mass.: Addison-Wesley, 1980.

——, ed., *The Economics of Information and Knowledge.* Harmondsworth, Middlesex, England: Penguin Books, 1971.

LAMBERTON, D. M., "National Policy for Economic Information," *Int. Social Sci. J.,* 28, no. 3 (1976), Unesco.

MACHLUP, F., "Uses, Value and Benefits of Knowledge," *Knowledge,* 1, no. 1 (1979), 62–81.

MARSCHAK, J., "Economics of Information Systems," *J. Am. Stat. Assoc.,* 66 (1979), 192–219.

MARSCHAK, J., and R. RADNER, *Economic Theory of Teams.* Cowles Foundation Monograph 22. New Haven, Conn.: Yale University Press, 1972.

NEAVE, E. H., and J. C. Wiginton, "Economic Evaluation of the Information Content of Alternative Sales Forecasting Techniques," *INFOR,* 17, no. 1 (February 1979), 35–41.

NEWMAN, G., "An institutional perspective" International Social Science Journal, 20, no. 3, (1976), UNESCO 466–492.

OSTWALD, F. P., *Cost Estimating for Engineering and Management.* Englewood Cliffs, N. J.: Prentice-Hall, 1974, Chap. 13.

SHARPE, W. F., *The Economics of Computers.* New York, N.Y.: Columbia University Press, 1969.

TOMITA T., "The Volume of Information Flow and the Quantum Evaluation of Media," *ITU Telecommun. J.,* 42, no. 6 (1975), 339–49.

WEINGRAD, D. E., *Marketing for Library and Information Agencies.* Norwood, N.J.: Ablex, 1983.

WEISER, A. L., "Assigning Priorities to Management Information Reports," in *Analysis, Design and Selection of Computer Systems,* ed. E. Joslin. Arlington, Va., College Readings Inc., 1971, pp. 39–44.

6

Cost-Benefit
Analyses

Determining the costs and the benefits is the recognized approach to choosing between alternative courses of action in management science, although a political scientist or a sociologist might adopt a different view or consider quite different factors in the accounting. The usual case is that costs are identified readily, but that benefits are more intractable because there are important ones which are intangible or unquantifiable. In situations where service centers are not operated as profit or cost centers, as happens in the public sector, even determining costs can present problems, because of accounting and budgeting rules which do not allow amortization of capital equipment or carryover of funds from one fiscal period to the next.

We start in Section 6.1 by identifying the economic factors that have to be considered in doing a cost/benefit study, and by looking at the criteria, based on investment analysis, which are commonly applied to make a go/no go decision. In the following section the techniques are applied to a number of instances where users have to make choices about use of computer facilities.

6.1. GENERAL APPROACH

Investigations for deciding whether a project should be undertaken are referred to as *feasibility studies*. A quantitative evaluation of costs and benefits is often part of a feasibility study, but it also includes factors which are not strictly quantifiable. Costs can basically be grouped into capital, one-time, and ongoing, but a finer structure is needed. Broadly speaking, benefits can be classified as cost saving or cost avoidance, both of which are usually quantifiable or tangible. Intangible benefits have quality features which are difficult to quantify, but a persistent effort can often show how to translate them into quantifiable ones. The mathematics of investment, based on dollar calculations of the quantifiable benefits, provides the initial criteria for judging whether a project should be undertaken. But this approach can be simplistic. Other criteria are discussed in Section 6.1.3.

6.1.1. Feasibility

There are important classes of carefully formulated management problems in which the term *feasibility* has a precise, mathematical meaning. Essentially, a solution is feasible when the values of certain variables satisfy constraints imposed by the nature of the problem. Examples are:

- Mix problems in linear programming, where the amount of an ingredient cannot exceed a given available supply.
- Class–teacher scheduling problems, where each teacher can meet with at most one class, and each class can meet with at most one teacher in a given hour. This constraint is imposed by the logic of the problem. There may be others introduced arbitrarily, for example, prescribed maxima and minima for the number of sessions in a week for any teacher.
- Routing problems, as in scheduling commercial aircraft, where the number of hours a plane may fly before it returns to its home base for maintenance is limited by regulation.

In each case the technique is to find, among the feasible solutions, the one (or perhaps the set) that satisfies some condition of optimality (e.g., least cost or fewest personnel required).

In project engineering there may be other kinds of constraints imposed on the solution of a problem. In a request for proposal, there may be constraints on the total budget, on the time taken to complete the project, on the available personnel with specified skills, or on system performance (e.g., the response time for 50% of the jobs submitted to a time-sharing computer must be less than a specified interval). Again, a solution meeting the constraints is said to be feasible, but the constraints may not be quite as rigid as those in mathematical programming. A *sensitivity analysis* of the solution, in which certain of the variables are changed, might reveal that if one of the constraints were to be relaxed by a very small amount, a considerable reduction could be achieved in cost. In such a case it might well happen that this alternative solution would be acceptable, illustrating that the term *feasible* has a somewhat weaker or more general meaning in project planning than it does in mathematical programming.

In projects relating to the acquisition and installation of computers the phrase *feasibility study* is also used commonly, and here the term has a still more general meaning. In the early days of computers feasibility studies were carried out, largely by management consultant firms, to determine whether the benefits to be had by installing a general-purpose computer justified the expenditures. An important part of the study was a comparative rating of vendors' hardware, usually submitted in response to a request for proposals. Such studies are still conducted today, but they are more likely to be on behalf of a small company, trying to decide whether to acquire a small business system or to determine whether a particular application (e.g., scheduling shift assignments) should be converted to a computer. A dollar calculation of costs and benefits is an important step, and ways of doing this will be elaborated in the section that follows. But in computer feasibility studies it is usually expected that factors other than cost will also be taken into consideration. Overall system performance is examined, including such features as throughput, response time, reliability, availability and quality of software, vendor support, possibilities of subsequent upgrades, and so on.

A key problem in conducting the study is how to reconcile such a diverse collection of criteria—how to compare apples and oranges. Several techniques are commonly used, all of them dependent on *feature analysis,* an enumeration of those features considered to be important in evaluating the system. Each feature is regarded as a category with several constituents, and in some situations the total number of constituents may run into the hundreds. To each constituent a descriptor is attached, considered to be appropriate for the system under investigation. This descriptor may be qualitative, chosen from a ranked set (e.g., very good, good, acceptable, poor, unacceptable) or it may be a numerical value lying within a designated range. As an example, Table 6.1(*a*) shows a feature analysis chart for small business systems. The result is a figure of merit for the system, which is then divided by the cost [Table 6.1(*b*)] to obtain a system rating. This FOM is calculated for the system proposed by each vendor, and the proposal with the best FOM is chosen. As another example, Boehm (1981) describes a very detailed feature analysis system, for which the main categories and weights are shown in Table 6.2(*a*). Each category in turn is subdivided, as illustrated in Table 6.2(*b*) for the supervisory category.*

The problems with feature analysis are obvious. If there are a great many features, when qualitative indicators are used it is difficult to make an overall judgment from the display. If numerical weights are used, we have the same problems we encountered before in using FOMs for computer systems (Section 1.1) and reports (Section 5.2). No matter how much effort is expended in trying to obtain a consensus about the weighting values, the result has to be regarded as arbitrary. Boehm points out another problem when the scheme illustrated in Table 6.2 was used to evaluate a number of competing systems. For the configurations under investigation the weighted scores ranged between 4.44 and 6.44, the highest being achieved by the IBM 360/67. But shortly after the study

*For still another enumeration of features, see Phister (1979, p. 89).

TABLE 6.1 (a) Feature Analysis Chart for Small Business Systems

		Maximum Rating[a]
Manufacturer		33
Delivery and installation	(7 max.)	
Overall experience	(4 max.)	
Experience with SBCs	(5 max.)	
Maintenance	(6 max.)	
Training provided	(4 max.)	
Documentation provided	(6 max.)	
Alternate site availability	(1 max.)	
Peripheral equipment		31
Data input devices		
Data output devices		
Auxiliary storage		
Central processor		24
Word size		
Main memory size		
Speed		
Instruction set		
Addressing capability		
Programmable registers		
Interrupts		
Software		12
Compiler languages		
Operating systems		
Utilities		
Figure of merit (FOM)	Maximum	100

[a]Rating = FOM/total cost.

(b) Cost Data for Small Business Systems

Monthly Lease Rates

Hardware	_____
Software	_____
Maintenance	_____
Training	_____
Documentation	_____
Total cost	_____

was done, it was discovered that TSS, the operating system for the 360/67, was very inefficient, and the throughput capacity would not even be equal to the load on the IBM 7044 which the new machine was destined to replace. Moreover, the hardware supervisor contributed a total of only $0.27 \times 0.03 = 0.0081$ to the total score so that with the given weights, this important feature of performance of the supervisor was, in effect, ignored. Essentially, there was an implicit throughput

TABLE 6.2

(a) Feature Analysis Categories and Weights

Category	Weight Factor
Hardware	0.27
Supervisor	0.27
Data management	0.08
Language processors	0.16
General programming support	0.02
Conversion considerations	0.12
Vendor reliability and support	0.08
Total	1.00

(b) Details for Supervisor Category

	Weight Factor	Point Value
Functional capability	0.58	
Command interpretation		0.13
Task scheduling		0.17
Interrupt handling		0.07
Storage allocation		0.16
Multiple processor capabilities		0.08
Program and data protection		0.14
Fail-soft mechanism		0.05
Self analysis and accounting		0.10
Debugging		0.05
System/operator interaction		0.03
Cold starting and stopping		0.02
Ease of revision	0.11	
Modularity		0.65
System editing		0.35
Reliability	0.12	
Ease of usage	0.16	
Command language		0.40
Appropriateness of response		0.20
Virtual memory		0.40
Hardware requirements	0.03	
Total	1.00	

Source: Example from B. W. Boehm, *Software Engineering Economics* (Englewood Cliffs, N.J.: Prentice-Hall, 1981).

constraint not represented in the scoring system, namely that the new system must have at least the throughput capacity of the old one. If such factors *are* recognized they can be given more weight—or a scheme based on multiplicative factors (rather than additive ones) might be devised, so that a critical feature will have a greater effect on the final score. Still, the arbitrary nature of scoring systems remains, and it is clear that they can only be used with reservations. Feasibility studies based on FOMs, or on qualitative judgments, can be useful tools for comparing systems, but the results have to be backed by quantitative calculations where possible, and at all times must be checked against common sense.

6.1.2. Economic Criteria

Debit and credit entries.   Table 6.3 itemizes the cost components involving acquisition or use of a computer facility. Capital costs are amortized over a period of years; one-time costs are related primarily to startup, and they may be amortized, or be written off wholly in one year; ongoing costs are those which are expected to recur throughout the project's lifetime. Some comments are in order:

- In the calculations that follow, a periodic payment interval is assumed (usually monthly or annually, as was done in Section 3.1), and it will be necessary to convert amortized costs (both capital and one-time) to this basis. Thus certain items (space, hardware) are shown in several places in Table 6.3, but on conversion only a single entry will be present for any

TABLE 6.3 COSTS FOR INFORMATION SYSTEMS

Capital
    Building
    Hardware (computers, communication systems, etc.)
    Software
One-time
    Planning (in-house, managerial, consulting, etc.)
    Site preparation (electrical, air conditioning, security, etc.)
    Testing
    Installation
    Staff hiring and training
Ongoing
    Maintenance (hardware and software)
    Rental and leasing (hardware, software, communications)
    Data preparation
    Operations (analysts, operators, program librarians, etc.)
    Space
    Utilities (electricity, air conditioning, telephone, etc.)
    Communications
    Education and training (professional development, etc.)
    Documentation (of system, for users, etc.)
    Quality control
    Supplies (cards, tapes, disks, paper, etc.)
    Overhead (purchasing department, library, security)
    Taxes

TABLE 6.4 TYPICAL COMPUTER CENTER BUDGETS

	Typical Expenditures (%)		
Category	Industry	Education	Government
Salaries	47	37	43
Operations			
Management			
Instructional			
Hardware	35	42	46
Purchased			
Leased			
Maintenance			
Software	6.2	9	
Purchased			
Leased			
Data communications	1.2	2	1
Supplies	6.5	7	9
Cards			
Paper			
Documentation			
Other	8	3	1
Site			
Space, utilities			
Purchasing			
Travel			
Advertising			
Education			

Source: Datamation, 26, no. 1 (January 1980).

given item. In particular, software may be purchased and be regarded as one-time cost (plus perhaps maintenance), but in some jurisdictions it is regarded as a capital asset, and taxed on this basis.

• The breakdown of Table 6.3 may not correspond to the way costs are itemized in the budgeting process. Thus in budgets all salaries might be grouped together whether they are ongoing for regular employees, or one-time payments for consulting personnel engaged during the planning phase. The breakdown here is on a project basis for planned program budgeting.

• The relative fractions spent on the various categories differ according to site size (large, medium, or small) or the sector in which the system operates (public, private, institutional). Table 6.4 illustrates the relative budget expenditures typical of installations in industry, education, and government. Other breakdowns are given in McLaughlin (1976) and Phister (1979*). Note the small fraction spent on salaries in education (not surprising

*Figs. 3.11.23, 3.25.10-22; Tables 3.25.2, II.3.25.1-4, etc.

TABLE 6.5 QUANTIFIABLE BENEFITS FOR A
COMPUTER APPLICATION OR INFORMATION
SYSTEM

Lower production costs deriving from:
    Reduced labor content
    Need for less managerial control
    Reduced inventory
    Fewer rejects
    Less labor turnover
Increased market share deriving from:
    New products
    Lower prices
    Better customer satisfaction with deliveries, service
Cost avoidance deriving from:
    Deferred equipment purchase
    Less breakage, pilfering, theft
    Lower insurance

---

because faculty and student users would not be shown in the computer center's budget) and the still relatively low expenditures for purchased or leased software.

Table 6.5 lists the quantifiable benefits from a computer application or information system.* There are other nonquantifiable or intangible benefits discussed in Section 6.1.3. The quantifiable benefits may be grouped into three main classes—those deriving from lower production costs, from increased market share, and from cost avoidance. Within each class several instances are given of how the benefits are actually realized. For a highly detailed enumeration of costs and benefits, see de Micheli (1978). Justification for installing a computer system is often advanced in qualitative terms. The computer will make it possible to have:

- Better management and auditing control
- Increased flexibility in planning
- Better labor relations
- Better public relations
- Less vulnerability to vandalism and disasters

In each of these examples, if the claims are accepted it should be possible to attach some dollar value to them. Better management control could result in a release of middle management time, in a reduced inventory, or in lower purchasing costs, but in *some* way it should be possible to show just how savings are effected. Similarly, better employee relations should eventually show up as

---

*For a somewhat different categorization of benefits, see King and Schrems (1978).

savings because of reduced labor turnover, smaller training costs, and fewer strikes, and it is reasonable to insist that the savings be estimated in dollars. It may take years to realize such savings, and they can be difficult to estimate, but it can be argued that unless *someone* is willing to pinpoint them, there is a lack of conviction about their reality.

In a commercial environment reduction in labor cost is probably the most important single reason for installing a computer or undertaking a new application. But for several reasons, statistics on the effectiveness of computers in this regard are few and far between. Often, total labor costs do not really go down—they are held constant even though the volume of work increases considerably. Thus the labor savings may take the form of cost avoidance. Many companies are sensitive to the loss of jobs due to the introduction of a computer, and when there are unions present, such reductions may have to be negotiated. Therefore, data on reduced labor costs may be hard to produce in the first place, and may be confidential when they do exist. In any case the direct *cost* of the labor is not the only job-related factor; other, nonquantifiable aspects discussed in Section 6.1.3, have to be included.

Decision rules.   Although comparing the net present value of cash flows, the method we saw in Section 3.1 for choosing financing options, is probably the most important technique, for reasons that will be obvious it is common in engineering investments (and also in other situations) to calculate other quantities (see, e.g., Busey, 1978). The calculations are rather simple if certain conditions are satisfied, but it is not always true that the conditions hold. In particular it is assumed that:

1. The benefits can be estimated with certainty. Otherwise, the problem becomes one of decision under risk, and as we saw in Section 5.2, this is a much more complicated question.
2. The project under consideration is independent of other projects; otherwise, cost accounting has to be brought in. This particular assumption is not always a good one. If installation of point-of-sale equipment is being considered, the principal savings might derive from the accompanying inventory management process. But the installation would undoubtedly affect the divisions of the company responsible for accounts receivable and for marketing. There are, in fact, joint applications; then, should the benefits (and costs) be distributed or should they all be attributed to the first project being considered? In what follows, we assume that they are all associated with a single project.

Payback Period.   The general pattern is that there is a period of initial payments, corresponding to investments, followed by a period during which savings are realized. Let Y_t, $t = 0,1, \ldots, N$, be the net profit (benefits) at each of the $N + 1$ time intervals. If Y_t is negative for some period, an investment is being made. In this case the payback period, P, is defined by

$$\sum_{t=0}^{P} Y_t = 0 \tag{6.1}$$

As an example, suppose that we have the following sequence:

t	0	1	2	3	4	5	6	7
Y_t	−50,000	−32,000	−1,500	25,000	35,000	45,000	40,000	35,000
$\Sigma\, Y_t$	−50,000	−82,000	−83,500	−58,500	−23,500	21,500	61,000	96,500

P can be determined by plotting (Fig. 6.1) or by simple linear interpolation. It is clear that P is between 4 and 5 years. Writing $P = 4 + x$, we have

$$\frac{x}{23,500} = \frac{1}{23,500 + 21,500} \quad \text{where} \quad x \approx \frac{23,500}{43,500} \approx 0.52 \text{ year}$$

Therefore, $P = 4.5$ years. It is usual to accept the project only if P is less than some predefined limit (e.g., 6 years). P may also be used to rank other

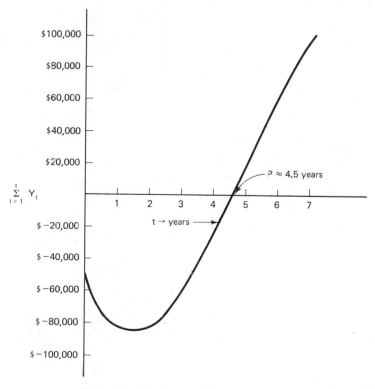

Figure 6.1   Calculation of the payback period

alternatives, each of which has been found to be acceptable by some other criterion. The shorter the payback period, the better the project. Note that in calculating P no consideration has been given to the value of money (i.e., the discount rate).

Net Present Value.   The net present value (NPV) is simply the sum, over the project's lifetime, of the discounted cash flows at each period. Let v, the discount rate $= 1/1 + i$, where i is the interest rate.

$$\text{NPV} = \sum_{t=0}^{N} Y_t v^t \qquad (6.2)$$

Using the cash flows of the example just given, Table 6.6 illustrates the calculation of NPV when $i = 0.1 = 10\%$ annually. It turns out to be $30,839. The acceptance criterion for a project is $\text{NPV} > 0$.

Benefit/Cost Ratio.   Let C be the present value of the accumulated investment outlays. Then the benefit/cost ratio, $\text{BCR} = \text{NPV}/C$. For the example given, $\text{BCR} = 30,839/80,331 = 0.383$.

Although NPV is the most widely used criterion for acceptance it is obvious why BCR is also of interest. Given two projects that differ only slightly in their NPVs, the one requiring the least outlay of capital is to be preferred. However, the time interval is also important. If it takes 10 years to earn back $1000 on a project, it would not be as good as one for which the time were 3 years. The amount invested and the time of investment are both taken account of in the next criterion, which is the internal rate of return.

Internal Rate of Return.   A company may be regarded as an enterprise which earns money on capital invested, at a rate defined to be the internal rate of return (IRR). Given a project that is described by a sequence of cash flows, suppose that we ask what interest rate, i^*, makes NPV, the discounted cash flow,

TABLE 6.6 CALCULATION OF NET
PRESENT VALUE

t	Y_t	v^t	$Y_t v^t$	$\Sigma Y_t v^t$
0	−50,000	1	−50,000	−50,000
1	−32,000	0.9091	−29,091	−79,091
2	−1500	0.8264	−1,240	−80,331
3	25,000	0.7513	18,782	−61,549
4	35,000	0.6830	23,905	−37,644
5	45,000	0.6209	27,941	−9,703
6	40,000	0.5645	22,580	+12,877
7	35,000	0.5132	17,962	+30,839

equal to zero (i.e., makes the project just worthwhile). An acceptance criterion for the project is $i^* \geq$ IRR. We have

$$\text{NPV}(i^*) = \sum_{t=0}^{N} Y_t(1 + i^*)^{-t} = 0 \tag{6.3}$$

Given the cash flows $Y_0 \cdots Y_n$, Equation 6.3 can be regarded as an equation for the *project IRR*. This polynomial equation can have multiple roots, no real roots, or no positive roots. Negative and imaginary values of i^* are meaningless but because of the possibility of multiple roots (and sometimes even when there is a single positive i^*) care has to be exercised in interpreting the quantity calculated by Equation 6.3 as an internal rate of return.

If the cash flows $Y_0, Y_1, \cdots, Y_k$ are all negative and $Y_{k+1} \cdots Y_N$ are all positive, the project may be viewed as one in which money is invested for a number of periods, after which there are (positive) returns until the end. Such an investment is said to be *conventional*. In a *nonconventional* investment there is one or more negative cash flows interspersed with the positive ones; that is, there is at least one occasion when money has to be invested again after returns have been experienced. An example of a nonconventional investment might arise when a software program that has been written and used for a while (during which there are savings) then has to be rewritten because of a change in the configuration or operating system. The rewrite makes it necessary to invest additional funds before returns can be realized again.

Nonconventional investments are very general, and it is possible that no meaningful IRR can be determined for them. Thus for the cash flow series

t	0	1	2	3	4	5
Y_t	0	50	50	−300	100	200

the only real roots of the polynomial equation

$$50(1 + i^*)^4 + 50(1 + i^*)^3 - 300(1 + i^*)^2 + 100(1 + i^*) + 200 = 0$$

are $i^* = -1.165884$ and $i^* = -4.044678$, so that the IRR is not defined and cannot be used to evaluate this project. It is not difficult to show that for conventional investments there is at most a single positive root, and there is no difficulty in interpreting the IRR for them. For example, the investment with cash flows of $-300, 100, 50, 150, 100, 100$ has the equation

$$-300(1 + i^*)^5 + 100(1 + i^*)^4 + 50(1 + i^*)^3$$

$$+ 150(1 + i^*)^2 + 100(1 + i^*) + 100 = 0$$

with one real root $i^* = 0.190179$ for the IRR. But conventional investments are too restrictive a class, and it would be desirable to have some other test which would allow one to examine an investment and determine whether the IRR is meaningful. There is no simple test based on the cash flows and their signs, and it is necessary to solve the polynomial equation for the roots. Even when there is only one positive root there are circumstances where there is some ambiguity in interpreting this root as an IRR for the project. Before examining this situation it is worth noting that the acceptance criterion for a project is $i^* \geq$ IRR, where IRR is the company's internal rate of return averaged over all its projects, and it should not be concluded that different projects can be ranked according to their IRRs. Thus consider projects (a) and (b), whose amortization schedules are shown in Table 6.7. For (a) the IRR is 0.149625, while that for (b) is 0.121104. But (a) yields $350 \times 4 - 1000 = \$400$ in 4 years, while (b) yields $3300 \times 4 - 10,000 = \$3200$ in 4 years, so that (b) has to be considered a better project, even though its IRR is less.

Suppose that a project has an interest rate i associated with it. The *unrecovered balance* $U_t(i)$ is defined as the value of the money invested at time t. Thus

$$U_t(i) = Y_0(1 + i)^t + Y_1(1 + i)^{t-1} + \cdots Y_t$$

Generally, $Y_0 < 0$, and $Y_1 \cdots Y_t$ may be positive or negative, so that $U_t(i)$ can be positive, negative, or zero for $t \neq 0$.

If $U_t(i) < 0$, the firm is lending funds to the project at time t.
If $U_t(i) > 0$, the project is lending funds to the firm, which is, in effect, borrowing money at time t.
If $U_t(i) = 0$, the firm has recovered its investment and no money is being borrowed or loaned at time t.

TABLE 6.7 TWO PROJECTS WITH DIFFERENT INTERNAL RATES OF RETURN

End of Period:	Project (a)			Project (b)		
	Y_t	$(1.149625)^{-t}$	$Y_t(1.149625)^{-t}$	Y_t	1.121104^{-t}	Y_t
0	−1000	1.000000	−1000.00	−10,000	1.000000	−10,000.00
1	+350	0.869849	304.45	+3300	0.891978	2,943.53
2	+350	0.756664	264.82	+3300	0.795625	2,625.56
3	+350	0.658160	230.36	+3300	0.709680	2,341.94
4	+350	0.572500	200.37	+3300	0.633018	2,088.96
Σ			0.00			−0.01
IRR		14.9625%			12.1104%	

Recall that for i^*, the IRR, $U_N(i^*) = 0$. For a *pure investment*

$$U_t(i^*) = \sum_{j=0}^{t} Y_j(1 + i^*)^{t-j} \leq 0 \qquad \text{all } t < N$$

$$U_N(i^*) = \sum_{j=0}^{N} Y_j(1 + i^*)^{N-j} = 0$$

Otherwise, the investment is *mixed*.

It is easy to show that a conventional investment is necessarily pure, but not vice versa, so that the term *pure* defines a more general class than conventional. The three distinct types are illustrated in Table 6.8. Nonconventional mixed investments, like mixed investments, can have negative or imaginary roots for their polynomial equations, but even when there is a positive root, as in example (c) of Table 6.8, caution has to be exercised in identifying this root with the internal rate of return. In that example at the end of the second period the unrecovered balance is +$13.61, meaning that the company has borrowed money from the project. In such circumstances the interest rate of concern to the company is normally the cost of borrowing money, *not* the internal rate of return. (Presumably, the cost of borrowing is less than the expected return on operations, or the company would refrain from borrowing.) Thus for a mixed investment there are times when the solution to Equation 6.3 cannot properly be regarded as yielding an IRR. For a pure investment [examples (a) and (b) in Table 6.8] the company is owed money for the whole duration of the project, and even though there may have been some repayment of funds [example (b)], the project is a true investment for its entire duration.

The examples show that the concept of internal rate of return has to be treated with some care. Its existence presumes that the company is *continuously* able to invest capital, and earn this return, taking into account all the opportunities open to it. On applying the concept to a single project, as we have done here, there are some implicit assumptions about the nature of the project.

TABLE 6.8 TYPES OF INVESTMENTS

End of Period:	(a) Conventional, Pure			(b) Nonconventional, Pure			(c) Nonconventional, Mixed		
	Y_t	v^{*t}	$\mathrm{NPV}_t(i^*)$	Y_t	v^{*t}	$\mathrm{NPV}_t(i^*)$	Y_t	v^{*t}	$\mathrm{NPV}_t(i^*)$
0	−300	1.00000	−300.00	−200	1.00000	−200.00	−200	1.00000	−200.00
1	+100	0.84019	−215.98	+100	0.81208	−118.79	+100	0.81328	−118.67
2	+50	0.70593	−180.68	+50	0.65948	−85.82	+200	0.66142	+13.61
3	+150	0.59312	−91.17	−200	0.53555	−192.94	−600	0.53792	−309.14
4	+100	0.49833	−41.88	+200	0.43491	−105.95	+300	0.43748	−177.90
5	+100	0.41870	−0.01	+300	0.35319	0.01	+500	0.35580	0.00
IRR	19.02%			23.14%			22.96%		

Some of these are, in effect, continuity conditions on the solution, which assure that whenever there are greater (positive) cash flows, the IRR increases. Other assumptions assure that the investments are realistic in different ways. In example (c) of Table 6.8, suppose that the project were terminated at the end of three payments. The equation for this truncated project is

$$-200(1 + i^*)^2 + 100(1 + i^*) + 200 = 0$$

which has the positive root $i^* = 0.28078$, corresponding to an IRR of 28.078%, which is greater than that for the project as a whole. The last three payments may be regarded as cash flows for a project whose equation is

$$-600(1 + i^*)^2 + 300(1 + i^*) + 500 = 0$$

corresponding to an IRR of 19.648%, less than that for the project as a whole. The company could do better by terminating the project after three payments, thereby earning a higher IRR. In a way, because the unrecovered balance has been positive, it can be argued that there are two separate projects and some doubt is cast whether the solution for the cash flow payments of example (c) can be regarded as a true internal rate of return on a single project. These reservations notwithstanding, the solution to Equation 6.3 *is* frequently taken as a criterion for investing in a project. Under appropriate conditions, certainly when the investment is a pure one, it can unambiguously be interpreted as an effective internal rate of return, and the meaning of the criterion is clear.

6.1.3. Other Determinants

Important as the quantitative decision rules just discussed are, as pointed out at the beginning of this chapter, there are other factors, both favorable and unfavorable, which have to be taken into consideration when evaluating a computer application. It could well be that these factors, although nonquantifiable and intangible, will be the determining ones in making the decision, and we consider them now. For additional discussion, see Parker (1982), where there is a bibliography on the subject.

Institutions, both private and public, are surrounded by a mesh of government regulations which often impose the requirement to submit highly detailed reports on operations. In the United States such reports are needed for the Internal Revenue Service, the Bureau of the Census, the Securities and Exchange Commission, and the Federal Communications Commission, to name only a few principal agencies. For many organizations the data needed for these reports can be gathered and organized only with the help of computers. It is difficult, almost pointless, to attempt to place a monetary value on reports produced for such purposes. The activity *has* to be undertaken for the organization to meet legal requirements and to exist. Perhaps some estimates could be made for the *cost* of producing the report, but almost invariably the data gathered will also be used for other, operations-related purposes, and we are back to the problem of trying to allocate joint production expenses discussed in Chapter 5. The benefits to be had from computers providing the ability to meet requirements of governmental reporting are clear, and are usually considerable, but they are difficult to assess quantitatively.

Another benefit that might come out of the implementation of an information system would be the ability to respond promptly to queries posed by the president or directors of the organization. No one would question the usefulness of such a capability, but it would require wild guessing to place a value on it. The queries might relate to long-range possibilities which are not followed up, and even for those which are, the benefits may not be visible for many years. Some of the query-processing abilities of a data base or information system relate to operations, and it may be possible to attach a quantitative value to these; others relate to strategy, and although the value may be high, it has to be accepted that they are probably unquantifiable.

The main driving force for automation in an industry may simply be that it is "in the air" and that any organization that fails to make the change will sense itself to be, and may really be, at a serious competitive disadvantage. In the early 1960s the airlines went to computerized reservation systems, and today no airline could hope to compete if it did not offer immediate confirmation of bookings. The quantifiable benefits of a computerized seat inventory were undoubtedly important in making the case for computerization, but the competitive factor was just as important. Conceivably, it might have been possible to estimate the loss of sales that would be experienced if manual reservation systems had been retained, but it is very doubtful if such calculations were ever attempted. The industry as a whole was making a change, and this fact overrode any cost/benefit analysis. More recently, the banking industry is finding itself in a similar situation. There is a strong trend toward computerized services, whether they are provided through tellers or self-service on-line terminals, and competitive factors play a key role. This is not to suggest that cost/benefit analyses are not carried out in banking applications or that the quantifiable benefits do not support the trend to computerization. But a look at banking advertising makes it clear that major competitive factors are at work. Even when competition is not directly present, the fact that an industry as a whole is moving toward computerization may be a driving force. This may well be the case in much office automation, where there are general feelings about computers and word processors increasing the productivity of office workers, but where hard data on cost savings are rare. Nevertheless, there is a sense that time has come for offices to be automated, and this sense may be the principal determinant when feasibility investigations are carried out.

Not all of the nonquantifiable influences favor computerization. It was stated earlier that one of the principal savings is reduction of labor costs. This benefit, from management's viewpoint, has a cost, from a societal viewpoint, in that there is an increase of unemployment. The effects of computers on employment levels (and on the quality of jobs) are examined in Section 11.1.2. Here it is only necessary to point out that job-related issues *should* enter into the picture when decisions to install a computer or implement an application are being made. Even where there is no legal requirement to consider such issues, it is increasingly likely that workers and unions will bring them to the fore. Beyond the job issues there are others relating to privacy, bureaucratization, and centralization of power (see Gotlieb and Borodin, 1973) where there are social costs and benefits arising from the introduction of computers. Usually, these are unquantifiable, but in some cases, notably where privacy is at stake, the social costs are already seen as being so high that computerization may be inhibited or even prohibited because of restrictions and technical measures that elevate costs.

In one sense the qualitative, nonquantifiable effects discussed in this section are secondary effects of computerization, because they do not enter directly into the cost calculations of Section 6.1.2. But at times they may be the primary determinants as to whether an application is undertaken, and the cost calculations may be carried out just to support a decision which has already been taken for more basic reasons. As a final point, there is a lesson about intangible benefits to be learned from public-sector projects, an area where they figure prominently. What has been learned there is not to attempt to combine quantitative benefits with intangible ones, by assigning arbitrary weighting factors to produce a single figure of merit for the project as a whole. For example, if among the benefits of a proposed transit system it is being argued that better service will be provided for disadvantaged persons, and that the aesthetic appeal of certain neighborhoods will be preserved, these advantages should be listed but not combined with quantitative benefits about tax revenues earned on appreciating property values. Similarly, for information projects, the intangible benefits (and costs), when identified, should be noted and kept distinct. An arbitrarily determined figure of merit, calculated as a single number, probably serves to reduce the credibility of a cost/benefit calculation rather than to increase it.

6.2. EXAMPLES

Very often a user is faced with choosing which one of several possible modes of operation he or she should select in undertaking a computer application. There are many situations when such choices can arise (Gotlieb, 1976), and here we examine four in detail. These are:

1. Deciding whether to establish an in-house computer facility or make use of an external service bureau
2. Determining whether the application should be run in a batch, an on-line, or possibly even in a real-time mode

3. Selecting what kind of data acquisition and data-entry devices to use
4. Choosing between the advantages of writing software in-house, or those to be had from a commercially available, packaged system

The general approach is a cost/benefit analysis, modified by the special circumstances of the problem at hand.

6.2.1. In-House Versus Service Bureau

Suppose that a company not having a computer facility, or a division of a company, without a computer but with sufficient budgetary authority to acquire one if it wished to do so, has satisfied itself that there are definite benefits in automating an application or set of applications. The decision as to whether the application should be run on an in-house facility acquired for the purpose or on an external facility ought to be regarded as a separate one in its own right, and subjected to the same kind of analysis that is undertaken for other projects. The main arguments for and against each option are conveniently summarized in the tabular form used to compare centralized and decentralized systems. These are shown in Table 6.9.

The choice envisaged here is between having to install a new facility and going to a large, well-established bureau that is already offering service to many clients. In these circumstances the service bureau will have on its staff specialists such as system programmers, data preparation experts, and program librarians. It will also have a large number of utilities and software packages available on an as-needed basis, so that clients will have the full range of services obtainable from a large system. It is to be noted that some points are listed as advantages

TABLE 6.9 IN-HOUSE COMPUTER SYSTEM VERSUS SERVICE BUREAU

	In-House System	Service Bureau
Advantages	Lower unit costs for large volumes	Costs proportional to volume processed
	Better control over schedules	Faster, more modern hardware
	Accessibility assured	Clear costing and tax position
	Better security possible	Utilities and package software on royalty basis
	Possible sale of excess time	Experienced help available
		Shorter lead time needed for changes
		More sophisticated services (e.g., security) available
Disadvantages	More space needed	Must negotiate priorities, backup, security, contracts, etc.
	Greater capital costs	
	Installation costs	Must arrange transportation for program, data
	More staffing, training	Conversion may be needed
	Operating responsibilities	Experience not transferable
	Backup needed	

for both the in-house system and the service bureau. For example, in principle it *should* be possible for the company to exercise greater security if all processing is done on site. In practice, it requires a great deal of effort to install the physical protection and the software techniques, such as data encryption, needed to ensure good security, and it is very possible that better security will be achieved through the service bureau.

The qualitative comparison of Table 6.9 can be converted into a quantitative one by estimating the costs for each alternative. When the proposed applications are being computerized for the first time, the calculation will in effect be part of the feasibility study. It will make a considerable difference to the outcome whether a single application is being considered or a related set of applications, such as accounts receivable, accounts payable, and inventory management. Once a system is installed, many of the disadvantages no longer hold for another application; the marginal cost of using the in-house computer for the additional purpose may be relatively low, so that whereas a single application is not financially justifiable, the set of applications will be. A set of related applications will undoubtedly be implemented over an extended period; development costs as well as operating costs have to be considered, the discount rate becomes important, and the cost calculations become more complicated. Alewine and Fleck (1976) illustrate the calculation of net present value on implementing a set of applications over an extended period on an in-house system.*

As the computer technology has changed because of the emergence of remote job entry systems and minicomputers, there have been shifts in the relative advantages of different operational modes, so it is not surprising that whereas in one study it is concluded that there are considerable savings to be effected in moving from a service bureau operation to an in-house computer, in a different study, carried out at another time in different circumstances, there are benefits seen in going from an in-house system to a service bureau. Table 6.10 illustrates a small business application where a savings of $6270, or about 39%, was effected by switching from an IBM 360/30 to a remote job-entry terminal connected to a service bureau. Hanna (1975) documents a study carried out in the U.S. Social Security Administration in which immediate savings of $54,000 would be realized on going to an in-house time-sharing system, and these would be more than doubled in 4 years (see Table 6.11, but note that costs for space are ignored). Other examples of cases where it was advantageous to change *to* a service bureau are reported in Abbot (1974) and Payne (1972). On the other hand, the computer trade literature is full of examples where it was advantageous to move from a service bureau to a stand-alone system, even for a single application. The continued growth in small business systems and microcomputers, the decreasing cost of hardware, and the increasing availability of packaged

---

*See also Phister (1979, Sec. 3.27) for a discussion of justifying data processing costs and how these are affected by implementing a number of different functions.

TABLE 6.10 COMPARATIVE MONTHLY COSTS OF AN IN-HOUSE FACILITY AND A SERVICE BUREAU OPERATION

In-House System		Service Bureau via Remote Job Entry	
Hardware		System usage—	
Leased IBM 360/30, 64k store	$12,000	310 hr at 24/hr	$7,440
6 tape drives		Volume discount	−900
Taxes—4%	480	Storage—	
Facilities		20 megabits	650
Space, power, air conditioning	500		
Security, insurance	200	Communications	
Staff	200	Port	250
Systems programming	800	Datanets: 2 at 260	520
Operators, librarians	1,600	Line charges	150
Program products	400	Terminal	1,800
Total	$16,180		$9,910

Source: Example from "Remote Batch Processing: An Applications Casebook," *Can. Datasys.,* June 1972, 42–46.

TABLE 6.11 MONTHLY COMPUTER COSTS USING AN EXTERNAL SERVICE BUREAU AND AN IN-HOUSE SYSTEM

	1971	1975
Current costs, using in-house computers and external time-sharing service		
In-house large-scale computer	$ 64,789	$156,073
In-house medium-scale computer	20,325	31,165
Program development	372,035	550,255
Terminals	20,000	20,000
Total	$477,149	$757,493
Costs using proposed in-house time-sharing system		
Hardware rental	$ 62,400	$150,000
Training	9,186	9,186
Systems support	10,105	18,189
Recompilation of programs	6,917	0
Operators	104,246	204,314
Program development	297,628	440,204
Production not connected to time sharing	21,356	0
Total	$423,230	$644,518
Savings on changing to in-house time-sharing system	$53,916	$112,975

Source: Data from W. E. Hanna, Jr., "A Case Study in Procurement," in *The Economics of Informatics,* ed. A. B. Frielink (Amsterdam: North-Holland, 1975).

software designed to be used by nonexperts in computers all point to the steady trend toward acquiring in-house facilities, even for very small enterprises which previously could not have considered this option. The continuing existence of service bureaus shows that they too can offer advantages in particular situations, although the trend away from commercial service centers, based on very large general-purpose computers, seems to be definite. It may be that the large general-purpose service bureau will be destined to serve a consortium of companies wishing to pool their resources, or government, which is often reluctant to establish permanent agencies.

6.2.2 Time-Sharing, Batch, and Real-Time Processing

The pervasive use of on-line transaction processing in so many areas—reservation systems, banking, and insurance, to name three—suggests that time sharing is becoming the dominant mode of computer processing. But each of the three modes of processing—time-sharing, batch, and real-time—has its place, and the choice of mode is essentially determined by the type of application and a cost/benefit analysis for the different alternatives.

The basic question concerns how important is it to achieve a rapid response time. We can regard the computer as one component in a system which includes people and which responds to events (such as a query being initiated) or to changes in the environment (such as detection of an oncoming vehicle). When it is essential that the system be able to respond quickly, even more quickly than a human being can react, there is no choice but to use a dedicated, real-time computer with appropriate sensors and activating mechanisms. Where the change takes the form of a query initiated by a human being or a transmission of new data to a file, and the response or acknowledgment can take place in a few seconds (as opposed to tenths or hundredths of a second in a real-time application), then an on-line, time-shared system is called for. When hours or weeks are permissible for the reaction time, a batch system can be completely satisfactory. Usually, the type of application determines in a clear-cut way which of the three modes should be employed. Table 6.12 summarizes the three situations.

TABLE 6.12 REAL-TIME, TIME-SHARED, AND BATCH PROCESSING

Type	Response Time	System Use	Representative Applications
Real-time	<1 sec	Dedicated, single-purpose	Manufacturing process control, patient monitoring, vehicle control
Time-shared	1 to 5 sec	Single-purpose or multipurpose	Airline reservations, banking, program development
Batch	>1 hr	Multipurpose	Customer billing

Time-shared systems imply the need for communications, and hence are more expensive. As costs have come down and it has become easier and cheaper to attach communication devices to computers, more and more systems which previously had to be operated in batch mode have been converted to an on-line mode. Historically, it has been a matter of debate, or rather of economics, whether certain types of applications should be carried out in a batch environment versus a time-shared environment. The fact that batch processing still survives for certain uses, such as customer billing in the retail trade, shows that there are still trade-offs to be considered in choosing the mode. In certain areas of applications, such as the processing of student computer jobs, the choice of mode is still influenced greatly by economic considerations. Thus it is interesting to apply the cost/benefit techniques that we have been considering in this chapter to the problem of choosing between time sharing and batch for computer processing.

One of the earliest studies of time-shared versus batch systems was carried out by Gold (1969), who compared the performance and costs for two groups of students who were using similar systems, one time-shared, the other batch, in a classroom situation. The subject was business management, taught in the form of a game in which a business is simulated and every (simulated) quarter year student-teams have to make a set of management decisions corresponding to the amounts of money that should be spent on marketing, plant investment, research, and so on. Using inherent equations that represent production functions, the business environment, and the effects of competition, the computer program for the game calculates, for each team, manufacturing quantities, sales, and profit figures resulting from its decisions. Performance on the game is determined by how well the team understands the workings of the game at the end of a teaching quarter when there has been the opportunity to play a number of rounds, and also by how well the team does financially in relation to its competitors. The business game existed in two versions. In the batch version teams met to make decisions and received the results after a few days; in the time-shared version the results came back immediately, so that the teams using this mode could reenter a new set, and consequently get more plays during an academic session. Statistical techniques were used to assign players to the batch and interactive teams so as to reduce the probability that any difference in results achieved would arise from differences in the backgrounds of the players. As well as tabulating decisions, game results, resource use, and other objective observations, Gold also asked the students to fill out questionnaires which reported on their subjective evaluation of the game as they played it themselves and as they sensed that it was being played by their classmates using the other version.

Table 6.13 summarizes the results of the experiment. The evaluations (rows 1, 2, 4 to 8) are based on a rating scale of 1 to 9; the grades are based on scales of 1 to 15 (rows 10, 11) and 1 to 10 (rows 12 and 13); the maximum performance (row 15) is the maximum profit scored by the team during its plays. Although there were no significant differences in the grades or understanding achieved by

TABLE 6.13 TIME-SHARING VERSUS BATCH-PROCESSING GROUP DIFFERENCES

Variable	Time-Sharing Group			Batch-Processing Group			Problem Mean Differential	Problem SD	Correlation
	N	Mean	SD	N	Mean	SD			
1. Batch evaluation	30	1.766	1.430	29	1.627	1.559	—	—	—
2. Time-sharing evaluation	28	6.928	1.644	28	5.321	2.373	0.008	—	0.36
3. Sufficient time	25	0.640	0.489	20	0.400	0.502	—	—	—
4. Computer system usefulness	25	7.800	1.625	22	4.161	2.174	0.001	—	0.68
5. Satisfaction with results	25	6.760	1.362	22	4.363	2.766	0.009	0.001	0.49
6. Usefulness of other system	24	3.125	1.848	22	8.090	0.9211	0.001	0.002	0.86
7. Batch evaluation	16	2.187	1.276	22	3.227	1.950	—	—	—
8. Time-sharing evaluation	25	8.000	1.040	22	7.545	1.010	—	—	—
9. Total problem time (hr)	26	16.03	7.022	27	19.23	8.188	0.070	—	—
10. Grade A: understanding model dynamics	26	9.500	3.313	24	9.958	3.168	—	—	—
11. Grade B: strategy with model	26	6.653	3.643	24	6.375	3.785	—	—	—
12. Grade C: flexibility	26	3.036	3.515	24	2.583	3.282	—	—	—
13. Grade D: perceptiveness and understanding	26	5.346	2.169	24	3.916	1.954	0.019	—	—
14. Sum of grades	26	26.53	10.15	24	24.63	9.785	0.003	—	—
15. Maximum performance ($)	25	1444.	203.2	20	1244.	226.7	—	—	0.43
16. CPU time (sec)	27	345.9	157.6	28	71.76	59.63	0.001	0.001	0.76
17. Elapsed time (days)	27	4.296	1.996	28	4.071	1.998	—	—	—

Source: M. Gold, "Time-Sharing and Batch Processing: An Experimental Comparison of Their Values in a Problem-Solving Situation," *Commun. ACM*, 12, no. 5 (May 1969), 249–59. Copyright 1969, Association for Computing Machinery, Inc., with permission.

the two groups, the time-shared system was regarded as being significantly better both by those using it and by the other group. The increase in maximum performance for the time-sharing group is statistically significant, as is the increase in CPU time used by that group. Corresponding to the increased CPU time, the time-shared group spent less total time on the problem. One way of interpreting the results is to calculate a value for students' time which will make the cost of the extra CPU time used, equal to the savings resulting from the reduced time spent on the problem. Let

R_m = Labor resources expended (19.2 hours for batch and 16.0 hours for time
  sharing)
V_m = value for labor
R_c = computer resource expended (0.0199 hour for batch and 0.0955 hour for
  time sharing)
V_c = value of the computer resource ($350 per hour for batch and $485 per
  hour for time sharing)

Equating, we have

$$R_m^t \times V_m^t + R_c^t \times V_c^t = R_m^b \times V_m^b + R_c^b \times V_c^b$$

where the superscripts identify the time-sharing and batch terms. Substituting values and noting that $V_m^t = V_m^b = V_m$ yields

$$16.0 \times V_m + 0.0955 \times 485 = 19.2 \times V_m + 0.0199 \times 350$$

where $V_m = \$12.30$ per hour. Thus if the students are regarded as managers, even in those early days of time sharing the benefits derived from a better perception of the system and less time spent on the problem compensated for the extra computer cost. Today, when computer costs are less, with a smaller difference between the cost of running on a time-shared versus a batch system, and labor costs are greater, the conclusions hold with even greater force.

Streeter (1972) analyzed computing costs for different modes of operation in another environment—that of the IBM T. J. Watson Research Center at Yorktown Heights, New York, where users are research scientists and engineers who can turn to a number of alternative systems for their computing needs. The need may be for (1) computation, (2) program development followed by computation, or (3) problem formulation, program development, and computation.

Streeter first discusses batch systems and shows how to derive an operating point on the system capacity curve such that there is trade-off between running jobs for high throughput and reduced turnaround versus lower throughput and faster turnaround. This can be done with the help of two curves. Figure 6.2(a) shows the relation between system utilization U (see Equation 2.7) and system response time R. This curve, which has the general shape to be expected for a

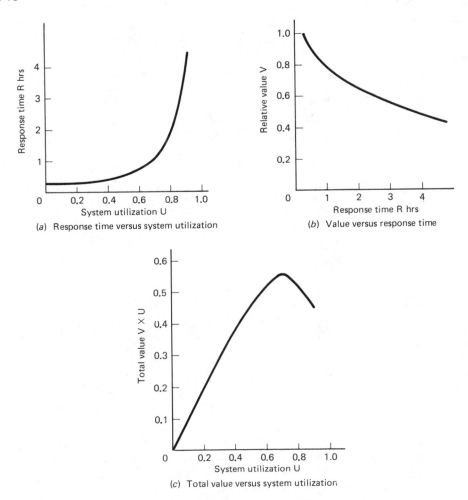

Figure 6.2   System utilization, response time and value

queueing system (see Fig. 2.6), can be derived from observations on the system. Also derived from observation, this time by conducting a survey of users, is Fig 6.2(*b*) which shows how the value of a result declines as the time to get it becomes longer. This curve is, in effect, a measure of the economist's utility or demand functions versus time. From Fig. 6.2(*a*) and (*b*) a table of U versus R and V can be constructed (Table 6.14), and this is in turn used to produce a curve of $V \times U$ versus U [Fig. 6.2(*c*)]. $V \times U$ can be interpreted as the *total* value for all jobs, and as can be seen, it goes through a maximum at $U \approx 0.7$. In other words, the system should be run at about 70% of its capacity so that the turnaround will be fast enough to make the results useful. Streeter also shows

TABLE 6.14 RESPONSE TIME AND RELATIVE VALUE FOR JOBS
VERSUS SYSTEM UTILIZATION

System Utilization, U	Response Time, R (hr)	Relative Value, V	Total Value, $V \times U$
0	0.25	1	0
0.1	0.28	1	0.1
0.2	0.30	0.98	0.20
0.3	0.35	0.92	0.32
0.4	0.45	0.91	0.36
0.5	0.50	0.90	0.45
0.6	0.70	0.85	0.51
0.7	1.0	0.80	0.56
0.8	2.0	0.65	0.52
0.9	4.0	0.50	0.45

how a different operating point would be chosen if one were to consider a batch system which accepts two classes of jobs, regular and express, each class having its own curve for V versus R.

This same conclusion, namely that system load should be limited in order to achieve maximum productivity, is emphasized in later studies of time-sharing facilities. Doherty and Kelisky (1979) measure load in terms of the *system expansion factor,* which is defined as the ratio of the actual time to do a unit of computer-limited work to the minimum time required to do that work in a stand-alone environment. [This is $(t_{CPU} + t_{I/O} + t_{queueing})/(t_{CPU} + t_{I/O})$, where t_{CPU} and $t_{I/O}$ are assumed not to be overlapped; as the load increases, $t_{queueing}$ increases, and this ratio is clearly a measure of the load.] Using data observed on a System/ 370 facility with TSO (time-sharing option) at Yorktown Heights, they show how the curve of productive time versus expansion factor goes through a maximum, and consequently how a curve of "lost dollars per hour" versus expansion factor goes through a minimum (Fig. 6.3). In a different study, Thodhani (1981) defines *productivity* as the number of interactions/user/hour. He made extensive observations on two systems, A and B, for what he calls *human-intensive* interactions because they consume small amounts of computer resources (as opposed to *computer-intensive* interactions, which consume large resources and take many seconds to complete). Figure 6.4 shows the observed curve of productivity versus response time for one of these systems, and it is clear that it is equivalent to the relative value versus response time curve of Fig. 6.2(*b*). It is interesting to note that Doherty and Kelisky, as well as Thodhani, confirm earlier observations that user response time (i.e., the think time of Chapter 2) increases linearly with system response time (see Fig. 6.5), a phenomenon that raises questions on how users behave on an interactive system (see also Boies, 1974).

In his 1972 study for a time-sharing situation in which the user is interested

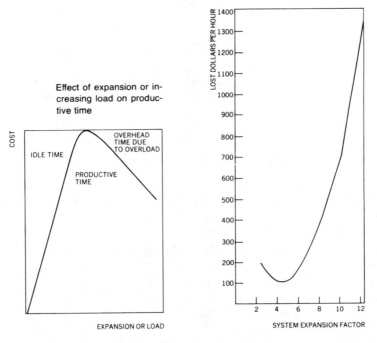

Dollars lost due to a combination of hardware operating points and user costs

Effect of expansion or increasing load on productive time

Figure 6.3 System load vs cost and dollars lost (From W.J. Doherty and R.P. Kelisky, "Managing VM/CMS Systems for User Effectiveness," *IBM System J.,* 18, no. 1 (1979), with permission.)

in computation only (i.e., where a job is submitted to be run using an already written program), Streeter breaks down the total cost, T, into five components:

$$T = S + C + U + D + A \qquad (6.4)$$

where

T = total cost for the computation
S = computing system costs ($t_{CPU} \times \text{rate}_{CPU}$)
U = cost of user's time
D = cost of delay (elapsed time $\times$ delay penalty charge)
A = auxiliary charges

D is a cost arising from the fact that the user's productivity is reduced because the results are not available (estimated as equal to $0.2U$); A is for keypunching.

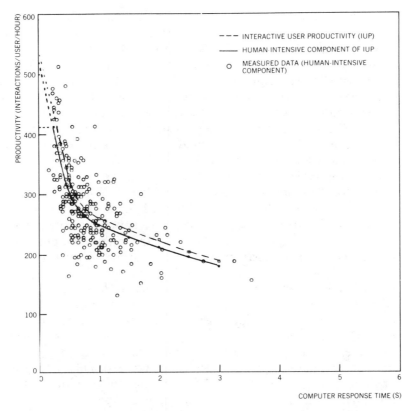

Figure 6.4   Interactive user productivity versus computer response time for human-intensive interactions (From A. J. Thodhani, "Interactive User Productivity," *IBM System J.,* 20, no. 4 (1981), 407–23, with permission.)

Effect of system response time on user response time

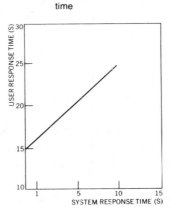

Figure 6.5   Effect of system response time on user response time (From W. J. Doherty and R. P. Kelisky "Managing VM/CMS Systems for User Effectiveness," *IBM System J.,* 20, no. 4 (1981), with permission.)

When a benchmark program called ETEST* was run, these cost components for the various systems available to a researcher at the IBM laboratory (in 1972) are shown in Table 6.15. There is a 2:1 ratio between the cost for the most expensive option compared with the least expensive. The most expensive was for using a dedicated IBM 1130, and this is the closest to the modern one of using a personal computer or a workstation. *However,* this mode assumes a 2-hour delay because of the need to wait for the 1130 to become available, corresponding to a penalty cost of $12.00. When this penalty is subtracted, and allowance is made for the low cost of the CPU time for a modern microcomputer, as well as the relatively high speed, which would mean a low charge for user's time, it is certain that a similar comparison today would result in lowest charges for the individualized system for Thodhani's human-intensive interactions.

When a time-shared system is used for both program development and computation, Streeter discusses the choice between an interpreter, such as APL, or a compiler, such as FORTRAN. With the interpreter, program development is much faster and less costly, but the running time for the program is considerably greater. Thus if the program has to be run only a few times, the interpreter will result in lower cost, but if many executions are required, the overall cost for the compiler will be less. Given the actual figures, it is easy to calculate a break-even number of executions, beyond which it is better to use the compiler. For this reason, on large computers it is common to have two versions of a language: for example, an interpreter (or fast-turnaround compiler) for development, and an optimizing compiler, which produces very efficient code, for run time. The obvious strategy is to employ the interpreter for development and switch to the optimizing compiler when the program is complete.

When program development is the *main* task, and the problem is essentially complete once the program has been written, a time-sharing interpreter makes the best use of the user's time. Since, increasingly, the cost of user's time is coming to dominate the total cost of a system, the arguments for going interactive become stronger and stronger. Figure 6.6 illustrates the trend for costs, starting in 1980 with a system that rents for $500,000 per month, requires data processing support costing $200,000 per month, with 35% of the costs designated for the time-sharing service, and where there are 70 users whose salaries average $4000 per month. Projecting that user and data processing support costs increase at 10% per year and that hardware costs decrease at 15% per year, it can be seen that by 1984 hardware costs equal data processing costs, and beyond this they are greater. The conclusion is that in a professional software development environment interactive computers are mandatory, and even for educational use they are now dominant.

Streeter also discusses the case where a time-sharing terminal is used for problem formulation, program development, and computation. This is the most difficult case, but it is also the most interesting, for it really corresponds most

---

*ETEST is a FORTRAN program to calculate e to 2500 decimal places using integer arithmetic.

TABLE 6.15 COSTS FOR RUNNING A BENCHMARK PROGRAM UNDER VARIOUS TIME-SHARED SYSTEMS

	System					
	360/91/OS	60/67/TSS	360/67/ CP/CMS	IBM 1130	360/67/191 TSS/OS	360/67 Batch
CPU time at $/min = system charge	0.25 min at $15/min 3.75	2.56 min at $10/min 25.60	2.26 min at $10/min 22.60	21 min at $0.40/min 8.40	0.25 min at $15/min 3.75	0.71 min at $10/min 7.10
Connect time at $0.06/min = connect charge		22 min 1.32	13 min 0.78		10 min 0.60	
User's time at $0.50/min = user time cost	21 min 10.50	10 min 5.00	8 min 4.00	35 min 17.50	16 min 8.00	21 min 10.50
Elapsed time at $10/min = delay cost	120 min 12.00	22 min 2.20	13 min 1.30	155 min 15.50 (2-hr-availability wait assumed)	85 min 8.50	120 min 12.00
Auxiliary charge: keypunching	2.00	—	—	—	—	2.00
Total cost	$28.25	$34.12	$28.68	$41.40	$20.85	$31.60

Source: D. N. Streeter, "Cost-Benefit Evaluation of Scientific Computing Services," *IBM Syst. J.*, 11, no. 3 (1972), 219–33, with permission.

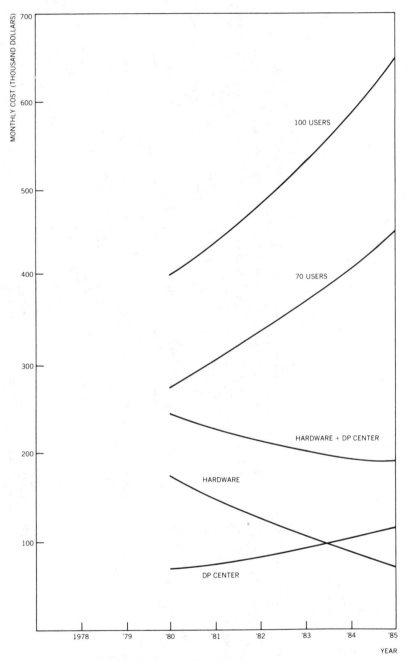

Figure 6.6 TSO cost trends and projections (From A. J. Thodhani "Interactive User Productivity," *IBM System J.,* 20, no. 4 (1981), with permission.)

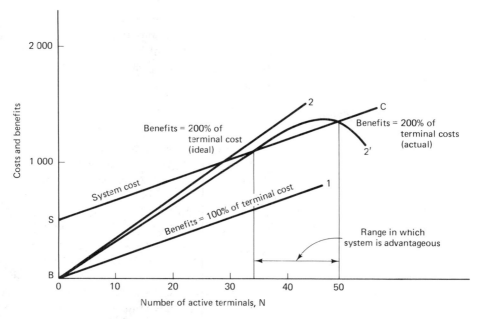

Figure 6.7   Costs and benefits for a time-sharing system

closely to today's office automation, where individual terminals or workstations are being considered for a variety of managerial and secretarial functions. A graphical presentation is helpful in portraying the economics. In Fig. 6.7 the line *SC* shows the system cost as a function of the number of users. This is based on the assumption that there is a basic overhead for the system as a whole, and then a fixed cost for each individual terminal. Suppose that the benefits that users derive from having a terminal at their disposal are just equal (i.e., are 100%) to the terminal cost. Then the line *B*1 represents the benefit. Note that it fails to intersect *SC;* there is no way to recover the fixed overhead. Suppose now that the benefits derived from a terminal are twice the cost of the terminal. The line *B*2 has twice the slope of *B*1; it intersects *SC* at $N \approx 28$, and for more users than this there is an overall advantage in using the system. In practice, as noted, the value of a system goes through a maximum as system utilization (no. of users) increases. Therefore, the line *B*2 should really look like *B*2′, and there is a range in the number of users for which the system offers positive benefits. When the number of active users is between 34 and 49, there is an overall advantage in using the system. The number of terminals that have access to the system can of course be larger, by a fraction that depends on the use factor of terminals. In an actual situation the difficult thing to determine is just how much benefits there are to be had in making a terminal available. Streeter quotes a figure of 100 to 300% as the productivity increase for a researcher on an interactive terminal. Although this estimate seems high, it will depend on the type of work that can be done on the terminal. As the range of activities broadens to encompass file management, communications, scheduling, and tasks relating to more and more aspects of the total job, the case becomes stronger for giving each researcher or manager a terminal for individual use. But in the absence of actual data on the productivity gains, it is difficult to estimate at what point expensive dedicated terminals for individuals are justified.

6.2.3 Data Acquisition and Entry

Due to the rapidly changing nature of the computer industry, a particularly frequent kind of choice that arises is when to replace an old device or technology by a new one which is gaining acceptance. The decision to change is dictated mainly by the type of application and costs, but other considerations, such as depreciation write-offs, reliability of maintenance, and the need for retraining staff enter. Technological improvement of various computer components—CPUs, memories, and peripherals—are discussed in Chapter 8, but in this section we examine data acquisition and entry. Perhaps nothing illustrates the diversity of the computer industry better than the almost bewildering variety of devices which are available for capturing data in machine-readable form. The devices can be categorized in different ways, but Fig. 6.8 shows an (almost) hierarchical classification according to whether the data are collected for batch submission to a computer, entered for on-line or transaction processing, or collected by automatic devices. Detailed descriptions and comparisons of these various families are to be found in *Datapro 70* (Sec. 70D4-010, Data Entry) and various sections of Auerbach (*Key-to-Storage, Optical Character Recognition,* etc.). Automatic data collection devices are a special case, for they often require digitizing and conversion equipment which has to be designed specially for the application. The need for devices suitable for on-line systems and transaction processors arose with time sharing in the middle 1960s. Before then, and even for a decade afterward, card punches dominated the keyboard entry equipment. With the development of mini- and microcomputers, key-to-diskette, and key-to-disk systems finally began to displace card punches as the chief source of data-entry equipment, and since the beginning of the 1980s CRT terminals and distributed processing terminals have become the principal mode of data entry.*

Because labor cost for the human operator is almost always the principal concern, the main feature of interest in key-entry equipment is the number of keystrokes per hour that can be sustained, or, what is equivalent, the number of records that can be expected to be handled at a keying station, with the ability to control format and correct mistakes important additional considerations. On a card punch an experienced operator attains a rate of 7500 to 12,000 keystrokes per hour, corresponding to an input rate of about 1000 records per day. On a key-to-disk system (where a minicomputer supports a variety of functions for a

---

*For statistics that trace the changes, see Phister (1979, Sec. 1.23) and "User Ratings of Key Entry Equipment," *Datapro 70,* Sec. 70D4-010-72a, October 1981.

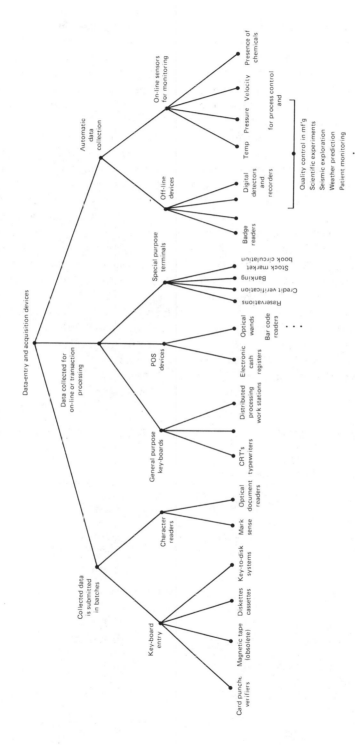

Figure 6.8 Types of data-entry and data acquisition devices

cluster of stations) an input rate of 8000 to 15,000 keystrokes per hour can be expected, corresponding to approximately 1000 to 15,000 records per day. With on-line CRTs the keystroke rate is similar to keypunches but there is greater flexibility in handling different formats. When data are entered via distributed processing terminals there is so much automatic handling of formats, and help through prompts, that attention can be focused on the data entry itself, and the input rate is increased, to perhaps 10,000 to 15,000 keystrokes per hour.

When it comes to point-of-sale (POS) equipment for the retail trade, many more factors than keystroke rate have to be considered. Department stores, where electronic cash registers are connected to a central computer, and grocery supermarkets, where cashiers use optical wands to read bar codes imprinted on packages, are two examples of the increasing use of POS equipment. In such situations the cost/benefit analysis centers on the extra capital cost for the equipment versus the advantages to be had from increased productivity, the ability to record much more data with POS devices, and the additional benefits to be had from analyzing the data and being able to make decisions based on the analysis. Circumstances vary from application to application. In a department store, each purchase takes a relatively long time. The ability to do extra tasks, such as checking credit or disabling the code on the merchandise tag which sets off an alarm if the item is taken out of the store without going by the cash register, is important, whereas in a supermarket productivity of the checkout cashier is a principal (but not the only) concern.

Several detailed studies have been done on the cost and benefits of introducing POS into supermarkets. The basic question is whether to use con-

TABLE 6.16 ESTIMATED COSTS (DOLLARS) FOR INSTALLING KEY-ENTRY CASH REGISTERS AND REGISTERS EQUIPPED WITH SCANNERS IN A SUPERMARKET CHAIN

(a) Costs Incurred at the Head Office

Description	Key-entry	Scanning
Fixed costs		
Studies	217,000	217,000
Communication equipment	60,000	60,000
Main-memory expansion	7,000	7,000
Total	284,000	284,000
Less tax reductions	153,360	153,360
Yearly costs		
Point-of-sale department	110,000	110,000
Committees	15,000	30,000
Electronic data division	30,000	75,000
Telephone lines	4,800	4,800
CPU time	53,820	53,820
Total	213,620	273,620
Less tax reductions	118,055	147,755

TABLE 6.16 Continued

(b) Costs Incurred at Each Store

Description	Key-entry	Scanning
Fixed costs		
Remodeling, including architectural changes, new check-out lanes, new bagging shelf with brackets, safes, turnstiles, and new shopping carts if needed	25,500	32,000
Promotion	—	9,350
Pricing controls	—	4,000
UPC equipment	—	122,360
Total	25,500	167,710
Less tax reductions	13,770	90,563
Yearly costs		
Operations	687	2,300
Maintenance	9,600	15,600
Rented computer equipment	16,908	16,908
Windows (average)	—	130
Pricing control	—	12,480
Total	27,195	47,418
Less tax reductions	15,074	25,606
Costs per lane		
Point-of-sale terminal	9,650	9,650
Backup calculator	100	100
Scanner equipment	—	4,078
Total	9,750	13,828
Less tax reductions	5,265	7,467
Cost per employee—		
Training	6.25	35.00
Total	6.25	35.00
Less tax reductions	3.38	19

Source: R. Gornitsky, "A Cost/Benefit Study on a Canadian Supermarket Point-of-Sale System," M.Sc. Thesis, University of Toronto, 1982.

ventional, stand-alone cash registers or to employ a bank of registers connected to a central minicomputer in the store, equipped with work scanners capable of reading the universal product code (UPC), which is now printed on about 75% of the items sold in a store. Table 6.16 compares the estimated costs for modernized key-entry cash registers with those for scanners, as incurred at the head office and at individual stores for a large supermarket chain, designated as ABC (Gornitsky, 1982). If, at the time of writing, ABC installed key-entry systems in all its supermarkets, it would have cost $17.7 million for installation and $3 million to operate. If the stores were fully automated with scanning systems, the cost would have been $39 million for installation, and $5.3 million annually for maintenance. Assuming a 10-year life for the equipment, the cost of installing and maintaining key-entry systems in all stores is $4.7 million per year (0.27% of sales), while implementation of a scanning system would come to $9.2 million per year (0.53% of sales). These estimates do not include costs for writing and operating computer programs for inventory analysis of the data recorded on the computerized system, since this function was not to be implemented in the initial stage.

These costs were estimates made on the basis of a few trial stores and they are reasonably firm, although it may be noted that many of the items were missing in earlier studies. The benefits are much harder to estimate. Table 6.17 shows estimates for savings resulting from the use of scanners derived from a series of simulation studies in the early days of the technology. ABC carried out a study of its own in 1975, and this was reviewed in part in 1981, and the results were quite different, as can be seen in Table 6.18. It is common to refer to *hard benefits*, those attainable directly as a result of the POS equipment, and *soft benefits*, those arising through better control of inventory. To start with, there were no immediate soft benefits because the communication equipment to transmit sales data to warehouses and head office were not installed, initially at least. Then one of the main hard benefits, savings due to removal of the need to

TABLE 6.17 ESTIMATED SAVINGS RESULTING FROM INSTALLATION OF SCANNERS IN SUPERMARKETS AS DERIVED FROM SIMULATION STUDIES

Category	Percent of Sales in:		
	1971	1973	1975
Cashier productivity			
Front-end	1.15	1.03	0.68
Misrings	0.14	0.19	0.20
Training	0.02	0.06	0.03
Item pricing			
Price marks	0.38	0.39	0.09
Repricing	0.14	0.21	0.08
Administration—			
bookkeeping	0.10	0.38	0.15
Gross savings	1.93	2.26	1.23
Costs			
Symbol marks	(0.44)	(0.42)	(0.26)
Depreciation/ maintenance/ administration	(0.86)	(0.56)	(0.34)
Gross costs	(1.30)	(0.98)	(0.60)
Net savings	0.63	1.28	0.63

Source: Data from R. Shaw, *Universal Product Code Scanning Systems: The Retail Experience 1974–1976,* Department of Agricultural Economics, Cornell University Agricultural Experiment Station, New York State College of Agricultural and Life Sciences, Staff paper.

TABLE 6.18 OBSERVED SAVINGS (PERCENT OF SALES) DUE TO INTRODUCTION OF SCANNERS IN SUPERMARKETS[a]

	Earlier Studies	ABC Supermarkets, 1971, 1975, 1981
Savings		
Removal of item pricing	0–0.50[b]	n.a.
Improved pricing accuracy	0.23	−0.01
Reduced keying errors	0.08	0.04
Increased cashier productivity	0.41–1.2	0
	(8–50% of salaries)	(9% of salaries)
Increased bookkeeper productivity	0.15	0.0
		(31% of salaries)
Item movement	0.09–0.40	0.0
Sales increase	n.d.	0–23%
Costs	0.37–0.43	0.55
Net savings		
(excluding sales increase)	0.59–2.13	−0.52

[a] n.a., not applicable; n.d., no data.

[b] 54% of supermarkets did not remove prices.

Source: R. Gornitsky, "A Cost/Benefit Study on a Canadian Supermarket Point-of-Sale System," M.Sc. thesis, University of Toronto, 1982.

price individually every item on the shelf, could not be realized, because consumer resistance to the removal of item pricing made it unwise to carry this out. There was a very small increase in the productivity of checkout personnel (as measured by the number of items processed per hour) and in store bookkeeper staff, but the increase was usually insufficient to reduce checkout staff and never sufficient to result in savings of bookkeepers, since there was only one bookkeeper per store. It did turn out that the experimental stores with scanners experienced increased sales, presumably because of customer satisfaction with faster checkout service. But it was felt that this benefit of scanners could not be counted on in the long run, because eventually the competition would introduce scanners.

The net result is that without removal of item pricing, and without the benefits of better inventory management, the overall value of introducing scanners in supermarkets, according to this study, is marginal. Although ABC was doubtful about the benefits of scanners and hesitated to increase the number of installations, its competitors continued to place scanners in their stores, perhaps because this was regarded as necessary to maintain competitive positions. Modern scanners have voice devices which speak out the prices, and print detailed sales slips which identify every item bought, so that the customers see even greater benefits.

These observations on supermarkets cannot be carried over into other areas without considering the special circumstances in these other places. For example, in department stores where clothes are sold, and seasons and styles are critically important, there are large savings to be had through better management of inventory. When daily inventory reporting and analysis is included (and advantage is taken of other benefits, such as rapid credit verification) POS equipment is definitely justified. On the other hand, in bookstore chains, although rapid response to inventory change is desirable for best-sellers, these constitute too small a fraction of total sales to justify the extra costs for fully automatic POS equipment (but electronic cash registers, with special features to aid cashiers and bookkeepers, *are* cost-effective).

Thus every industry segment and every application area needs its own cost/benefit study to determine the best mode of data acquisition. Moreover, as the technology changes, what is true at one time may no longer be true later. What is observed is an increasing trend toward more fully automated data acquisition and recording. Even if the benefits to be derived do not fully justify a move immediately, many feel that in the long term, the change will have to be made, and competitive factors help to bring about the change even in cases where the immediate dollar benefits are marginal.

6.2.4. Make or Buy Software

As a final illustration of evaluating the costs and benefits of a project, we consider the advantages and disadvantages of buying a software package to carry out a computer application versus having the application programmed by an in-house team of analysts and programmers. In many respects the choice here is similar to that of acquiring an in-house computer versus contracting with an outside service bureau, and the same matrix format that was presented in Table 6.9 will be used here. For a full comparison each matrix entry that refers to a cost should be accompanied by an actual estimate. The most important entries, of course, are those for acquisition (purchase or rental), maintenance and modification in the buy alternative, and those for determining the labor expenditures in the development option. The latter costs are very difficult to estimate, and how to do this is the subject of the next chapter. Here we content ourselves with drawing up, in tabular form, a checklist of the factors that have to be considered, as shown in Table 6.19.

The advantages of making hinge on the fact that a custom-made product is more likely to fit the particular needs of the company, and the experience in constructing the product can be a valuable one, useful when modifications are needed or other products are wanted. The advantages of buying center on the fact that greater confidence can be attached to costs and timetables when purchasing an off-the-shelf product. Further, since the seller of software can amortize development costs over a number of customers, the vendor can afford to put greater effort into documentation and fine-tuning performance. As in other four-way tables of this type, an entry in one box is often matched by a complementary entry in the box diagonally opposite.

Each of the arguments can be elaborated—see, for example, Guide on Edp

TABLE 6.19 ADVANTAGES AND DISADVANTAGES OF MAKING AND BUYING SOFTWARE

Choice	Advantages	Disadvantages
Buy	Costs more predictable—often less, resulting in a faster payback	Packaged software will probably not match the requirements exactly—modifications may be difficult, costly
	Time to implement more predictable	Package evaluation is difficult—perhaps expensive
	Approach encourages clear project definition	Benefits of learning through do-it-yourself lost to company
	Product is likely to have better computer utilization	Software industry has high mortality; vendor may go out of business, not be available for backup
	Superior documentation	
	Easier to discontinue project if necessary	
	Allows management to concentrate on prime responsibility	
	Possible tax advantage through capitalization	
Make	More likely to fit the need now—easier to modify in future, if necessary	Less incentives to draw up specifications and go through formal acquisition process
	Learning benefits reside in the company (department)	More difficult to control costs and schedules
	May cost less if budget is tightly controlled	

Administration (1974) and Datapro's "An Overview of the Make vs. Buy Decision" (1979). The Datapro article describes the decision process in the form of a flowchart in which a sequence of questions is asked, the answers to which lead to a decision to make, or to enter into a contract with a software vendor, development house, or service organization. For a comprehensive survey of the make-or-buy decision in manufacturing environments, see Gambino (1980). The trend, however, is very clear. As will be seen in Chapter 9, the decreasing cost and improving quality of packages, coupled with the increasing difficulty of maintaining custom software, is resulting in a pronounced shift away from making and toward buying in software acquisition.

PROBLEMS

1. An optimizing compiler costs $15,000 and has an annual maintenance charge of $1000. It has an expected lifetime of 4 years. It is estimated that using it saves 12% of the running costs for the programs to which it is applied. The value of these programs is currently $50,000 a year and their volume is increasing at 10% per year.

   (a) Assuming that money is worth 15% p.a., what are the payback period and the NPV for investing in this compiler?
   (b) What is the internal rate of return for the investment?
   (c) Should the compiler be purchased?

2. For a proposed software project it is estimated that:

(1) The project will require 2 years for completion with expenditures of $50,000 and $20,000 in the period. (Assume payments at the end of the year.)

(2) The project will be useful for 3 years after implementation, with maintenance costs of $2000 per year.

(3) Once the project is implemented there will be salary savings of $3000 per month initially. Salaries are expected to rise 10% annually.

(a) Determine the class of investment.
(b) Calculate the payback period.
(c) What is the NPV assuming that money is worth 16% p.a.?
(d) Calculate the internal rate of return.
(e) Should the project be undertaken?

3. A company has the opportunity of purchasing a program now at a cost of $5000 for a computer which will not be installed for 4 years. Thereafter, starting with the fifth year, there will be annual savings of $2500 for the indefinite future. What is the internal rate of return for this investment?

4. The Crystal Ball Company, which carries out consumer surveys, radio and television ratings, and public opinion polls, is examining alternatives for recording its data in machine-readable form. This is presently done by a service bureau at a cost of $1.45 per thousand keystrokes. Its volume of work currently averages about 12 million characters per month, with a minimum of 8 million and a maximum of 20 million characters per month. The possibilities have been narrowed down to:

(1) Card keypunches, renting at $195 per month.
(2) KEY-EDIT system, marketed by Consolidated Computer, with output in the form of magnetic tape.
(3) IBM 3740 data-entry system, with output on diskette.
(4) SCAN-DATA OCR system, with typewriter stations and output on magnetic tape.

DATA FOR OPERATING STATIONS IN EACH OF THESE MODES ARE AS FOLLOWS:

	Keypunch	KEY-EDIT	Diskette	OCR
Equipment cost ($/station/month)[a]	$195	See Auerbach	See Auerbach	$50
Operating rate (keystrokes/hr)	9000	12,000	12,000	15,000
Operator salaries ($/hr)	5.50	6.00	6.00	5.50
Supplies ($/Kcharacter)	0.20	0.15	0.20	0.10

[a]In addition to the basic units for KEY-EDIT and OCR.

Prepare a brief report on the costs and benefits of the various systems. Your report should include:

(1) Calculations and a graph showing the cost of operations versus volume (millions of characters per month)

(2) A table indicating the advantages and disadvantages of the various modes

(3) Consideration of future possibilities

(4) A recommendation of what the company should do, with reasons

(Assume 165 hours per month and that all equipment is rented under the shortest contract offered.)

5. Use the data given in Section 6.2.3 on the costs for key-entry and scanner equipment for ABC supermarkets, and on the benefits of scanners, to determine whether or not it is better to install scanners by calculating the difference in NPVs for the two alternatives. Assume that:

(1) The equipment has a 10-year life.

(2) The increased sales due to scanners will diminish by 20% per year as the competition also installs them.

(3) Money is worth 10% p.a.

(4) The profit margin is 4% of sales.

(5) The productivity gains for cashiers and bookkeepers do not result in reduced labor costs.

Suppose that as a result of the productivity gains, it is possible to reduce the labor costs (which are 1.1% of sales) by 25%. Does this make any difference to the choice?

6. For a time-shared system with n users the response time, R, is given by $R = \dfrac{an}{1 - bn}$ where a and b are constants. For a single user, the productivity, measured in interactions/user/hour, is given by

$$P = \frac{c}{d + R}$$

where c and d are the same constants for each user.
 a) What is the maximum number of users on the system?
 b) When $a \ll 2bd$ show that

Optimal number of users $= \frac{1}{2} \times$ maximum number of users.

7. Examine the standard contracts (purchase and rental) from a mainframe supplier with respect to the following features: warranties, preventive and remedial maintenance, transportation and installation costs, commencement of charges, price escalations, extra usage charges, rental credits, penalties for nonperformance, and consequent damages. In what respects does there seem to be insufficient protection for the purchaser? Which of the foregoing points are addressed in the warranty that comes with a personal computer? (See Auer and Harris, 1981.)

BIBLIOGRAPHY

ABBOT, H. L., "Who Needs a Computer," *Datamation,* 20, no. 11 (November 1974), 85–90.

ALEWINE, T., and R. A. FLECK, JR., "Service Bureau or In-House Data Processing," *Comput. J.,* 19, no. 3 (August 1976), 198–201.

AUER, J., and C. E. HARRIS, *Computer Contract Negotiations.* New York: Van Nostrand Reinhold, 1981.

AUERBACH, "Key to Storage," 1978; "Optical Character Recognition," 1978. Auerbach *Computer Technology Reports.* Pennsauken, N.J.: Auerbach.

BOEHM, B. W., *Software Engineering Economics.* Englewood Cliffs, N.J.: Prentice-Hall, 1981.

BOIES, S. J., "User Behavior on an Interactive Computer System," *IBM Syst. J.,* 13, no. 1 (1974), 1–18.

BUSEY, L. E., *The Economic Analysis of Industrial Projects.* Englewood Cliffs, N.J.: Prentice-Hall, 1978.

DATAPRO, "An Overview of the Make vs. Buy Decision," *Datapro 70,* Sec. AS30-100, November 1979, Datapro Research Corp., Delran, N.J.

DATAPRO, "All about Data Entry," *Datapro 70,* 70-D4-010, January 1982, Datapro Research Corporation, Delran, N.J.

DE MICHELI, F., La réduction des couts informatiques. Paris: Enterprise Moderne d'Édition, 1978.

DOHERTY, W. J., and R. P. Kelisky, "Managing VM/CMS Systems for User Effectiveness," *IBM Syst. J.,* 18, no. 1 (1979), 143–63.

GAMBINO, A. J., *The Make-or-Buy Decision.* The Society of Management Accountants of Canada/New York: National Association of Accountants, 1980.

GOLD, M., "Time-Sharing and Batch Processing: An Experimental Comparison of Their Values in a Problem-Solving Situation," *Commun. ACM,* 12, no. 5 (May 1969), 249–59.

GORNITSKY, R., "A Cost/Benefit Study on a Canadian Supermarket Point-of-Sale System," M.Sc. thesis University of Toronto, 1982.

GOTLIEB, C. C., "Modal Choices," *Proc. Spring Tech. Meet.*, 1976, Share European (SEAS), pp. 101–11.

GOTLIEB, C. C., and A. BORODIN, *Social Issues in Computing.* New York: Academic Press, 1973.

Guide on Edp administration, CH IV, Treasury Board, Ottawa, Information Canada, 1974.

HANNA, W. E., Jr., "A Case Study in Procurement," in *The Economics of Informatics,* ed. A. B. Frielink. Amsterdam: North-Holland, 1975, pp. 156–70.

HANZLEK, C., "Evaluation of Facilities Management: A Cost Perspective," Public Policy Research Organization, University of California, Irvine, WP-80-92, 1980.

KING, J. L., and E. L. SCHREMS, "Cost-Benefit Analysis in Information Systems Development and Operation," *Comput. Surv.,* 10, no. 1 (March 1978), 19–34.

KLEIJNEN, J. C., *Computers and Profit: Quantifying Financial Benefits of Information.* Reading, Mass.: Addison-Wesley, 1980.

McLaughlin, R. E., "1976 Budgets," *Datamation,* 22, no. 1 (January 1976), 57–58.

Parker, M. M., "Enterprise Information Analysis: Cost-Benefit Analysis and the Data Management System," *IBM Syst. J.,* 21, no. 1 (1982), 108–23.

Payne, D. V., "From 11440 to O/S-RJE without Any Regrets," *Can. Datasyst.,* June 1972, 32–35.

Phister, M., Jr., *Data Processing Technology and Economics,* 2nd ed. Santa Fe, N. Mex.: Santa Monica/Bedford, Mass.: Digital Press, 1979.

Streeter, D. N., "Cost-Benefit Evaluation of Scientific Computing Services," *IBM Syst. J.,* 11, no. 3 (1972), 219–33.

Thodhani, A. J., "Interactive User Productivity," *IBM Syst. J.,* 20, no. 4 (1981), 407–23.

7

Software Development and Maintenance

We have already examined the trade-offs between making software in-house, and purchasing or leasing it, and in this chapter we explore further what is involved in writing one's own software. While the economic criteria developed earlier still apply, there are some special considerations that come into play for software. Software projects are notorious for being delivered late and for running over budget. This has been so endemic that there is a whole literature on the subject (see Brooks, 1975) and various strategies such as "structured programming" (Dahl et al., 1972) and "chief programmer teams" (Baker and Mills, 1973) have been proposed to deal with the disease. Another special aspect to software is the relatively large effort that has to be expended on *maintaining* systems even after they have been nominally completed. In part this is because hardware has been changing so rapidly, and it is a major task to keep the software compatible with system upgrades and conversions. Since an organization's *files* have a relatively long life (often just to meet legal requirements), software to access the files and keep them up to date should be correspondingly stable—a goal that is not always met. But the high maintenance costs for software are also due to problems in its design methodology. It has taken a long time to learn to build large programming systems in a modular fashion, so that the various segments interface properly and so that a seemingly minor correction in one place does not propagate a sequence of changes that can hardly be controlled. There are those who claim that this lesson has not yet been learned.

The emphasis in this chapter will be on economics, not on the engineering methods which have been evolved for controlling and managing software projects. We shall be concerned with measurements of effort and costs, and techniques for estimating effort, time, and costs before a software project is initiated, while it is under way, and after the product has been released.

7.1. THE DEVELOPMENT CYCLE

A feature that software projects *do* have in common with other kinds of projects—computer, engineering, or scientific—is the concept of a *life cycle*. There are distinct stages in the evolution of a software project, and identification of these stages is helpful in design and scheduling. In fact, the stages, names, and the aspects that mark the end of one stage and the beginning of the next are very much the same as those found in other disciplines. But the relative amounts of effort spent on the various stages are not.

The first column of Table 7.1 names the stages of a software project. Although the terminology is not standard, the names are descriptive of the activities they stand for, and can usually be matched against terms used by other writers. The stages are often used as checkpoints for the project, to review the progress formally, and confirm that it has been carried out as intended. The listing in Table 7.1 suggests that the process is sequential, each new stage being started after the completion of its predecessor. This is not necessarily the case. As part of the validation, after any stage it might be advisable to return to an earlier one, so the whole progression ought to be viewed as a series of (potentially) iterative loops rather than as a sequential process. Implicit in this process is a maintenance phase which will usually continue over a far longer interval than that taken to construct the project, and for which the overall cost, as will be seen later, can be significant.

The other columns in Table 7.1 show the relative distributions in effort as reported in a number of sources.* Effort here is measured in person-months. As will be noted in the next section, the rate at which effort is committed is not uniform (generally there are fewer people involved in a project toward the beginning and end). Therefore, the relative expenditure of *time* would be different, and the numbers here should be regarded as the integral of the labor versus time curve, for the various intervals indicated.

Although there is a general consistency between the numbers as reported from different sources, there are some considerable differences in detail. Boehm reports a significantly higher percentage devoted to coding than do other sources.† He is the only one who attempts to make explicit how the percentages

---

*Boehm's numbers, as he gives them, add up to 106%, 6% being assigned to the proposal and requirements study, all the rest adding up to 100%. This may be because from management's viewpoint the effort on proposal and requirements represent "sunk costs" which are expended whether or not the project is undertaken. We have multiplied Boehm's numbers by 100/106 so that his figures will be comparable with the others in the table.

†He describes coding as "a complete verified set of components." It may be that others include verification under different headings. The opinion that too much design time is spent on coding, and too little on requirements study and product specification, has often been expressed.

TABLE 7.1 RELATIVE EXPENDITURE OF EFFORT IN STAGES OF A SOFTWARE PROJECT

| | Expenditure of Effort (%) As Reported in: | | | | | | Boehm[f] | | | | |
| Milestone | Wolverton | | | Zelkowitz[d] | Gotlieb[e] | Small | Intermediate | Medium | Large | Problems in This Book |
	[a]	[b]	[c]							
Proposal	12		10	10	12	5	5	5	5	5
Requirements study		42			6					5
Product specification	18		10	10	13	15	15	15	15	10
Detailed design	16	33	15	15		25	24	23	22	15
Coding	20		20	20	19	40	38	36	34	25
Module test	20	13	25	25	19	15	18	21	24	20
System test					19					10
Installation	14	12	20	20	12					5
Acceptance										5

[a] 1974.
[b] 1974—Sage.
[c] 1974—Gemini II.
[d] 1979.
[e] Based on a project for developing a large data base system in the telephone industry (unpublished report, 1979).
[f] 1981. The number of source language statements in small-, intermediate-, medium-, and large-size programs are, approximately, 2k, 8k, 32k, and 128k, respectively.

vary from small to large program size. Clearly, there are some factors which will greatly influence the difficulty of a project and affect the distribution of effort among the various stages. A rewrite or conversion of an existing program will not need as much effort spent on proposal, requirements, and specification as would a new project. A project undertaken for a large number of users will need much more time for product specification, as a consensus is sought among users, than will a project designed for a single user. Software tools can reduce the effort devoted to coding. Such factors will influence not only the time of the project but also the effort devoted to various stages. Some writers have attempted to categorize projects as being easy, standard, or difficult, according to the presence of these features. Presumably, there will be a different effort distribution for each category. For the purposes of problems in this book the entries in the last column of Table 7.1 will be taken as representing the relative distribution of effort, regardless of project size or difficulty.

7.2. EFFORT AND TIME ESTIMATES FOR SOFTWARE PRODUCTION

Although Table 7.1 is useful, much more is needed for estimating the cost of a project and for projecting the rate of expenditure. Some way of estimating the *total* cost of a project is wanted, as well as a method for judging what the cost is likely to be, or should be, for each stage. These estimates can only be derived from data gathered from projects considered to be similar to the one in mind, and in this section we examine such empirically based data.

7.2.1 Estimating the Total Effort

Two conventions have been adopted by almost everyone writing about estimating software costs:

1. Effort will be measured in person-months.
2. Equations will be based on the number of instructions in the program wanted. (The unit that is taken almost universally is *thousands* of lines of code.) This implies that lines of code per person-month is a productivity measure for programmers.

The reason for the first is obvious. With inflation a factor in every country, equations developed for dollars need constant revision. The justification for the second is less obvious. One might think that the number of instructions might be the *end* result of an estimating process rather than the beginning, and at one level this will certainly be so. But to estimate the number of instructions required for a piece of software it will clearly be necessary to examine its functions, segment the program into modules, and compare each module with existing modules that do the same kind of thing. All of this assumes a backlog of experience with similar programs. This dependence on experience has to be built into empirically derived formula; without such experience there is no basis for estimation, and it is therefore reasonable to take the number of instructions, say I, as the independent variable. This immediately raises other questions. How will a relationship expressed in terms of lines of code depend on the particular programming language used (assembly language, COBOL, FORTRAN, APL, Pascal, etc.)? What is to be counted as an instruction? Currently, most programs are written in a high-level procedural language, and most of the data on developing estimation equations is based on such programs. Thus we follow most writers in taking I to be the *number of source language instructions, in thousands* (as distinct from the number of compiled instructions). Also, to be specific, we count in I all instructions, data declarations, and job control statements but omit comments.*

With this understanding the basic equation for estimating effort is written as

$$M = af_1 \cdots f_k I^{f_d} \tag{7.1}$$

where M = total number of person-months of programming effort for the project
I = number of source language instruction, thousands
a = a constant

$f_d, f_1, \cdots, f_k$ are factors depending on such features as the difficulty of the project, the language used, the experience of the programming team, the type of system on which the development is being done, and so on. In standard situations $f_1 \cdots f_k$ will be unity, but wherever there is evidence that the project is being developed under conditions that differ from the standard, appropriate f factors, different from unity, will be introduced. The conditions may be favorable or unfavorable so that the f factors may be less than or greater than 1. Essentially, Equation 7.1 contains $k + 2$ parameters $(a, f_d, f_1, \cdots, f_k)$. When enough data about the size and effort expended on a collection of existing programs is available, by regression techniques the values of $a, f_d, f_1, \cdots, f_k$ can be determined. Then, if the program being developed is like those used to derive the formula, given I, M can be estimated for it. If desired, statistical techniques can be used to judge how good the estimator is, for example by stating confidence intervals, between which say 90% of the estimates can be expected to lie.† With variations, this is the technique proposed by most authors on estimating software costs. See Boehm (1981), Phister (1979), Schneider (1978), Chrysler (1978), Halstead (1977), and Doty (1977).

As a first simplification to Equation 7.1, consider the situation where the only parameter present is f_d, corresponding to project mode, all other conditions

---

*Some authors include comments in I, but we follow Boehm (1981) in omitting them. For a discussion of the alternatives, see Jones (1977).

†Another way of describing how good the equation is, is to state how much of the variance (i.e., the deviation between the observed and calculated estimate) is accounted for by each parameter.

being assumed standard. As experimentally derived form of Equation 7.1 with one parameter is*

$$M = 2.54I^{f_d} \tag{7.2}$$

where $f_d = 1.05$ for a project in the standard mode
$\quad\ f_d = 1.12$ for a project in the intermediate mode
$\quad\ f_d = 1.20$ for a project in the constrained mode

Standard projects are assumed to be carried out by small, experienced teams that can communicate easily with the users about specifications, where there are good programming facilities, and no stringent constraints on the project (time, memory size, etc.). Constrained projects have some tight constraints (in time, memory, or reliability) which cannot be changed easily because, for example, a large community would be affected (as might happen in a banking project). Intermediate projects, as the name suggests, lie between the two. There may be some constraints present, or perhaps a mixture of experienced and inexperienced staff on the project.

Equations 7.1 and 7.2 are inverses of an economist's *production function,* that is, an equation which relates the quantity of a product to the inputs supplied. If, for $f_D = 1.05$, we invert the function, then†

$$I = 0.41 M^{0.95} \tag{7.3}$$

Since the exponent of M is less than 1, this implies that programming is an activity showing diseconomies of scale—there is less relative output for a given relative expenditure of effort on a large project than on a small one. This aspect of program behavior, and the related one of programmer productivity (which may be defined as I/M), are of some interest. Most, but not all authors quote values just over unity for f_d in Equation 7.1, corresponding to diseconomies of scale. Doty (1977) gives a value of f_d as low as 0.781, and Schneider (1978) a value as high as 1.83. Halstead (1977) in an attempt to establish a theoretical basis for software (and hardware) design comes up with a value of 1.7.‡ The diseconomy of scale is consistent with the difficulties experienced with large software products.

The factors $f_1 \cdots f_k$ of Equation 7.1 correspond to variables which, by observation, have been found to affect programmer productivity significantly. These can be grouped into categories: those which depend on the computer used

---

*These values for a and f_d correspond to those proposed in Boehm (1981) in what he calls the basic COCOMO model. However, we have multiplied Boehm's value of a by 1.06 because, as mentioned earlier, he excludes the time for the proposal and requirements stages in his estimates of M. Also, Boehm uses the terms "organic," "semidetached," and "embedded," corresponding to our "standard," "intermediate," and "constrained."

†This is a particular case of the well-known Cobb–Douglas function, $Q = A K^\alpha L^\beta$, where K and L are the capital and labor inputs, and α and β are the corresponding elasticities.

‡Boehm (1981, p. 88) lists values from a number of sources, as does Phister (1979, Fig. 4.22.2a), who also reports on programmer productivity [see Fig. 4.22(a), Tables II-4.22.1, II-4.22.3(a)–7(a)].

for programming, those which depend on the experience of the programming team, and those which depend on project management style. Within each category there may be several separate variables. To illustrate, experiments carried out within IBM suggest that when the chief programmer team was adopted, the programmer productivity increased from 219 instructions per month to 408 (Phister, 1979, Table II.4.22.6a). If this result is representative, we may conclude that reduction factor $f_{\text{chief prog.}}$ to be applied when such a technique is used = 219/408 = 0.54. Similarly, when a formal structured programming approach was used, productivity increased from 169 to 301 instructions per month, corresponding to a factor $f_{\text{str. prog.}} = 0.56$. Other f values dependent on management style are as follows:

	Extent of Use		
Technique	Less Than Normal	Normal	More Than Normal
Top-down development	1.21	1	0.74
Design and code inspections	1.36	1	0.88

Nevertheless, it would be unwise to conclude that if all four favorable practices were used to their fullest, the programming effort can be decreased by a factor of $0.54 \times 0.56 \times 0.74 \times 0.88 = 0.20$. These multiplicative factors have been derived by different investigators, each basing their results on their own set observations. Thus for personnel experience, the IBM data give the following f values:

	Degree		
Feature	Minimal	Average	Extensive
Overall experience and qualifications	1.95	1	0.63
Previous experience with languages	1.84	1	0.58
Previous experience with like projects	1.51	1	0.54

However, for this same factor of personnel experience, Boehm (1981) quotes the following f values:

	Rating				
Attribute	Very Low	Low	Normal	High	Very High
Analyst capability	1.46	1.19	1.00	0.86	0.71
Applications experience	1.29	1.13	1.00	0.91	0.82
Programmer capability	1.42	1.17	1.00	0.86	0.70
Virtual machine experience	1.21	1.10	1.00	0.90	—
Programming language experience	1.14	1.07	1.00	0.95	—

Even with features having similar names (e.g., programming language experience), quite different factors emerge in the two cases. These differences are a reminder of the care that has to be exercised when using equations based on empirically fitted regression curves.

To emphasize the arbitrariness that is inevitable in dealing with empirically based equations, note that whereas the dependence of M on the complexity of the program was absorbed in the f_d factor in Equation 7.2, it is equally possible to absorb complexity into one or more of the f_i factors of Equation 7.1. Thus Daly (1982), rather than changing f_d from 1.05, proposes f_i factors depending on whether various features, as noted in Table 7.2, are present. The different *form* for Equation 7.2 means that a different result for M will be calculated for a given situation.

The empirical nature of Equation 7.2 means that special attention has to be paid to the variance between the computed and observed results. When using Equation 7.2 to calculate M from observed data, Boehm notes that only 29% of the computed results are within a factor of 1.3 of the observed times, and 60% are within a factor 2. With the extended model, where up to $15f_i$ factors are introduced, the fit to the 63 cases on which the observations are based is of course much better.

Putnam and Fitzsimmons (1979) suggest that one way to handle the uncertainties is to calculate a range for M, assuming that the I's are governed by a beta statistical distribution. At different times during the development cycle *three* estimates should be made for I: for example, upon commencement, at the end of the project definition phase, and at the end of the detailed design phase. The three estimates can be designated as I_{min}, the smallest number of instructions, I_{prob}, the most likely number expected, and I_{max}, the largest number. Then it can be shown that for the beta distribution the expected number

$$I_{exp} = \frac{I_{min} + 4I_{prob} + I_{max}}{6}$$

TABLE 7.2 FACTORS INFLUENCING PROGRAM COMPLEXITY

Feature	f Factors					
Interactive support tools available	Yes	0.8	No	1		
Number of programmers	1	0.95	> 15	1		
Number of modules, D	$5 \geq D$	1.0	$10 \geq D > 5$	1.1	$D > 10$	1.2
Real-time application?	No	1	Yes	1.25		
Complex algorithm?	No	1	Yes	1.5		
Significant hardware interface?	No	1	Yes	1.5		
Module unlike previous work?	No	1	Yes	1.2		
Module is a rewrite and only new instructions contribute to I?	No	1	Yes	1.5		
Memory size critical?	No	1	Yes	1.25		
Development is batch; turnaround > 4 hr	No	1	Yes	1.1		

Also, the standard deviation, σ, as given by

$$\sigma = \frac{I_{max} - I_{min}}{6}$$

Moreover, if separate estimates are made for the different modules M_i of a program ($i = 1, \cdots, N$), the standard deviation for the entire system,

$$\sigma_{system} = \left(\sum \sigma_i^2 \right)^{1/2} \qquad i = 1 \cdots N$$

Given the beta distribution, there is a 68% chance that an expected value lies within the range $I_{exp} \pm \sigma$ and a 99% chance that it lies within the range $I_{exp} \pm 3\sigma$.

The basic question is whether an estimation model derived from a set of observations in one programming environment will give good results when applied to another. The answer will depend on how close the projects in the two sets resemble each other and how much consistency there is in the definition for measured quantities such as I, programmer experience, and so on. Although the form of Equation 7.1 seems to be generally accepted, no standard way of defining the f values has yet gained acceptance. Until standards emerge, the actual parameters for $a, f_d, f_1, \cdots, f_k$ in Equation 7.1 must be regarded as valid only in the situation where they were derived. We thus have the same caveat that was present in calculating FOMs by Equation 1.1, also derived by regression techniques.

7.2.2. Effort as a Function of Time

An estimate of the total effort for a project is useful in itself, but more is needed for detailed planning. We need some way of determining how much effort to commit at each stage of the development cycle. Experience certainly shows that doubling the effort for a stage will not complete it in half the time. Adding personnel increases the need for communication, and individual productivity lessens. It is this which gives validity to Brooks' law—"adding manpower to a late software project makes it later" (see Brooks, 1975, and Problem 4). It is for this reason that software management techniques such as the chief programmer team and top-down development have emerged.

In the early stages of a project fewer people will be involved than during the middle, and toward the end the number will fall again, so that the curve of effort versus time should have a maximum. Norden (1970) proposed the Rayleigh equation (Equation 7.4 and Fig. 7.1) as a suitable one for expressing effort as a function of time in project development. Putnam and Wolverton (1977), and others, report that experience shows that it *does* reflect the way effort is distributed for large software projects. The Rayleigh curve is expressed as

$$N = 2Eate^{-at^2} \qquad (7.4)$$

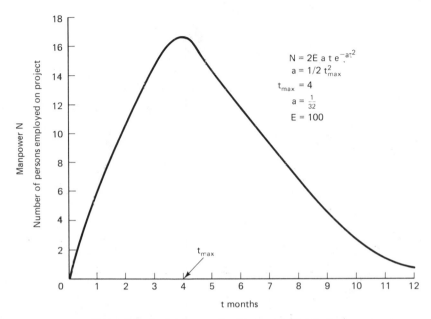

Figure 7.1   Rayleigh curve for Manpower Distribution

where N = number of persons employed at time t
$\quad$ E, a = constants

One useful feature of this curve is that there are simple interpretations to the constants E and a. We have

$$M = \text{total person-months employed} = \int_0^\infty N\, dt = E \int_0^\infty e^{-at^2}\, d(at^2) = E$$

Also, $dN/dt = 2Eae^{-at^2}(1 - 2at^2)$, so that at maximum employment, $1 - 2at_{max}^2 = 0$ and $a = 1/2t_{max}^2$. Thus we may rewrite Equation 7.4 as

$$N = \frac{M}{t_{max}^2}\, te^{-t^2/2t_{max}^2} \tag{7.5}$$

Since there are two constants it should require just two observations of N and t to determine M and t_{max}. In practice we rewrite Equation 7.4 as

$$\ln\left(\frac{N}{t}\right) = \ln(2Ea) - at^2$$

and by plotting a regression line of $\ln(N/t)$ versus t^2, we find a from the slope and $\ln(2Ea)$ from the intercept. Thus one possible use of the Rayleigh equation is to

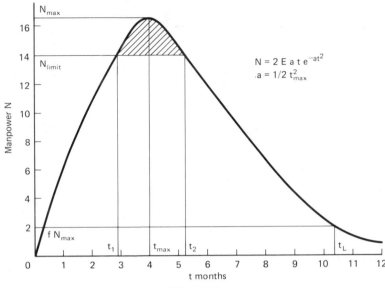

$$N = 2\,E\,a\,t\,e^{-at^2}$$
$$a = 1/2\,t_{max}^2$$

Figure 7.2

estimate the *total* cost of the project from a few observations made relatively early in the development stage. Alternatively, the equation may be regarded as a guide for determining how many persons to assign at each stage of the project.*

Although the mathematics is simple enough, and the interpretation satisfying, there are problems in using the Rayleigh equation in real situations. The long tail of the curve, and to a lesser extent the initial buildup, do not quite seem to correspond with experience. In particular, the curve does not reach $N = 0$ in any finite time, so that there is no immediate concept corresponding to the lifetime, L, of a project. There are good reasons why an expression for the lifetime is needed, for with it the milestones corresponding to the end of stages can be determined. As shown in Figure 7.2, we could declare the project ended when N reaches some designated fraction, f, of N_{max}, but this seems arbitrary (see Problems 8 and 9).

Equation 7.4 assumes that people are both available and added as needed, but this is hardly realistic. Although programmers can be assigned part time, additions and subtractions are discrete rather than continuous. On a small project the staff may vary between $\frac{1}{2}$ person and 3 persons, and even on a large project there may be a limit to the number of people available. We might try to incorporate this last into the model by assuming that the real curve is flattened off.

*Besides wanting to know how many people to have at any time, presumably the project is divided into teams, each working on a different module. It would be desirable to know how many modules there should be and how large the modules should be in number of instructions. (The number of people to assign to each module can then be determined from Equation 7.2.) This question of project segmentation is considered by Phister (1979, p. 588).

Thus

$$N = \begin{cases} 2\,Eate^{-at^2} & \text{for } t \le t_1 \\ N_{\text{limit}} = N(t_1) = 2\,Eat_1 e^{-at_1^2} = N(t_2) & \text{for } t_1 \le t \le t_2 \\ 2\,Eate^{-at^2} & \text{for } t \ge t_2 \quad \text{(Fig. 7.2)} \end{cases}$$

But again this is arbitrary, and some of the simplicity of the Rayleigh curve is lost because E no longer has the interpretation of being the total effort for the project.

Another possibility is to pick two milestones corresponding to points in the development cycle and assume that the Rayleigh curve will be used to model personnel assignments only between these times. If the first milestone is the completion of the initial requirements stage t_{req}, and the second is the lifetime t_L, it is easily seen that the parameter E in the Rayleigh equation is related to $E_{t_{\text{req}}}^{t_L}$, the effort in person-months from requirements to completion, by

$$E_{t_{\text{req}}}^{t_L} = E(e^{-\tau_1^2} - e^{-\tau_2^2}) \tag{7.6}$$

where $\tau_1 = t_{\text{req}}/\sqrt{2}\,t_{\text{max}}$ and $\tau_2 = t_L/\sqrt{2}\,t_{\text{max}}$. Also, the total person-months is given by

$$M = E(1 - e^{-\tau_2^2}) \tag{7.7}$$

and if f_0 is defined as the fraction of M devoted to the project until the requirements phase ($=0.05$ from Table 7.1), then

$$f_0 = \frac{E_0^{t_{\text{req}}}}{E_0^{t_L}} = \frac{1 - e^{-\tau_1^2}}{1 - e^{-\tau_2^2}} \tag{7.8}$$

This is similar to an approach of Boehm (1981), who uses the portion of the Rayleigh curve between $0.3t_{\text{max}}$ and $1.7t_{\text{max}}$ to fit the development curve between t_{req} and t_L, and in doing so finds that the curve corresponds well with the labor deployment on certain projects.

Still another way of bringing the lifetime t_L into the calculations is to assume that it is one more empirically determined, dependent variable, to be found from a regression fit of t_L versus the total effort M. This is suggested by Boehm, who derives the result

$$t_L = 2.5(M)^{0.38} \tag{7.9}$$

where t_L is in months.

With any of these assumptions regarding t_L, it is possible to convert Table 7.1, showing the effort expended in achieving various stages, to one showing the fraction of t_L needed to arrive at the different milestones. In this form the table can be used to judge whether the project is on schedule.

Useful as these estimates are, it is necessary to remember that these calculations have only an empirical basis and that the various equations can be applied to a given project only when the project is similar to those used to determine the parameters. It is also necessary to be aware of the effects of variations and uncertainties in the variables on which the quantity depends, that is, of the *sensitivity* of the dependent variable to changes in the independent variables. Mathematically, if V is a function of $v_2 \cdots v_k$, knowledge of the partial derivatives $\partial V/\partial v_i$ allows us to calculate the relative change, $\Delta V/V$, arising from a change, $\Delta v_i/v_i$, in one of the independent variables. In Equation 7.1 M is linearly dependent on $f_1 \cdots f_k$, so that a 1% change in one of the f_i's $(i = 1 \cdots k)$ causes a 1% change in M. But $\Delta M/M = f_d(\Delta I/I)$ and since $f_d > 1$, changes in M are more sensitive to changes in I than they are to changes in the f_i. Further, $\Delta M/M = f_d \times \log_e I \times \Delta f_d/f_d$, so that relative changes in M can be highly sensitive to changes in f_d, the variable that reflects project complexity. On the other hand, if project complexity is accounted for by a linear factor which is a product of individual factors such as those displayed in Table 7.2, M will not be nearly as sensitive to changes in this variable.

7.3. SOFTWARE MAINTENANCE

So far the focus has been on software development costs, but, like hardware, software that is in continuous use requires regular maintenance. Results of a survey conducted by Lientz and Swanson (1980) over 487 business organizations showed that for application software, 49% of the total effort was expended for maintenance compared with 43% for development and 8% for other purposes. Software changes arise from reasons that can be categorized under four headings:

1. Changes in the functional specifications
2. Changes to correct errors in performance
3. Changes in hardware or software environment
4. Changes to enhance performance

Ideally, good design and programming practices would avoid changes for the first two reasons, and this is the goal of structured programming and techniques for proving program correctness. But for large software projects the goal is still elusive, and maintenance is needed to incorporate changes for all these reasons. Changes for the first three may be seen as required, compared with changes for the fourth, which is optional, and which could be viewed as a contribution to development rather than a need for correction. In the Lientz and Swanson survey mentioned earlier, approximately 40% of the changes were required (Table 7.3).

TABLE 7.3 REASONS FOR CHANGES IN RELEASED SOFTWARE

Reason	Software Maintenance Effort (%)
Enhancements for users	41.8
Changes arising from changes in input data	17.4
Emergency program corrections	12.4
Routine program debugging	9.3
Changes arising from changes in hardware	6.2
Changes to improve documentation	5.5
Improve performance	4.0
Miscellaneous	3.4

Source: Data from B. P. Lientz and E. B. Swanson, *Software Maintenance Management: A Study of the Maintenance of Computer Application Software in 487 Data Processing Organizations* (Reading, Mass.: Addison-Wesley, 1980).

Models of different complexity can be used to derive estimates for the effort devoted to software maintenance. A simple model is to assume that no enhancements are added, so that the number of instructions, I, is fixed. Let n be the number of errors corrected by time t, and N the number still remaining. It is reasonable to assume that

$$n + N = \epsilon I$$

and that $dn/dt = kN$, where ϵ and k are constants. Then $dN/dt = -kN$, with $N = \epsilon I$ at $t = 0$. It follows that $N = \epsilon I e^{-kt}$ and $n = \epsilon I(1 - e^{-kt})$. The initial error rate reduction is $k\epsilon I$, and the remaining errors decrease at an exponential rate governed by the time constant k. Every $1/k$ months the errors are reduced by a factor of e. When software is used frequently the rate of error discovery should be high, so that k should be shorter for system software than for application software. Phister (1979) quotes data on two application programs and two operating systems, with constants as shown in Table 7.4.

According to this model, the number of errors eventually falls to zero and no further maintenance is needed. In practice, maintenance continues to be

TABLE 7.4 CONSTANTS IN PROGRAM MAINTENANCE

Constant	Application Program		Operating System	
	1	2	1	2
Number of instructions, I	2000	20,000	100,000	40,000
Error incidence, ϵ	0.005	0.005	0.001	0.0039
Observed time constant, $1/k$ (months)	13.6	45.5	3.9	8

Source: Data from M. Phister, *Data Processing Technology and Economics,* 2nd ed. (Santa Fe, N.Mex.: Santa Monica/Bedford, Mass.: Digital Press. 1979), Fig. 4.22.18, Table 11.4.22.4.

needed, in part because enhancements are being added and the program grows in size. Suppose, as before, that

$$\frac{dn}{dt} = k_1 N \quad \text{and} \quad n + N = \epsilon I$$

but now I grows linearly at a relative rate of k_2 instructions per year, so that

$$I = I_0(1 + k_2 t) \tag{7.10}$$

Then $dN/dt = \epsilon k_2 I_0 - k_1 N$ with $N = \epsilon I_0$ at $t = 0$. The solution to this equation is

$$N = \epsilon I_0 e^{-k_1 t} \left(1 - \frac{k_2}{k_1}\right) + \epsilon I_0 \frac{k_2}{k_1} \tag{7.11}$$

Eventually, $N = \epsilon I_0(k_2/k_1)$, a constant, implying a constant maintenance effort. If it is assumed that each error needs five instructions to correct it, the ratio of the number of instructions undergoing modification each year to the original size of the program is $5\epsilon_0 k_2/k_1$. Using the values for application program 2 of Table 7.4 for ϵ and k_1, and assuming that I_0 increases at a rate of 10% per year, this works out to $5 \times 0.005 \times 45.5 \times 0.1 = 0.11$ or 11%. In the Lientz and Swanson survey cited, approximately 9.2% of application software underwent modification each year. Other data (Boehm, 1981, Chap. 30) show this ratio varying between 10 and 40%.

It is clearly possible to elaborate the model still further by making additional assumptions about the mechanics of software change. Such exercises are worthwhile only if there is enough statistical data to enable one to distinguish between different maintenance models, and data of this kind are only beginning to become available. Belady and Lehman (1976) report on the experience in IBM with maintaining OS/360. Successive releases of the operating system are identified by the release sequence number R. M_R is the number of modules in the system at release R (this is closely correlated with the number of lines of code), and D_R is the number of elapsed days between release R $-$ 1 and release R. A regression fit of M_R against R is given by

$$M_R = 760 + 200R \tag{7.12}$$

The cyclical and stochastic fluctuations in M_R are suppressed in this trend-line fit. If D is the number of elapsed days from release 1 to release R ($D = \Sigma_{R=1}^{R} D_R$) and M_D the number of modules at day D, an alternative fit for the system size is given by

$$M_D = 89 + 1350 \log\left(1 + \frac{D}{51}\right) \tag{7.13}$$

Note that this implies a slower-than-linear growth of system size with time, as against the linear form of Equation 7.12.* The difference arises because the interval between successive releases increased (polynomially or nearly exponentially) with R. Belady and Lehman also give curves for HR_R, the number of modules handled for release R, and C_R, the fraction of the modules that were changed. Regression lines for these quantities are given by

$$C_R = 0.14 + .0012R^2 \qquad \text{or} \qquad C_R = 0.037 + 0.0013\ R^2 + 0.008\,HR_R$$

$$\sum_{R=1}^{R} HR_R = 1100 + 11D$$

Belady and Lehman summarize their observation on OS/360 in three "laws," the first of which they call the *law of continuing change:* "A system that is used undergoes continuing change until it is judged more cost effective to freeze and recreate it."

The important point to note is that as experience with the maintenance of software accumulates and data are gathered on program growth size, error correction rates, and related observations, it becomes possible to measure and hence control the balance between effort devoted to program development and that devoted to program maintenance.† These efforts influence the longevity of the software, a factor that is important in estimating the value of software products and the feasibility of embarking on an application needing software.‡

PROBLEMS

1. When the coding on a project has been completed, the record of expenditures per month is as follows:

Month	1	2	3	4	5
Expenditures	$2900	$5300	$6900	$7400	$7100

A budget of $50,000 has been set for the project. Use the data above to obtain *two* independent estimates for the total cost. Is the project on budget?

*Although the size of OS/360 increased at a slower-than-linear rate, for another ALGOL-based system it was found that system size grew linearly with time.

†For additional data on maintenance, and other models, see Ohba (1984).

‡There are few data on the lifetime of software. A survey by Frost and Sullivan (1977) reported that users expected software packages to be useful between 5 and 10 years (except for operating systems, where a 2½-year lifetime was expected), while suppliers estimated a 6- to 8-year lifetime for packages, with 4 years for an operating system. In the Lientz and Swanson survey, the mean age of application systems was 4¾ years, but there were a significant number of systems over 12 years old. (See Problem 11.)

2. With reference to Equation 7.2, Boehm (1981) proposes the following f factors relating to the computer on which the project is being programmed:

	Rating				
Computer Attribute	Low	Normal	High	Very High	Extra High
Execution-time constraint	—	1.00	1.11	1.30	1.66
Main storage constraint	—	1.00	1.06	1.21	1.56
Virtual machine availability	0.87	1.00	1.15	1.30	—
Computer turnaround time	0.87	1.00	1.07	1.15	—

Taking into consideration the project mode (standard, intermediate, constrained), experience of the programming team, management style, and computer, estimate the least and greatest times for a project with 26,000 instructions. Comment on the differences.

3. In general, different estimates are derived for M according to whether program complexity is accounted for by Equation 7.2, with constrained $f_d > 1.05$, or by the factors shown in Table 7.2, with $f_d = 1.05$. However, in a given situation the two methods yield the same M for *one* value of I. Assuming a highly constrained environment, such that all the f factors in Table 7.2 are at their maximum values (and with a large number of modules), what is this value of I? If I is increased by 10%, what is the percentage difference between the two estimates of M?

4. The fact that a programmer, B, who joins a team, needs time to learn the new job can be expressed by writing the productivity (measured in instructions delivered per person-day) in the form

$$P_B = P_b(1 - e^{-bt})$$

where b and P_b are constants, characterizing B's education, experience, and skill. Assume that B, while learning, is taught by another programmer, A, who for all practical purposes has reached peak productivity, but because of the time spent in teaching, P_A is reduced to $fP_a, f < 1$.

(a) Derive an expression for T_1, the time required for P_{A+B}, the productivity of the team $A + B$, to reach P_A. If $a = b = \frac{1}{100}$ day^{-1}, $P_a = P_b$, and $f = 0.7$, what is T_1?

(b) Under what conditions will P_{A+B} *never* equal P_A?

(c) Suppose that A continues teaching to T_2, when M_{A+B}, the *work* of $A + B$, is equal to that which would have been done by A alone. (*Note:* $M_{A+B} = \int_0^t P_{A+B}\,dt$.) Derive an equation for T_2. Find T_2 for the parameters in part (a).

(d) In a more realistic model, at T_3, when P_B reaches FP_b (where F is a constant), teaching is no longer necessary. What is the condition of F for $T_3 < T_1$? (Gordon and Lamb, 1979)

5. Suppose that we define the lifetime of a project, t_L, as the time at which the labor hours are down to a fraction f of that at the peak. Show that t_L is determined by the solution of the equation

$$\ln x = \frac{1}{2} (x^2 - 1) + \ln f$$

where $x = t_L / t_{max}$. Calculate t_L for $t_{max} = 100$ days and $f = 0.05$.

6. (a) Show that for the Rayleigh curve approximately 40% of the effort is expended between $t = 0$ and $t = t_{max}$.
   (b) If the only part of the Rayleigh curve between $t = 0.3t_{max}$ and $t = 1.7t_{max}$ is taken to correspond to the labor distribution curve between t_{req} and t_L, what fraction of the effort is expended to t_{max}?

7. Suppose that Equation 7.5 is assumed for the labor distribution curve. Given a value t_1, find an iteration to determine t_2, where $N(t_1) = N(t_2)$.

8. Assume that the Rayleigh distribution corresponds to labor assignment until N falls to $0.05N_{max}$, and that the time for this corresponds to t_L, the life of the project. Given the relative distributions of *efforts* in the last column of Table 7.1, calculate t_M/t_L, where t_M is the milestone *time* corresponding to the beginning of each of the developed stages.

9. Let t_d be the milestone when detailed design is complete, and let t_s be the milestone when system test is complete. Some observations of Putnam (1979) suggest that

$$\frac{t_d}{t_L} = 0.43 \qquad \text{and} \qquad \frac{t_s}{t_L} = 0.67$$

Assuming the model of Equations 7.6 to 7.8, how consistent are these observations with the relative distribution of effort as shown in the last column of Table 7.1?

10. A software project with an estimated I Kinstructions (thousands of instructions) contains two modules. Module I, consisting of fI Kinstructions, is of the constrained type. Module II, with $(1 - f)I$ Kinstructions, is standard. The project manager is considering whether he ought to concentrate his best team on module I. If he does, the effort for module I will be reduced to half, while the effort for module II will be multiplied by 1.5.
    (a) Assuming the relation between effort and I given by Equation 7.2, show that the concentration should be done when

$$\ln I \geq 7 \ln (1 - f) - 8 \ln f$$

   (b) What is the value of I for $f = 0.3$? Show that for $f \geq 0.6$ the team should always be divided.

11. Accepting the model for software maintenance which assumes that program size grows at a constant rate, derive an expression for $n/\epsilon I_0$, where n is the number of program corrections made at time t. A decision is made to keep the software for a time, T, such that $n(T) = I_0$. Derive an equation for T, and applying a reasonable approximation, solve for T. If $\epsilon = 0.001$, $1/k_1 = 4$ months and $1/k_2 = 10$ months, what is T? Is the approximation condition satisfied?

12. Suppose that program size grows *logarithmically* with time, as indicated by Equation 7.13, instead of linearly, as in Equation 7.10, and that the rate of error detection is proportional to the number of errors remaining. Derive an expression for the number of errors remaining corresponding to Equation 7.11.

13. The following data were gathered when testing a large program:

Test Hours	276	652	911	1226	1432	1754	2117	2400	2800	4000
Major Errors	13	21	30	46	57	66	75	80	86	93
Minor Errors	31	47	66	89	101	114	125	129	136	146

Assuming the simple model (constant program size), determine the constants k, and ϵl for major, minor, and total number of errors. Estimate the rate of decrease of errors for each 1000 hours of program testing. [P. N. Misra, "Software Reliability Analysis," *IBM Syst. J.* 22, no. 3 (1983), 262–70.]

BIBLIOGRAPHY

BAKER, F. T., and H. D. MILLS, "Chief Programmer Teams," *Datamation,* 19, no. 12 (December 1973).

BELADY, L. A., and M. M. LEHMAN, "A Model of Large Program Development," *IBM Syst. J.,* 15, no. 3 (1976), 225–52.

BOEHM, B., *Software Engineering Economics.* Englewood Cliffs, N.J.: Prentice-Hall, 1981.

BROOKS, F. P., Jr., *The Mythical Man-Month.* Reading, Mass.: Addison-Wesley, 1975.

CHRISTENSEN, K., G. P. FITSOS, and C. P. SMITH, "A Perspective on Software Science," *IBM Syst. J.,* 20, no. 4 (1981), 372–87.

CHRYSLER, E., "Some Basic Determinants of Computer Programmer Productivity," *Commun. ACM,* 21, no. 6 (June 1978), 472–73.

DAHL, O. J., E. W. DIJKSTRA, and C. A. R. Hoare, *Structure Programming.* New York: Academic Press, 1972.

DALY, E. B., "Organizational Philosophies Used in Software Development," in R. Goldberg and H. Lorin, *The Economics of Information Processing,* Vol. 2. New York: Wiley, 1982, pp. 124–36.

DOTY, D. L., "Software Cost Estimation Study," *NTIS AD/A-044,* Vol. 11, 1977.

Frost and Sullivan Inc., Computer Software and Packaged Services Market 1977.

GORDON, R. L., and J. C. LAMB, "A Closer Look at Brooks' Law," *Datamation,* 23, no. 6 (1977), pp. 81–86.

GRIFFIN, E. L., "Real-Time Estimating," *Datamation,* 26, no. 6 (1980), pp. 188–98.

HALSTEAD, M. H., *Elements of Software Science.* New York: Elsevier North-Holland, 1977.

JONES, C., "Productivity Measurements," *Guide 44,* Session MA-5, San Francisco, 1977.

LIENTZ, B. P., and E. B. SWANSON, *Software Maintenance Management: A Study of the Maintenance of Computer Application Software in 487 Data Processing Organizations.* Reading, Mass.: Addison-Wesley, 1980.

LINGER, R. C., H. D. MILLS, and B. I. Witt, *Structured Programming: Theory and Practice.* Reading, Mass.: Addison-Wesley, 1979.

NORDEN, P. V., "Useful Tools for Project Management," in *Management Production,* ed. M. K. Stan. New York: Penguin, 1970, pp. 71–101.

OHBA, M., "Software reliability analysis models," IBM J. Res. Develp., 28, no. 4 (July 1984), 428–443.

PARKIN, A., "The Probable Outcomes of a Data Processing Project," *Comput. J.,* 20, no. 2, 1977, 98–101.

PHISTER, M., *Data Processing Technology and Economics,* 2nd ed. Santa Fe, N. Mex.: Santa Monica/Bedford, Mass.: Digital Press, 1979.

PUTNAM, L., and A. Fitzsimmons, "Estimating Software Costs," *Datamation,* 25 (1979), Pt. 1, September; Pt. 2, October; Pt. 3, November, 137–40.

PUTNAM, L. H., and R. W. WOLVERTON, "Quantitative Management: Software Estimating," tutorial presented as *COMPSAC '77,* IEEE Computer Soc. First Int. Comput. Software Appl. Conf., Chicago, November 8–10, 1977.

SCHNEIDER, V., "Prediction of Software Effort and Project Duration: Four New Formulas," ACM SIGPLAN Notices, June, 1978, pp. 49–59.

SUDING, A. D., "Hobbits, Dwarfs and Software," *Datamation,* 23, no. 6 (June 1977), 92–97.

WOLVERTON, R. W., "The Cost of Developing Large-Scale Software," *IEEE-TC C-23*, June 1974, pp. 615–36.

ZELKOWITZ, M. V., "Perspectives on Software Engineering," *Comput. Surv.,* 10, no. 2 (June 1978), 198–216.

ZELKOWITZ, M. V., "Principles of Software Design," in *Principles of Software Engineering and Design,* M. Zelkowitz, A. Shaw, and J. Gannon, eds. Englewood Cliffs, N.J.: Prentice-Hall, 1979.

Part III

THE INDUSTRY

In Part IV of this book the costs and benefits associated with computers and their use are examined from the point of view of national interests, because they must be viewed from that light in order to comprehend why the technology is seen to be so important. Computer companies, and the industry as a whole, are organizations which are intermediate between the user and service centers we have studied so far and the countries we shall be looking at later. The principal computer companies are multinational enterprises, and the industry is really global, transcending national boundaries. Nevertheless, it is useful to examine the industry at the national company level, particularly the U.S. industry, before turning to the international stage. Partially, this is because a country's capabilities and aspirations must be built around its industrial realities. But it is also because the U.S. industry has played, and continues to play, such a dominant role worldwide. In this section we set out to identify the components of the computer industry and their interrelationships, to chart the growth, and to examine the technological forces responsible for the growth. The main focus will be on computers, but for reasons that will soon be obvious if they are not so already, it is necessary to give major attention to the communications industry. That the growth in computers *has* been driven primarily by technical innovation rather than by prior perception of markets or needs is generally accepted. In other words, the history of development is one of devices being invented, and new and faster systems being conceived and built because it was recognized to be technically feasible to do so. As faster and larger computers were built for narrow and special purposes, eventually there were commercial versions built to satisfy wider-based demands. During the early days of computers the view was expressed that a few large electronic digital computers would meet the computational needs of the whole world. Multinational computer centers were advocated, and funded, because of the conviction that even an advanced country could not justify the expense, or generate enough work, for a computer by itself. But this was when computers were seen to be numerical computing engines rather than general information-processing systems. As the technology developed, the market for computer products has expanded continuously, to the point where the information-based industries now make up a significant sector of all industry. Their growth rate assures that this sector will increase for decades, and it is commonly held that before the end of the century the information sector will be exceeded only by that for energy.

8

Technological Developments in Information Processing

Even in a world which, in the span of only half a century, has seen incredible developments in communications, transportation, medical science, and space exploration, the nature and pace of change in information-processing technology stand out. As we saw in Table 1.3, within 30 years there have been at least four generations of computers, each generation being characterized by an order-of-magnitude increase in performance, accompanied by comparable decreases in cost. In our efforts to rate computer performance in Chapter 1 we looked at the changes in processor speed, but in this chapter we take a more general look at how improvements in the technological performance of computer systems have come about.

Computers are complex devices, built from basic logical units such as flip-flops, gates, and registers, which are organized into structures of higher and higher complexity—adders, arithmetic and logic units, memories, chips, channels, unit processors, multiprocessor systems, and networks. It is important to realize that enormous technological improvements have taken place everywhere in this hierarchy. At the same time there has been a progression of developments in programming languages and operating systems and an enormous proliferation of computer applications. Although these developments in software have not produced the same dramatic increases in *speed* as have those stemming from hardware, they have resulted in systems which are more flexible, easier to use, and capable of handling larger and more varied tasks. All of this has contributed to the growth of computer use and to the diffusion of computer technology into other sectors of the economy. Paralleling these developments in computers there have been equally dramatic improvements in communication speed and channel capacity during the last three decades. From the combined developments in computers and communications there have emerged the multitude of *services* which are the most visible manifestations of the information-processing technology. The most far-reaching development has been the steady convergence of the computer and communication technologies.

8.1. HARDWARE IMPROVEMENTS

Figure 8.1 shows the cost of a flip-flop between 1955 and 1978 as eight different technologies were introduced. The figure is a typical one for technological replacement, not only in computers but in the aircraft, communication, and other industries, and the following features can be observed:

- As a technology is used there is a learning curve for it, so the costs go down. It is usual to fit a straight line to the logarithm of the cost so that the slope of the line corresponds to the exponential rate of decrease.
- A newer technology is introduced during the lifetime of the older one. At first the cost is higher, but it decreases at a faster rate, and eventually the new technology replaces the old.
- In the meantime a still newer technology is introduced, with costs decreasing at a still faster rate; and eventually *it* becomes dominant.
- It is important to realize that the succeeding technologies not only cost less, but show superior performance—in this case the switching speed of the flip-flop decreases, as do the size and power consumption.

Obviously, this cycle cannot continue indefinitely. Eventually, fundamental factors such as the speed of light and the size of molecules will limit performance. At any given stage it is impossible to be sure that a new technology will emerge, but it is impressive to realize that there have been so many cycles in such a short time span; and apparently, the limit has not yet been reached. The average decrease in cost over the last 25 years has been about 22% per year.

As noted, there are factors other than cost that can be taken as measures of technological improvement. Noyce (1977), citing an observation of Gordon Moore made in 1964 to the effect that the number of components in the most advanced integrated circuits has doubled every year since 1959, presents a graph to show that the trend was still continuing in 1977. Figure 8.2 shows a similar trend in the number of components in a chip of constant cost, between 1972 and 1978. Chip area, the number of bits in a bipolar chip, and the number of components in an MOS logic chip all increase at exponential rates. The number of components on an MOS (constant cost) chip increased from 30 in 1962 to 8000 in 1974, corresponding to a growth rate of 160%, not quite doubling, but still impressively large. Noyce suggests that the rapid rate of technological improvement in chip performance arises because of the very high volumes of

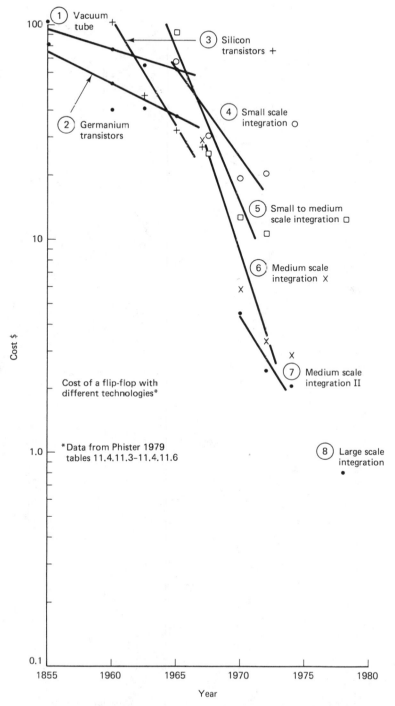

Figure 8.1 Technology Replacement (Data from M. Phister, *Data Processing Technology and Economics,* 2nd ed. (Santa Fe, N. Mex.: Santa Monica/Bedford, Mass.: Digital Press, 1979), Tables 11.4.11.3 11.4.11.6.)

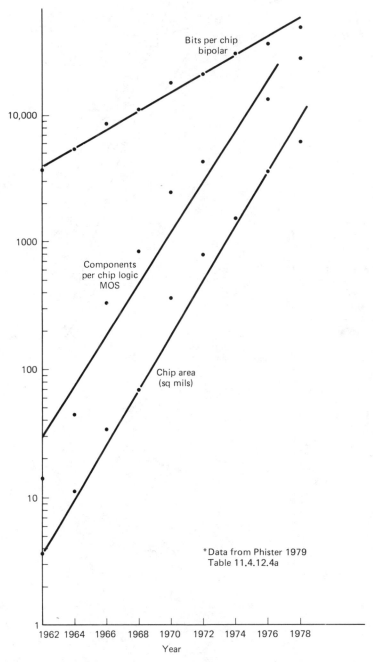

Figure 8.2 Number of components in a chip of constant cost (Data from M. Phister, *Data Processing Technology and Economics*, 2nd ed. Santa Fe, N. Mex.: Santa Monica/Bedford, Mass.: Digital Press, 1979), Table 11.4.12.4a.)

chips produced. Many industries follow a learning curve in which price decreases exponentially with quantity, the reduction factor corresponding to a decrease in cost of about 28% each time the number of units produced doubles. Since chips are manufactured in *very* large numbers each year, the rate of learning is high.

From Fig. 1.2, showing Knight's performance index for the years 1962–1966, we were able to estimate the technological improvement rate in total computer power (at constant price) for that period. Figure 8.3 is a plot of the number of additions per dollar (which can be regarded as a very simple measure of processor speed/cost) for systems appearing between 1955 and 1975. The improvement factor is 1.58 or 58% per year (compared to 2.15 calculated from Fig. 1.2). Although the spread of the points in Fig. 8.3 is very large and the performance measure is crude, the trend line is still instructive. Any system that departs widely from the line, either below or above, can be regarded as unusual. For example, the RCA 501 (the BIZMAC) is well below this line. To reach the line going horizontally, one goes a distance of about $6\frac{1}{2}$ years, which can be interpreted as saying that when the RCA 501 was introduced it was about $6\frac{1}{2}$ years behind the state of the technology for commercial systems. By the same token, the PDP/8 was almost 9 years *ahead* of the state of the art. It should therefore be no surprise that the RCA 501 was a commercial failure, whereas the PDP/8 was a great success.* Figure 8.3 is also useful for estimating the rate of diffusion of the technology within the computer industry: that is, the time lapse between the appearance of a high-performance state-of-the-art product and the launching of a commercial product with equivalent performance. Most of the computers shown in Fig. 8.3 are commercial systems. But also shown are points corresponding to systems such as the IBM 704, the IBM 7090, and the CDC 6600, which were the supercomputers of their day. The average horizontal distance from these points to the line is 5 years, an estimate of the rate of technological diffusion.

In the historical development of computers, memory has always presented a special problem. At any stage, CPU speed has been considerably greater than I/O speed (i.e., rate of transfers in and out of secondary storage), so systems have invariably been I/O bound. (Recall the illustrative calculation in Section 2.1.) The general solution to this problem is to provide a hierarchy of storage devices, starting with a relatively small amount of expensive storage with very short access time, and going in stages to very large, low-cost devices (e.g., magnetic tapes) with long access times. The architecture is then designed so that instructions and data needed by the CPU are cascaded down from the high-capacity devices to the high-speed registers, using techniques which are invisible to the user (e.g., cache memory and virtual storage). In essence there are two desiderata for memory, short access time and large capacity; achieving either is expensive, so there is a conflict, requiring a trade-off. This trade-off is illustrated in Fig. 8.4. For the cascading to work well it is necessary to have reliable devices which overlap in the areas from the top right to the bottom left. Figure 8.5 shows

---

*Of course, there were other reasons for the PDP/8's success. It filled a gap in the market. These factors are discussed further in Chapter 10.

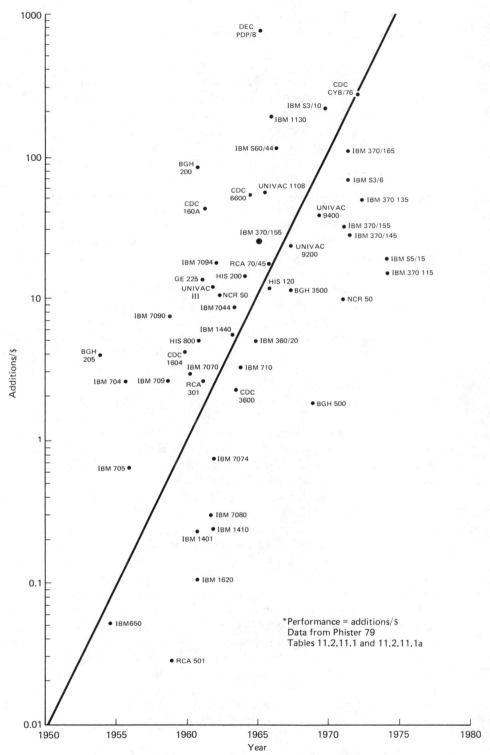

Figure 8.3 System performance trend (Data from M. Phister, *Data Processing Technology and Economics,* 2nd ed. (Santa Fe, N. Mex.: Santa Monica/Bedford, Mass.: Digital Press, 1979), Tables 11.2.11.1, 11.2.11.1a.)

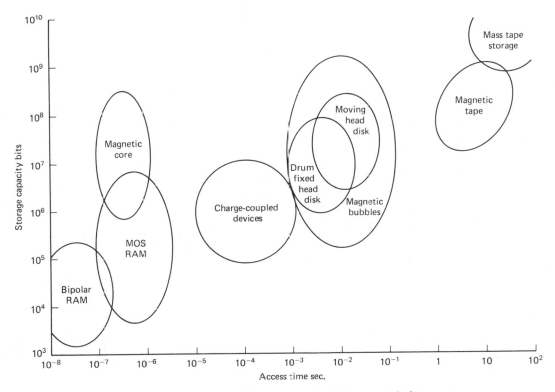

Figure 8.4   Performance trade-offs in storage devices

price in cents per bit plotted against access time. In fact, there have always tended to be gaps in the regions corresponding to different storage technologies and this is why so much effort has been devoted to the search for new devices (Theis, 1980).

Figure 8.6 shows cost trends for various storage technologies. Note the sudden disappearance at about 1972 of magnetic core as the main high-speed memory, with the appearance of semiconductor memories which are both faster and cheaper.* Note also the leveling off in cost for magnetic tapes as physical limitations on the number of bits that could be stored per inch (due to the presence of dust particles in even clean environments) and in the speed at which tape can be moved took over. After 1980 thin magnetic films were introduced, allowing higher recording density, and the tolerances in mechanical systems became even finer, so that the leveling trend was reversed and cost again continued to decrease for a time. In 1973, IBM introduced Winchester disk systems which were completely enclosed from the outside environment, significantly increasing reliability.

*However, semiconductor memories are volatile (i.e., their contents are lost when power is switched off), while magnetic cores retain their contents, so that the displacement has posed some technical problems.

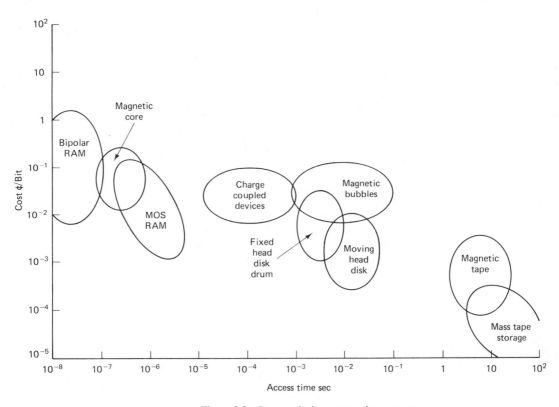

Figure 8.5   Storage devices access time vs cost

Dramatic decreases in cost for large storage systems are possible with optical disks, in which data are recorded in the form of extremely fine holes burned on the disk with a laser beam. However, this technology does not permit rewriting data, so its primary use is as a mass archival storage medium, and it is not likely to completely replace magnetic disks.

Figure 8.7 shows the performance and price trends for a particular storage technology, large moving-head files.* Besides the access time, maximum data transfer rate is plotted as a performance measure. This is in addition to the other measure that we have already noted for storage, cost/capacity, so the overall performance behavior depends on *three* factors—access time, storage cost, and data rate—complicating the situation. Brechtlein (1978) observes that there is an almost inverse relation between price and capacity. We could determine a regression where price per bit depended on both access time *and* total capacity, but the

---

*The considerable spread is due to several reasons. There *is* a systematic difference in the performance from disks of different manufacturers. Also, when a new model is introduced, there is likely to be an appreciable difference in the price of disks based on the older model.

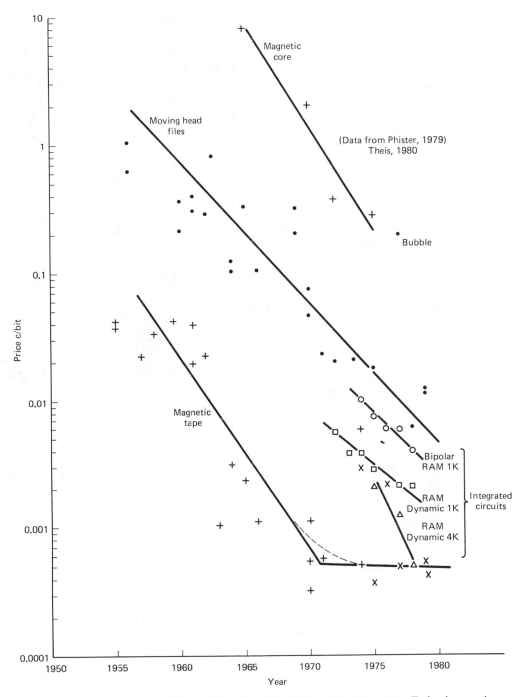

Figure 8.6 Storage cost trends (Data from M. Phister, *Data Processing Technology and Economics,* 2nd ed. (Santa Fe, N. Mex.: Santa Monica/Bedford, Mass.: Digital Press, 1979): and D. Theis, "An Overview of Memory Techniques," *Datamation,* 26, no. 1 (January 1980), 113–29.)

plots shown in Fig. 8.7, where performance is defined in terms of a single variable, make it simpler to examine the trade-off between performance and price.

As mentioned in connection with the system performance trend, Fig. 8.3, and as pointed out in Bell et al. (1978), such trend lines are useful in marketing analysis. Besides being able to pinpoint systems which are most marketable, the performance versus time line and the price versus time line together imply a performance versus price trade-off, since increments in performance and price can each be expressed as an increment in time. Suppose that for the price, P, the trend line $P = P_0 e^{-p(t - t_0)}$ is observed ($P = P_0$ at $t = t_0$), while performance X has the line $X = X_0 e^{x(t - t_0)}$. Then $\ln P = \ln P_0 - pt + pt_0$ and $\Delta P / P = -p \, \Delta t$ or $\Delta P / pP = -\Delta t$. Similarly, $\Delta X / xX = \Delta t$. Thus at any given time a decrease in performance, ΔX, can be compensated for by a corresponding decrease in price of $\Delta P = (pP / xX) \, \Delta X$.

For example, from Fig. 8.7, the price, P, in dollars per kilobytes, for moving-head files is approximated by the equation

$$P = 2e^{-2.67(t - 1965)} \qquad \$/\text{Kbytes}$$

Also, the maximum data rate, D, in Kbytes per second, is approximated by

$$D = 90e^{0.215(t - 1965)} \qquad \text{Kbytes/sec}$$

In the marketplace a decrease in maximum data rate of $\Delta D = 10$ Kbytes/sec should be accompanied by a decrease in price of

$$\frac{2.67}{0.215} \times \frac{P}{D} \times 10 = 124 \, \frac{P}{D}$$

In 1970, when $P = 0.58$ \$/Kbyte and $D = 265$ Kbytes/sec, a decrease in the maximum data rate of 10 Kbytes/sec should have meant a price decrease of $124 \times 0.58 / 265 = 0.27$ \$/Kbyte. A similar calculation could be carried out using the average access times as a performance measure, or as suggested above, using a measure based on access time, maximum capacity, and data transfer rate.

As a final example of performance trends for hardware, Fig. 8.8 shows the increase in printing speed for commercial line-at-a-time (as distinct from character-at-a-time) printers between 1950 and 1979. As different mechanisms were introduced there was a systematic increase in printing speed, leading off at about 1200 lines per minute in 1965. For each mechanism there has been a tendency to market two or more versions of the printer: a high-speed version and lower-speed versions at less cost.

During the interval a variety of low-speed printers using different technologies have evolved for use with terminals. In these situations lower-quality printing is often acceptable, so that the costs per character are significantly less than the costs for line printers. Alternatively, screens are common with

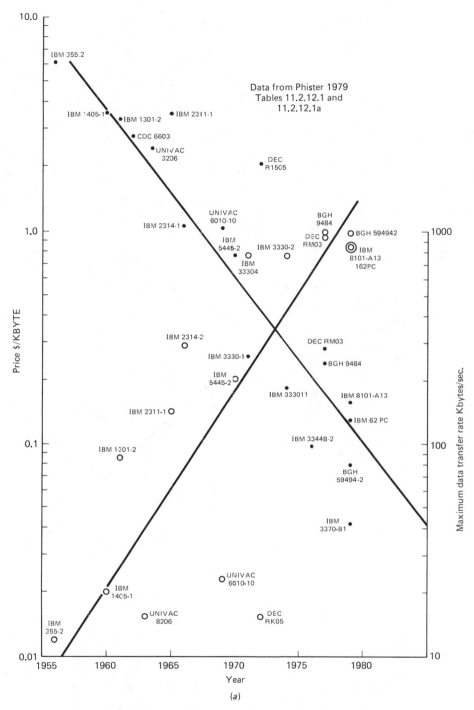

Figure 8.7 (a) Large moving-head files trends in price and maximum data transfer rate; (b) Large moving-head files trend in average access time (Data from M. Phister, *Data Processing Technology and Economics,* 2nd ed. (Santa Fe, N. Mex.: Santa Monica/Bedford, Mass.: Digital Press, 1979), Tables 11.2.12.1, 11.2.12.1a.

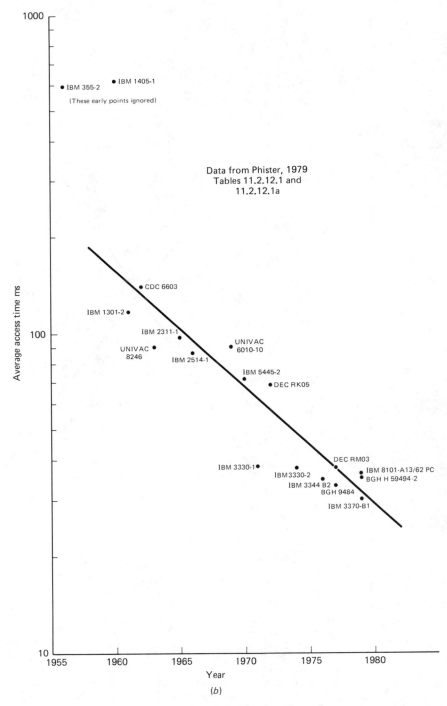

Figure 8.7 (Continued)

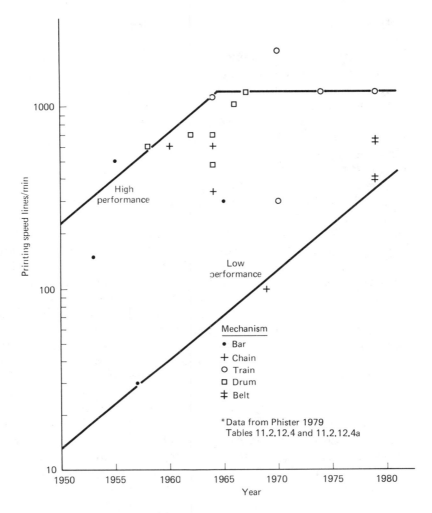

Figure 8.8   Price trend for mechanical line printers (Data from M. Phister, *Data Processing Technology and Economics,* 2nd ed. (Santa Fe, N. Mex.: Santa Monica/Bedford, Mass.: Digital Press, 1979). Tables 11.2.12.4, 11.2.12.4a.

terminals, and for these it would be possible to trace the improvements in resolution, number of characters per line and per page, color presentation, and so on. More recently, there have been very high speed laser printers, based on xerographic and fiber-optic principles. For very high volume products these compete with impact printers.

In a similar way, cost and performance trends could be plotted for all the many peripheral units associated with computers. What has been illustrated here suggests the kind of information that can be derived from observing these hardware trends.

8.2. SYSTEM AND APPLICATION SOFTWARE

The need to program computers was recognized as soon as they were conceived, but initially this task was thought to be less challenging and less demanding than getting the machines to work or making them compute faster. It was therefore left to women! Lady Lovelace's dissertation on programming Babbage's analytical engine is a fascinating historical record, and in the early days of computing in the United States, the Harvard relay computers and ENIAC were programmed almost exclusively by women.* Through the 1950s and 1960s software was either provided free by manufacturers together with hardware, or it was exchanged informally at users' group meetings. It is generally accepted that the cost of this so-called "free" software is really included in the hardware purchase price, and it is estimated that approximately 25% of the hardware price can be attributed to software. The *possibility* of a software industry emerged in 1969 when IBM, partly in response to continued threats of antitrust actions, "unbundled" software from hardware (i.e., introduced the policy of charging separately for some of the software distributed with its computers). Although this move was of ultimate benefit to users, for it encouraged the commercial production of high-quality software, the software industry grew very slowly, partly because of uncertainty as to whether software, as an intellectual property, is best protected through patents or through copyrights. The main form of protection now adopted for software is through trade agreements, and through certain technical features incorporated into the programs. There are still some important unresolved issues about protection and whether software is to be regarded as a tangible or intangible asset (the distinction is reflected in different rules for investment tax credits, depreciation, and sales tax†). Nevertheless, these uncertainties have not prevented the software industry from growing rapidly since the late 1970s. The amount and variety of packaged software is increasing sharply, and this growth in volume and variety is an indicator of the increased use of computers and the technological dissemination of knowledge about computer application skills.

Much software is still distributed by computer manufacturers who either continue to make it available without cost together with hardware, or who do not report separately on software revenues. Software houses that market packages may also do contractual programming for individual customers, so revenues are not in themselves a good measure of the volume of software distributed. Some statistics on revenues are presented in Chapter 9, but for this section, to indicate the technological development of software, attention is focused on the variety of software and on the changing nature of the product.

Software is designated as belonging to either of two classes: system software

---

*For a discussion of the sociology of programming, see Kraft (1977).

†In the United States, different states apply different rules for taxing software. For example, in 1982 California exempted custom software from state sales tax, but continued to levy sales taxes on packaged software ("Software Tax Break," 1982).

or application software. System software programs help the computer carry out all tasks efficiently. Examples are assembling routines and data so that they are brought into high-speed storage when needed, translating the statements of a procedure-oriented language such as COBOL into the machine language code capable of being executed by the computer, and managing resources such as memory and I/O devices. Table 8.1 lists the principal kinds of system software. Application software consists of specialized programs dedicated to well-defined processes needed by users. Examples are systems for production control, calculating payrolls, or for carrying out statistical analysis and predictions on market reports.

Chapter 1 detailed the reasons why it is so difficult to rate the overall performance of computer hardware, although, as seen in the preceding section, there are obvious rating factors for individual components. Software performance and quality are even more difficult to judge. It is easy enough to define some simple measures of speed and program compactness:

- The number of statements compiled per minute
- The time to compile and execute the null statement

TABLE 8.1 SYSTEM SOFTWARE

Type	Functions	Examples (Supplier)
Operating systems	Program and data read-in	MVS/XA (IBM)
Resource managers	Job scheduling and accounting	Unix (AT&T)
Communication handlers	Memory management; resource scheduling (I/O devices, channels, communication devices)	CP/M 86 (Digital Research)
Performance monitors	Evaluating system software	Look (Applied Data Research)
Language processors	Programming, compiling, interpreting, executing statements in high-level programming language	Fortran, COBOL, APL, Pascal, Basic
Utilities		
Report generators	Report preparation	RPG (IBM)
Sort generators	Sorting and merging files	SynSort (SynSort Technology)
Program development aids	Program development	
File management systems	File and data base management	Mark IV (Informatics)
Librarians	Tape and program library management	Panvalet (Pansophic Systems Inc.)
Data-entry systems	Data preparation	

- The number of lines of code in the source program
- The number of lines of code in the object program

Even when comparative figures on these measures are available it is difficult to draw conclusions about performance because there is so much variation in the conditions under which the measurements are made. But as machine speed and size of memory have increased, such factors have become less important, and there is general agreement that the *quality* of the software should be the principal concern. Quality is determined by correctness, reliability, and ease of use. The last, especially, is subjective and very difficult to measure. If n_f failures are observed in n runs of a program, the reliability R can be defined as $R = 1 - \lim_{n \to \infty} n_f/n$ (Ramanworthy and Bastani, 1982). Eventually, reliability is determined by the number of corrections that have to be issued for the program, and it very much influences the cost of maintenance. It would be desirable to have measures that would recognize when software is complex, so that the complexity could be reduced or the software subjected to more strenuous testing before release. Considerable work has been done in attempting to define software metrics which would measure complexity and correlate well with reliability (see Bowen, 1978). Halstead defines a number of counts for a program module, and then derives quantities intended to measure complexity and difficulty (see Halstead, 1977). If, for the module,

$$n_1 = \text{number of } distinct \text{ operators in a program}$$
$$n_2 = \text{number of } distinct \text{ operands}$$
$$N_1 = total \text{ number of operators}$$
$$N_2 = total \text{ number of operands}$$

then the number of distinct tokens, $n = n_1 + n_2$, is defined as the *vocabulary* of the module; $N = N_1 + N_2$ is the *length* of the module and $V = N \log_2 n$ is the *volume*. Halstead suggested that $N = n_1 \log_2 n_1 + n_2 \log_2 n_2$ would be a good estimator for length, and V a good estimator for the number of lines of code. Observations on programs show that these quantities *are* correlated as suggested (Christensen et al., 1981). Halstead went on to argue that the *difficulty, D,* of a program is estimated by $n_1 N_2 / 2n_2$. McCabe defines a different complexity measure based on the decision structure of the program when viewed as a flow graph. If e is the number of edges in the graph, n the number of nodes, and p the number of components, the cyclomatic number of the graph, $C = e - n + 2p$, is taken as the measure. (For a single-component program, C = number of decisions + 1.) Comparisons of the number of errors found in actual programs with measures such as C and $D,$ or with other measures based on different counting rules, show some correlation (see Gross et al., 1982; Hartman, 1982; and Lipow, 1982). Hall and Preiser (1984) also discuss the Halstead and McCabe measures of program complexity, as well as some others, and give indications of their usefulness, but there is no generally accepted metric of program complexity derivable from an a priori analysis of the program code* which can serve as a precise indicator of the number of errors to be expected in the program. Other, more subjective features of the quality of software, such as ease of use, quality of documentation, and satisfaction with the product and vendor, are reported in user surveys conducted by Datamation, Auerbach, and Datapro. The most effective ways of improving ease of use have centered on better displays, such as those developed around Xerox's Star and Apple's Lisa computers (depending on such features as windows which allow several programs to be worked on simultaneously, and icons as mnemonic aids), together with alternatives to keyboard inputs, such as the "mouse."

In evaluating software it is important to note the role that standards have played for language processors especially, but to a lesser degree for operating systems as well. Standards make software more acceptable because costs are lowered where programs are portable and when people trained in the standardized procedures are available. In a report published by the Bureau d'Orientation de la Normalisation en Informatique, France's standards office, the cost of incompatibility was estimated to be 26% of the total resources expended on computers. COBOL, which is used in an estimated 80% of business applications, gained acceptance from its very beginnings because of the insistence of the U.S. Department of Defense that COBOL be provided on any computer that it bought. At the Compiling Testing Center of the General Service Administration (GSA), programs are submitted to tests containing about 300 programs, with some 350,000 lines of code, designed to utilize every function of the 1974 ANSI COBOL Standard. Intensive standardization is still being done on COBOL, on other languages such as FORTRAN and Pascal, and on Ada, which is to be an eventual replacement of COBOL. For operating systems the standards are not as formal as those for languages, but particular systems are emerging as de facto standards. Two operating systems, CP/M (Control Program, Microcomputers), developed by Digital Research, and MS/DOS, developed by Microsoft, have become widely accepted micro and personal computers. Also, Unix, developed by the Bell Telephone Laboratories and marketed through AT&T, has moved beyond the scientific computing establishments, where it was first used, to become a de facto standard for systems of all sizes, although it exists in many variant forms.

If the trend toward standardization is a sign of the growing maturity of system software, the *variety* of packages and the number of suppliers are indicators of the growth and spread of application software. As the number of computer installations has grown, the uses to which computers have been put has increased correspondingly. But for a long time most application software continued to be custom made, written by the user. What is striking since 1980 is

---

*Surprisingly, V. Basili and B. Perricone present empirical data to suggest that during program development the number of errors per 1000 executable lines of code *decreases* with cyclomatic complexity. See "Software Errors and Complexity: An Empirical Investigation," *Commun. ACM,* 27, no. 1 (January 1984), 42–52.

the sharp increase in the number of vendors of *packaged* software and in the number of products they offer. The categories shown in Table 8.2 just begin to suggest the available applications. Many directories are published regularly (see *Datapro 70, International Directory of Software, International Software Directory, LIST,* and the *Software Catalog*). In March 1979, *Datapro* listed about 900 vendors offering 5000 packages; in September 1982 about 2000 vendors offered 6200 packages for programs on minicomputers and larger systems. The number of packages for minicomputers and personal computers is growing even faster, and listings of the International Software Database are available through the Lockheed DIALOG service. Some industries are particularly receptive to packaged software; a survey taken by the American Bankers Association in 1978 showed that of the 1040 banks that responded, 583 had acquired 6257 packages which were used in 46 different applications.

Programming started as a branch of mathematics concerned with the representation and analysis of algorithms capable of being executed on computers. Logic and mathematical reasoning are still central to programming, but during the 1960s and 1970s the activity expanded to become what is best described as "software engineering." The size of programs and programming teams, and the magnitude of the effort needed to produce programs, made it necessary to bring in techniques developed in engineering for managing projects where scientific knowledge, technical skills, and economic factors are all important. With the spread of packages, software entered into a new phase where the ability to use a computer to carry out a task does not depend on the existence of an algorithm or on being able to construct the program, but rather on the ability to *use* an existing product, possibly without fully understanding how it works. This spread significantly affects the rate of introduction of best practices in science, engineering, and management to everyday situations. It means that methodologies that are known only to researchers and experts, or used mainly by organizations with considerable resources at their disposal, become much more generally available. This diffusion of best practice to become common practice is just what is meant by technological dissemination. It can be illustrated by the remarkable way in which VisiCalc, Multiplan, and similar programs, marketed first for microcomputers, then for other systems, found immediate acceptance. VisiCalc is a financial planning program. Amounts are displayed on a screen in matrix format; the effects of changing a variable or parameter are calculated by the computer and displayed at once. In this way it is very easy to carry out a planning process under a whole variety of "what if" conditions, and the powerful techniques of scenario and sensitivity analyses become available to those who might never have heard of them.

Although the software side of computer technology is just as old as the hardware, few would argue that it has developed to the same degree of excellence. Much remains to be done in evaluating software and in improving production techniques and the quality of products. Yet it has progressed from a mathematical, problem-solving activity, through an engineering methodology, to an industry

TABLE 8.2 CATEGORIES OF APPLICATION SOFTWARE PACKAGES

Accounting
  Accounts payable/receivable
  Billing
  Contractor/construction
  Fixed assets
  General
  Ledger
  Professional accounting/billing
  Tax
  Utility billing/municipal
Banking and finance
  Check credit
  Commercial loans
  Customer information file
  Demand deposit
  Financial control/planning
  Funds transfer
  Installment loans
  Integrated systems
  General banking systems
  Mortgage loans
  On-line terminal control
  Savings/time deposits
  Stock/bond management
  Trust accounting
Database management
Editing and word processing
  Indexing
  Letter writing/mailing
  Office management aids
  Subscription fulfillment
  Text/file editing
  Word processing
Educational applications
  Administration
  Admissions
  Career guidance
  Computer-aided instruction
  Computer training
  Counseling
  Financial management
  Inventory control
  Library circulation control
  Response evaluation
  Skills testing
  Student information systems
  Test scoring
Energy conservation and management
Engineering and scientific applications
  Aerospace
  Automotive

Engineering and scientific applications
  (Continued)
  Aviation
  Chemical
  Communications
  Construction/architecture
  Electrical engineering
  Flow analysis
  Graphic arts
  Petroleum/fuel industry
  Pipeline networks
  Textiles
Facilities security and protection
Farming
Games
  Arithmetic
  Mathematical
  Musical
  Word games
Government
  Court administration and scheduling
  Patents and trademarks
  Public safety
Graphics
Hotel and motel management
Insurance
  Contract administration
  Estate planning
  Finance/accounting
  Financial planning
  Group benefit programs
  Independent agents and brokers
  Investment portfolio management
  Life and health insurance
  Mortgage loan systems
  Property and liability
  Statement generation
Library
  Cataloging
  Circulation management
  Indexing
  Interlibrary loan
  Medical
  Periodicals
  Reference
Mailing lists
Management sciences
  Employee productivity assessment
  Forecasting, modeling, and simulation
  Project planning and control

TABLE 8.2 (Continued)

Manufacturing
  Activity planning
  Bill-of-materials processing
  Customer order survey
  Financial operating
  Information systems
  Inventory management
  Job cost control
  Master production scheduling
  Material requirement planning
  Packaging management
  Plant equipment maintenance
  Testing and quality control
  Tool engineering
Mathematics and statistics
Media management
  Film booking
  Film library management
Medical and health care
  Admissions/discharge/transfer
  Ambulatory care
  Appointment scheduling
  Blood banks
  Claims administration
Payroll and personnel
  Employee services and benefits
  General payroll
  Personnel management
  Special payrolls
Personal
  Astrology
  Biorhythms
  Health and diet
  Hobbies

Personal (Continued)
  Household management
  Music
  Sports
Programming aids
  Application program development
  Conversion
  Cross-assemblers
  Cross-compilers
  Cross-reference lists
  Flowcharting
  High-level languages
  Preprocessors and program generators
  Program documentation
  Screen-oriented aids
  Simulators
  Testing and debugging
Real estate management
Sales and distribution
  Distributor information systems
  Food and beverage systems
  Inventory management
  Order processing
  Real estate
  Retail systems
  Sales accounting
  Sales management
  Special-purpose distribution systems
  Tracking systems
  Warehouse management
  Wholesale distributor systems
Statistics
Time management
Transportation
Word processing

with a strong market base. The boundary line between software and hardware is not static. Many functions that start by being carried out in software end up by being realized as hardware, or perhaps embedded in read-only memory in what is known as *firmware*. But software, always an integral part of the computer technology, is perhaps the aspect that is now developing most rapidly. The growth of technology will undoubtedly be critically dependent on advances in the design, production, and dissemination of software.

8.3. DATA COMMUNICATIONS

Traditionally, the communications industry has been regarded as an example of what economists call a "natural monopoly." Users are better off if a single agency operates a network, for then they will be able to communicate with all other subscribers to the service. As a result, in most countries communication organizations are government run, by the so-called PTTs (Postal, Telephone, and Telecommunication) agencies. In the United States and Canada different types of services are allotted to different private companies—the common carriers—and because of the monopoly (which can be regional or depend on the type of service), a regulatory agency ensures that profits are not excessive and that there is no discrimination in offering service.* This historical picture of a government-owned or highly regulated communication industry is, of course, quite different from that of the computer industry, which in the industrialized (nonsocialist) countries has been relatively free of regulation.

When the need arose, in the 1950s, to exchange data between computers, the communication networks, built to handle analog voice data, were adapted to take digital information by providing termination devices in the form of data sets or modems (modulator/demodulators) which converted the digital signals into the continuous waveforms needed for transmission over telephone lines. The capital investment needed for a communication network is very high, and originally the common carriers and PTTs were the sole providers of both channels and termination devices for converting data. But computer users came to feel that the carriers, concerned mainly with voice and video traffic, were not responsive to the special requirements of data communications. Data traffic, as compared with voice traffic, is much more "bursty" (i.e., less continuous), is more penalized by the comparatively long time needed to establish a connection, and is much more sensitive to errors in transmission. Eventually, governments were prevailed upon to open up the market by allowing private companies to compete in offering interconnection devices between computers and the carriers lines and, first in the United States and then in other countries, to establish other, specialized common carriers (OCCs) which concentrated on data needs in restricted areas.

The largest common carriers in the United States are American Telephone and Telegraph (AT&T), General Telephone and Electric (GTE), and United Telecommunications. The largest specialized carrier is TYMNET, a subsidiary of the Tymshare computer services company. AT&T and its former Bell subsidiaries have dominated telephone service, accounting for some 80% of local calls and 96% of long-distance calls. With the separation of AT&T (together with Bell Telephone Laboratories and its manufacturing arm, Western Electric) from the 7 local operating companies as a result of the 1982 consent decree of the Justice Department (see Section 10.3), the operating companies continue to be the major providers for home telephone service. However, major technological developments, such as digital transmission, satellite broadcasting and optical fibers, and rapidly growing markets for data communications, cable and long-

*The FCC (Federal Communications Commission) in the United States and the CRTC (Canadian Radio and Telecommunications Commission) in Canada.

line services, and specialized networks, have provided opportunities for many new suppliers and carriers. So rapid is the pace of change that the communications technology and industry are expected to continue in a state of flux for decades, both in the United States and in other countries.

8.3.1. Basic Services and Tariffs

Because communication equipment and services are so important to a computer system, we wish to examine some of the options. Designing the communications segment of a computerized network is a highly technical task. Factors such as the choice of multiplexers or concentrators (devices intended to make more efficient use of telephone channels by sharing them among terminals), or the actual configuration of a network, will not be considered here. For such designs, see Martin (1972), Schwarz (1977), or Tanenbaum (1981). Only some of the simpler aspects of communication costs will be discussed: those relating to the cost of the lines and of the termination equipment. Even then, only illustrative rates will be given, because the tariff system is enormously complicated and detailed, and any attempt to describe it in depth would be well beyond the scope of this book. Phister (1979) presents a good overview and comparison of the multiplicity of offerings in historical perspective, but services and prices are subject to constant revision, all the more so since the 1982 consent decree, and for accurate information it is necessary to go directly to the providers of the services.

Data transmission may be simplex (one way), half duplex (either way, but in only one direction at a time), or full duplex (simultaneous, two-way). The cost for full duplex is usually about 10% greater than that for half duplex, and it is the generally accepted mode for data because of the need to acknowledge receipt of messages. Line costs depend on four principal factors—line speed (measured in bits per second, bps, or baud*), distance, duration of service, and time of service—but the exact tariff structure is extremely complicated, depending on which points are being interconnected (high traffic density rates have lower unit costs), the existence of competition, government regulation, and history.

The carriers provide low-speed transmission facilities (e.g., 1200-baud voice-grade channels or 60-bps teletype channels) by dividing up the bandwidth available from high-speed links, and the cost per bit transmitted at high speed

---

*Baud and bits per second are synonymous here. It is important to realize that neither is actually the data rate. Every communication protocol carries with it a certain overhead. This overhead takes the form of start/stop bits, synchronization and block delimiting characters, error-checking characters or bits (parity, checksum) and line-turnaround time (when communicating two-way on a half-duplex line). Thus, if we assume that 8 bits are required for 1 byte, 300 baud implies $300/8 = 37.5$ bytes/sec transmitted, but the actual number of data bytes transmitted will be less, by up to 30% for reasonable protocols. Higher overhead occurs in specialized systems where correctness of data is paramount and the communications channel is noisy. In such cases much redundant information is transmitted, and overhead can reach hundreds of percent. Assuming an overhead in the range 5 to 20%, the number of data bytes transmitted is the baud rate divided by 8, with 5 to 20% subtracted from the result.

can be very much less than the cost per bit for low speed. In other words, it is cheaper (per channel) to acquire one high-speed channel and subdivide it than to acquire several low-speed channels. As technological invention in the last three decades made it possible to transmit at higher and higher frequencies (through UHF, to microwave and optical frequencies), the cost savings available from the ability to subdivide channels became more and more important. With the appropriate equipment this subdivision can be done by the computer service center (using purchased or rented equipment), by the computer supplier, by a specialized carrier, or by a common carrier. Moreover, some of the principal tasks of the termination equipment relating to handling protocols, storing messages, and correcting errors can be done by either hardware or software. All of this enormously increases the range of options open to users and, of course, the complexity of the already complicated pricing calculations.

The most widespread communication service is direct dialing (DD), which, through a hierarchy of telephone exchanges, provides point-to-point, half-duplex, voice communication capability (typically 1200 baud) all over the world. Using datasets or modems, the DD network can be used for transmitting digital data from terminals or other I/O devices, and voice-grade channels can be combined to provide higher data rates, as would be needed, for example, when a magnetic tape unit of one computer is read by another situated remotely. A DD call starts with a setup phase, during which a connection is established between the communicating stations. A message exchange phase ensues, during which a channel is dedicated to the call, and a disconnect phase completes the transaction. Very often the *local loop* that connects a telephone to the nearest exchange has to be adjusted if the error rate for transmitting digital data is to be kept to a satisfactorily low level, a process known as *conditioning*. Within a small geographic region, whose size depends on the density of telephones, there is a flat monthly rate for DD service. Outside this region the charges vary with distance and time of day and increase incrementally with duration. Until January 1984, when the consent decree that separated AT&T from its operating companies went into effect, both local and long-distance rates were subject to strict regulation, and they were generally allowed to increase slowly with inflation. Since then, there has been much competition and change in long-distance rates, but it is useful to examine the earlier rate structure to obtain an idea of the types of services available.

Phister notes that the AT&T line charges for DD service at speed from 300 to 4800 baud are given (approximately) by an equation of the form

$$C_L' = t(a + b \log_{10} D)f_p \tag{8.1}$$

where C_L' = cost for the line, dollars

t = time, minutes

D = distance between service points, miles

f_p = a factor dependent on the period of service ($f_p = 1$ for daytime, 0.67 for evenings, and 0.40 for nights and weekends)

In 1980, a equaled 0.07 and b was 0.095. To these costs there needs to be added C_S, the monthly rental for the data set, which depends on the speed of service. For DD service, C_S for the two data sets (one at each end) was, in 1980:

Speed (baud)	300	1200	2400	4800
C_S ($/month)	54	78	117	257

Heavy users of communication facilities can use a variety of services which are advantageous under different conditions. WATS (wide-area telecommunication service) permits low-cost use of the DD system over a specified area. For example, using 4800-baud WATS within a radius of 124 miles there is a 10-hour minimum use costing $130, after which the rate is $10 per hour. Thus

$$C_L' = 130 + 10t \qquad t \geq 10 \text{ hours}$$

Besides this "measured time" WATS, there is also an unlimited-use service for which the costs range between $500 and $850 per month in a 100-mile radius. In addition, there is 50,000-baud service, which, in the 124-mile radius, comes to $0.80 per minute.

Instead of using the DD network between two cities, a customer can lease a dedicated private line from the carrier. At each end of the line there can be a data set or a private branch exchange (PBX) giving access to the local DD network. Although the DD local rates did not change significantly for two decades, AT&T charges for private lines have continued to decrease dramatically, particularly for high-speed facilities. Private-line charges are at two levels, depending on whether service is between cities of high-density traffic (there are about 350 of these in the United States) or between localities with low-density traffic. For private lines the line charge, in dollars per month (1980), was

$$C_L = 128 + 0.85D \qquad \text{high density}$$

$$C_L = 88 + 2.5D \qquad \text{low density}$$

(8.2)

for line capacities up to 9600 baud, where D is the distance in miles. The additional cost, C_s, for data sets is

Speed (baud)	300	1200	2400	4800	9600
C_s ($/month)	44	32	123	275	545

For a restricted number of cities AT&T offers DDS, another version of private-line service, for which

$$C = C_S + D \times F_s \qquad (8.3)$$

where

Speed (baud)	2400	4800	9600	56,000
C_S	201	261	331	594
F_S	.60	.90	1.30	6.00

In addition to these (and many other) AT&T services, in certain areas of high-traffic volume there are the offerings of the specialized common carriers. These services are generally similar to those of AT&T, competing in price, availability, or quality.

Beside the basic line and termination costs, for which examples have been given, certain other costs have to be taken into account in calculating the overall costs of a communication system. There are installation costs, almost invariably line conditioning costs, and in some cases software costs. Moreover, just as the effective data rate of a computer I/O device is less than the nominal data rate because of start/stop or seek times, interrecord gaps, and extra characters, the effective rate of a communical channel is less than the nominal rate because of protocols, line turnaround times (for half duplex), and error checks. Considerable savings can be realized by using multiplexers or concentrators to share a high-speed line among several terminals. The exact calculation of costs for a communication system is a highly technical and specialized activity, but some rules of thumb can be observed about the line charges.

1. For very low volume use, DD with the slowest dataset (300 baud) is adequate. As the number of bits transmitted in a month increases, at some point it pays to go to a higher-speed data set, then to switch to private lines, then to go on to still higher speed services.

Between each two service levels there is a break-even point. For example, let N be the number of megabits (Mb) in a month for the break-even between the lowest-speed DD 300-baud and the 1200-baud service. Since 300 baud correspond to 18 kb/min, the time to transmit N megabits (assuming completely efficient lines) = $55.5N$ minutes. The cost for the 300-baud service is $55.5N(0.07 + 0.095 \log D) + 54$. The cost for the 1200-baud service is $55.5N/4(0.07 + 0.095 \log D) + 78$. For $D = 300$ miles these are equal when

$$0.16.94N = 4.23N + 24 \text{ or } N = 1.89 \text{ Mb}$$

corresponding to 105 minutes at 300 baud.

2. From these break-even points it is possible to derive a curve showing the cost/bit $vs.$ volume transmitted, using the cheapest mode for a given distance. For example, at 300 miles, since 300-baud DD service is least costly until 1.89

Mb is transmitted in a month, the time to transmit 1 Mb at this service $= 10^6/$ $300 \times 60 = 55.5$ minutes. The cost for this service (300 miles, daytime) is $71, so that one point on the 300-mile curve is 1 Mb per month and $71 per month. In the resulting curve the cost per megabit decreases sharply as the monthly volume increases, starting at $71 per megabit for 1 Mb per month and dropping to about $0.01 per megabit for 100 billion megabits per month.*

3. The dependence of the cost upon distance is complicated because of the existence of low-density rates and DDS in selected cities. DDS, where it is offered, always costs less than a low-density private line. Going from A to B, it may be preferable to use an available DDS service to an intermediate point C rather than using low-density service between A and B.

When the existence of WATS, other services, such as TELEPAC (which is cost advantageous for high-speed lines over long distances) and the packet-switched services described in the next section, are taken into account, the possibilities increase, and choosing the least-cost service becomes even more complicated. In general, the addition of higher-grade services has brought communication costs down steadily for high volumes, a trend accelerated by the entry of the specialized carriers. But the cost for the low-speed services (voice grade and below) was fairly constant for two decades, previous to deregulation.†

8.3.2 Value-Added and Other Networks

The specialized services offered by OCCs are not merely different in price from those of AT&T. They can be different in quality, and OCCs can provide them over their own lines or over lines leased from AT&T but which are configured into networks with additional capabilities: that is, *value-added networks* (VANs). Examples are the packet- and message-switching services marketed by Tymnet and International Telegraph and Telecommunications (ITT) in the United States and by TransCanada Telephone System (TCTS) in Canada.

Packet-switched networks operate differently from those discussed previously in one crucial aspect: There is no logical (much less physical) continuous path between communicating points. Data take the form of blocks, typically 1000 to 2000 bytes in length. These blocks are sent from source to destination by being passed along from node to node, each node being a computer capable of executing a variety of tasks, including receiving, checking, storing, and forwarding the packets. Because of the intelligence at each node, dynamic rerouting is possible: If the shortest route is busy or nonfunctional the computer at that node can reroute the packet, perhaps in a roundabout manner. This allows great

---

*For a given distance there is an approximately linear relation between log (cost/Mb) and log (number of bits transmitted per month). See Phister (1979, Fig. 2.14.5).

†However, AT&T has argued that long-distance charges have, for a long time, subsidized local charges. With the divestiture of the local operating companies, the long-distance rates, subject to competition, are decreasing appreciably (see Section 10.3). The local operating companies, with success, are arguing for significant increases and for charges to access the local net.

flexibility and robustness in the system. At no time is there a direct path established between sender and receiver. The system depends on the speed of the nodal computers for its fast response time, and on the flexibility of routing for its reliability. Packet-switching networks are advantageous for transaction-type processing and for sending relatively short messages. The pricing structure reflects this.

For a typical packet-switching service there are charges for:

- Terminal access (from user site to the local processor based on connect time and terminal speed)
- The carrier's processor, depending on its speed, number of users, and so on.
- The number of kilobytes transmitted (e.g., 10 cents per kilobyte for the first 80,000 in the month, with a lower rate for additional bytes)

Alternatively, a subscriber may lease a dedicated port and line to the host processor for a fixed monthly rate, with no extra charges for connect time or characters transmitted. Unlike AT&T's charges, distance is a relatively unimportant factor in the rate structure.

Packet switching grew more slowly than was anticipated when commercial service was introduced in the late 1970s. But as well as advantages in reliability and the ability to handle a variety of equipment, there are distinct savings for large volume over long distances, and this service has become an increasingly important segment of data communications.

The volume of data communication traffic has been less than 10% of the total communications traffic, and it is not expected to exceed that fraction by much. This has important consequences. Economies of scale dictate that it is more efficient to build *integrated service networks*—those which combine voice, video, and data traffic—rather than separate networks for each type of service. This, in turn, means that companies which have traditionally operated in one range are attracted by opportunities elsewhere, so there is a blurring of the lines of distinction between different carriers. Another consequence is that the advantages of digital versus analog transmission for data communications favor the installation of digital networks generally, so that they become *integrated data service networks* (IDSNs). The most economical way of introducing digital networks is to bring in new exchanges through evolutionary upgrading. Just as the 4-KHz voice channel is the main building block of the older analog networks, the 64-kbps channel is the accepted building block for digital networks. In the United States approximately 2% of main lines were connected to digital exchanges in 1980; this is expected to increase to approximately 9% by 1985 and to 25 to 30% by 1990.

Nothing illustrates the proliferation of communication companies and services in the United States better than the number of domestic communication satellites. Table 8.3 lists U.S. operating and proposed satellite systems at the end of 1982. For an international listing, see Jansky (1983). While the earlier

TABLE 8.3 OPERATING AND PROPOSED SATELLITE SYSTEMS IN
THE UNITED STATES

Satellite	Date of Launch	Operated by:	Mission
WESTAR-I WESTAR-II WESTAR-III	4/74 10/74 8/79	Western Union Telegraph Company	Fully integrated satellite/terrestrial communications, network voice, video, message, and data (12 C-band transponders)
WESTAR-IV	2/82		Replace Westar I and II (24 C-band transponders)
WESTAR-V	Proposed		Increase capacity (24 C-band transponders)
Advanced WESTAR I and II	Proposed		Increase capacity (12 C-band transponders) and DBS video service (6 K-band transponders)
SATCOM-I SATCOM-II	12/75 3/76	RCA American Communications, Inc.	Full video, voice, and data network between major U.S. cities (24 C-band transponders)
SATCOM-IV	11/81		Primarily television relay, video, and audio distribution (24 C-band transponders each with 1 video and 1 FM audio)
SATCOM-IR, IIR, IIIR	2/82		Replacements for SATCOM I, II, and III; primarily video and audio distribution to cable and TVROs (24 C-band transponders)
SATCOM-V	Proposed		Primarily television relay, video, and audio distribution (24 C-band transponders each with 1 video and 1 FM audio)
COMSTAR D-1 COMSTAR D-2 COMSTAR D-3 COMSTAR D-4 COMSTAR D-1R COMSTAR D-2R, D-3R	5/76 7/76 6/78 2/82 Proposed replacement for D1 Proposed replacement for D2, D3	COMSTAT for AT&T/GTE	Primarily long-haul telephone/data network service for AT&T; also provides private networks (24 C-band transponders)

TABLE 8.3 (Continued)

Satellite	Date of Launch	Operated by:	Mission
SBS-1 SBS-2 SBS-3	11/81 9/82 11/82	Satellite Business Network (IBM, Aetna Life, and Comsat General)	Integrated private satellite communications network; digital transmission system for telephone, computer link, electronic mail, and video teleconferencing (10 K-band transponders)
MARISTAT-1 MARISTAT-2 MARISTAT-3	2/76 6/76 10/76	COMSAT	Provide global communications for ships with U.S. mainland
GALAXY-1 GALAXY-2 GALAXY-3	1983 1983 1984	Hughes Communications	Primarily a CATV satellite, intended for video/audio program distribution (24 C-band transponders)
GSTAR I GSTAR II, III	Proposed Proposed	GSAT (GT&E Satellite Corporation)	Provide satellite circuits for GTE's Telenet network (16 K-band transponders)
SPACENET-I SPACENET II, III, IV	1984 Proposed	SPCC (Southern Pacific Communications Company)	High-capacity spacecraft with 24 transponders operating at C and K bands; both business and private users of data, message, and video
ASC-1, ASC-2	Proposed 1985–1986	ASC (American Company)	Full communications services in C and K bands

Source: Telespace Information Ltd., Toronto, 1982.

launches were mainly for voice and video services, the second-generation systems, launched since 1981 by Satellite Business Systems, RCA, Macomnet, and others, are targeted at data communications.

Other types of networks are the private local area networks (LANs) offered mainly by computer-based companies for linking together electronic office equipment (printers, terminals, copiers, computers, electronic files) within a building or a closely spaced group of buildings. Typical is Xerox's ETHERNET, operating at 10 Mbps, for which Xerox, Digital Equipment Corporation, and Intel produce compatible equipment. Other examples are PRIMENET (Prime Computer Co.) and WANGNET (Wang Laboratories). ETHERNET works in the "contention mode"; one device wanting to communicate with another waits until the connecting bus appears to be quiet, and then broadcasts its message. Sometimes collisions between messages arise, and it is then necessary to retransmit. Other LANs are built on the "token-passing" principle. A device transmits only when it is in possession of a circulating token which gives it authority to do so. Alternatives to both of these types of LANs are offered by the common carriers in high-speed digital PBXs, which can more easily carry voice and be linked into the public networks. Reception and transmission through rooftop antennas, communicating with direct broadcasting satellites (DBS), increases further the ways in which LANs can communicate remotely.

8.3.3. Standards

Mention has already been made of the role of standards in software. In communications, standards are much more critical; when they are in force, equipment made by different suppliers is compatible and the arguments for monopoly are greatly diminished. Standards are needed for such developments as local area networks to determine both technical and economic directions. So great is the need that on some matters considerable progress has been achieved in a relatively short time. The principal agencies are the International Standards Organization (ISO) and the Comite Consultatif International de Télégraphique et Téléphonique (CCITT). The main contribution of ISO is the adoption of a conceptual seven-layer model, called the Reference Model of Open System Interconnection (OSI), describing how two application processes communicate with one another. The layers reflect the existence of multiple levels in any communication process, even between human beings. At the top level is the semantic exchange of ideas; below that there is a means for communicating by an agreed-upon language; below that there is an agreed-upon mode (voice, telephone, etc.).

The OSI model is illustrated in Fig. 8.9. Although there are protocols and virtual communication between peers at the same levels, only at the lowest level is there physical communication resulting in the flow of data from one machine (called a host) to the other. In between, data flow across the layer interfaces. The physical layer protocol specifies the voltage levels and time durations for the bit stream making up the signal. The data link protocol is designed to deal with transmission errors between the user's equipment and the network. The network protocol specifies methods of addressing, controlling direction, confirming delivery, handling interruptions, and so on. The transport layer deals with breaking up the message into smaller units, if necessary, and reassembling them. The session and presentation layers deal with other aspects of message handling, such as initiating, authenticating, and terminating sessions, or data compression and encryption. The application layer is the responsibility of the individual user.

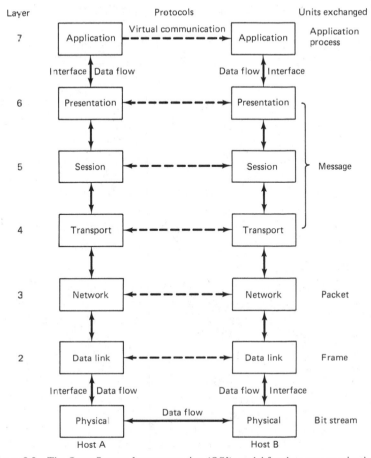

Figure 8.9 The Open System Interconnection (OSI) model for data communications

CCITT initially set protocol standards only for the bottom three layers. Collectively, these are known as X.25; that for the physical layer is X.21. Since much existing equipment does not conform to X.25, interim standards have been described. The X.75 protocols are addressed at the next three layers. It is not likely that standards will be set for the application layer. For a more detailed description of the function of the protocols at the different layers, as well of the standards and how existing networks correspond to these standards, see Tanenbaum (1981) and Martin (1981). Here it is sufficient to realize just how much the existence of these standards influences the marketing opportunities and decisions of computer and communication companies. The need to make existing networks compatible with standards by transforming protocols has greatly broadened the VAN marketplace (VAN, 1982).

8.4. MERGING OF COMPUTERS AND COMMUNICATIONS

The growth of data communications traffic is only one aspect of the merging of the computer and communications technologies. There are at least three major ways in which this convergence is manifest.

1. The underlying technologies, based on very large scale integrated circuits, on pulsed code techniques for handling digital information, and on software and firmware, are common to the two.
2. As a result, companies which have traditionally operated in one of the two areas have had to acquire expertise in the other, and in so doing have naturally expanded their marketing efforts.
3. Users see integrated services which depend equally on the two technologies and expect to have their needs met from one source. This reinforces the trend toward a common supplier.

We examine these in turn.

1. Throughout this book there have been repeated references to the presence of communication equipment in computers; see, for example, the discussions of computer networks in Chapter 4, of time sharing in Section 6.2.2, and of terminals in Section 6.2.3. In like manner it is hardly an exaggeration to regard every modern piece of communication equipment as a special-purpose digital computer. Just as computers have integrated circuit boards, read-only and random-access memories, control units, and programs that may be wired in as firmware or programmable routines, so communication devices such as digital PBXs, concentrators, and front-end processors have these same types of components. The store-and-forward, routing, and error-checking operations carried out in the node of a packet-switched communication network are really specialized computer applications. A "gateway" that connects two computer networks carrying out code conversion, error checking, and protocol interpretation may be regarded as a component of the communication system or an extension of the computer processor. Ownership of the gateway equipment can be vested in the user, a computer company, a common carrier, or a specialized common carrier operating a value-added network. In some countries (e.g., Canada) it has been regarded as important, for regulatory purposes, to be able to draw a sharp distinction between "content" and "carriage" in a communication system. The idea is that the information provider is responsible for the content of a message, while the carrier is responsible for transporting the message. Among other things, this distinction can help in determining obligations for obeying censorship, copyright, libel, and obscenity laws. But the operations that an information provider such as a news agency might do in selecting, preparing, editing, and storing a textual message, perhaps translating it from one language to another, are not very different in kind from the code conversion, store-and-forward functions, routing, error checking, and message disassembly and

assembly performed by the carrier. Without suggesting that the creator of a textual message plays no special role, it is still almost impossible to divide the many tasks which can take place in communicating that message into unique responsibilities for all the parties involved. In particular, the *information-processing* tasks and the *communications* tasks can be apportioned almost arbitrarily. Thus one consequence of the merging of computer and communications is that an information provider responsible for content can easily be engaged in tasks which might, in other circumstances, be done by the carrier.

2. There have also been illustrations, in the preceding section, of computer companies entering the communications field—IBM with its stake in Satellite Business Systems, and even more centrally, with its System Network Architecture (SNA), where it has nontrivial differences with the ISO data-link protocols. Other examples are Digital Equipment Corporation with DECNET, and Wang Laboratories with WANGNET. The reverse is also true. One of the most far-reaching results of the 1982 consent degree was that AT&T became free to engage in the nonregulated computer market. It acted promptly to do so, through its restructured company, which offered the Advanced Information Systems, AIS/NET 1000. It also has declared its interest in videotex. We shall see other examples of communication industries staking out claims on computers in later chapters.

3. It would be impossible today to list *all* the services that depend on the linkage of computers and communications—new ones surface daily. For an overview, see Dordick et al. (1981, Chaps. 9–12), and following the classification given there, they may be grouped into business network services, government network services, consumers network services, and the network marketplace. Many business and consumer services are illustrated by the software application packages listed in Table 8.2. For U.S. government network services it is sufficient to name some principal agencies which routinely use on-line data capture, data processing, and information retrieval. These include law enforcement agencies (e.g., FBI's National Crime Information Center), the Bureau of the Census, the Internal Revenue Service, the Social Security Administration, the Federal Reserve, the Department of Defense, Congress, and the U.S. Postal Service. Consumer services are those that can be delivered into the home, and they are just becoming common through teletext (via broadcast and cable channels) and videotex (where telephone lines provide two-way communication channels). The debate as to when, if at all, videotex services will be an economically feasible market, and which, if any, real social needs it satisfies, has been the subject of lengthy reports and full-length books (see Gotlieb, 1978; Wolfe, 1980; Mosco, 1982). Here we need only mention the usual cornucopia of promises: shopping, banking, electronic mail, games, education, house protection, calendar, news, real estate, home management, patient monitoring, job hunting, work at home, library, and so on. Regardless of when or whether all these consumer-based services materialize in the home, millions of people already draw on them daily in their work, schooling, through their contacts with

government, and in conducting their personal affairs. The fraction of time that people spend, either directly or through the intermediary of another person, in sessions on a terminal communicating with a computer, is growing at a phenomenal rate. It is *this* fraction that is the clearest manifestation of the merging of the computer and communication technologies.

PROBLEMS

1. Using the data in Fig. 8.7, estimate the increase in average access time which should accompany a decrease of 10 cents/Kbyte for a moving-head disk file in 1970.

2. For IBM tape drives the trend line for price is determined by the following points:

Model	Year	Rental Price (dollars/month)
2420-7	1968	1050
729-2	1957	700

The trend line for transfer rate is determined by the following points:

Model	Year	Transfer Rate (kcps)
2420-7	1968	320
729-6	1962	90

   (a) Calculate the equations for price and transfer rate versus time.
   (b) Calculate an expression that relates the change in price to the change in transfer rate, assuming that the units follow the trend lines.
   (c) The 729-4 model, offered in 1959, had a transfer rate of 62.5 kcps. What should its rental price be, assuming that the expression in part (b) is valid? Its actual rental was $900 per month. By what percentage was it overpriced or underpriced?

3. Suggest a performance measure for moving-head disks in which capacity, access time, and maximum data transfer rate enter as independent variables. Using the data in Phister (1979), plot the trend line of cost versus performance. Is the fit to the trend line using this measure better than those obtained using access time or maximum data transfer rate alone? Express the difference in statistical terms (i.e., reduction of variance).

4. Halstead (1977) predicts that the number of faults, B, in a program is given by

$$B = \frac{V}{3000}$$

Here V = volume = $N \log_2 n$, where

n_1 = number of distinct operators n_2 = number of distinct operands
N_1 = total number of operators N_2 = total number of operands
$n = n_1 + n_2$ $N = N_1 + N_2$

Also $N = KP$, where P is the program length in lines of code, and K is a constant characteristic of the language. (For FORTRAN, K is observed to be 7.5, and for assembly languages, $K = 2.7 \approx 3$.) Assuming, for simplicity, that $n_1 \approx n_2$, show that

$$KP = n \log_2 n - n$$

and B/P, the number of faults per line of code = $K/3000 \log_2 n$. Calculate n for a 2000-line FORTRAN program, and hence estimate B/P. By what percentage is the number of faults reduced if the program is divided into two 1000-line modules?   (Lipow, 1982)

5. A company is sending data to a branch plant 300 miles away, using the 9600-bps DDS service. The line is in use 22 days a month, 7½ hours a day.
   (a) What is the cost per M bits for the transmission?
   (b) If the data volume is increased by 30%, what changes should it make in the service (overtime use is ruled out)? What will the cost per M bits be then?
   (c) At what volume will the 56 kbps be justified? What will the cost be at this volume? What is the cost if the 56-kbps line is used at maximum capacity?

6. In Section 8.3.1 it was shown that for a distance of 300 miles, DD service with a 300-baud dataset is cheapest ($71 per month) for data volumes to 1.89 Mb/month, after which it is advantageous to upgrade to the 1200-baud service. Using the constants in Equations 8.1 and 8.2, calculate the break-even time between 4800-baud DD service and 300-baud private-line high-density service. Hence determine another point on the curve of cost per bit, using the cheapest mode, versus data volume transmitted.

7. Between two cities, A and B, 1200 miles apart, only low-density private-line DD service is available. However, there is DDS from A to a third city, C, which is 1300 miles away from A and 500 miles from B. What is the cost saving in going from A to B through C, rather than directly, for a 4800-baud line? (From C to B there is also low-density service.)

BIBLIOGRAPHY

BELL, C. G., J. C. MUDGE, and J. E. MCNAMERA, *Computer Engineering*. Bedford, Mass.: Digital Press, 1978, Chap. 2.

BOWEN, J. B., "Are Current Approaches Sufficient for Measuring Software Quality?" in Proc. of the Software Quality Assurance Workshop, *Performance Evaluation Review*, 7, nos. 3 and 4 (November 1978), 148–55.

BRECHTLEIN, R., "Comparing Disk Technologies," *Datamation*, 24, no. 1 (January 1978), 139–50.

CHRISTENSEN, K., C. P. FITSOS, and C. P. SMITH, "A Perspective on Software Science," *IBM Syst. J.*, 20, no. 4 (1981).

Datapro 70, Datapro Research Corp., Delran, N.J.

DORDICK, H. S., H. G. BRADLEY, and B. NANUS, *The Emerging Network Marketplace*. Norwood, N.J.: Ablex, 1981.

GOTLIEB, C. C., *Computers in the Home.* Montreal: Institute for Research on Public Policy, 1978.

GROSS, D. R., M. A. KING, M. R. MURR, and M. R. EDDY, "Complexity Measurement of Electronic Switching System (ESS) Software," in Workshop on Software Metrics, Score 82, Pt 2, *Performance Evaluation Review,* 11, no. 3 (Fall 1982), 75–85.

HALL, N. R., and S. PREISER, "Combined Network Complexity Measures," IBM Journal of Research and Development, 28, no. 1 (January 1984), 15–27.

HALSTEAD, M. A., *Elements of Software Science.* New York: Elsevier North-Holland, 1977.

HARTMAN, S. D., "A Counting Tool for RPG," in Workshop on Software Metrics, Score 82, Pt 2, *Performance Evaluation Review,* 11, no. 3 (Fall 1982), 86–100.

International Directory of Software. Princeton, N.J.: Computing Publications, 1983.

International Software Directory, Vol. 1: *Microcomputers;* Vol. 2: *Minicomputers.* Fort Collins, Colo.: Imprint Software, 1983.

JANSKY, D., ed., *World Atlas of Satellites.* Dedham, Mass.: Artech House, 1983.

KRAFT, P., "Programmers and Managers," in *The Routinization of Programming in the U.S.A.* New York: Springer-Verlag, 1977.

LIPOW, M., "Number of Faults per Line of Code," *IEEE Trans. Software Eng.,* SE-8, no. 4 (July 1982), 437–39.

LIST (Redgate Publishing Co.), 1, no. 1 (Spring 1983).

MARTIN, J., *System Analysis of Data Transmission.* Englewood Cliffs, N.J.: Prentice-Hall, 1972.

——, *Computer Networks and Distributed Processing.* Englewood Cliffs, N.J.: Prentice-Hall, 1981.

MOSCO, V., *Pushbutton Fantasies.* Norwood, N.J.: Ablex, 1982.

NOYCE, R. R., "Microelectronics," *Sci. Am.,* 237, no. 3 (September 1977), 63–69.

PHISTER, M., *Data Processing Technology and Economics,* 2nd ed. Santa Fe, N. Mex.: Santa Monica/Bedford, Mass.: Digital Press, 1979.

RAMANWORTHY, C. V., and F. B. BASTANI, "Software Reliability—Status and Perspectives," *IEEE Trans. Software Eng.,* SE-8, no. 4 (July 1982), 354–70.

SCHWARZ, M., *Computer Communications Network Design and Analysis.* Englewood Cliffs, N.J.: Prentice-Hall, 1977.

The Software Catalog: Microcomputers, Minicomputers. New York: Elsevier, 1983.

"Software Tax Break," *Datamation,* 28, no. 11 (November 1982), 96.

SOMA, J. T., *The Computer Industry.* Lexington, Mass.: Lexington Books, 1976.

TANENBAUM, A. S., *Computer Networks.* Englewood Cliffs, N.J.: Prentice-Hall, 1981.

THEIS, D., "An Overview of Memory Techniques," *Datamation,* 26, no. 1 (January 1980), 113–29.

TURN, R., *Computers in the 1980s.* New York: Columbia University Press, 1974.

"VAN Market Grows," *Datamation,* 28, no. 12, (Dec. 1982), 46–47.

WITHINGTON, F. P., "The Golden Age of Packaged Software," 26, no. 12 (Dec. 1980) 131–134 *Datamation.*

WOLFE, R., *Videotex.* London: Heyden, 1980.

9

Industry
Structure

In the preceding chapter we examined hardware devices, communications, information processing systems, and services in order to get a sense of the transformation of the computer technology as witnessed by the nature and the quality of its products. This chapter examines the computer industry from the point of view of the manufacturers and sellers of products and services, and looks for measures of the volumes produced and consumed. Perhaps more than in most industries there is a long chain between the manufacturers of the most basic components of computers and the end users of information systems. Anyone on an intermediate point along this chain will be both a consumer to one group and a supplier to another. Thus the computer center is a customer for hardware, software, and supplies, but a dispenser of services to those who want to use computer systems to solve problems.

There already has been, to this point in the book, considerable use made of tables and surveys containing data gathered from government statistical reports, supplied by manufacturers, or collected and interpreted by observers of the technology. Even greater use is made of such material in this chapter, and here it is necessary to repeat a caveat given by Phister (1979) about uncertainties in economic data in general, and economic data about computers in particular. It frequently happens that there are several independent sources for what is presumably the same statistic—for example, the number of general-purpose computer systems installed in the United States at a given date. The more highly aggregated the statistic, the more likely it is that there will be significant differences in the values reported by different sources. Some of these differences reflect the fact that different things were counted. Estimates of the number of computer systems obviously depend on the definition of what a computer is. In the early days of computers it was mainly necessary to differentiate between them and conventional accounting and tabulating machines. To do this it was sufficient to define a computer as a machine with a stored but changeable program, as distinct from one in which the program was permanent or set up by plugboard connections. But later, machines came to be categorized more exactly—general-purpose systems, small business computers, and minis; also intelligent terminals with highly sophisticated stored programs appeared, and then microcomputers and hand-held calculators with completely programmable memories. Thus the count of computers eventually came to be broken down into counts for general-purpose systems, small business computers, mini- and micro computers, terminals, and hand-held calculators. If different reporting sources arrive at this classification at different times, it is obvious that there will be discrepancies in the counts. Even when there is no ambiguity about the product counted will there be differences. Some companies, notably IBM, do not release information about the number of units shipped, installed, or returned. Estimates of the population of a particular IBM system, such as the 360/40, must be derived from secondary sources (e.g., customer surveys). It is hardly surprising, then, that three counts of the number of IBM/360 systems installed in the United States on June 30, 1970, show considerable variation (18,189 by DP Focus, 22,593 by EDP/IR, and 26,715 by ADP/N). Such differences make it clear that all statistical tabulations have to be used with caution. As explained in the preface, many of the statistics quoted here are based on those appearing in Phister, who, while quoting sources and attempting to reconcile different results or choose among them, still ends with a disclaimer about their accuracy. We are forced to do the same, pointing out, as Phister does, that although these uncertainties weaken the conclusions that can be drawn from the data, they do not make it impossible to draw any conclusions whatever. Often the *differences* between two values of a quantity given at two times can be more trustworthy than the absolute value, and the most interesting quantity is the growth *rate*. The inconsistencies in the data do mean that it is seldom possible to attach confidence to results beyond the first or second significant figures, but even such accuracy helps to make abstract concepts more real.

9.1. INDUSTRY SUBSECTORS AND INTERRELATIONSHIPS

Before presenting details about the computer industry and its history, it is necessary to understand the nature of the basic data and the sources from which these are drawn. The principal data relate to annual shipments and revenues arising out of the sales of computer products and services. Such statistics are gathered in the normal course of keeping track of the economy in many countries, and they cover domestic production and consumption, imports and exports. However, a great deal of interpretation is needed to derive precise information about the computer industry from data on production, exports, and imports. The Standard International (Trade) Classifications (SICs) are very broad. For a long time computers were in SIC 318, which comprised office machinery, and included typewriters, duplicating equipment, and so on. The subdivision still included hand calculating machines, accounting machines, and devices other than electronic computers, and not all countries reported trade figures to this degree of refinement. Often, revenues from computer sales were included with revenues on other electronic equipment, such as television sets. More recently, computers are assigned to SIC 335 (while services are SIC 772 and communications SIC 335). Although there have been successive refinements in the categories, in general, the classifications are too coarse, and the figures reported by governments do not give a clear picture of the dynamic computer industry. Therefore, nationally gathered statistics must be supplemented with estimates produced by professional organizations, trade publications, and market analysts. The most detailed and comprehensive reports from nongovernmental agencies are those published by the International Data Corporation (IDC). Useful statistics are also gathered by the Association of Data Processing Service Organizations, Inc. (ADAPSO), the American Federation of Information Processing Societies (AFIPS), and by consultants who prepare reports for their clients. Usually, data are aggregated in the major categories shown in Table 9.1 and are reported annually, both as dollar amounts (revenues or expenditures) and in number of units, with domestic shipments separated out from the worldwide figures, which include exports. Imports are reported separately, but not necessarily under the same categories.

Some comments are in order about the classifications of Table 9.1.

- Since many SBCs are built around minis, the minis in SBCs have to be subtracted from entries under 1.1 to obtain totals for complete systems.
- Hardware is the total of complete systems and peripherals.

TABLE 9.1 DATA PROCESSING INDUSTRY
STATISTICS: MAJOR CATEGORIES

1.	Hardware
1.1.	Computer systems
	General-purpose systems
	Minis
	Small business computers (SBCs)
	Minis in small business computers
	Other
1.2.	Peripherals
	Plug-compatibles
	Other
	Original equipment manufacturers (OEMs)
	End-user revenues
2.	Services
	Batch
	On-line
3.	Software
4.	Data communication
5.	Supplies

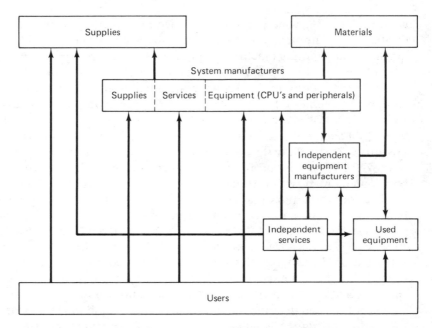

Figure 9.1   Flow of funds from users to suppliers of computer equipment and services (from B. Gilchrist and R. E. Weber, *The State of the Computer Industry in the United States* [Montvale N.J.: AFIPS Press, 1973]).

- Plug compatibles are devices made by competing independents as substitutes for components provided by complete system manufacturers.
- Other and OEM peripherals include terminals, data-entry equipment, and so on.
- Within each category more detailed statistics about subcategories are usually available. Supplies consist of cards, paper, ribbons, magnetic tapes, disks, and so on; communications can be broken down into numerous categories, details being available from the common carriers and the communication industry. Chips are basic components of hardware, but like data communications, comprise an industry in itself and statistics are reported separately.*
- As noted already, basic national figures separate production, exports, and imports. It is necessary to take all three into account to derive figures on consumption.

Within the categories there is a complicated flow of revenues. Service bureaus are customers for hardware, peripherals, supplies, and communication services. End users are customers for items under all five major categories. Figure 9.1 shows the flow of funds between the various subsectors of the computer industry. Figure 9.2 shows the structure of the computer service subsector.

*For details on the chip industry, see Wilson et al. (1980) and Hazewindus and Tooker (1982).

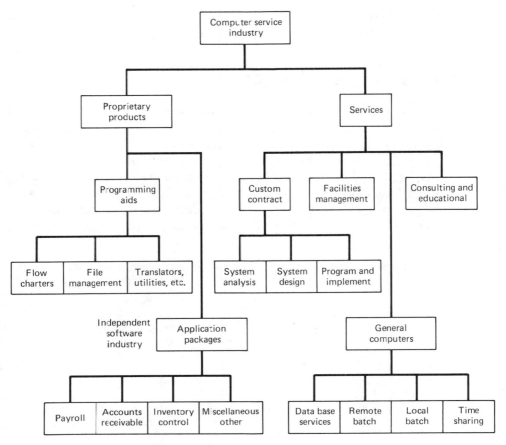

Source: Auerbach Info. Inc., with permission

Figure 9.2 Structure of the computer service subsector (from Auerbach Info. Inc., with permission).

In addition to aggregated data for the industry as a whole, separate figures for individual manufacturers and suppliers are of interest, as well as breakdowns according to systems size. Beside the statistics about equipment and services listed in Table 9.1, data on user expenditures are important. Distributions of costs according to type (salaries, hardware, software, etc.) and statistics showing the market composition (industries where the equipment is used) are also of considerable interest. Finally, data on the labor force, makeup, and distribution are needed to have a composite picture of the data processing industry.

The totality of available data is enormous, and, of course, continually being updated, and it is beyond the scope of this book to attempt to present it to any great detail in either tabular or graphical form. However, in the next section representative tables and figures are presented so that some appreciation of the scale of the industry, its rate of growth, and the relative positions of different suppliers can be gained. In this chapter, with a few exceptions, we deal principally with the United States, but in Part IV, data for other countries are given.

9.2. REPRESENTATIVE STATISTICS

First we consider data showing the installed base (i.e., total number of systems) derived from annual shipments of computers. Detailed compilations include breakdowns according to value, the number of units, the size or class of systems, and country of origin, but we give illustrations only, not the complete set. Table 9.2 lists, since 1959, the number of computers in use provided by U.S.-based manufacturers (i.e., cumulative shipments, less systems taken out of service). Data are given for general-purpose systems, minis, and small business computers for the United States and worldwide. The same information is displayed graphically in Fig. 9.3.

TABLE 9.2 COMPUTERS IN USE (THOUSANDS): U.S.-BASED MANUFACTURERS

Year	Total		General Purpose		Minis		Small Business Computers	
	U.S.	Worldwide	U.S.	Worldwide	U.S.	Worldwide	U.S.	Worldwide
1959	3.80	4.50	3.1	3.8				
1960	5.40	6.50	4.4	5.5				
1961	7.55	9.15	6.2	7.8				
1962	9.90	12.35	8.1	10.5				
1963	13.80	17.45	11.7	15.2				
1964	19.20	24.80	16.7	21.9				
1965	24.70	33.40	21.6	29.6	0.2	0.2		
1966	31.67	44.85	27.1	39.1	1.2	1.4		
1967	37.79	56.70	31.0	48.0	3.0	3.5		
1968	46.50	71.40	37.0	59.0	5.2	6.2		
1969	56.40	87.30	40.0	66.8	11.5	13.5		
1970	67.08	106.40	41.9	74.7	20.0	24.3		
1971	79.16	127.83	45.0	84.2	28.5	35.5	0.3	0.3
1972	102.53	163.03	50.2	94.2	45.0	58.5	0.7	0.9
1973	133.64	208.99	58.3	106.0	65.1	89.6	1.5	2.0
1974	171.24	264.69	61.5	111.3	96.1	135.3	4.5	6.2
1975	208.64	323.74	62.1	115.4	126.3	181.4	12.4	16.8
1976	253.38	392.83	59.6	112.5	162.3	235.3	27.2	39.2
1977	322.32	496.76	58.2	112.8	214.5	311.2	48.8	71.7
1978	401.46	619.32	58.0	113.2	275.3	402.3	72.8	110.3
1979	849.56	1,276.22	53.3	105.5	345.2	518.0	104.3	167.0
1980	1,283.75	1,929.96	56.5	115.1	419.7	651.7	139.8	230.3
1981	1,875.34	2,798.21	60.8	124.8	508.8	809.7	181.8	304.5
1982	2,655.41	3,938.46	64.8	134.1	613.0	997.30	230.1	390.7

Source: M. Phister, *Data Processing Technology and Economics,* 2nd ed. (Santa Fe, N. Mex.: Santa Monica/Bedford, Mass.: Digital Press, 1979—derived from various sources, principally the International Data Corporation.

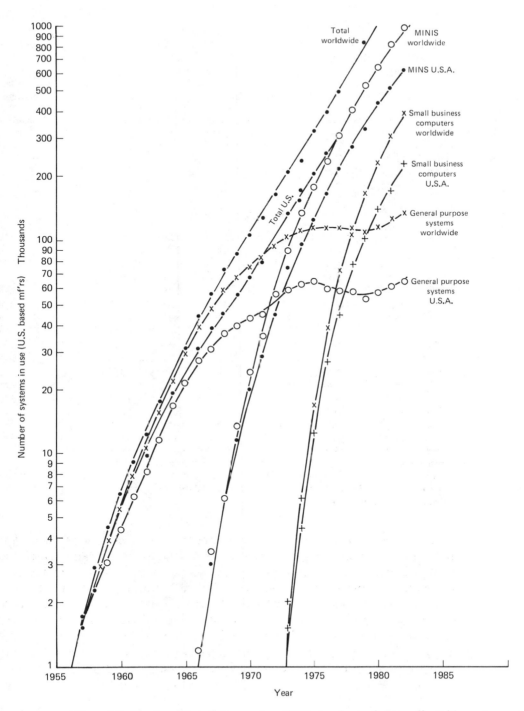

Figure 9.3 Number of installed computers of U.S.-based manufacturers (from M. Phister, *Data Processing Technology and Economics*, 2nd ed. [Santa Fe, N. Mex.: Santa Monica/Bedford, Mass.: Digital Press, 1979.]

TABLE 9.3 COMPUTERS IN USE (BILLIONS OF DOLLARS):
U.S.-BASED MANUFACTURERS

Year	Total		General Purpose		Minis		Small Business Computers	
	U.S.	Worldwide	U.S.	Worldwide	U.S.	Worldwide	U.S.	Worldwide
1959	1.38	1.60	1.3	1.6				
1960	1.94	2.27	1.9	2.2				
1961	2.71	3.21	2.6	3.1				
1962	3.62	4.40	3.5	4.2				
1963	4.76	5.96	4.6	5.7				
1964	6.30	8.14	6.0	7.8				
1965	8.23	11.15	7.8	10.6	0.01	0.01		
1966	9.96	13.75	9.4	13.1	0.04	0.04		
1967	13.08	18.42	12.4	17.6	0.09	0.10		
1968	16.56	23.56	15.7	22.6	0.16	0.18		
1969	20.18	30.52	19.1	29.2	0.31	0.35		
1970	22.68	36.17	21.4	34.6	0.48	0.56		
1971	24.82	41.37	23.3	39.5	0.65	0.77	0.01	0.01
1972	26.58	45.84	24.3	43.5	0.97	1.19	0.04	0.04
1973	29.62	51.77	27.3	48.7	1.32	1.76	0.08	0.10
1974	33.31	58.48	30.2	54.2	1.90	2.67	0.23	0.30
1975	37.81	67.06	33.8	61.3	2.54	3.78	0.53	0.70
1976	43.25	76.58	37.9	68.6	3.40	5.24	1.11	1.58
1977	50.30	88.99	42.9	77.8	4.77	7.36	1.95	2.86
1978	58.63	104.18	48.7	88.9	6.52	10.18	2.95	4.52
1979	67.2	120.9	52.2	97.4	8.7	13.8	4.6	7.3
1980	78.7	141.4	58.2	108.8	11.5	18.4	6.4	10.3
1981	92.1	165.1	63.9	120.2	15.0	24.1	8.6	14.1
1982	108.4	193.0	70.1	132.2	19.2	31.2	11.1	18.4

Source: M. Phister, *Data Processing Technology and Economics,* 2nd ed. (Santa Fe, N. Mex.: Santa Monica/Bedford, Mass.: Digital Press, 1979)—derived from various sources, principally the International Data Corporation.

Table 9.3 gives data for the same headings, but lists the *value* of the equipment rather than the number of systems, and Fig. 9.4 shows the information graphically. It will be observed that minis (for which figures start in 1965) and small business computers (for which figures start in 1971) are continuing to grow at exponential rates, corresponding to a growth rate of about 27% per year, but there is a leveling off in the value, especially the number of general-purpose computers since 1970, when the minis made their first significant appearance. Note also that in all categories (except for number of general-purpose computers in the last 3 years) the installed base (of machines supplied by U.S.-based manufacturers) is greater for the United States than for the rest of the world combined.*

*In some countries, notably the United Kingdom and Japan, computers produced by indigenous manufacturers form an appreciable fraction of the installed base, but generally, most computers are supplied by U.S.-based companies.

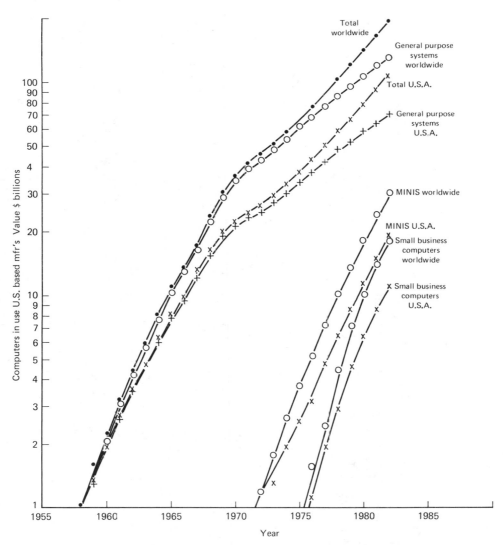

Figure 9.4 Value of installed computers of U.S.-based manufacturers (from M. Phister, *Data Processing Technology and Economics*, 2nd ed. [Santa Fe, N. Mex.: Santa Monica/Bedford, Mass.: Digital Press, 1979] derived from various sources, principally the International Data Corporation).

Table 9.4 shows the data processing revenues for the largest U.S. data processing companies for the years 1976–1982, and Fig. 9.5 shows the cumulative distribution when the companies are ranked according to these revenues for the year 1981. Note that this list includes hardware manufacturers whose business is mainly or solely computers (e.g., IBM and Wang Laboratories), hardware companies that derive most of their overall revenues from other products (e.g., General

TABLE 9.4 LARGEST DATA PROCESSING COMPANIES IN THE UNITED STATES

1983 Rank	Company	Data Processing Revenues (millions of dollars) for:							
		1983	1982	1981	1980	1979	1978	1977	1976
1	IBM	35,603	31,500	26,340	21,367	18,338	17,072	14,765	12,717
2	Digital Equipment Corp.	4,827	4,019	3,587	2,743	2,032	1,437	1,059	736
3	Burroughs Corp.	4,000	3,848	2,934	2,478	2,442	2,107	1,844	1,630
4	Control Data Corp.	3,500	3,301	3,103	2,791	2,273	1,867	1,513	1,331
5	NCR Corp.	3,333	3,173	3,072	2,840	2,528	1,932	1,574	1,100
6	Sperry Corp.	2,780	2,800	2,781	2,552	2,270	1,807	1,472	1,430
7	Hewlett-Packard Corp.	2,496	2,165	1,875	1,577	1,147	657	402	335
8	Wang Laboratories, Inc.	1,793	1,322	1,008	682	280	168	114	82
9	Honeywell, Inc.	1,666	1,685	1,774	1,634	1,453	1,294	1,037	1,428
10	Xerox Corp.	1,200	1,300	1,100	770	570	236	209	120
11	Apple Computer, Inc.	1,085	664	401	175	—	—	—	—
12	TRW, Inc.	1,015	825	855	377	440	466	350	295
13	Tandy	945	725	460	220	150	—	—	—
14	Commodore International Ltd.	927	368	184	99	—	—	—	—
15	Storage Technology	887	1,079	922	603	480	300	162	122
16	Data General Corp.	867	804	764	673	540	380	255	161
17	Texas Inst. Corp.	850	900	667	562	425	204	155	66
18	General Electric Corp.	820	862	750	475	350	190	200	185
19	Automatic Data Processing	816	704	613	505	401	290	238	178
20	American Telephone & Telegraph	807	802	—	—	—	—	—	—

Sources: Datamation, various issues, June 1977–1984.

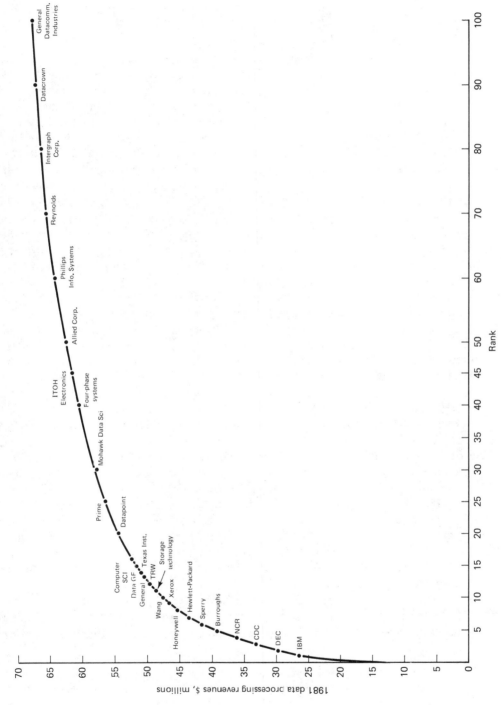

Figure 9.5 Cumulative data processing revenues of leading U.S. data processing companies, 1981 (from *Datamation*, June 1982).

Electric Co., ITT, Xerox, and TRW) and companies engaged primarily in making peripherals or components (e.g., Storage Technology and Texas Instruments). The largest software company, Computer Sciences Corp., ranked sixteenth overall in 1981. Table 9.5 shows the revenues and ranking for the leading mainframe companies for 1982, 1981, 1980, and 1975. Whereas IBM has approximately 60% of the total for this group, the older mainframe companies which come after DEC, the second larget company (Burroughs, UNIVAC, NCR, Control Data and Honeywell, or the BUNCH, as they are sometimes called), have only 4 to 7% each. Digital Equipment Corporation achieved second place in 1981. As a fraction of the revenues of the top 100 companies, IBM had 38.8% in 1981 and 42.1% in 1982.

The distribution of data processing revenues by product segment is shown in Table 9.6 for 1979 and 1980. Revenues from mainframes, although increasing in dollar value, constitute a decreasing fraction of the total market. Whereas in 1975 general-purpose mainframes comprised 83% of the systems market, in 1980 they made up only 59%, and in 1982 it was projected that by 1985 they would contribute only 36%.* Microcomputers, word processors, and software products show the largest growth rate, but in 1980 each of these made up only a few percent of the total. In fact, the decline in mainframe revenues has been even more precipitous than expected. Data compiled by International Data Corporation show them leveling off in 1982, with slow growth projected after 1984 and being exceeded by sales in personal computers after 1984 (Table 9.7).† Tables 9.8 and 9.9 show the 1981 and 1982 revenues for the principal companies making personal computers (microcomputers) and office systems (word processors). The absence of the BUNCH group from the list, except for Burroughs in Table 9.9, is noteworthy.

Table 9.6 shows software product revenues for 1980 of $1738 million, making up 3.1% of total computer revenues. Other surveys estimate software revenues somewhat higher. Frank (1983), citing data collected by IDC, estimates 1981 software product revenues as $3465 million, of which $2195 million was earned by hardware manufacturers and $1270 million by independent suppliers. Further, it is projected that by 1986, growing at an annual rate of 31% they will come to $8575 million and $4985 million, respectively, for a total of $13,560 million. Table 9.10 shows a still different set of estimates for software revenues. The spread between estimates derived from different sources is presumably because costs for custom software are included with service in some tabulations. Allowing for this ambiguity, 1982 software revenues were between 7 and 15% of all data processing revenues, with an annual growth rate of about 30%, the greatest growth being experienced in packaged products.

In evaluating the market it is useful to know where computers are used. Table 9.11 shows the distribution of computer installations in Canada for 1982, classified by industry and monthly rental. The data come from the Canadian Information

*Business Week, February 15, 1982, p. 78.

†Note that the 1980 estimate for mainframe revenues is considerably different from that of Table 9.6, indicating that different things have been included in the two counts.

TABLE 9.5 DATA PROCESSING REVENUES OF THE PRINCIPAL MAINFRAME
COMPANIES (MILLIONS OF DOLLARS)

Company	1982			1981			1980			1975		
	Revenues	%	Rank	Revenues	%	Rank	Revenues	%	Rank	Revenues	%	Rank
IBM	31,500	60.0	1	26,340	57.9	1	21,367	56.3	1	11,116	61.2	1
Digital Equipment Corp.	4,019	7.7	2	3,587	7.9	2	2,743	7.2	4	534	2.9	7
Burroughs Corp.	3,848	7.3	3	2,934	6.5	5	2,476	5.5	6	1,447	7.4	2
Control Data Corp.	3,301	6.3	4	3,103	6.8	3	2,791	7.3	3	1,218	6.7	5
NCR Corp.	3,173	6.0	5	3,072	6.6	4	2,640	7.5	2	960	5.3	6
Sperry Corp. (UNIVAC)	2,800	5.3	6	2,761	6.1	6	2,552	6.7	5	1,295	7.1	4
Hewlett-Packard Corp.	2,165	4.1	7	1,875	4.1	7	1,577	4.2	7	250	1.4	9
Honeywell, Inc.	1,685	3.2	8	1,774	3.9	8	1,634	4.3	6	1,324	7.3	3
Total	52,491			45,465			37,962			18,144		

Source: Data from *Datamation*, 1976–1983.

TABLE 9.6 DATA PROCESSING REVENUES BY PRODUCT SEGMENT
(MILLIONS OF DOLLARS)

	1980		1979		Percent Growth Rate
	Revenues	%	Revenues	%	
Systems					
Mainframes	15,148	27.2	13,312	29.0	13.8
Minicomputers	8,840	15.9	6,916	15.0	27.8
Microcomputers	769	1.4	416	0.9	84.9
Word processing	881	1.6	538	1.2	63.8
Total systems	25,638	46.1	21,182	46.1	21.0
OEM peripherals	3,968	7.1	3,128	6.8	26.9
End-user peripherals	6,910	12.4	5,943	12.9	16.3
Data communications	1,141	2.1	927	2.0	23.1
Software products	1,738	3.1	1,347	2.9	29.0
Maintenance	8,888	16.0	7,372	16.0	20.6
Service	6,432	11.6	5,329	11.6	20.7
All other	911	1.6	772	1.7	18.0
Total	55,626	100.0	46,000	100.0	20.9

Source: Data from *Datamation,* 27, no. 6 (June 1981).

Processing Society, which maintains an almost complete inventory of computers in the country. Comparison with earlier distributions derived from sampling computer installations in the United States shows that the patterns in the two countries are similar (see Nyborg et al., 1977, Fig. 2-3).

Of special interest is the number of people employed in the computer industry and those engaged in computer-related activities in other industries. From data provided in 1977 by the Bureau of Labor Statistics, U.S. Department of Labor, for the year 1974, the following estimates were given (see Nyborg et al., 1977, Fig. 3-1, Table 3-1):

Total work force in computer manufacturing and service industries	348,000
Computer labor force in computer manufacturing and service industries	111,000
Computer labor force in *all* industries	853,000
Total U.S. labor force	85,936,000

TABLE 9.7 ESTIMATED U.S. SALES OF MAINFRAMES AND PERSONAL COMPUTERS (BILLIONS OF DOLLARS)

	Year[a]							
	1980	1981	1982	1983	1984	1985	1986	1987
Mainframe	8	8	12	12	12	13	15	15.5
Personal computers	1	2	4	7	11	14	17	19

[a]Projected data for 1984–1987.

Source: Estimated from a graph in *The New York Times,* February 5, 1984, provided by the International Data Corporation, Framingham, Mass.

TABLE 9.8 PRINCIPAL U.S. MANUFACTURERS OF PERSONAL COMPUTERS

Company	Revenues (millions of dollars) for: 1982	1981[a]
Apple Computer	664	401.1
IBM	500	n.a.
Tandy	466	293
Commodore	368	184
Hewlett-Packard	235	196
Texas Instrument	233	144
Digital Equipment	200	n.a.

[a]n.a., not available.

Source: Data from *Datamation*, 29, no. 6 (June 1983).

TABLE 9.9 PRINCIPAL MANUFACTURERS OF OFFICE SYSTEMS

Company	Office System Revenues (millions of dollars) for 1982	1981
IBM	1800	1600
Wang Laboratories	585	456
Motorola	275	232
Lanier	241	228
Burroughs	200	50
Xerox	200	132
Philips Information Systems	176	123
Exxon	165	165
Northern Telecom	134	162
CPT	127	103
NBI	120	77
Digital Equipment	100	n.a.[a]

[a]n.a., not available.

Source: Data from *Datamation*, 29, no. 6 (June 1983).

TABLE 9.10 ESTIMATES FOR U.S. SOFTWARE REVENUES

	Year[a]			
	1980	1982	1983	1985
System software				
revenues (millions of dollars)	1,500	2,630	3,430	5,800
% Growth	36	31	30	29
% Total	25	29	31	35
Application software				
revenues (millions of dollars)	1,100	2,360	3,320	5,770
% Growth	22	44	41	26
% Total	18	26	30	35
Custom-built software				
revenues (millions of dollars)	3,500	4,090	4,320	4,940
% Growth	30	7	6	11
% Total	57	45	39	30
Total (millions of dollars)	6,100	9,080	11,070	16,510

[a]Projected data for 1983 and 1985.

Source: Data compiled by Input, Mountainview, Calif., 1982.

TABLE 9.11 COMPUTER INSTALLATIONS IN CANADA CLASSIFIED BY INDUSTRY AND BY MONTHLY RENTAL (AS OF DEC. 31, 1982)

Industry	Less than $1,000	$1,000 to $1,999	$2,000 to $4,999	$5,000 to $9,999	$10,000 to $19,999	$20,000 to $49,999	$50,000 to $99,999	$100,000 and Over	Other and Not Identified	Total	Percent
Primary or resource (includes agriculture, forestry, fisheries, and mining)	19	319	179	69	29	23	10	3	3	674	4.4
Construction	27	75	69	30	16	2	1	—	3	225	1.5
Manufacturing	157	655	754	363	205	103	40	8	31	2,316	15.3
Transportation	26	96	73	39	41	50	21	5	10	363	2.4
Utility	68	504	158	62	26	53	17	24	10	924	5.1
Communication (includes printing, TV, publishing, radio, and newspaper advertising)	26	96	142	83	27	34	7	1	6	424	2.8
Distribution (wholesale, retail)	72	593	466	162	66	56	16	14	20	1,487	9.6
Financial (banks, trust companies, investment dealers, stock exchanges)	5	56	69	66	82	42	22	15	3	382	2.5

										Total	%
Insurance	36	40	101	26	42	32	14	23	12	330	2.2
Other services (unions, professions, associations)	55	98	61	41	27	8	3	3	10	325	2.2
Service bureau (Computer systems and software companies)	504	379	411	186	76	79	50	39	27	1,751	11.6
Government (federal, provincial, municipal, but excluding utilities and school boards)	289	537	439	142	86	74	41	29	44	1,683	11.1
Petroleum	18	134	141	92	71	55	12	11	21	555	3.7
Educational	1,215	400	249	137	90	39	23	5	97	2,255	14.9
Medical	16	91	102	47	14	17	2	1	2	291	1.9
Legal	14	4	9	—	—	—	—	—	—	27	0.2
Accounting	37	31	19	3	1	3	1	—	4	95	0.6
Hospitality	—	9	15	7	4	—	7	—	2	41	0.3
Other	33	59	51	46	13	7	7	2	10	228	1.5
Industry class not identified	59	306	171	66	46	30	15	11	46	776	5.2
Total	2,876	4,466	3,721	1,713	990	707	302	194	364	15,154	100.0

Source: 1983 Canadian Computer Census of Canadian Information Processing Society, with permission.

TABLE 9.12 EMPLOYMENT IN THE COMPUTER
INDUSTRY, 1980

Company	Employment (thousands)
IBM	278
NCR	66
DEC	60
Burroughs	57
Control Data	49
Sperry	47
Honeywell	29
Hewlett-Packard	28
Computer Sciences	15
Data General	14
Total top 10	643
Total	863
Number of companies reporting	83
Percent DP revenues represented	93.3

Source: Datamation 27, no. 6 (June 1981).

Also, the projected figures for 1985 are;

Total work force in computer manufacturing and service industries	620,000
Total U.S. labor force	103,355,300

Table 9.12 gives the work force for the 10 largest computer companies in 1980, as estimated from a survey conducted by *Datamation,* together with the number of people employed by the 83 responding companies, which was 863,000. These companies accounted for 93.3% of the total data processing revenues for that year, and if the assumption is made that the work force was proportional to revenues, it follows that the total work force in computer and manufacturing for 1980 was approximately $863,000 \div 0.933 = 925,000$. Note that this is already considerably greater than the projection of 620,000 made in 1977 for the year 1985, indicating that the computer industry has grown much more rapidly than expected. In fact, the 1980 U.S. census figures revealed that the computer labor force (key-entry operators, computer operators, programmers, and systems analysts) in all industries was 1.4 million. This was an increase of 700,000 over the corresponding figure from 1970, and it is projected to increase to 3.1 million by 1990.*

Thus there has been a substantial and rapid growth in the data processing population within the computer industry and in industry in general. But since 1980 the overall unemployment rates in the United States (as well as in other countries) have been unusually high, ranging between 7% and 10% of the labor force (see

*B. Gilchrist, A Dayli, and A. Shenkin, *Datamation*, 29, no. 9 (September 1983), 100–110.

OECD, 1982, pp. 34–36). The extent to which automation and increasing computerization of white-collar jobs has contributed to these high figures, and will continue to depress employment, is a subject of much controversy. This question is examined in greater detail in Section 11.1.2.

The preceding examples will serve to illustrate the size and growth rate of the computer industry. Additional tables and statistics are given in the remaining chapters of this book, but for a really comprehensive overview it is necessary to go to the sources cited earlier.

9.3 MICROECONOMIC MODELS

Whereas industry reports usually take the form of periodic statistical tables, of the kind just given, to obtain real insight about an industry it is usually regarded as desirable to have microeconomic models of it. In spite of the importance of the computer industry, theoretical studies, or mathematical models of either the technology as a whole, or of particular segments, are rare. There are a few, however.

In *The International Computer Industry,* Harman (1971) studied the computer industry as an example of technical innovation, where performance of a machine model m, at time t, X (m, t), is determined by such factors as R, the research and development expenditure of the firm, $g_R(t)$, the proportion of cash flow devoted to innovation, and τ, the period during which past expenditure on R&D remains useful. Included also are economic environmental factors such as the industrial production of the country, $I(t)$, the cost of capital, $r(t)$, and wage rates, $w(t)$. The principal input data to the model are Knight's performance indexes over a span of years for the various computer models produced by each manufacturer (these are taken as measures of X), observed and projected research expenditures, and observed production (i.e., demand) for computers in different countries. The basic outputs are the equilibrium number of machines for a country to possess, calculated on the assumption that firms act to maximize their profits over a time horizon T. Projections based on the model include the maximum computer performance that could be achieved by different companies, starting from 1966, the base year, to 1980, and the increased demand resulting from the then imminent entry of the United Kingdom into the European Economic Community. Interesting as the model is, it suffers from the fault noted in Chapter 2, that Knight's index is an inadequate measure of performance in the light of the major technological changes that have taken place in the industry. Moreover, the evolution of the industry into different segments, such as general-purpose machines, small business computers, microcomputers, software, terminals, and other services, mean that a single statistic (even an aggregated one such as total revenues) is not an adequate description of the market state. There has been too much *structural* change in the technology, and too much change in the total computer/communications environment, for the model to continue to be useful for detailed descriptive or predictive purposes. This is a serious weakness in most economic models.

Brock, in a now-classic book, *The U.S. Computer Industry* (1974), devotes a chapter to IBM's pricing policy, in recognition of the dominant role that IBM plays in the industry. The assumption is that IBM maximizes the discounted present value of its profits over the indefinite future by adopting prices that yield high profits, but not so high as to attract competition in spite of barriers to new entrants. Brock extends an earlier model of an industry with a dominant firm to take into account the high technological growth characteristic of the computer industry. In both Brock's and the earlier model there is a *limit price,* defined as the price for which neither entry nor exit of competition takes place. The total market is expanding because of price reduction due to technological improvements at a rate a and exogenous growth at rate g. The mathematical formulation is fairly detailed, but essentially it requires the solution of a pair of simultaneous, nonlinear differential equations for $p(t)$, the dominant firm's price, and $x(t)$, the competitive firm's market share. Parameters are estimated by fitting regression curves to observed variables. Thus the industry demand function $= Ap(t)^b e^{gt}$, where A and g are constants, is found to be $7440p^{-1.44}e^{0.147t}$ for the time period 1954–1966. For the function used to represent the average total cost of production $c(t) = c_o e^{-at}$, c_o is estimated as 2.15 and a (as determined from several performance measures, including Knight's index) is 0.237. The remaining quantities of interest are r, the dominant firm's discount rate, and the function which gives the response of competitive market share to differences in price and limit price, $k(t) = k^o e^{at} = 0.3e^{0.237t}$. To fit the data it is necessary to set $r = 0.2733$, a high rate of return, which comes about because of the high growth rate of the industry. When the equations for $p(t)$ and $x(t)$ are solved with the parameters given above, the time curves for price and market share correspond reasonably well with those observed.[*] According to the theory, IBM's market share should decrease slowly to a long-term equilibrium which is below the initial (1956) share by an amount that increases as the exogenous growth factor decreases. For the given values of $g = 0.147$ and $r = .2733$, IBM's share declines from its initial value of 75% to an equilibrium value of 65.4%, but this is very slow and the early rate of decrease is only about $1\frac{1}{2}$% per year (compare the decrease rate shown in Table 9.5). In this important respect of market share the theory does have predictive value.

Section three of *The Economics of Information Processing* by Goldberg and Lorin (1982) is devoted to two microeconomic models of the information processing industry.[†] The first is a series of models constructed by Dunn and Fronistas (1982) for information services offered through computer networks. In the models a variety of assumptions are made for:

- The type of services (homogeneous or differentiated)
- Management objectives (maximization of profits, total surplus, or revenues)

---

[*] In practice, new product generations introduce jumps in price which are not present in the continuous variables assumed for the theory.

[†] In the section three models are described, but the third is not quantitative and hence, strictly speaking, it is not a microeconomic model.

- User demand (a linear function of cost, where costs arise from supplier costs, transmission costs where the supplier is remote, and congestion costs due to waiting time)
- Production costs (assumed to be at most a quadratic function of the supplier's output level)

Using *hypothetical* data, calculations are presented for a network market where there are four centers, with both local and remote users, and with competing producers keeping track of maximum cost incurred by users' but not of competitors' prices. With appropriate parameters all four producers capture market share, but assuming unrestricted entry and the arrival of a new, profit-maximizing producer with low production costs, a number of interesting cycles can arise. These include capture of a large share of the market by the new producer, cessation of operations by firms experiencing losses, attempts to create monopolies by lowering prices on the part of the efficient producers, price wars, reversion to profit maximization, and other situations characteristic of such a competitive environment. Another sample calculation is given for a nine-center network, first where producers act as local monopolists, and second where the network is interconnected and producers act competitively or in collusion. The Dunn and Fronistas model is typical of those used for studying the way competition operates in the economic environment, and it is made applicable to the computer/communications industry by taking appropriate forms for the functions used to represent production cost and user demand. There was no indication of an attempt to apply the model to a real situation, where the assumption of no barrier to entry would certainly have to be changed (see Section 10.1).

The second of the models in *The Economics of Information Processing* is a description by Sassone and Williams (1982) of a regression model developed to explain and forecast f_{ij}, the sales of computer systems when categorized by industry size i, and producer size j (see Table 9.9). In their study the industries selected were manufacturing (SIC 23, 25, 31, 34, and 39), wholesale distribution (SIC 50 and 51), and banking (SIC 60 and 61). Product size was specified by using the IBM convention for classifying systems according to points (i.e., dollar cost of monthly rental); industries are classified according to the number of employees. A key requirement is that in the matrix of the computed estimates for f_{ij}, the sales for customer size i of all products ($\Sigma_j \, f_{ij}$), and of product size j, summed over all customers ($\Sigma_i \, f_{ij}$), be consistent with separately computed estimates for these aggregates. Given i and j a regression curve could be fitted for f_{ij} using a number of possible independent variables, including:

- Industry size
- Industry ability to buy (measured by profits, data processing budget, etc.)
- Price
- Industry stock of data processing equipment

- General economic conditions (GNP, prime rate, etc.)
- Industry needs (measured by transaction volumes, for example)
- Managerial characteristics
- Marketing effort

In the actual model only the first five of these factors were used since data were not available for the other three. Also, although there were six establishment size codes, and five system size codes, it was impractical to attempt to produce regression fits for 42 observables (recall that the column and row sums are also observables) since there were too many missing data over the period, 1965–1978, for which the study was done. Therefore, establishment and systems sizes were aggregated by a method which still preserved useful distinctions. The basic technique was to carry out initial forecasts using the previously found regression curves, and then to adjust the forecast by adding missing entries and adjusting them so as best (in a least-squares sense) to make the row and column sums consistent. Table 9.13 shows the initial forecasts for total points in the manufacturing sector, and the final, adjusted values. Since the predictions for the totals in Table 9.13(*a*) are made independently, they are not equal to the sums of the predicted table entries; in Table 9.13(*b*) these sums are forced to be equal by the consistency conditions.

TABLE 9.13 FORECASTS FOR TOTAL 1982 SALES OF IBM COMPUTERS TO THE MANUFACTURING SECTOR (Monthly rental in thousands of dollars)

(a) Initial Prediction

Establishment Size	System Size		Total
	S1	S2	
E1	319	46	206
E2	64	115	189
E3	182	—	181
Total	437	225	500

(b) Adjusted Prediction

Establishment Size	System Size		Total
	S1	S2	
E1	236	3	239
E2	37	129	166
E3	141	29	170
Total	414	161	575

By applying statistical tests of significance to the observed and predicted values for 1982, the authors conclude that the model does have significant predictive powers and hence could be used by IBM as a reasonably detailed sales forecasting technique.

There are other examples of models constructed to help a company in its marketing and financial analysis. Champine (1977) describes a financial model developed by UNIVAC to predict revenues and profitability of new systems going through their product development cycle. The model has four main components (computer system performance, user cost/benefit, system revenue, and manufacturer cost) for which nearly 100 variables have to be specified. The output includes total and component performance and financial quantities such as cost, profit, maximum investment, and optimum price. A sensitivity analysis revealed that the profit was most sensitive to the variables representing (in order of importance):

1. Interest rate
2. System price
3. Development schedule
4. Total market revenue
5. Number of competitors
6. Competitors' prices
7. Product life

Technical performance was *not* an important factor and came well down on the list. When the model was used on a particular system under development it turned out to be a good predictor for performance and cost, but at the time of reporting there were no data on how well it predicted revenues and profitability.

Perhaps models for predicting sales or financial performance are not uncommon in the computer industry, but published reports on such models and on their effectiveness are rare. Although the computer/communications industry is being very closely monitored, much remains to be done in building a theoretical framework which can be used to explain developments and predict the course of events. The high rate of technological development is undoubtedly a key reason for this lack. While it continues the industry cannot achieve stability, either with respect to the type of products or the number of suppliers, and without this it is impossible to obtain the statistics or produce a structure that can model the industry except in some very general respects.

PROBLEMS

1. Using an appropriate equation, extrapolate Fig. 9.5 so as to obtain R_{1981}, the total data processing revenues for 1981. Using Table 9.4 and assuming that the sums of the revenues for the 15 largest data processing companies are proportional to the total revenues each year,

estimate $R_{1976} \cdots R_{1982}$ and hence the annual growth rate for data processing revenues for the interval. Check the assumption by consulting *Datamation* for June 1982 and June 1981, where the data processing revenues for the 100 largest companies are listed.

2. In an interesting attempt to chart the total volume of data processing activity in business, Phister (1979, Suppl. Sec. 3.0, p. 561) introduces three parameters:

   (1) *D*—average number of bytes stored in an organization's files, normalized by annual revenue or number of employees
   (2) *f*—fractions of bytes processed during a year
   (3) *S*—number of elementary operations (by human beings or machines) to process one byte

Estimates for the total activity, *fSD*, by human beings and machines are presented. The data suggest an S-shaped curve between 1950 and 1980, leading to the conjecture that "*over the past ten years the rate of growth of processing has slowed, and that it will decrease further during the coming decade*" (original italics). Phister's arguments do not take into account the implications of the merging of the computer and communication technologies. What additional parameters are needed to allow for this? Considering growth trends for personal workstations, SBCs, and data communications does the conjecture seem reasonable for the next decade? Eventually? What data might be collected to formulate an alternative conjecture and test it? Are there similar arguments to suggest that limits to the rate of data processing for home computer services and services on behalf of government are in sight?

BIBLIOGRAPHY

BROCK, G., *The U.S. Computer Industry: A Study of Market Power.* Cambridge, Mass.: Ballinger, 1974.

CHAMPINE, G. A., "Univac's Financial Model for Computer Development," *Datamation,* 23, no. 2 (February 1977), 53–57.

DOLOTTA, T. A., M. I. BERNSTEIN, R. S. DECKSON, JR., N. A. France, B. A. ROSENBLATT, D. P. SMITH, and T. B. STEEL, JR., *Data Processing in 1980–1985: A Study of Potential Limitations to Progress.* New York: Wiley, 1976.

DUNN, D. A., and A. C. FRONISTAS, "Economic Models of Information Services Markets," in *The Economics of Information Processing, Vol. 1: Management Perspectives,* ed. R. Goldberg and H. Lorin. New York: Wiley, 1982, pp. 141–62.

FRANK, W. L., *Critical Issues in Software.* New York: Wiley, 1983.

GILCHRIST, B., and R. E. WEBER, *The State of the Computer Industry in the United States.* Montvale, N.J.: AFIPS Press, 1973.

GOLDBERG, R., and H. LORIN, *The Economics of Information Processing, Vol. 1: Management Perspectives.* New York: Wiley, 1982.

HARMAN, A., *The International Computer Industry.* Cambridge, Mass.: Harvard University Press, 1971.

HAZEWINDUS, N., and J. TOOKER, *The U.S. Microelectronics Industry.* Elmsford, N.Y.: Pergamon Press, 1982.

Nyborg, P. S., P. McCarter, and W. Erickson, eds., *Information Processing in the United States—A Quantitative Summary.* American Federation of Information Processing Societies, Inc., (AFIPS) Montvale, N.J., 1977.

OECD Economic Outlook, 32 (December 1982). Paris: OECD.

Phister, M., Jr., *Data Processing Technology and Economics,* 2nd ed. Santa Fe, N. Mex.: Santa Monica/Bedford, Mass.: Digital Press, 1979.

Sassone, P. G., and F. E. Williams, "Economic Modelling of the Small Computer Industry," in *The Economics of Information Processing,* Vol. 1: *Management Perspectives,* ed. R. Goldberg and H. Lorin. New York: Wiley, 1982. pp. 163–76.

Soma, J. T., *The Computer Industry.* Lexington, Mass.: Lexington Books, 1976.

Wilson, R. W., P. K. Ashton, T. P. Egan, *Innovation, Competition, and Government Policy in the Semiconductor Industry.* Lexington, Mass.: Lexington Books, 1980.

10

Corporate
Strategies

Since the growth of the computer industry in the last 25 years has been almost unprecedented, this market expansion should have, and has, presented great opportunities. Yet the record shows that it has been extremely difficult for very many companies to capitalize on them. Large corporations with enormous assets and extensive experience in electronics have entered the computer field, stayed a few years, and withdrawn. In the United States, Raytheon, Philco, RCA, General Electric, and Xerox all eventually gave up competing for the sale and manufacture of general-purpose computers. In Europe the story has been the same—English Electronic and Facit, to name two companies, have come and gone from the computer scene. For small companies life in the computer industry has been just as precarious as it has been for large ones.

In the last two chapters some salient facts about the computer industry were emphasized. First, it has displayed and continues to display an extraordinarily rapid pace of technological change. This pace has quickened because of the convergence with another industry which is itself in great flux, communications. Second, since the beginnings of the industry, the computer market has been dominated to a significant degree by one country, the United States, and within that country by one company, IBM. High rates of change and dominant enterprises are not unique to the computer industry. But the *extent* to which these are present in the computer field *is* unusual, and it is these factors that we examine in attempting to see why the industry has been in constant turmoil, and how companies in the field have tried to deal with the consequences. The focus here will be on the U.S. computer industry because it is the largest part of the international industry and documentation on it is best. There are strong simi-

252

larities elsewhere with what has happened in the United States, but, in the main, considerations about other countries will be deferred to Part IV.

10.1. COST ADVANTAGES OF ESTABLISHED COMPUTER FIRMS

Table 9.4 showed the market shares for the major U.S. mainframe computer manufacturers. In his interesting and well-documented study of the U.S. computer industry (mainly about the hardware sector, and before communications assumed the major role that it now plays) Brock (1974) examined the reasons why a company which has a dominant share of the market is in a favored position, and he estimated how the factors translate, quantitatively, into cost advantages for IBM over its competitors. Brock identified three major factors: economies of scale in production, marketing advantages, and capital availability.

Before looking at these it is helpful to have some idea of how the revenue of mainframe computer companies is apportioned. Table 10.1 shows the distribution for four companies, IBM, Digital Computer Equipment, Prime, and Tandem, in 1978. These are only representative. IBM, of course, has consistently had the largest revenue; DEC ranked sixth for 1978 (it was second in 1981); while Prime and Tandem are smaller (Prime ranked forty-sixth in 1978 and twenty-fifth in 1981 and Tandem was thirty-eighth in 1981) they are interesting in that they are both relatively young, aggressive companies with highly rated products and with high growth rates.

10.1.1. Economies of Scale in Production

Although a large market share certainly results in economies of scale in manufacturing, mainly because of the opportunity to make or purchase components at lower costs, experience in most industries is that there are definite limits

TABLE 10.1 REVENUE DISTRIBUTION (PERCENT) OF FOUR MAINFRAME COMPUTER COMPANIES, 1978

	IBM	DEC	Prime	Tandem
Cost of revenue (labor, parts, software)	37	56	42	37
Product development (R&D)	7	8	8	8
Marketing, administration, general	33	20	30	37
Interest (net)	1	—	—	2
Taxes	11	6	7	9
Earnings	13	10	11	9
Total[a]	102	100	98	102

[a]Differences from 100 due to round-off effects.

Source: Revenue Recognition Policy, September 1, 1979.

beyond which there are no further advantages to be had by building larger and larger plants. The curve of unit cost versus volume of production is U-shaped rather than one which approaches an asymptotic value determined by the cost of materials and labor. The reason for the (rather shallow) minimum is that the administrative costs for very large organizations tend to rise rapidly because of the necessary hierarchical structure, and because of the need to maintain communication between the different subunits. In other industries it has been found that minimum unit costs are reached when about 20% of the market share is attained; beyond that there are no further economies of scale to be had from concentrated production. Typically, a firm with about 10% of the national market (i.e., half the most efficient scale) experiences costs which are increased by 1 to 8%, while a firm with 2% of the market (one-tenth the efficient scale) would have cost elevations of 2 to 35%.

Some evidence about IBM production costs comes from depositions in an antitrust suit of *Telex* v. *IBM* (see *Telex* v. *IBM*). Although there are suggestions that for complete systems economies of scale continue to be present for quite large market shares, for peripherals they seem to be fairly small. Overall, Brock estimates that with regard to mainframe manufacturing, which accounts for 10 to 15% of the revenues earned, a firm with 10% of the market would have cost elevations of about 5 to 15% compared to one with 100% of the market.*

However, economies of scale manifest themselves for reasons other than production. Since the computer industry functions by direct sales from the manufacturer to the end user rather than by a network of middle-level distributorships which is often present in other industries,† the costs for sales force, customer engineering, and maintenance are important. There are significant economies of scales to be had for all of these, and it is not difficult to construct simple models to estimate what they might be. A company with a large market share will have a high density of customers and can establish a service area (for either sales or maintenance) with a smaller radius, reducing travel costs for personnel and improving the quality of service. Let D be the customer density for a firm with 100% of the market. Then the density for a firm with a fraction f of the market will be fD. The number of customers in a circle of radius r for the 100% firm will be $\pi r^2 D$. The corresponding circle, to include the same number of customers for the low-market-share firm, will have radius R, where $\pi r^2 D = \pi R^2 fD$. Thus $R/r = 1/f^{1/2}$. If we assume that the costs are proportional to radius, then when $f = \frac{1}{4}$, the costs ratio will be $(\frac{1}{4})^{1/2} = \frac{1}{2}$ (i.e., a firm with 25% of the market will experience double the travel-time costs). Of course, travel time is only an addition to the time the salesperson or maintenance engineer spends at the site.

For maintenance another effect arises out of queueing theory, which has

---

*Note that the costs for revenue are higher in Table 10.1, but the latter include maintenance and software costs.

†But note that for personal computers retail outlets are crucial.

already been mentioned in assessing the reliability of large systems compared to small (Section 4.2). For a given response time, the cost per customer for servicing a queue with a high arrival rate of calls is less than that for a queue with a low arrival rate.* The disadvantage is mitigated because a great deal of maintenance on computers is preventive, and for this there is no random fluctuation component.

Taking all factors into consideration, Brock estimates that the economies of scale due to sales (which he estimates account for 10 to 15% of computer revenue) are such that a firm with 10% of the market experiences cost elevations of 2 to 5% compared to the firm with 100% market share. The corresponding figure for maintenance (accounting for 7 to 10% of computer revenues) is 15 to 20% cost elevation.

The greatest economies of scale for high market share come from software. Here, by far most of the costs are for development, and the incremental cost for an additional customer is very low. Brock's estimate is that for software (to which 10 to 15% of revenue must be devoted) the 10% market share firm has cost elevations of 50% compared with those for the 100% firm.†

When the cost elevations for each of these four factors (manufacturing, sales, maintenance, and software) are weighted by their importance (i.e., the fraction of revenue that must be devoted to them) the result is that a firm with 10% of the market suffers a disadvantage of about 20%, due to the economies of scale enjoyed by the firm with 100% market share.

10.1.2. Economies of Scale in Marketing

As noted in Table 10.1, marketing costs are usually included in indirect expenses due to administration. Of the 33% devoted to these purposes by IBM, it is estimated that 13% is for sales promotion. The main expenses are those for sales personnel. With the simple model used for maintenance, a company with 24% of the leader's share finds its marketing costs increased by 4.3%; one with 5.5% of the leader's costs has its marketing expenses raised by 12% and for a company with only 1 to 2% of the leader's share, marketing costs are elevated by 31%.

There are other marketing advantages that established firms possess. Costs of retraining, reprogramming, and data conversion are effective deterrents to switching manufacturers. A 1971 Datamation survey showed that 91% of Burrough's customers replaced their computers with a Burroughs machine; corre-

---

*Because of statistical fluctuations, the low-arrival-rate queue will experience a larger fraction of the time when the queue is empty and the server is idle. It is to overcome this effect that banks, for example, have adopted a single queue for a set of tellers, rather than having a separate queue for each wicket, as used to be the case.

†According to Brock, the combined cost of sales and maintenance (including software) for the firm with 100% of the market is 27 to 35% of revenues earned. Phister quotes costs in the range 35 to 40% for these as experienced by IBM (1979, Fig. I.311.8a). With manufacturing costs of 10 to 15%, this means that the cost of revenues is in the range of 37 to 50%, which agrees with the percentage shown in Table 10.1.

sponding figures for IBM, Honeywell, NCR, and UNIVAC were 82%, 79%, 76%, and 61%, respectively.

The most important factor in marketing generally is product differentiation. This is strong when there is an inability to evaluate products accurately, integration of the retail dealer organization with the manufacturing firm (as is found in the automobile industry), and when there is conspicuous consumption, as happens with many kinds of consumer goods. A study of the relative importance of characteristics such as rental costs, demonstrability, system support, delivery time, value of installed equipment, reciprocal purchasing arrangements, and execution time revealed strong preferences for:

- The current supplier
- An up-to-date system
- Extensive system support

The weight attached to these factors is different (i.e., less) for plug-compatibilities (disks, memories, printers) than it is for complete systems, and it is also different for smaller machines. As users have become more experienced they have gained confidence and become more independent, and the advantages of established firms have decreased. Nevertheless, customer loyalty has tended to remain high. A 1982 survey* of 3278 minicomputer users taking delivery of 13,242 systems revealed that 82.6% indicated they had no plans to switch suppliers. Table 10.2 shows the percentage of sites where a switch of manufacturer was being planned or considered, together with reasons cited for the dissatisfaction.

10.1.3. Capital Requirements as a Barrier to Market Entry

For several reasons the need for capital is especially great in the computer industry. One is the high rate of technological development, as documented in Chapter 8. This means that the R&D costs are greater than they are in most other industries. Table 10.3(*a*) shows the 1980 R&D expenditures for the 10 largest hardware manufacturers: other types of computer companies spend even more [Table 10.3(*b*)].

Another reason for large capital requirements is that a high percentage of computer products (and this even includes software) have traditionally been leased rather than sold. This means that a large amount of capital must be invested, and the cash flow problems can become especially acute when sales are rising rapidly. For a large enough growth rate the profit margin can actually dwindle to zero! (See Problem 1.) A company with great success in marketing its products through leases can find itself in a very unfavorable position when it has to go to the money markets for capital. This is a principal reason for the eventual

*_Datamation,_ 28, no. 11 (November 1982), 34–48.

TABLE 10.2 CUSTOMER LOYALTY TO MINICOMPUTER VENDORS

Manufacturer[a]	Percent of Sites Planning or Considering Switch	Percentage of Switching Sites Dissatisfied with:					
		Delivery	Price	Hardware Reliability	Software Support	Sales/ Service	Other
Tandem[a]	7.5	—	—	33.3	33.3	—	33.3
DEC	11.0	5.8	23.1	22.4	34.0	24.4	25.6
IBM	11.1	6.8	31.5	15.1	38.4	21.9	24.7
SEL	13.6	—	—	—	100.0	—	66.7
Prime	14.1	3.4	31.0	31.0	37.9	17.2	27.6
Hewlett-Packard	14.3	2.5	22.8	16.5	30.4	24.1	36.7
Honeywell	15.7	—	4.8	33.3	66.7	9.5	19.0
Wang	16.1	6.5	16.1	19.4	22.6	38.7	29.0
Texas Instruments	16.8	5.6	38.9	11.1	11.1	44.4	22.2
Perkin-Elmer[a]	18.0	—	—	22.2	66.7	33.3	11.1
Total sites[b]	17.4	5.0	20.5	22.6	39.5	22.2	27.8

[a]Fewer than 10 sites.

[b]Only 10 of the 23 manufacturers listed are shown here.

Source: Data from J. W. Verity, "1982 Mini-micro Survey," *Datamation,* 28, no. 12 91982), 34–48.

TABLE 10.3 R&D EXPENDITURES OF DATA PROCESSING COMPANIES

(a) Ten Companies with Largest Expenditures, 1980

Rank	Company	Expenditure (millions of dollars)	Expenditure as Percent of DP Revenue
1	IBM	1277	6.0
2	DEC	217	7.9
3	Sperry	216	8.5
4	NCR	201	7.1
5	Control Data	183	6.6
6	Burroughs	175	7.1
7	Honeywell	150	9.2
8	Hewlett-Packard	139	8.8
9	Data General	68	10.1
10	Amdahl Corp.	63	16.0

Source: Datamation, 27, no. 6 (June 1981), 91–103.

(b) Ten Companies with Largest Expenditure as Percent of Revenue, 1981

Rank	Company	Expenditure (millions of dollars)	Expenditure as Percent of DP Revenue
1	Management Science America	15.6	21.3
2	Applicon	11.0	17.1
3	Amdahl Corp.	75.1	16.9
4	Cray Research Inc.	16.3	16.0
5	Flosley Point Systems	8.8	16.0
6	Dypan Corp.	15.8	15.1
7	Intergraph Corp.	12.0	13.1
8	Teletype Corp.	27.3	12.3
9	Computervision Corp.	27.2	10.0
10	Computer Automation, Inc.	7.2	10.0

Source: Datamation, 28, no. 6 (June 1982), 115–25.

bankruptcy of Consolidated Computer Co., a Canadian-based company manufacturing key-editing systems for data entry.

A third reason for high capital requirements in the mainframe industry, especially, is the need to develop a large product line so that users can upgrade smoothly as their data processing activities grow. It is especially difficult to maintain compatibility across hardware, software, and data communications simultaneously, yet users demand this because they do not want to convert files and programs, or retrain staff. The net result of this last demand is that only companies with *very* large amounts of capital have chosen to stay in the across-the-board mainframe business, and this is why even the giant companies mentioned in the introduction to this chapter eventually withdrew from competition. In many cases the investment was *too* large, the payback period *too* protracted, and there were better prospects of return in other ventures. But for

TABLE 10.4 SUMMARY OF COST DISADVANTAGES FOR A NEW ENTRY,
RELATIVE TO IBM

Constraint	Integrated Systems	Peripherals	Minicomputers
Economies of scale in production—disadvantage	20%	10%	50%
Marketing disadvantages	20–30%	10–20%	5–10%
Capital requirements	Blocked	Moderate	Minor
Total evaluation	No entry possible	20–30% disadvantage	10–15% disadvantage

Source: Reprinted with permission from G. W. Brock, *The United States Computer Industry: A Study of Market Power,* copyright 1974, Ballinger Publishing Company, Cambridge, Mass.

minicomputers and peripheral equipment, the capital needs are not nearly as great.

Table 10.4 summarizes the cost disadvantages for entry of new firms compared with the costs of IBM. Note the judgment that (by 1975) entry to the total integrated system market was no longer possible. Actually, just about that time Amdahl entered to stay, but the company had to turn to Japan for capital to survive. In fact, as we shall see in the next two chapters, the only *survivors* in the integrated systems market, besides IBM, have been companies such as ICL and Fujitisu, which in a sense have the financial backing of a whole country behind them, and it is generally conceded that *new* entries to the total market are practically impossible—practically, but not completely ruled out. We have seen the reasons why communication companies are being led into the computer industry, and there is evidence that telecommunication giants such as AT&T are deciding to compete across a very broad spectrum of computer products and services. See *AT&T in the Computer Market* (1984). But the situation is quite different for makers of minicomputers, peripherals, and others who are prepared to look for sales in specialized areas. Here new industries abound.

10.2. MARKETING APPROACHES

In view of IBM's dominant position in the computer industry, other companies have two obvious courses of action—develop products which are compatible with those of IBM and attempt to compete on the basis of performance and price, or seek innovations to open up new markets which IBM has not yet entered. Different companies have concentrated on one or the other of these approaches. In general, the mainframe companies such as Control Data Corporation, Digital Equipment Corporation, and Tandem have pursued the latter course, seeking to develop products that would differentiate them from IBM, but inevitably having also to compete with IBM along the way. On the other hand, manufacturers of components and peripheral equipment, such as memories, disk drives, and printers, have *had* to be compatible with IBM if they were to have any hope of placing their devices in a user's installation.

Given a niche in the market, companies also have two choices regarding pricing. The first is geared to expansion, achieved by keeping prices low, forgoing short-run profits, and hoping to build up a significant market share. The second, which is possible on possession of a product clearly superior to, or different from, that offered by IBM, is to concentrate on high, short-term profits, in the hope of building up enough capital to gain a permanent place in the market.

All four of these strategic combinations are to be found in the histories of computer companies.

10.2.1 Compatibility

.The relatively short lifetime of computer products makes timing crucial when attempting to compete with IBM by offering compatible equipment. A product introduced late in the life cycle will have too short a lifetime to recoup the research and development costs. But a product introduced early in the life cycle, or better still, one that is competitive with the *next* generation of IBM's equipment, stands a good chance of being successful.

The IBM 650, introduced in 1954, had phenomenally high sales and more than anything else convinced IBM that its future lay with electronic computers rather than punched-card equipment. UNIVAC, which to begin with was even more closely identified with computers in the public mind than was IBM, tried to compete with the IBM 650 by introducing the UNIVAC Solid State 80 in 1959. Although this was based on the superior solid-state technology, it was priced too high for a machine which otherwise did not perform better. A few months later the IBM 1401 arrived, also a solid-state machine, and one which, with its variable word length, was clearly designed for business applications. The UNIVAC timing was too late. On the other hand, in December 1963 Honeywell introduced the H-200, a machine it advertised as the "Liberator" because it freed users from dependence on IBM. Priced the same as the 1401, but with better performance, it was a serious contender right up to 1972, and its success was partially responsible for an acceleration in the release of the IBM System 360. Other examples of the importance of timing are to be found in RCA's Spectra 70 (introduced unsuccessfully in 1965 to compete with the 360, but with difficult-to-compare compatibility and doubtful performance improvement) and the Amdahl, successful against the IBM 370/168 because of good timing and superior price/performance characteristics.

The compatibility approach, whether used by mainframe companies or makers of plug-compatible equipment, is essentially a price war. A competing product either sells for less or has better performance for the same price. Where the device is strictly compatible (high-speed memories, disk drives, printers, etc.)

the competitor has the advantage of asking the customer to risk very little. The device can be wheeled in and tried on short notice and little cost, so its advantages are easy to demonstrate. IBM's ability to respond by direct price cuts is limited. Any reductions made to gain new customers (or hold old ones being wooed) must also be offered to the large installed base, which, due to customer loyalty, is probably contemplating no change, and the *overall* effect of a price cut could mean a substantial drop in revenue. But through the years IBM has developed an impressive set of other countermeasures to meet the challenges posed by competitors offering price advantages.

Among the possible responses are:

- Midlife kickers (upgrading the performance of installed machines)
- Proprietary diagnostics (making it difficult for a customer to place responsibility when the system goes down)
- Movement and integration of interfaces (making it difficult for the competing device to be attached
- New leasing plans (offering price reductions to customers willing to commit themselves to longer-term contracts)

All these techniques have been used by IBM at different times against such competitors as Telex, Memorex, Potter, and leasing companies, sometimes with devastating effect, as could be seen when the share price of one of the competitors plummeted immediately after IBM announced a new policy. It was evidence of tactics like these, often employed by IBM to meet the threat of a particular company against a particular product, which has formed the basis of many of the antitrust actions launched against IBM by the government and by different companies.*

10.2.2. Innovation

If the key to compatibility is timing, the key to innovation is pricing. Any technical advance must be achieved at reasonable cost, but here too timing is important, for the market must be ready to receive the new product.

It is well known that achieving a technical breakthrough by research is not enough to assure market success, and that there are numerous cases where the innovating company was not the one to reap the principal rewards of its invention. In computers Philco was the first company to produce a transistorized machine, but it did not stay in the market for long. Again GE, working with M.I.T., produced the GE 645, the first commercial time-sharing machine, but this achievement was not enough to sustain the company in the mainframe computer business.

On the other hand, there are also cases where a better product, or one that

*For details, see Brock (1974. Chaps. 7, 8).

defined a new market, *has* had a lasting effect on the company's fortunes. The Control Data 6600, introduced in 1964, had a Knight's scientific index of 7020, compared with IBM's 7094 II, with an index of 217, introduced in the same year. The CDC 6600 established Control Data as a leading producer of the number-crunching machines used for computations in nuclear physics and meteorology, a position it has maintained. The Burroughs B-5000 had stack compilation, was the first computer with multiprocessing, and had a clean logical design which led to good software, giving Burroughs a reputation that is has enjoyed ever since. In 1965 Digital Equipment introduced the PDP-11, the first of the minicomputers, offering excellent performance at the price, and this laid the foundation for the DEC machines, which have opened up vast markets of new users. In the late 1970s Tandem's Non-Stop systems met the needs of users who had to have 24-hour assured operation (e.g., banks with unattended terminals) and in doing so earned a solid place for the company. Also, Prime offered, in its 50 Series of minicomputers, architectural features which until then could be found only in the most expensive supercomputers (pipeline processing, cache memories, many levels of program interrupts, virtual memory) achieving a price/performance factor so outstanding that the company was an immediate success. Most recently, the personal computer market was opened by a new set of manufacturers—Commodore, Osborne, Apple, and Tandy—who produced microcomputers based on a single processor chip for hobbyists. It was not until the 1980s, when the potential for such machines in business applications became apparent, that IBM, DEC, and traditional mainframe manufacturers entered the field for personal computers.

It is reasonably clear from these examples that IBM's dominance in the computer field is not due to the overwhelming technical superiority of its product or its innovative designs. Since we have seen that economies of scale are also not enough to account for its lead, it is fair to ask what the reasons *are*. There is general agreement that IBM is superior in at least two respects. It is an extremely well managed company. Time and time again it has reorganized itself almost from top to bottom, in order to meet the new conditions of a changing marketplace. This it has done both domestically and internationally, responding to the demands of each level. To give examples of IBM's flexibility it is only necessary to recall how it was able to respond to the unbundling pressure by introducing separate pricing for software in a way that has kept revenues intact. Further, when it introduced the Personal Computer, it was ready to accept and market both hardware and software from other sources, in recognition of the fact that this was an area where, not having its usual market share, it could not expect to set standards, as was its custom. Also, of all the computer companies, IBM, with its ubiquitous presence in international markets and strong client base of multinational companies, was the first to recognize the importance of communications in computing, and through its interest in Satellite Business System and emphasis on System Network Architecture, has made the most direct entry into the telecommunications field. But in attempting to explain the reasons for IBM's dominance, there is also agreement that IBM's superb marketing is a major factor. Of all computer companies it has been the most successful practitioner of a *product differentiation strategy*. This is a sales approach based on the concept that the company offers a unique product, different from that of its competitors in that it emphasizes not machine cycles but users' needs. In doing so it is ready to provide hardware, software, education, consulting help, and whatever is required to help solve the *user's* problems. Together with a product differentiation strategy has come *constant pricing* (initially low in the product life cycle and latterly high), capitalizing on the reluctance of most users to change suppliers, *functional pricing* (based on performance rather than cost of production), and *asset ownership* (a predisposition, but not a fixation, toward renting rather than selling). Essentially, past strategy has been noncompetitive, and to a large extent it was made possible because, as has been emphasized throughout this book, computer products and services are difficult to rate objectively. As users have become more sophisticated, evaluation methods more common, and the variety of products has increased, the product differentiation strategy has had to be modified, but IBM has been able to react appropriately. The basic strategy is to compete in all segments of the information processing industry, but there is also an emphasis on *low cost* products, along with a much greater readiness to have these made by carefully chosen suppliers. The effect is that IBM has been able to maintain and even increase its dominance of the marketplace.*

10.3 SHIFTING PATTERNS

Changeable as the computer industry has been before convergence with the communication technology, since then it has been in an even greater state of flux. In part this is because telecommunications has a strong international component, and this brings more actors onto the stage. The international aspects will be examined in greater detail in Part IV. But within the United States itself the presence of telecommunications in computers has brought the common carriers onto the scene, especially the largest of the carriers, AT&T. To understand recent developments it is necessary to know a little of the background of AT&T, a company that profited greatly because of regulation, and which is being transformed radically as a consequence of deregulation. Similarly, it is useful to understand something of the history of IBM, whose actions have been limited, in part, because antitrust suits were always in its background, and for whom the release from threats of antitrust action presents new opportunities and challenges.†

---

*For an historical overview of IBM's strategy, see M. G. Schulman, "Big Blue's Big Bucks." *Datamation*, 29, no. 2 (Feb. 1984), 131–36.

†For histories of IBM, see Sobel (1981) and Fishman (1981, Part II).

10.3.1. IBM and AT&T

In the United States the Sherman and Clayton Acts have proven to be powerful instruments for protecting consumers against monopolistic practices. They have enabled government to break up large corporations and can result in awards, to a winning company, of amounts which are triple the damages caused by a losing defendant. The history of IBM's involvement in antitrust actions either initiated by the government or by other companies is long and complex.* As early as 1936, the Clayton Act was used to prohibit IBM from insisting that users of its punch-card machines had to purchase their cards from IBM. A significant event was the 1956 consent decree,† one result of which was that IBM undertook to sell, as well as rent, its equipment. The CDC versus IBM suit filed in 1968 was also noteworthy because of the vast collection of evidence (25 to 40 million IBM documents examined by Control. Data, and 120 million Control Data documents examined by IBM), enormous expenditures ($15 million by Control Data and an estimated $60 million by IBM), and the magnitude of the out-of-court settlement, which took place in 1973. As a result of that settlement IBM sold its subsidiary, Service Bureau Corporation, to Control Data for its very low book value, paid Control Data $101 million and Control Data destroyed its computerized data base of evidence, a serious loss to the government, which in 1969 had filed its own suit against IBM. Cases against IBM were also launched by Greyhound (1971), Telex (1972), Memorex (1973), Calcomp (1973), and others. IBM has never lost a case in court‡, but through the 1950s, 1960s, and 1970s all these actions and threats of action constrained IBM's conduct. In attempts to stave off the 1969 government suit, IBM withdrew a 60% discount offered to educational institutions, unbundled software from hardware, and established the Service Bureau Corporation as a distinct company. The case dragged on for over a decade, challenged at every level by IBM, and pursued with varying amounts of diligence by successive U.S. administrations, until January 1982, when it was dismissed as being "without merit." It is commonly felt that it was no accident that dismissal came at a time when the U.S. computer industry was being challenged seriously for the first time, especially by the Japanese, and there had emerged a feeling that it was time to stop placing U.S. companies at a disadvantage in the international marketplace because of domestic antitrust constraints. IBM's response was immediate; within a short time it reentered the service bureau business¶, increased its activities in communications, and reinstituted policies of making substantial gifts to universities and other educational institutions.

---

*For details, see Gilchrist and Wessil (1972), Brock (1974), and Pantages (1979).

†A consent decree is like a settlement in that guilt is neither proven nor admitted, but the defendant understakes certain actions as a result of which the suit is dropped.

‡Although there were temporary losses, later reversed on appeal (e.g., to Telex).

¶In Canada, IBM never did give up its service bureau operations.

Whereas government, through antitrust actions and threats, has served to constrain IBM, until recently at least, through regulation, it has been a help to AT&T by protecting it from new competitors. The early history of telephone and telegraph communications is a complicated story of the making and breaking of monopolies (see Brock, 1981, Chaps. 4, 6). In 1907, AT&T was the largest single company, but independents owned almost half of the telephones in the country. About then AT&T accepted the limitations imposed by regulation on price and service so as to be able to engage in mergers which absorbed the competition. This umbrella of regulation, together with acquisition of basic vacuum-tube patents, allowed it to become the controlling firm in telecommunications by 1934, when it owned 80% of the telephones in the United States and had the only important long-distance network. That year is significant because it also marked the formation of the Federal Communication Commission. Investigations initiated by the FCC led to an antitrust suit against AT&T, with the aim of making it divest itself of Western Electric, its manufacturing arm. But under the terms of a 1956 consent decree, AT&T was allowed to remain an integrated company, retaining Western Electric (and Bell Laboratories), while it agreed to restrict its activities to those governed by regulation and to license its patents to competitors. AT&T thrived as a regulated monopoly, so that by 1981 it and its 22 operating companies controlled 80% of the local service in the United States; it provided 96% of the long-distance calls, and its assets of $138 billion and revenue of $59 billion placed it among the largest companies in the country.

The development of microwave techniques greatly increased the available electromagnetic spectrum and lessened the arguments that a scarce resource justified a communications monopoly. Also, under the very complicated rate structures that had grown up, the rates for local calls were subsidized by long-distance rates. In 1956 the FCC began a review of microwave frequency allocations, and in 1959 decided to allow private microwave carriers but did not at first provide for interconnection with the common carriers. This decision was opposed by AT&T (and other carriers) and it began to offer cheaper long-distance service (e.g., Telpak) and engaged in long delaying tactics in the courts. It was not until 1972 that Microwave Communications Inc. (MCI) established an operating facility between St. Louis and Chicago to become the first of the specialized common carriers. Other entrants followed (Southern Pacific, Datatron), but their share of the total market has continued to be small. Nevertheless, FCC's decision to remove regulative barriers to competition, and to insist on interconnection, was far-reaching. Particularly important was the 1968 Carterphone decision, which allowed the use of a cradle-type modern as long as there were no unfavorable impacts on the telephone network, for this presented the opening for new entrants into the market for PBXs and other attachments. The overlap between computer and telecommunications services led the FCC to hold two inquiries, and after long hearings rules were promulgated (in 1971 and again in 1979) which attempted to distinguish between services which were primarily telecommunication-like and subject to regulation, and those which were primarily computer-like and were therefore free of regulation. This distinctions proved unworkable. In the meantime there were court decisions allowing competitors to subdivide high-capacity channels purchased from AT&T and resell them, and conflicting bills were introduced into Congress, one that would have effectively reaffirmed AT&T's monopoly and others which would have had the opposite effect of weakening it. Technological advances in computers and satellite transmission made it increasingly difficult to maintain or justify a monopolistic position with respect to long-distance lines, although the case for regulation of *local* telephone traffic continued to have validity. Finally, in a far-reaching consent decree which became effective in January 1984, AT&T divested itself of its local operating telephone companies (which remained under state regulation) and retaining its long-haul lines, Western Electric and the Bell Laboratories, became a new company, AT&T Information Services, free of regulation. This move was welcomed both by AT&T, which had been seeing its monopoly eroded without being able to enter into new fields that might compensate for the loss, and by other companies seeking to enter the market for long-distance lines. Many of the implications, such as the effect on costs for local service, have yet to be seen, but there is a general agreement that freer competition will give consumers greater benefits from the technological advances in computers and communications and more say in how the industries develop.

The immediate consequence was that IBM, the dominant company in computers, could engage more freely in telecommunication activities, and AT&T, the dominant U.S. company in communications, was freed to enter the computer market. Many feel that head-on competition in such areas as office automation is inevitable. Estimates on the projected communications traffic in offices suggested that by 1990 the data component, which makes up 10 to 20% of the total currently, will increase by approximately an order of magnitude and will equal or surpass the voice component.* This growth will come from increased use of personal computing, electronic messaging, and document distribution. Both IBM and AT&T are staking claims against this growth, as are other companies, such as Xerox, Wang, and Digital Equipment Corporation, to say nothing of companies in other countries. The prospects for competition are all the greater because of the emphasis being given to intergrated system data network (ISDNs). Two services, the Information Network, launched February 1982 by IBM, and the Advanced Information System, introduced in June 1982 by AT&T, show how each company is enlarging its range of activities into areas that potentially intersect with those of the other. Figure 10.1 shows a map of information products and services, together with the domains occupied by IBM and AT&T. The overlap is noteworthy. Whatever the form of competition, it is clear that IBM and AT&T will each have to take account of the strategic interests of the other in planning future operations and markets.

---

*S. A. Smith and R. I. Benjamin, "Telecommunications Demand in Automated Office," in *Proceedings of Eleventh Telecommunications Policy Conference, 1983* (Norwood, N.J.: Ablex, in press).

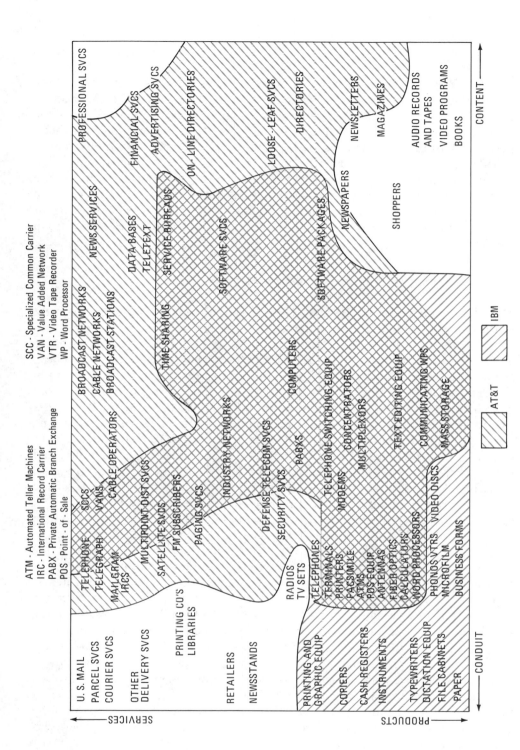

Figure 10.1 Information products and services IBM and AT&T (from J. F. McLaughlin and A. E. Birinyi, "Mapping the Information Business," 1980 Program on Information Resources Policy, Harvard University, Cambridge, Mass., with permission).

267

But it is not only AT&T and IBM that have moved to take advantage of the opportunities created by the deregulation of communications. Other companies, attracted by the predictions of rapid market growth, have sought to enter the competition whenever they feel that there is some special entry point for them. Banks and insurance companies are expanding their financial operations to offer a wide variety of services based on electronic transfer of funds; hotels are offering facilities for teleconferencing; all the major time-sharing networks are competing for electronic mail. For a graphic description of the market explosion and the way in which companies, that until now have been customers of telecommunications, are scrambling to become providers of services, see Irwin (1983).

10.3.2. Diversification, Integration, and Joint Agreements

Major companies such as IBM, AT&T, and ITT, already strong in one segment of the computer/communication industry, are clearly well placed to expand into those sectors where new markets arise, and this they do. This is also the approach of companies outside the United States which traditionally have been strong in communications (e.g., C.F. Thomson in France and L.M. Ericsson in Sweden) or in specialized areas (Olivetti in Italy). Even companies not engaged primarily in computers or communications have acted to diversify their interests by staking out claims in the information technologies, either by acquiring existing companies and building on them or by launching new enterprises. Thus Exxon, the world's largest oil company, acquired Zilog semiconductors, and made a major thrust into office automation with Exxon Office Systems. McDonnell-Douglas Automation Company was initially a service arm of the parent aircraft company, but in expanding its activities to outside customers it earned $476 million of data processing revenues in 1982, ranking twenty-fourth in the list of U.S. companies. The Harris Corporation, engaged primarily in defense-related industries, actively entered the information sector, both in the United States and abroad to market superminicomputers, interactive terminals, distributed data processing systems, word processors, digital telephone switches, supervisory control systems, and so on. In 1982 it ranked thirty-fourth among U.S. companies with data processing revenues of $332 million. General Electric, which left the mainframe market in the 1960s, came back into the information sector, concentrating on microelectronics, CAD/CAM equipment, and industrial robots, aggressively pursuing market share. In 1982 it ranked thirteenth in data processing revenues with earnings of $862 million and unusually high profits.

In the highly competitive information industry, with so many different facets to it, no company, not even IBM, has attempted to assure its place by complete vertical integration. There are simply too many areas where expertise is required, too many types of components from chips to printers, too many geographical regions where it is important to compete, to make vertical integration an effective strategy. Instead, there has been a steady stream of mergers, alliances, and joint undertakings where two or more companies with complementary strengths have pooled their efforts. The advantages are obvious—high research and development costs make it attractive to acquire expertise quickly from others; the presence of one company in a market or country offers possibilities of penetration for the other; capital available in one company may be needed by the other. Examples of such joint undertakings are:

- The agreement between AT&T with the Dutch giant Philips and with Olivetti in Europe to market each other's products, giving each company entry into regions where it had not been visible previously. In addition, AT&T has associated itself with Wang in the United States so as to gain better entry into the office automation sector.
- The technological cooperation agreements between Northern Telecom, a company whose expertise lies in electronic switches, with computer companies such as Digital Equipment Corporation, Sperry, and Data General
- The joint venture between L.M. Ericsson Telephone Co., the Swedish company mentioned earlier, and Anocada, a U.S.-based subsidiary of Atlantic Richfield oil company, whose main activity in telecommunications had originally been in cabling and related equipment for the interconnect market
- The purchase of warrants by Burroughs and NCR of Convergent Technologies, a company which supplies them with systems
- The 12% equity position taken by IBM in Intel, assuming the former of guaranteed supplies, and providing capitalization for the latter, and the acquisition of Rolm, a major telecommunications company

Because of the shift away from mainframes, and the many new Japanese entries into that market, the principal computer companies, those listed toward the beginning of Table 9.4, have had to review their positions and strategy continually to retain market share. DEC has attempted to reduce its dependence on minicomputers by entering the market for personal computers and office automation equipment. Hewlett-Packard has focused on 32-bit desktop computers and workstations, especially aimed at the engineering milieu, where its noncomputer products have long had a good reputation. UNIVAC's computer sales declined to the point where the name was dropped in favor of that of the parent company, Sperry Corp., but it has continued to sell large mainframes to the Air Force and to banks and government agencies, and has emphasized systems and software, while turning to other manufacturers for small computers. The BUNCH group of companies, particularly, has been slow to enter the microprocessor competition, but they have acted in different ways to maintain their positions.* Control Data Corporation has emphasized peripherals, service bureaus, and educational software, the last stemming from its long-term

*The New York Times, February 5, 1984.

investment in Plato, a system for computer-aided instruction. NCR has sought to exploit its strong presence in financial and retailing systems, POS terminals, and electronic fund transfer systems. Burroughs has concentrated on office and bank systems and IBM-compatible products, as evidenced by its acquisition of Memorex, a company that specialized in IBM-compatible peripherals.

In summary, the steady increases in data processing and communication revenues have not meant that companies with appreciable market share could count on their established customer base for continued growth. The industry has been in such a great state of flux, because of rapid technological obsolescence of existing products, new entrants into the market, and multiple sources for new customers, that companies have had to invest heavily in research and development and be constantly alert for shifts in trends. Although the worldwide recession that started in 1980 was slow to affect the computer/communications industry, the results were definitely felt by 1982, when many large companies suffered at least a temporary slowdown in growth and even more drastic reductions in profits. Also important is the fact that the scale of operations of companies in the computer/communications field has, increasingly, become internationalized. Both the revenues of U.S. companies originating from abroad and the presence in the United States of foreign multinational companies have grown. It is to these international aspects that we turn next.

PROBLEMS

1. Let

Q = initial monthly sales for a computer manufacturer
q = monthly growth rate of sales
P = sales price when machines are purchased
R = rental not including maintenance
f_R = number of machines rented/number sold
i = monthly interest rate
f_P = fraction of price covering production costs
f_O = fraction of price covering overhead
L = lifetime of the machine in months = break-even between purchase and rental
PM = profit margin = profit/earnings per unit sold

Brock (1974, p. 59) shows that when $f_R = 1$, $P/R = 48$, $f_P = 0.35$, $f_O = 0.45$, and $i = 0.75\%$, then $L = 60$, and the steady state PM is given by

$$\text{PM} = \frac{0.015}{q} (1 - e^{-60q}) - 0.45 \qquad (A)$$

(In doing so he assumes that monthly depreciation = production cost/L.)

(a) Show that in general

$$\text{PM} = f_R \left[\left(\frac{R}{P} - \frac{f_P}{L} \right) \frac{1 - e^{-qL}}{q} - f_O \right] + (1 - f_R)(1 - f_O - f_P)$$

(*Hint:* First calculate V_R = value of machines on rental for $t > L$.)

(b) Show that this reduces to Equation (A) for the values given.

(c) Assume that $i = 1\%$, $f_R = 0.75$, $f_p = 0.35$, $f_O = 0.45$, and $P/R = 48$. Determine the value of q for which PM = 0. Explain the meaning of the result.

BIBLIOGRAPHY

AT&T in The Computer Market, Northern Business Information, New York, N.Y., 1984.

BROCK, G. W., *The United States Computer Industry: A Study of Market Power.* Cambridge, Mass.: Ballinger, 1974.

——— *The Telecommunications Industry.* Cambridge, Mass.: Harvard University Press, 1981.

FISHMAN, K. D., *The Computer Establishment.* New York: Harper & Row, 1981.

GILCHRIST, B., and M. R. WESSIL, *Government Regulation of the Computer Industry.* Montvale, N.J.: AFIPS Press, 1972.

HARMAN, A. J., *The International Computer Industry.* Cambridge, Mass.: Harvard University Press, 1971.

IRWIN, M. R., *Telecommunications America: Markets Without Boundaries.* Westport, Conn.: Quorum Books, 1983.

JOHNSON, J., "IBM—AT&T: Strategies in the Services Realm," *Datamation,* 28, no. 7 (July 1982), 24–30.

MEYER, J. R., R. W. WILSON, M. A. BAUGHAIM, E. BURTON, and L. CAWETTE, *The Economics of Competition in the Telecommunications Industry.* Cambridge, Mass.: Oelgeschlager, Gunn & Hain, 1980.

"Moving Away from Mainframes," *Business Week,* February 15, 1982, 78–94.

PANTAGES, A., "Justice vs. IBM: Still Many Questions," *Datamation,* 25, no. 1 (January 1979), 84–87.

PHISTER, M., JR., *Data Processing Technology and Economics,* 2nd ed. Santa Fe, N. Mex.: Santa Monica/Bedford, Mass.: Digital Press, 1979.

SOBEL, R., *I.B.M. Colossus in Transition.* New York: Times Books, 1981.

Telex v. *IBM,* 72-C-18 and 72-C-89, Northern District of Oklahoma.

WITHINGTON, F. G., "IBM—AT&T: Sizing Each Other Up," *Datamation,* 28, no. 7 (July 1982), 8–16.

Part IV

NATIONAL POLICIES
FOR COMPUTERS
AND COMMUNICATIONS

Our vantage point for looking at information technology now shifts to that of the country or nation. In Chapter 11 the reasons information technology is so strongly linked to national economic well-being are first examined. Because of this linkage, almost all countries, industrialized and developing, are attempting to formulate policies and take actions with respect to information technology. But these actions are constrained by the tremendous changes in the world economic order generally, and by the realities of the computer and communications technologies in particular. In Chapter 12 government involvement in computer development is traced for the principal countries participating in the developments. Their actions are interpreted in terms of national policies and efforts to formulate new policies.

11

Issues, Goals, and Constraints

It is easy to list the goals countries want to achieve by using and producing computers. It is much more difficult to know how to arrive at them. The difficulties arise from the constraints that any country experiences because of global interdependencies of national economies, participation in trading agreements and blocs, and from special features of the information technologies. One serious concern is the concentration of the production capacity for information products within a few multinational corporations. Most actions taken by individual countries on information technology reflect this concern. Another growing concern is the degree to which transnational data flows influence national sovereignty. The measure of this influence, and what steps might be taken to counteract it, are still under investigation. Although the range of actions that can be taken to deal with information technology is large, it is very difficult to ensure that together these form a coherent plan to address the major problems.

We start by examining why so much of economic policy has become a preoccupation with information technology.

11.1. THE INFORMATION ECONOMY

The Information Economy is the title of a thesis and of a series of reports by Marc Porat (1977) detailing the expenditures and contributions of the U.S. labor force devoted to the production and dissemination of information. There are important antecedents to Porat's work. In a seminal book, *The Production and*

Distribution of Knowledge in the United States (1962), Fritz Machlup identified knowledge-based industries as a distinct and growing force in the economy. In subsequent writings, Daniel Bell (1967) and Peter Drucker (1969) emphasized the centrality of knowledge as a resource even more important than capital or labor, and the evolution of a service-oriented rather than a production-oriented economy. An illuminating way of highlighting changes in the structure of the economy over the past century has been to chart shifts in the labor force, first away from the primary and extractive industries of agriculture, forestry, and mining, to the secondary manufacturing industries, and then away from manufacturing to tertiary service industries as exemplified by transportation, utilities, communications, government, and marketing. By focusing on activities relating to the production and dissemination of information and knowledge, Machlup, Drucker, Bell, Porat, and others extended the traditional primary, secondary, and tertiary industry categories to a new sector, the information sector, in which the computer and communications industries play a central role.

11.1.1. *A Two-Sector Description of Economic Structure*

The concept of the information economy, as a sector derived from the three traditional groupings, is reinforced in an OECD report, *Information Activities, Electronics and Telecommunications Technologies* (1981), which applied Porat's analysis to the economies of OECD countries other than the United States. In that report information occupations are grouped into four main classes— *producers, processors, distributors,* and *infrastructure occupations*—each class having several subclasses. The specific occupations within each class and subclass, together with the International Standard Classification of Occupations (ISCO) codes assigned to these occupations by the International Labor Organization, is shown in Table 11.1. It will be noted that the definition of information worker is very broad and includes occupations which belong to all three sectors, although the service sector is most strongly represented. Figure 11.1 shows the work force makeup in the United States for four sectors—agriculture, industry, service, and information—over the period 1860–1980 based on categorizations used in Porat's report. Figure 11.2 shows the work force makeup according to a two-sector economy (information workers and noninformation workers) for the same period. The bands for each sector reflect different interpretations of which occupations should be included in the information sector. The lower edge of the band for information workers corresponds to a fairly restrictive definition, and it is associated with the upper edge of the band for noninformation workers. Figure 11.3 shows that the trend toward an increasing fraction of the labor force being devoted to the information sector is occurring in the other OECD countries.

Referring to Fig. 11.1, it is useful to identify different stages in the evolution of the work force. During stage I, ending at 1905, the largest component is from the primary sector; during stage II, ending about 1955, industry contributes

TABLE 11.1 INFORMATION OCCUPATIONS AND CODE NUMBERS

I. Information Producers
   Scientific and Technical

0-11	Chemists	0-29	Engineers N.E.C.
0-12	Physicists N.E.C.[a]	0-51	Biologists, zoologists, and
0-13	Physical scientists N.E.C.		related
0-22	Civil engineers	0-52	Bacteriologists, pharmacolo-
0-23	Electrical and electronic engi-		gists
	neers	0-53	Agronomists and related
0-24	Mechanical engineers	0-81	Statisticians
0-26	Metallurgists	0-82	Mathematicians and actuaries
0-27	Mining engineers	0-90	Economists
0-28	Industrial engineers (except	1-92	Sociologists, anthropologists,
	0-28.30)		and related

   Market Search and Coordination Specialists

4-10.20	Commodity broker	4-41	Insurance and stock agents,
4-22	Purchasing agents and buyers		brokers, and jobbers
4-31	Technical salesmen and ad-	4-42	Business services/advertising
	visors		salesmen
		4-43.20	Auctioneers

   Information Gatherers

0-28.30	Work study officers	0-33.20	Quantity surveyors
0-31	Surveyors (land, mine, hydro-	4-43.30	Valuation surveyors
	graphic, etc.)		
1-39.50	7-54.70		
3-59.30	8-59.20 Inspectors, viewers, and testers (various)		
3-59.45	9-49.80		
3-91.50	5-89.20 Information gatherers N.E.C.		

   Consultative Services

0-21	Architects and town planners	0-84.20	Computer programmer
0-32	Draftsmen	1-10	Accountants (except 1-10.20)
0-61	Medical practitioners	1-21 and	Barristers, advocates, solici-
0-69	Dietitians and nutritionists	1-29	tors, etc.
0-75.20	Optometrist	1-39.20	Education methods advisor
0-83	Systems analyst	1-62	Commercial artists and de-
			signers

   Information Producers N.E.C.

1-51.20	Authors	1-71.20	Composers

II. Information Processors
    Administrative and Managerial

1-22	Judges	2-12	Production managers
1-39.40	Head teacher	2-19	Managers N.E.C.
2-01	Legislative officials	3-10	Government executive
2-02	Government administrators		officials
2-11	General managers	4-00	Managers (wholesale/retail
			trade)

TABLE 11.1 (Continued)

II. Information Processors (Continued)
     Process Control and Supervisory

0-33.40	Clerk of works	3-5	Transport and communica-
0-41.40	Flight and ship		tion supervisors (except
0-42.30	Navigating officers		3-59.30 and 3-59.45)
		3-91.20	Dispatching/receiving clerk
3-0	5-20 6-00.30 Supervisors: clerical, sales		
4-21	5-31.20 6-32.20 and other		
7-0	Supervisors and general foremen (production)		

Clerical and Related

1-10.20	Auditor	3.93	Correspondence and report-
3-21	Stenographer, typists, and		ing clerks
	teletypists (except 3-21.50)	3-94	Receptionist and travel
3-31.10	Bookkeeper (general)		agency clerks
3-31.20	Bookkeeper (clerk)	3-95	Library and filing clerks
3-39.20	Cost computing clerk	3-99.20	Statistical clerk
3-39.30	Wages clerk	3-99.30	Coding clerk
3-39.40	Finance clerk	3-99.40	Proofreader
3-91.30	Stock records clerk		
3-92.20	Material and production		
3-92.30	Planning clerks		

III. Information Distributors
     Educators

1-31	University and higher educa-	1-34	Preprimary teachers
	tion teachers	1-35	Special education teachers
1-32	Secondary teachers		
1-33	Primary teachers		

Communication Workers

1-51.30	Journalists and related	1-73.50	Storyteller
1-59	writers (except 1-59.55)	1-74	Producers, performing arts
1-73.30	Stage director	1-79.20	Radio, television announcers
1-73.40	Motion picture, radio, televi-		
	sion director		

IV. Information Infrastructure Occupations
     Information Machine Workers

1-63	Photographers and camera-	9-21	Compositors and typesetters
	men	9-22	Printing pressmen (except
3-21-50	Teleprinter operator		9-22.70)
3-22	Card and tape-punching ma-	9-23	Stereotypers and electrotypers
	chine operators	9-24	Printing engravers (except
3-41	Bookkeeping and calculating		9-24.15 and 9-24.30)
	machine operators	9-25	Photoengravers
3-42	Automatic data-processing	9-26	Bookbinders and related
	machine operators	9-27	Photographic processors
3-99.50	Office machine operators		
8-49.65	Office machine repairmen		
8-62	Sound and vision equipment		
	operators		

TABLE 11.1 (Continued)

IV. Information Infrastructure Occupations (Continued)
    Postal and Telecommunications

3-70	Postmen, mail sorters, messengers	8-56	Telephone and telegraph installers/repairmen
3-80	Telephone operators	8-57.40	Telephone and telegraph linesmen
8-54	Radio and television repairmen	8-61	Broadcasting station operators

[a]N.E.C., not elsewhere classified.

Source: International Standard Classification of Occupations (ISCO), rev. ed. (Geneva: ILO, 1968). It includes 284 "unit groups" embracing 1506 "occupational categories."

the largest fraction, and since stage III, starting in 1955, the largest component derives from the information section. Looking at Fig. 11.2 it may be noted that in the United States since about 1970 (using the most inclusive interpretation of information worker) more than 50% of the labor force has been engaged in the information sector. Just as the shift of the labor force from agriculture to industry has traditionally characterized an industrial economy, so the shift to the information sector can be seen as characterizing Bell's postindustrial society. The noticeable leveling off in the information sector since the early 1970s (see Fig. 11.1) is significant, and it is displayed in another form in Fig. 11.4, which shows the growth rate of information occupations relative to the growth rate of

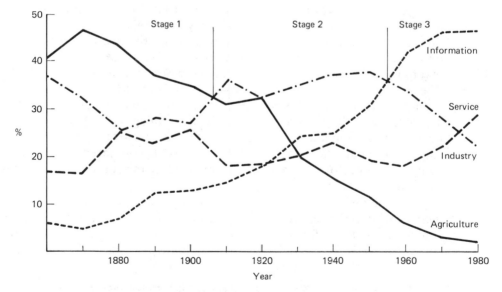

Figure 11.1 Four-sector aggregation of the U.S. work force by percent 1860–1980 (using median estimates of information workers). (From M. Porat. *The Information Economy,* Washington, D.C.: U.S. Government Printing Office, 1977.)

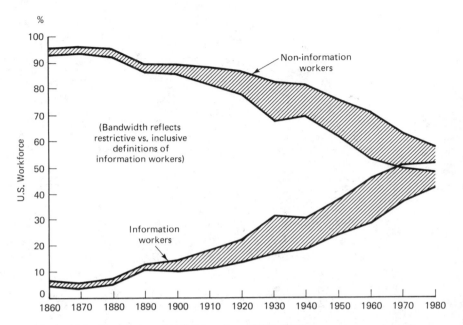

Figure 11.2 Time series of U.S. labor force (1860–1980) two-sector aggregate by percent (from M. Porat, The Information Economy, Washington, D.C.: U.S. Government Printing Office, 1977).

the total work force. Parker (1981) argues that this leveling off is related to a declining productivity in the labor force, and this in turn is because earlier productivity increases have arisen mainly in the manufacturing sector (as opposed to the information sector); as the work force has shifted away from manufacturing, the opportunities for increases in productivity have lessened. The need to increase the productivity of information workers has frequently been cited, and in part this need has justified the drive toward office automation. The argument is that increases in productivity in agriculture and manufacturing have been accompanied by (and in significant measure are due to) increased capitalization in these sectors, and we must be prepared to invest more on equipment for information workers if an increase in productivity in that sector is to be attained.*

Displaying shifts in the labor force is not the only way to show the increasing importance of the information economy. Porat also considers the contribution that information-based *industries* make toward the national income, but it is not as easy to classify industries into those which produce

---

*OECD data confirm that between 1963 and 1976 there has been greater productivity in manufacturing than in private (as distinct from government) services, while at the same time there has been a greater increase in capital investment per employee in manufacturing than in private services (see *Information Activities*, 1981, Tables 11.6, 11.8).

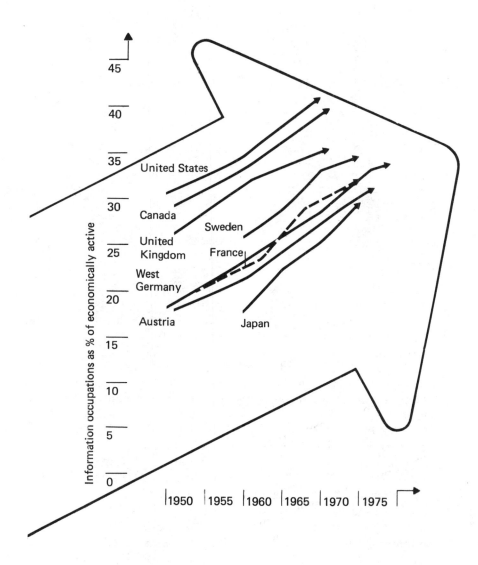

Figure 11.3   Changes in the share of information occupations in the labor force over the postwar period (from *Information Activities, Electronics and Telecommunications Technologies* [Paris: OECD, 1981, with permission]).

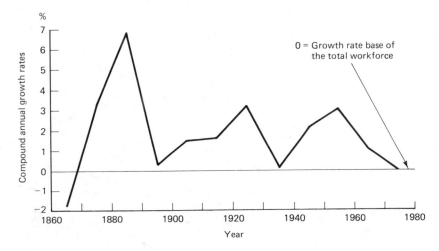

Figure 11.4 Net growth rates of information occupations (from M. Porat, *The Information Economy*, Washington, D.C.: U.S. Government Printing Office, 1977).

information goods and services and those which do not as it is to distinguish information occupations. The reason is that industries which make even consumer products engage in activities relating to the production and dissemination of information, so that a portion of their value-added output should be attributed to the information sector. In the OECD report a distinction is made between the *primary* information sector (PIS) and the *secondary* information sector (SIS). The primary information sector is that proportion of the total gross domestic product which conveys information or contributes to the production, processing, or distribution of information, and which further results from transactions on established markets. The secondary information sector is the proportion of the GDP recording the value added by reason of information activities undertaken while producing noninformation goods and services. Table 11.2 shows the PIS and SIS for selected OECD countries and dates. Because of the differing nature of the sectors (e.g., in one the goods and services are sold on the open market, while in the other the products are used within the producing industry) the percentages are not summed, but the overall increase in the information sector is clear. Jonscher (1983) presents the clearest estimates of the contribution of information activities to production. Figure 11.5 shows his representation of the flows between the production and information sectors of the U.S. economy for 1947 and 1972. In that 25-year period the increase in the value-added component for information was 270% (compared with 113% for production), and since then the information component has grown even larger. Jonscher also goes on to discuss productivity, and his calculations show that after 1980 a slow but steady rise in information worker productivity will have the effect of increasing overall economic productivity, even though production worker productivity remains constant.

TABLE 11.2 INFORMATION SECTOR AS A PERCENTAGE SHARE OF GROSS DOMESTIC PRODUCT: SELECTED COUNTRIES AND DATES[a]

(a) Percentage Share of Primary Information Sector in GDP at Factor Cost

Australia	France	Japan	Sweden	United Kingdom	United States
(1968) 14.6	(1962) 16.0	(1960) 8.4		(1963) 16.0	(1958) 19.6
	(1972) 18.5	(1965) 14.4	(1970) 16.9	(1972) 22.0	(1976) 23.8
	(1974) 19.1	(1970) 18.8	(1975) 17.8		(1972) 24.8

(b) Percentage Share of Secondary Information Sector in GDP at Factor Cost

Japan	United Kingdom	United States
(1965) 21.8	(1963) 13.8	(1958) 23.1
(1970) 16.2	(1972) 10.9	(1974) 24.4

[a]For an explanation of "Primary Information Sector" and "Secondary Information Sector," see the text.

Source: Information Activities, Electronics and Telecommunications Technologies, Vol. 1 (Paris: OECD, 1981, with permission).

The disaggregation of the economy into information and noninformation constituents is useful in studying and explaining a number of important phenomena relating to technological change, and ultimately justifies introducing the concept. These phenomena are examined in greater detail in the Porat, OECD, and Jonscher references cited, but we shall limit ourselves to discussing only one in the next section, that which has been of greatest concern everywhere.

11.1.2. Impact of Information Technology on Employment

Reports, studies, and books about the effects of information technology on jobs stream from individuals, labor groups, government at all levels, and international organizations in a steady flow.* The fear is that the increase in total demand, which has historically made up for reductions in employment arising out of technological improvements in agriculture and manufacturing, can no longer be projected. This suggests that current productivity increases achieved through the application of microtechnology will result in *permanent* reductions in the demand for labor. The issues are complex; not only do aggregated employment levels have to be considered, but also structural changes in the labor force and organizations, and changes in the quality of work life.

The results of studies by Kendrick and Grossman (1980) on the historical relations between real gross product, productivity due to labor and capital, and

---

*See, for example, *In the Chips* (1982), *Microelectronics, Productivity and Employment* (1981), Roda (1980), and Sherman et al. (1979).

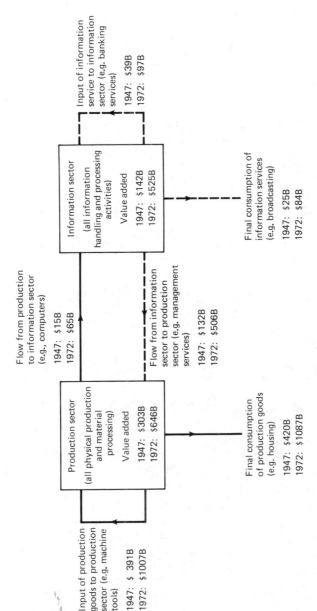

Figure 11.5 Schematic representation of the production and information sectors of the economy, with examples of flows of goods and services (data refer to United States economy, and indicate values of flows of goods and services in constant [1972] dollars) (from C. Jonscher, "Information Resources and Economic Productivity," *Information Economics and Policy,* 1, no. 1 [1983], 13–35, Elsevier Science Publishing Company, Inc. with permission).

prices in the U.S. economy are typical of those reported for other industrialized countries. The general observation is that, traditionally, there is a high *negative* correlation between rate of technological advances and unemployment rates, because productivity improvement results in stronger demands for goods and helps sustain profit levels, to spur investment and create a need for labor. This general observation is consistent with what happened during the early stages of computerization (i.e., until 1970). In spite of the growing use of computers in industry, government, and business, aggregate unemployment levels were comparatively low (less than 5%) and the total labor force was actually growing. This was true for all but a few industries; a U.K. survey (*Computers in Offices,* 1965) of the results of introducing over 600 computers into offices showed an 8% increase in aggregate number of staff employed (it was estimated that without computers there would have been a 13% increase).

Since 1970 the picture is more complex, and it is necessary to separate information occupations from those which are noninformation. Until 1975 at least, the information occupations continued to grow, as a fraction of the labor force (recall Fig. 11.3), and in total numbers. There are several reasons for this.

- Demand for information products continued to be high. When information activity goes into manufacturing, information labor is a complement (rather than a substitute) for labor.
- Growth of productivity for information-related tasks has been demonstrably low.
- The cost of labor relative to that of capital was low. Thus although computers were still expensive, the available work force for information occupations was increasing, in large measure because women continued to enter the labor market.
- There was a low elasticity of substitution between capital and labor; devices to save labor in the office were not yet generally available.

For manufacturing the picture has been different, both to 1975 and since. Generally, but more especially in industries such as printing and watchmaking, the introduction of computers and microtechnology has meant higher productivity followed by lower total employment. Table 11.3 illustrates this for the production of electronic switches in the United States and color television receivers in Japan. In other industries, such as automobile manufacturing, the introduction of robotics has had just as great effect on productivity, and a simultaneous sharp reduction of demand made the impact on employment particularly severe. Projection of these experiences to manufacturing as a whole, and then to information-related activities, has led to disaster scenarios about national and global unemployment levels (see Jenkens and Sherman, 1979; Osborne, 1979).

Since 1980 there has been a worldwide, often polarized debate about the long-term effects of microtechnology on employment levels. The answer is by no

TABLE 11.3 JOB REDUCTIONS AND PRODUCTIVITY INCREASES

(a) United States—Western Electric Switching Division

Year	Number of Employees	Reduction	Productivity Increase
1970	39,200		More than doubled
1976	19,000	50%	
1980 (projected)	17,400		

Source: Freeman, C. "Technical Change and Unemployment," in Proceedings of Conference on "Science, Technology and Public Policy," University of New South Wales, Australia, December 1977.

(b) Japan—Color TV Factories[a]

Company	1972	1976
Hitachi	9,051	4,299
Mitsushuta Panasonic	9,875	3,900
Sony	4,498	2,778
Other four large firms	24,462	14,700

[a]Production volume raised by 25% from 8.4 million sets in 1972 to 10.5 million in 1976.

Source: B. Sherman et al., *Technological Change, Employment and the Need for Collective Bargaining* (London: ASTM, 1979).

means clear. It is not obvious that introducing microtechnology into information occupations meets *all* the conditions that create technological unemployment. The laborsaving contribution has not been clearly demonstrated but there *are* capital savings (due to reductions in power, space, and fewer malfunctions), so that the motivation for bringing in the equipment is still there. Reductions in the costs for labor or in hours worked could be important, even though these have traditionally been resisted with new technology. It would be contrary to previous experience if increased productivity does not result in greater demand, although (with some exceptions, such as computer games) there is as yet little evidence of final demand for products of the information economy.

There *is* evidence that microtechnology is bringing about changes in the structure of the work force, in large measure because of the changes in skills it requires. For industrial production the low-skilled, rote activities of assembly work are needed less. Even highly skilled craft operations such as those performed by machinists are being incorporated into the machine intelligence of robots, so that the result can be a *deskilling* of workers. This illustrates that the effects on skill levels are complex and depend on the industry and application, although there is a general agreement that upgrading of skills is more usual. Within the service sector, again the more routine data capture and information-handling operations are being done by machines, so a more versatile set of skills is expected from those who work with them. In managerial ranks also, more routine tasks of supervision, scheduling, and preparation of daily reports are being transferred to machines, so that the skills of junior and middle managers are less in demand. But the ability to install, maintain, and operate the machines calls on the skills of the information infrastructure component of the labor force, and these are obviously needed more. The overall effect is to make certain segments of the labor force more vulnerable to the new technologies. Women, who generally have lower scientific and technical qualifications than men, are at higher risk, as are unskilled workers. As a result, significant pressures are being put on the educational systems at all levels to become responsive to the skill requirements of the changed workplace.

In summary, the transition to an information economy is characterized by major changes in the structure of work forces. The long-term effect on total employment levels is not clear, but the impact on employment has to be considered as the most important of the economic consequences of computers and microtechnology. There is continuing apprehension that if increased demand is *not* forthcoming, society will have to change in major ways to cope with permanently high levels of unemployment.

11.2. NATIONAL PRIORITIES IN A GLOBAL CONTEXT

Given the importance of the information sector and the key role that computer and communications technologies have, it becomes obvious why countries have focused so much attention on these technologies. In a general way the goals are easily summarized. Briefly, governments want to:

- Exploit the computer and communications technologies to make national industries strong and competitive
- Use technologies effectively for administration and defense
- Promote public awareness about the significance of the technologies
- Increase education, training, research, and development
- Control adverse side effects (e.g., unemployment, erosion of privacy, and centralization)

Actions to further these goals must be taken in the light of the special circumstances surrounding information technology. We have already discussed some of these circumstances in Chapter 8: the extremely high rate of technological growth and the strong trend toward merging the computer and communications industries. In this section we examine two others which, like the impact on employment, have been the subject of much study and have figured largely in attempts to formulate national policies on information technology. These are patterns in international trade for information products, and flow of data across national boundaries.

11.2.1. International Trade in Information Products

The ability to compete in both domestic and international markets for information goods and services is crucial to industrialized and newly industrialized countries. The market as a whole is important because so many jobs are tied to the information sector; the domestic market is important because of the triggering effect computers and communications have on other industries; the international market is important because few countries can rely on the domestic market to achieve economies of scale in production, and because trade in information goods is a growing factor in the balance of payments. For these reasons countries and trading blocs are sensitive to such indicators as the fraction of domestic consumption of information products which is satisfied by indigenous industry, the contribution of information products to exports as a whole, and the balance of payments due to trade in information products and services. Unfavorable trends in these statistics bring about pressures to strengthen or create domestic communications and computer industries.

Just as information activities encompass a broad range of occupations in the information economy, so do information products comprise a wide variety of goods relating to information. These include goods that intrinsically convey information (books, films, television programs, software) and equipment that is directly useful in its production (telephones, terminals, radio and television receivers, office machinery, watches, scientific instruments, computers). Although our interest is primarily in communications and computer equipment and services, these are often combined with other categories in trade statistics. The situation with respect to communications is different than it is with computer-based goods and services. Because the carriers are nationally owned by the PTTs or have been subject to regulation, home markets for telecommunications and services have traditionally been protected and domestic suppliers of equipment strongly favored. From the very beginning U.S. companies and their subsidiaries abroad have far and away been the principal suppliers of computer equipment. For electronic equipment, the role first of Japan, and then of newly industrialized countries such as Taiwan, Hong Kong, Malaysia, Singapore, and Brazil, has grown dramatically since the 1970s, principally because of exports in consumer electronic products.

A few examples will illustrate the trends. Table 11.4 shows that until 1974 the

TABLE 11.4 WORLDWIDE NUMBER OF COMPUTER INSTALLATIONS PRODUCED BY U.S.-BASED MANUFACTURERS AS A FRACTION OF THE TOTAL NUMBER INSTALLED WORLDWIDE

Year	1957	1959	1961	1963	1965	1967	1969	1971	1974
%	69	69	68	68	69	72	74	74	67

Source: M. Phister, *Data Processing Technology and Economics,* 2nd ed. (Santa Fe, N. Mex.: Santa Monica/Bedford, Mass.: Digital Press, 1979), Table 11.1.28.

TABLE 11.5 FRACTION OF THE APPARENT DOMESTIC MARKET FOR COMPUTERS SUPPLIED BY INDIGENOUS MANUFACTURERS

(Shipments—exports)/(shipments—exports + imports)

Country	1971	1972	1973	1974	1975	1976	1977	1978	1979
U.S.[a]	94.3	93.2	94.3	93.7	94.8	95.1	94.9	—	94.9
Japan[b]	78.2	82.1	81.1	79.7	79.9	81.4	82.2	88.3	87.1
U.K.[c]			35.9	29.7		36.1	40.1[d]		
France[e]				57.3			18.8[d]		
Canada[f]	13	15	14	18	13	12	2		

[a]U.S. Bureau of Census data.

[b]From data in *Japan Electronics Almanac* (Tokyo: Dempa Publications, 1981).

[c]C. C. Gotlieb and Z. P. Zeman, *Towards a National Computer and Communications Policy: Seven National Approaches* (Halifax: The Institute for Research on Public Policy, 1980), Table UK-6 based on data from U.K. Dept. of Trade and Industry.

[d]Data from *Mackintosh Yearbook of West European Electronics Data* (London: Mackintosh Publications Ltd., 1980).

[e]C. C. Gotlieb and Z. P. Zeman, ibid. Table F-6 based on data from Documentation Française.

[f]Electrical and Electronic Industry, Abstract of Industry and Trade Statistics, Dept. of Industry, Trade and Commerce, Ottawa.

U.S.-produced share in the worldwide number of computer installations hovered about 70%. Since then it has declined somewhat. Table 11.5 illustrates the fact that only the United States and Japan have come close to being self-sufficient with respect to computer equipment. Even among the industrialized countries, only in the United Kingdom and France is there an appreciable domestic production capability, and much of this originates with subsidiaries of U.S.-based multinational companies. Tables 11.6 and 11.7 show that although the average annual contributions of electronics-based goods* to the GPD has generally increased, only in Japan among the (larger) OECD countries has there been a trend to increased exports. In the United States exports of electronic capital goods and electronic components were relatively stable, but there was a decline in exports of consumer electronic products (especially TV sets) for the period. Figure 11.6 charts the trade balances for the electronic goods in selected countries. More detailed breakdowns according to the class of electronic goods are given in Ergas (1981) and in collections of national statistics cited in the next chapter. Table 11.8 illustrates the increase in exports and imports of *services* which are mainly information related. Since the beginning of the 1980s attention has focused on such services as are provided by computer bureaus and software companies in the belief that these will ultimately make up a significant component of consumption. In 1981 the seven largest software vendors in the United States were all hardware companies, so it is not surprising to find the United States as the major interna-

*These comprise office machines, telecommunications equipments, and electronic components.

TABLE 11.6 ELECTRONIC INDUSTRIES' CONTRIBUTION TO THE GROSS DOMESTIC PRODUCT

Country	Value of Shipments, 1975 (billions of current Canadian dollars)	1965 (%)	1975 (%)	Average Contribution, 1965–1975 (%)	Average Annual Growth Rate, 1965–1975 (%)
Canada	2.4	1.7	1.5	1.7	10.9
France	7.8	1.6	2.3	1.9	17.2
Japan	21.3	3.0	4.3	4.5	23.0
U.K.	6.4	2.1	2.8	2.7	11.7
U.S.	40.4	2.9	2.7	2.9	7.4
West Germany	9.0	2.1	2.1	2.3	14.0

Source: A report by the Sector Task Force on the Canadian Electronics Industry, Department of Industry, Trade and Commerce, Ottawa, 1978; based on OECD data.

tional supplier for software as well as hardware. In 1982, U.S. software and service companies, showing a growth rate of 85%, did an export business of $200 million.

These facts and trends about market share have meant that there are two basically different sets of goals about computer-based technologies. For the United States the problem is to maintain the technological lead it has enjoyed and to protect the favorable trade balance needed to offset losses incurred by importing energy and strategic materials. There is a need to resolve the conflict arising from the desire to preserve competition between the diverse, innovative industries which

TABLE 11.7 TRADE IN ELECTRONICS-BASED GOODS[a]

	Country		
	OECD Europe[b]	U.S.	Japan
Share in OECD exports (%)			
1965	61	30	15
1976	49	22	25
Ratio of exports to imports			
1965	1.17	1.86	3.68
1976	0.95	1.05	8.73

[a]Office machines, telecommunications equipment, and electronic components.

[b]The OECD countries are: Australia, Austria, Belgium, Canada, Denmark, Finland, France, the Federal Republic of Germany, Greece, Ireland, Italy, Japan, Luxemburg, the Netherlands, New Zealand, Norway, Portugal, Spain, Sweden, Switzerland, Turkey, the United Kingdom, and the United States.

Source: H. Ergas, "The Role of Information Goods in International Trade," in *Information Activities, Electronics and Telecommunications Technologies,* Vol. 2 (Paris: OECD, 1981, with permission).

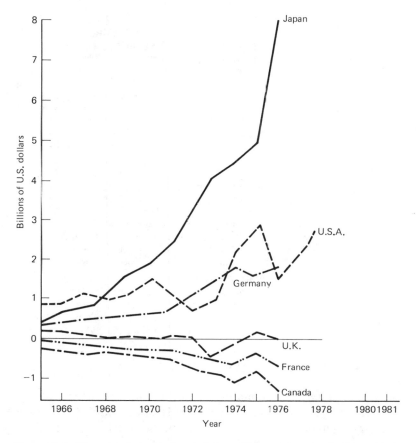

Figure 11.6 Electronic industries' trade balance (from a report by the Sector Task Force on the Canadian Electronics Industry, Department of Industry, Trade and Commerce, Ottawa, 1978. Based on OECD data).

have been the source of the U.S. strength, and the desire to let U.S. industries restructure themselves so as better to meet the challenges posed by companies in Japan and Europe. For other countries the problem is to capture a share in the new information technologies. We shall examine the methods which are taken to achieve this in the next section and in the next chapter, but two principal means have been to designate national champions in the vital computer and communications industries, and to gain access to U.S. technology and markets through licensing and through joint production and distribution agreements. In the United States the emphasis in the past, at least, has been on a pluralistic, laissez-faire approach, whereas in other countries there has been a history of government intervention and active involvement. Table 11.9 summarizes these two different approaches.

TABLE 11.8 ANNUAL PERCENTAGE INCREASE IN EXPORTS AND IMPORTS OF "OTHER SERVICES,"[a] SELECTED OECD COUNTRIES, 1960–1977

Country	Percent Increase in: Exports	Imports
Canada	16	14
France	12	14
Germany	19	17
Japan	25	20
United Kingdom	11	10
United States	12	9

[a]These are other than financial and transport services and are mainly information related (technical and professional, cultural and entertainment, communications, and data processing), but they include certain leasing, rentals, and charges for processing and repairs. See H. Ergas, "The Role of Information Goods in International Trade," in *Information Activities, Electronics and Telecommunications Technologies,* Vol. 2 (Paris: OECD, 1981).

11.2.2. Transborder Data Flows

This was first perceived mainly as a legal issue relating to privacy. After the state of Hesse in Germany, Sweden, the United States, and other countries enacted privacy legislation which placed limitations on the collection, storage, and dissemination

TABLE 11.9 DIFFERENCES IN APPROACHES TO COMPUTER/COMMUNICATION STRATEGIES

United States	Other Countries
Maintain technological lead	Establish a place in the international information economy
Maintain exports of hardware, software to counteract negative balance of payments due to energy, raw materials	Limit balance-of-payment problems and dependence on foreign suppliers
Maintain diverse, innovative industries	Promote indigenous creativity
	Gain access to U.S. technology and markets through joint ventures, cross-licensing, etc.
Pluralistic, unregulated, laissez-faire	Select "national champions"
Competition encouraged	Government support for coordinated actions
Diverse supporting actions by government	National policies adopted or wanted
Consistent calls for free international trade, free flow of information, allowing market forces to prevail	Unwillingness to give up selective protectionism
Isolated calls for national policy	

of data about individuals held in computers, a concern arose that some countries would act as data havens. In such countries personal data about foreign nationals might be stored in data banks which would be illegal in the countries where the data originated. Even when there are transfers of data within one state there are legal questions relating to privacy, copyright, security, and ownership. Insofar as different countries are at different stages in resolving these questions, it is inevitable that there will be legal issues when data are transferred across national boundaries. But as attempts were made to address these questions, it soon became clear that there were economic interests at stake as well, interests so large that transborder data flow began to be viewed as a political issue, affecting national sovereignty. The economic aspects are many:

- Some countries, notably Austria, Denmark, and Norway, extended their privacy legislation to cover "legal persons" as well as "physical persons" or individuals. This immediately meant that corporations were affected.

- At several conferences concern has been expressed that multinationals were exporting "raw data" from one country, processing it elsewhere, and returning it as "finished information" to the country of origin. The result is a reduction in the service bureau activity of the first country. Any action to restrict the export of data for this reason is a form of protectionism, and the classic arguments of free trade versus protectionism come into play.

- The numerous differential tariffs on telecommunications in many countries, and regulations which restrict interconnection with external networks, *are* in effect restrictions on the flow of data. Thus Euronet, a communications network operated by the European community, excludes foreign vendors from using computers outside Europe. Access to the DIALOG data base, for example, is denied to encourage the buildup of European bibliographic data bases.

- As another example, since January 1, 1982, international leased lines cannot be connected to German public networks unless the connection is made via a computer in Germany which does some processing of data; moreover, there must be a guarantee that leased lines will not be used to transmit unprocessed data to foreign public telecommunications networks.

- Data in their own right, especially machine-readable data, are increasingly seen as a strategic national resource. There is sensitivity about government operations and development plans, government-supported industries, and certain economic indicators. Equally vital are data about natural resources, and the fact that much can be learned about resources and agricultural conditions by remote sensing from satellites, a technique available only to the few countries with satellite programs, only heightens the sense that nation sovereignty is involved.

Beyond existing regulations, which require that certain types of data reside or be processed in the country of origin, such as those in Germany and Canada pertaining to bank records, there have been numerous occasions when much more general and stringent restrictions on transborder data flows have been advocated.* Like privacy, transborder data flow is an extremely difficult issue to resolve because of the need to satisfy two conflicting sets of goals. On the one hand, there are the desires to protect national industries and national interests; on the other hand, there is the recognition that data about international activities, whether these emanate from governments or from multinational companies, *must* have minimum freedom of movement or the world's business will grind to a halt. Some measure of the nature, volume, and essential character of international data flows can be gathered from the papers in *Usage* (1979) and *Policy Implications* (1980). Most of the flow takes place through special telecommunication networks such as SWIFT (Society for Worldwide Interbank Financial Telecommunications), SITA (Société International de Télécommunications Aéromatiques), TYMNET (an international time-sharing service bureau operated by Tymshare), and the private networks that all multinational corporations maintain. The trend toward electronic mail ensures that the traffic in public services such as Telex and Telenet will grow sharply.

Just as the position of the United States with respect to trade in information goods differs from that of other nations, so does its perspective on the international flow of data, and on telecommunication services, differ from that of many other countries. Freedom from censorship of news is a highly cherished American tradition and free flow of information is a major element of U.S. foreign policy. In the light of the trend toward integrated communication networks noted in Section 8.3, it is felt that monitoring the data content of telecommunications traffic would inevitably be a form of censorship. This fear is not lessened by concerted attempts in UNESCO for exercising more national control over international news agencies, as part of what is called the New Information Order. Just as important is the conviction that the lower costs and greater diversification of communications services in the United States, compared with those in other countries, owe much to the climate of reduced regulation. Most important, the vital role of data flows for the multinational companies and information industries which contribute so heavily to the U.S. economy is clearly recognized. For these reasons policy statements about international data movement from officials and others in the United States have emphasized the desirability of maintaining freedom of flow, subject to a minimum of regulation that might be needed for reasons of copyright protection or national security.† On the other hand, spokespersons from other

---

*See, for example, the reports on the 1978, 1980, and 1983 SPIN Conferences in the *Intergovernmental Bureau of Informatics (IBI) Newsletter,* Rome, together with the analyses of the recommendations in Chapter 8 of Schiller (1981); also Recommendation 24 of *Telecommunications and Canada,* report of the Consultative Committee on the Implications of Telecommunications for Canadian Sovereignty, Ministry of Supply and Services, Ottawa, 1979.

†For examples, see de Sola Pool (1980), *Towards an American Agenda* (1980), Eger (1979), and Colby (1979). There are nevertheless some contrary trends. Among the databases available through Lockheed's DIALOG is the Foreign Trade Index (FTI), which the U.S. Department of Commerce's Export

countries highlight the need to uphold privacy laws, including those applicable to legal persons (Stadler, 1979; Freese, 1979), the implications for data processing service and other industries (Cundiff and Reid, 1979, p. 22; Antonelli, 1981), and the crucial importance of data banks for national sovereignty.*

Several countries are attempting to formulate a position on transborder data flows as a necessary component of an overall strategy with regard to information. The level of activity is such that, since 1978, two periodicals, *TDF News* and *Transnational Data Report,* have been devoted exclusively to the subject. International conferences are frequent, and reports from national and international bodies numerous,† but there has as yet been only partial agreement on guidelines formulated by OECD countries. Transborder data flow problems are not new, but they have become more urgent because of the global developments in telecommunications described in previous chapters, and particularly because of the deregulation of the industry in the United States. Other countries are experiencing difficulties in responding to the U.S. moves, but they are under considerable pressure from multinational corporations, and even from indigenous companies, to weaken or end the monopolistic control of their own PTTs. For an account of the issues and the ways in which different countries are attempting to resolve them, see Ergas and Okayama (1984), and *Telecommunications* (1983).

11.3. INSTRUMENTS AND MODALITIES

In order to promote national objectives with respect to computers and communications, governments have at their disposal a large choice of actions. For the most part these are the usual mechanisms for pursuing industrial strategy, but special circumstances make some more attractive than others.

The actions can range from incentives that are strongly positive (i.e., directed to favor indigenous industry and help adapt the work force to the new technologies) to barriers that are strongly negative (i.e., directed at minimizing or even eliminating the penetration and influence of foreign companies). In most cases the actions require commitment of funds, but they can also take forms which are not primarily financial, such as regulation, increasing public awareness, or erecting nontariff barriers. A number of examples of specific actions have already been mentioned in this chapter; in Table 11.10 we classify them more systematically,

---

Information Division maintains about 150,000 companies in 130 countries. Under the terms of Lockheed's agreement, access to FTI is restricted to U.S. organizations [*Online Review,* 3, no. 1 (1979), 7]. Also, there has been a noticeable lessening in the information U.S. computer companies are willing to see released, and in December 1981 Reagan issued an Executive Order on Security Classification with the intent of extending the class of information that should be restricted for reasons of national security.

*Nora and Minc (1978, Chap. 3) and *Telecommunications and Canada,* op. cit. This has been the particular thrust of developing countries as voiced in the SPIN conferences convened by the Intergovernmental Bureau of Informatics, Rome.

†In addition to these already cited, see Turn (1979) and *Transnational Corporations* (1981).

TABLE 11.10 GOVERNMENT ACTIONS FOR ACHIEVING NATIONAL GOALS IN COMPUTERS AND COMMUNICATIONS

(a) Positive Actions and Incentives

Type of Action	Examples
Restructure industry	Telecommunications rebuilt around CGE, Thomson—CSF, France
Complete ownership and management of production or operating companies	National PTTs in most countries Nationalization of CGE—France, 1982
Taking equity position in private companies; joint ventures	25% ownership of Ferranti-Packard—U.K. Joint Systems Development Corp. for software—Japan 50% of interest in Datasaab—Sweden, 1977
Establishing public research institutes for basic R&D and transfer of new technologies	INRIA—France
Awarding research grants, subsidies, or non-competitive contracts to special groups and companies	University research grant programs—most countries R&D contracts to U.S. computer manufacturers for supercomputers in nuclear and space programs
Purchasing policies that favor indigenous companies	U.K. rules favoring ICL equipment for local and regional governments Buy American Act—U.S. Buy Japanese policies by Nippon Telegraph Telecommunications
Tax laws with accelerated write-offs for research or other expenses	West Germany, Canada, Japan, Israel, United States
Low-cost loans against export sales	Export Development Bank—U.S.
Creating or funding research, education, and training programs	Second Computer Plan—Germany, 1971–1975 Programs to introduce microcomputers in secondary schools—U.K., France, Canada, U.S., etc.
Heightening awareness by commissioning reports, conferences, conducting public seminars, etc.	Creation of Ministry of Information—U.K., 1981 U.K. Information Technology year, 1982 Le Semaine Informatique, Paris, 1979
Creating instruments for government/industry cooperation	Japan Electronic Industry Development Association (JEIDA)
Providing information about markets and competition to help exporters	Foreign Trade Index—U.S.
Encouraging competition within country	Diversified government procurement—U.S. Deregulation of communications—U.S., U.K.

(b) Negative Actions and Barriers

Type of Action	Examples
Imposition of tariffs	European community 17% tariff on integrated circuits 25% tariff on optical fibers—U.S. Duties on automated reservation equipment—Israel, Italy, Spain, Greece

TABLE 11.10 (Continued)

(b) Negative Actions and Barriers (Continued)

Type of Action	Examples
Insistence of local ownership or control of DP or communication industries	India, Nigeria (40%), Mexico, PTTs most countries
Regulations governing entry of foreign firms	Network controls on availability, degree of interconnection of leased lines (Japan, Germany, European community)
	Insistence that IBM patents be made available to Japanese firms—Japan
	Brazilian law prohibiting manufacture of minicomputers unless companies met certain conditions (e.g., establish *design* capability in Brazil)
	Foreign Investment Review Act (FIRA), Canada
Application of standards and inspection procedures for equipment; licensing rules for personnel; restrictions on commercial visas	All countries in varying degrees—Canada, Belgium, Brazil, Germany, Switzerland
Protective measures to keep activities in the country	Application of privacy laws—Sweden, Austria
	Bank information must be kept within country (Korea)

and for each type one or more instance is cited where that particular instrument has been used. Additional examples are to be found in the next chapter.

Because of participation in trading blocs and adherence to international agreements, governments may be restricted in the extent to which these instruments are used. The greatest freedom is in the area of telecommunications, where the existence of national PTTs has set a historical precedent for protectionist measures. The most comprehensive agreements for reduction of barriers are the General Agreement on Trade and Tariffs (GAAT), to which most countries adhere. The 1980 Tokyo round of negotiations, concluded after 10 years, established limited rules about trade in electronic products. One of the most important outcomes was that countries which had protective tariffs in place agreed to their gradual reduction and eventual removal. For example, the Japanese tariff for mainframes was 15% initially, but over an 8-year period it was agreed to reduce it to 4.9%; similarly, the tariff for peripherals was scheduled to become 6%, compared with the initial value of 25%. The U.S. and Canada tariffs are to be lowered to 3.9% from 5.5%. For the European Economic Community (EEC) the final tariff on CPUs will be 4.9%, but the 17% tariff on semiconductors will remain unchanged, in recognition of an accepted need to stimulate semiconductor industries in Europe. A principal result expected from the agreement is better entry of U.S. companies to the Japanese domestic market. Relatively few concessions were made by developing countries in the Tokyo round.

The Tokyo round, however, may have been a high point in the movement toward free trade. Since then a worldwide recession, and an increased awareness of the importance of information technology for overall industrial strategy, have led to suggestions, in the United States and in other countries, that more nationalistic approaches have to be taken with respect to information technology, and that perhaps there ought to be bounds on the transfer of the technology to other countries. Examples of these trends are given in the next chapter; if these trends persist, the effects on how the technology develops in the future, and on national market shares, are bound to be major.

BIBLIOGRAPHY

ANTONELLI, C., *Transborder Data Flows an International Business—A Pilot Study.* Paris: OECD, 1981.

BELL, D., "Notes on the Post-industrial Society," *The Public Interest,* Part I (Winter 1967), Part II (Spring 1967).

————, The Coming of Post-Industrial Society. New York: Basic Books, 1973.

COLBY, W., "International Information—Free Trade or Protectionism," International Conference on Transnational Data Flows, Washington, D.C., 1979.

Computers in Offices, Manpower Stud. 4, Ministry of Labour, Great Britain. London: H.M. Stationery Office, 1965.

CUNDIFF, W. E., and M. REID, *Issues in Canadian/U.S. Transborder Computer Data Flows.* Woburn, Mass.: Butterworth, 1979.

DE SOLA POOL, I., and R. SOLOMON, "Transborder Data Flows: Requirements for International Co-operation," in *Policy Implications of Data Network Developments in the OECD Area.* Paris: OECD, 1980, pp. 79–92.

DRUCKER, P. F., *The Age of Discontinuity.* New York: Harper & Row, 1969, Chap. 13.

EGER, J., Position paper in *Issues in Canadian/U.S. Transborder Computer Data Flows.* Woburn, Mass.: Butterworth, 1979, p. 75.

ERGAS, H., "The Role of Information Goods in International Trade," in *Information Activities, Electronics and Telecommunications Technologies,* Vol. 2. Paris: OECD, 1981.

ERGAS, H., and J. OKAYAMA, (eds), *Changing Market Structures in Telecommunications,* Proceedings of an OECD Conference held Dec. 13–15, 1982, Amsterdam, North-Holland, 1984.

FREESE, J., *International Data Flows,* Studentlitteratur Lund, Sweden, 1979.

GILCHRIST, B., and M. R. WESSIL, *Government Regulation of the Computer Industry.* Montvale, N.J.: AFIPS Press, 1972.

Information Activities, Electronics and Telecommunications Technologies, 2 vols. Paris: OECD, 1981.

International Standard Classification of Occupations (ISCO), rev. ed. Geneva: ILO, 1968.

In the Chips: Opportunities People Partnerships. Ottawa: Labour Canada, 1982.

JENKENS, O., and B. SHERMAN, *The Collapse of Work.* London: Eyre Methuen, 1979.

JONSCHER, C., "Information Resources and Economic Productivity," *Inf. Econ. Policy,* 1 (1983), pp. 13–35.

KENDRICK, J. W., and E. GROSSMAN, *Productivity in the United States: Trends and Cycles.* Baltimore, Md.: Johns Hopkins University Press, 1980.

MACHLUP, F., *The Production and Distribution of Knowledge in the United States.* Princeton, N.J.: Princeton University Press, 1962.

Microelectronics, Productivity and Employment. Paris: OECD, 1981.

NORA, S., and A. MINC, *L'Informatisation de la société.* Paris: La Documentation Française, 1978. Also published as *The Computerization of Society: A Report to the President of France.* Cambridge, Mass.: MIT Press, 1980.

OSBORNE, A., *Running Wild—The Next Industrial Revolution.* Berkeley, Calif.: Osborne/ McGraw-Hill, 1979.

PARKER, E. B., "Information Services and Economic Growth," *Inf. Soc.,* 1. no. 1 (1981), 71–78.

Policy Implications of Data Network Developments in the OECD Area. Paris: OECD, 1980.

PORAT, M., *The Information Economy,* 9 vols. U.S. Department of Commerce. Washington, D.C.: U.S. Government Printing Office, 1977.

RODA, J., *The Impact of Microelectronics.* Geneva: I.L.O., 1980.

SCHILLER, H. I., *Who Knows: Information in the Age of the Fortune 500.* Norwood, N.J.: Ablex, 1981.

SERAFINI, S., and M. ANDRIEU, *The Information Revolution and Its Implications for Canada.* Communications Economics Branch, Department of Communications, 1980.

SHERMAN, B., et al., *Technological Change, Employment and the Need for Collective Bargaining.* London: ASTM, 1979.

STADLER, G., "From National to International Legislation on Information Flow and Data Protection," in *Transborder Data Flows and the Protection of Privacy.* Paris: OECD, 1979, pp. 42–50.

TDF News, Information Gatekeepers, Brookline, Mass.

Telecommunications: Pressures and Policies for Change. Paris: OECD, 1983.

The Usage of International Data Networks in Europe. Paris: OECD, 1979.

Towards an American Agenda for a New World Order in Communications. The U.S. National Commission of UNESCO, Department of State, Washington, D.C., 1980.

Transborder Data Flows and the Protection of Privacy. Paris: OECD, 1979.

Transnational Corporations and Transborder Data Flows: An Overview. Geneva: United Nations Commission on Transnational Corporations, 1981.

TURN, R., ed., *Transborder Data Flows: Concerns in Privacy Protection and Free Flow of Information,* 2 vols. Washington, D.C.: American Federation of Information Processing Societies, 1979.

12

National Policies and Their Effectiveness

In the preceding chapter general objectives that countries seek with respect to computers and communications were identified, and examples of government actions taken to achieve these goals were given. For any particular country, the extent to which its actions address *all* the major issues about computers and communications, are consistent with the objectives, and are sustained over time measures the degree of commitment to a national policy. For a policy to exist it is not necessary that there be a comprehensive, explicit formulation of it, although it is more easily recognized when there is one. More important are the range and continuity of the actions and progress toward goals. Although all the industrialized countries and many of the developing ones have turned their attention to computers and communications at one time or another, they are at very different stages in arriving at an information policy and achieving the results that are sought from it. It is these differences that we examine now.

It is useful to start by reviewing what one should expect a national policy to accomplish. This will help establish criteria for assessing actions and observing their effectiveness. The following are the principal goals (see Section 11.2), but it need hardly be said that government is not the only agent. Private industry, public institutions, professional organizations, labor groups, consumer groups, the media, and individuals all have their essential roles. With this understanding, a national policy may be seen as a plan for a country to:

- Acquire and maintain the *technological capability* to produce as broad a range as possible of information goods and services, both for domestic consumption and export markets.

- Sustain the *infrastructure* necessary for this capability by:

   Promoting research and development

   Supporting education and training programs to produce professionals and a skilled work force

   Assuring the availability of capital

   Making the public aware of the importance and implications of the shift to an information economy

- Encourage the *application* of information technology in industry, government, and the home. In doing so, steps should be taken to counteract possible adverse effects (loss of privacy, sectoral unemployment, and establishment of monopolies) and to promote results that are in harmony with social and cultural goals.

We wish to compare how different countries have articulated such plans and progressed toward realizing the objectives outlined in it.

12.1. THE UNITED STATES

Evidence has already been presented in Chapter 9 of the strong, nearly dominant, position of the United States with respect to computer hardware, software, and telecommunications relative to other countries. To understand why, in the light of such strength, there is growing concern about erosion in this position, it is necessary to examine the infrastructure for the technologies, historically and currently.

12.1.1. Infrastructure for the Computer and Communication Technologies

It is generally recognized that throughout the 40 years of the computer industry, technological innovation has been the main driving force. New markets have been identified and exploited as new products, more reliable, with greater capabilities, and costing less, have been developed. Behind this innovation lies research and development. The commitment of funds for research and development of computers has been widespread and continuous in the United States. Government and the private sector have both shared this commitment. One of the principal ways the government has shown its support is by funding the costs for successive generations of supercomputers needed for the nuclear, space, and defense industries. At one time or another, IBM, Sperry Rand, Control Data, Burroughs, Cray Research, and other companies have all proposed very large computers to be used in some special application, often defense related, such as the atomic energy, weather prediction, or space programs. Almost invariably these proposals have been accepted, with the government contributing a substantial fraction of the costs of developing the new machines. Eventually, the techniques learned in making the new computers, techniques for architectural innovations which allow new devices to be used more simply, for miniaturization and quality control, find their way into commercial versions of new systems. From the very beginnings of computers, agencies such as the Office of Naval Research and the National Science Foundation have funded basic research in mathematics and computer science, with approximately half of such funds going to researchers in universities and colleges. The same type of support has served to advance telecommunications. The foundations for the packet-switched data communication services offered by Telenet and Tymnet were laid in the long-term support of Arpanet by the Advanced Research Projects Agency of the Department of Defense (DOD). Generally, the government views its research and development role as (*Long-Range Goals,* 1983, p. 203):

- "Providing a climate for technological innovation which encourages private-sector R&D investment
- "Focusing its direct R&D support in areas where there is likely to be significant economic gain to the nation, but where the private sector is unlikely to invest adequately because of long-term risks
- "Maintaining a growing technological base in categories where government and industry must cooperate fully
- "Promoting basic science and engineering research"

In 1980 the U.S. government spent $2.8 billion for telecommunications R&D in the private sector and $1.5 billion in the federal government—mainly through the Department of Defense (DOD). The 1981 DOD budget for R&D in intelligence and communications was $1.13 billion, and the 1983 budget $2.77 billion. The private-sector contribution to information technology R&D is even greater than that of government. The 1980 expenditures for computer R&D by the companies was $2.7 billion, matching that of the government for *both* computers and communications, and the fraction of revenue devoted to R&D continued high subsequently, in spite of economic recession (Table 10.3). The research activities of IBM and AT&T are illustrative of the importance attached to R&D by the information industries. IBM devotes 6 to 7% of its revenues to research and maintains some dozen laboratories throughout the world. Of these, three (at Yorktown Heights, New York; San Jose, California; and Zurich, Switzerland) are engaged in basic research, and the others are development laboratories, tending to have restricted mandates that link them to products in defined markets. AT&T's Bell Telephone Laboratories (BTL) has for 50 years been one of the most renowned research centers in the world, and from it have come Nobel laureates and inventions such as the transistor. The 1982 BTL budget was $2 billion, of which $156 million was for basic research. By the terms of the 1982 consent decree AT&T retained Bell Laboratories as a single entity, but there are suggestions that the focus may shift to more applied directions, with less publication in the scientific and engineering literature (*Long-Range Goals,* 1983, p. 218).

Patent awards are another useful indicator of technological research activity. The number of U.S. patents relating to telecommunications (including those of both U.S. and foreign origin) increased from an average of 174 annually in 1969–1970, to 420 in 1981–1982. During this period the proportion of foreign-origin to U.S.-origin patents increased, from 30% to 36%, with (for 1981–1982) slightly more than 50% of the foreign patents originating in Japan. Of greater concern, and indicative of what is seen as an inequality between the U.S. position and that held by other countries, is the effect of licensing patents. Often, as a result of antitrust actions, U.S. companies are required to license patent to other companies, including foreign owned. This is the situation with Comsat, and until recently, with AT&T, which has 400 agreements in effect with U.S. companies and nearly 200 with overseas corporations. Reciprocal licensing arrangements are not common in foreign countries. A survey of 161 U.S. companies conducted in 1982* revealed that the long-term effects of overseas licensing were seen as damaging to the companies granting licenses. Frequently, the result was to allow the startup of new companies much sooner than would otherwise have been the case, companies which eventually competed in the U.S. market.

In almost every country, including the United States, the scarcity of trained personnel has been a limiting factor in the application of computer technology. Recent emphasis on techniques such as menu selection as seen in VisiCalc, or the use of a "mouse" to make choices in the Xerox Star and Apple Lisa and Macintosh systems, have reduced the extent to which users have to be familiar with programming languages. But expertise and trained personnel are still needed in large numbers, including application specialists, analysts, system and application programmers who develop new software, maintenance technicians, design engineers, and researchers. Although degree programs in computer science and related disciplines have been available in the United States since about 1964, and it is still the country where there are the most offerings, graduates of the postsecondary system do not begin to fill the need for personnel in the computer field. Of the estimated 853,000 computer specialists in 1974 (see Section 9.2) only about 125,000 had *any* type of university degree; the others received their training at junior colleges, for-profit trade schools, or on the job. The shortage of specialists continued into the 1980s even when unemployment levels were generally very high. Moreover, a decline in the number of students taking science and mathematics at the secondary level, and the quality of science education at that level, threatens to exacerbate the situation, not only for computing but for engineering and science as a whole. A forecast made by the National Science Foundation in 1983 projected that the need for systems analysts and programmers in the United States would grow at an annual rate of 5 to 6% to 1987, creating a

*Forbes, August 1, 1982.

shortfall of 15 to 30% in the number of people needed.* These deficiencies led, in 1982 and 1983, to the creation of the National Commission on Excellence in Education under the Department of Education, and of the Commission on Pre-College Education in Mathematics, Science and Technology by the National Science Board, as well as to numerous proposals for dealing with the issues in Congress. Actions such as these, even if they are not put forward under the umbrella of a national policy for information technology, can be viewed as integral components of an overall approach.

A great strength of the U.S. information industry is the continuing availability of capital. The steady earnings of the major computer companies, especially IBM† (and AT&T as well), are an obvious reason for this. But just as important is the venture capital that new high-technology enterprise centering on computers has been able to attract. Every technological advance has spawned a large number of companies ready to market devices based on the advance, and each year hundreds of them are to be seen at giant trade shows such as the National Computer Conference (NCC) run by the American Federation of Information Societies, exhibiting their products alongside the older firms. The usual fate of the small company is to last only a few years or perhaps be absorbed by one of the large companies, but every once in a while there is a spectacular success and these examples keep the funds coming for new ventures. Thus Digital Equipment and Data General, formed in the late 1960s to exploit the invention of the minicomputer, were instant successes, soon growing to large size, and the high return they yield to anyone who bought their stock in the early years has encouraged investors to look for like examples. Wang Laboratories, specializing in word processors and office automation products, increased its revenues from $76 million in 1975 to $1321.5 million in 1982, when its return on equity was 20.6% and it ranked ninth among U.S. companies in data processing revenues; Apple Computer, Inc., formed in 1978 with the idea of making microprocessors based on a single chip, had a 175% increase in its revenues in 1980, and by 1982 earned $664 million, ranking nineteenth in data processing revenues. The terms "explosion" and "fever" were used to describe the startup situation in 1982, so great was the number of companies and the range of products being offered.‡ These included everything from LSI disk controllers, color printers and graphic systems, to CAD/CAM software and, especially, a very large number of personal computers, many of them compatible with the Apple. This readiness to invest in personal computers was present in spite of the large number of competitors, the fact that IBM's personal computer, although comparatively new, had already captured a significant share of the market, and the certainty that the Japanese were poised to enter the market with models that were likely to be low in price and high in performance. Although there has been some fluctuation in the availability of entrepreneurial

---

*The estimates are influenced by the extent of the economic recovery and the degree to which wage incentives attract entry into the field.

†IBM's earnings have generally been in the range 12 to 15% of sales.

‡*Business Week,* August 2, 1982, 53–54; *Datamation,* 28, no. 9 (September 1982), 180.

capital, since the 1980s investors have been anxious to move away from the "smokestack" industries (steel, utilities, automotive products, chemicals) to the "sunrise" industries, based on biotechnology, lasers, and especially, information technology. Over the years the computer industries, sparked by their growth and performance, have been able to find the capital needed to finance their continuing expansion. This is of no little importance. It has meant that there has not been in the United States the need or the pressure for government to come in as a partner with industry. As we shall see, the experience of most other countries in this regard has been quite different.

12.1.2. Policy Articulation

Two key factors have to be recognized in examining the extent to which there is or might be an explicit formulation of policy with respect to computers and communications in the United States:

1. Jurisdiction over computers and communications is shared among multiple agencies of the federal government.
2. There is a basic distrust of centralized planning with regard to economic matters, a distrust that extends to planning for the information technology sector, no matter how important that sector is seen to be.

In the report *Long-Range Goals* (1983) no fewer than 26 departments and agencies of the federal government are identified as having some responsibility for the development and implementation of U.S. policy on information and international telecommunications. Of these, the principal actors are:

1. The National Telecommunications and Information Administration (NTIA), a division of the Department of Commerce. Among its responsibilities it is to:
   a. "Develop and set forth . . . plans, policies and programs which relate to international telecommunications issues, conferences and negotiations
   b. "Assign frequencies to radio stations . . . operated by the United States
   c. "Develop and set forth telecommunication policies pertaining to the Nation's economic and technological advancement and to the regulation of the telecommunications industry
   d. "Conduct studies and make recommendations concerning the impact of the convergence of computer and communications technology"
2. The Department of State, for which a 1978 Executive Order specifies that: "With respect to telecommunications, the Secretary of State shall exercise primary authority for the conduct of foreign policy, including the determination of United States position and the conduct of United States participation in negotiations with foreign governments and international bodies . . ." and further that the Secretary of State "is responsible for instructing the

Communications Satellite Corporation in its role as the designated United States representative to the International Telecommunications Satellite Organization. . . ."

3. The Federal Communications Commission, which was created in 1934 for "regulating interstate and foreign commerce in communication by wire and radio. . . ."

4. The United State Trade Representative, a cabinet-level official in the Executive Office of the President who has "primary responsibility for developing and for considering the implementation of United States international trade policy. . . ."

In addition, national security considerations may at times override all others, as happens when high-technology goods such as computers are prohibited from being exported to communist bloc countries. With these overlapping mandates it is hardly surprising that there is no one locus in the U.S. federal government where decisions about U.S. information policy can be made. Sometimes, especially in domestic matters, the actions of the FCC have been decisive, as we have seen in the move to deregulation. But when negotiations take place with other countries on such matters as allocations of frequencies in the radio spectrum, access to markets for information products and services, and movement of data across national borders or transfer of technology, different agencies come into play, sometimes with conflicting goals. One of the stated intentions of the Communications Act of 1934 was, in part, "for the purposes of securing a more effective execution of this [i.e., Executive branch] policy by centralizing authority heretofore granted by law to several agencies." In the last few years particularly, there have been repeated calls from within government and from industry for greater government intervention in the information technology industry, along with arguments for consolidating authority so as to allow a clear national policy on information to evolve. We have already seen many examples of the kinds of actions sought, but it is useful to review some of the principal ones.

- Amend or relax antitrust legislation so as to permit and even encourage greater technical cooperation between U.S. companies*
- Modify tax policies (e.g., by increasing depreciation write-offs, educational allowances, and foreign tax credits) so as to promote new industries and decrease the risk of starting them up†
- Adopt trade policies (e.g., based on reciprocity) which emphasize free market access abroad and reduce penetration of U.S. markets due to unfair trade practices‡

---

*Diebold (1982); W. Norris, "Keeping America First," *Datamation,* 28, no. 9 (September 1982), 280–3; "The Birth of Silicon Statesmanship," *The New York Times,* February 27, 1983.

†Diebold (1982); Norris, op. cit.; "The Dangers of Sharing American Technology," *Business Week,* March 14, 1983.

‡Diebold (1982); "Birth of Silicon Statesmanship," op. cit.; *Long-Range Goals* (1983, Chaps. 4, 7).

- Protect vital industries (e.g., semiconductors) from the damaging effects of competitors (particularly Japan) inhibiting the transfer of technology where necessary*

- Examine patent and copyright laws and make changes to promote innovations†

- Promote greater industry–university cooperation and provide greater funding of university research‡

- Formulate a coherent, well-integrated policy recognizing the interests of the market, national security, and the need for regulation¶

The argument for a national information policy is part of the larger argument advanced at the same time, to the effect that the United States needs to adopt a national *industrial* policy.‖ The proponents look for a new institution (e.g., a "National Strategic Planning Board," a "Federal Industrial Coordination Board," or an "Economic Cooperation Council") with a principal function of promoting high-technology industries by actions, along the lines of those listed above. But the objections to centralized planning in the United States are deeply rooted. There are strongly held beliefs that such planning is inevitably protectionist and elitist, and that it legitimizes government's role in an area where there is no evidence that the government can do better than free enterprise. The latter view is consistent with that held by the Reagan administration, which sought to achieve the *results* of a national policy by encouraging private industry to adopt the necessary measures. Certainly, some actions along the desired lines have emerged from industry. The private-sector increase in funds for research and development has already been noted. In 1983 a consortium of electronics companies, called Microelectronics and Computer Technology Corporation (MCC),# was formed with specific long-range objectives for computer-aided design and manufacture, software productivity improvement, microelectronics packaging, and computer architecture research. These efforts were supported by assurances of immunity from antitrust litigation and by the "Strategic Computing and Survivability Project" of the Department of Defense, a direct response to the Japanese call for the "fifth-generation computer." Also, various bills are continually being put

*"SIA Urges U.S. onto Protectionism," *Computing,* February 1983, 2.

†Diebold (1982).

‡"Birth of Silicon Statesmanship," op. cit.; "How Will the U.S. Respond to the Fifth Generation?" *Commun. ACM,* 26, no. 4 (April 1983), 323.

¶*Toward an American Agenda for a New World Order of Communications* (Washington, D.C.: U.S. National Commission for UNESCO, Department of State, 1980); Diebold (1982); *Long-Range Goals* (1983, Chaps. 4, 7); "How Will the U.S. Respond?", op. cit.

‖"Debate Grows over Adoption of National Industry Policy," *The New York Times,* June 19, 1983.

#The companies are Advanced Micro Devices, Inc.; Digital Equipment Corporation; Harris Corporation; Honeywell, Inc.; Motorola; NCR Corporation; National Semiconductors Corporation; RCA; and Sperry UNIVAC. For a detailed account, see E. Holmes, "MCC: One U.S. Answer to the Japanese," *Abacus,* 1, no. 1 (1983), 65–67.

forward in the U.S. Congress, as well as in state legislatures, for support of high-technology industries.

The creation of a *centralized* institution in the United States, responsible for articulating overall policy about information technology and overseeing the implementation of recommendations somehow achieved through national consensus, would be a break with the past. In fact, from the objectives and events described in this and the preceding chapter, some genuine conflicts can be discerned. The desire for international freedom of access to, and transfer of information, important to U.S.-based multinationals in their daily operations, conflicts with growing concerns about national security and the need to conserve industrial strength by inhibiting dissemination of the results of research. The traditional position of the United States on free trade is compromised by those seeking to protect U.S. markets from competition seen as unfair. But it would be wrong to infer that there is *no* U.S. policy with respect to information technology from the absence of a single body with the responsibility for creating policy and following through on implementation. A great many actions of the executive and legislative branches of the U.S. government, of private industry, and of professional organizations are specifically designed to maintain and strengthen the infrastructure supporting the computer and communication technologies and to achieve just those results that a national policy would seek to promote. It can be argued that together, these actions make up a de facto policy, which just because it is not monolithic can be more effective in maintaining the U.S. lead in information technology.

12.2. JAPAN

Among the countries with free market economies, Japan has had the most carefully engineered industrial strategy. So successful has it been in one sector after another—steel, shipbuilding, automobiles, and electronics—that other countries, including even the United States, keep coming to examine the process and to try and learn lessons that can be applied at home (see Edelstein et al., 1978). Of all sectors, the electronics industry has received the greatest attention in Japan, and it has been chosen as the principal target for future development. Japanese output of electronics and information technology products has closely followed the plans laid down for them, so it is natural in this case to examine the planning process before looking at the capabilities.

12.2.1. The Planning Process

The Japanese industrial success is based on a complex mix of circumstances, some of them peculiar to Japan, and of deliberate policies adopted by government in a dedicated effort to achieve economic sovereignty. Any summary risks being an oversimplification, but some of the key factors are readily identified.

TABLE 12.1 MAJOR JAPANESE INDUSTRIAL GROUPS AND ASSOCIATED ELECTRONICS COMPANIES

Industrial Group	Computer Company
Dai-Ichi Kangyo	Fujitsu
Sumitomo	Nippon Electric Co.
Fuji	Hitachi
Mitsui	Toshiba
Sanwa	Oki
Mitsubishi	Mitsubishi Electric

- The presence of strong industries, largely focused into six major groups each with 20 or more subsidiaries, including a bank, one or two trading companies, and not coincidentally, one of the six main domestic Japanese computer companies. These groups and their associated electronic companies are listed in Table 12.1.

- A steady commitment by the Diet, the Japanese parliament, going back as far as 1957, to protecting and strengthening electronic industries. This commitment is shared by many branches of government, including the Prime Minister's Office, the Ministries of Finance and of Post and Telecommunications, Industrial and Economic Councils, and research agencies, but the most prominent agent has been MITI, the Ministry of International Trade and Industry.

- A consensus by which industry operates within MITI's administrative guidelines. These guidelines are not reached through some monolithic or hierarchical apparatus. Rather, they have been set out in legislative actions aimed at protecting and strengthening emerging industries and have been described in a sequence of visionary reports which have served to publicize the goals.* The broad objectives have been first to catch up, then to equal, and finally be first in technological capabilities. Besides encouragement of indigenous industries, restriction of foreign investment and control of imported goods have been principal instruments. It is important to note that a willingness to abide by MITI's incentives, awarded largely upon a demonstrated ability to export, does not prevent Japanese companies from competing fiercely with one another during the early stages of product development. The result has been that Japan has been able to achieve the advantages of both free enterprise (e.g., competitive industries) and planned economies (e.g., low unemployment).

- A variety of special organizations that promote innovation or harmonize relations between the public and private sectors. There are some 120 publicly

*See, for example, *The Industrial Structure in Japan,* ISC, 1963; *The Vision of MITI Policies for the 1970's,* ISC, 1971; *Outlook,* JERC, 1975; *Twenty First Century,* NIRA, 1979; *The Vision of MITI Policies in the 1980's,* ISC, 1980.

owned companies in Japan, many of which use their profits to catalyze new departures in industrial strategy. The Keindanren (Federation of Economic Organizations) is a powerful advocate for the business community, and it often offers alternative framing of emerging issues and acts to coordinate individual sectors. Keiretsu, an interesting arrangement between large companies and their smaller satellites, is also conducive to the formulation of overall strategy. Finally, nonprofit, nongovernmental organizations such as JACUDI, the Japan Computer-Usage Development Institute, have also contributed significantly to the formulation of policy.*

- The continuation of industrial patterns which contribute to stability. Examples are the practice, in the very large industries at least, of lifetime employment and the willingness of companies and investors to accept low returns for a long time during which market share is being built up.

If the relations between the government and Japanese industry are highly developed and complex, those between government and foreign-controlled industries have been much less subtle. For example, IBM Japan is forced to manufacture its most advanced products in Japan, is excluded from government procurement, has a restricted market share (29% in 1977), must license its technology to Japanese competitors, and is expected to develop Japanese-language processing. In contrast, Fujitsu has been designated as a chosen company, a "national champion," and it receives government subsidies, is a leader in computer communication sales to the government, and receives backing for global marketing efforts. The giant Nippon Telegraph and Telephone Public Corporation for a very long time restricted purchases to a closely knit family of Japanese suppliers, frustrating all foreign access to its $2.5 billion annual procurement budget.†

Although financial aid for research and development and for industry subsidation is an instrument in planning, it is not the only tool or even the most important one. The key is a carefully orchestrated approach to new products, starting with imitation, followed by product improvement, and finally innovation. At the same time there is *controlled competition,* whereby a few firms use foreign technology and other indigenous firms are encouraged to develop competitive products which were sold first in domestic and third-world markets, and then to industrialized countries. High-volume exports are emphasized because they make it possible for industries to automate and move rapidly up the learning curve so that unit costs decrease. In 1979, government spending on R&D was 2% of the GNP. But of this 64% went to development, and at the same time 0.2% of the GNP was spent on licensing foreign technology. As in the United States, most research is carried out in the private sector, where 70% of researchers are employed.

*A 1972 JACUDI paper, *The Plan for Information Society—A National Goal toward the Year 2000,* called for a $65 billion investment in information technology between 1972 and 1985.

†*Business Week,* August 9, 1982.

Another characteristic of Japanese planning is targeted sectors. Five critical areas of service and technology have been identified:

1. Aerospace
2. New energy
3. New materials
4. Biotechnology
5. Computers/communication

Within computers/communications technology itself there are major thrusts in very large scale integration (VLSI) fabrication, artificial intelligence (robotics, pattern recognition, speech synthesizers, and recognition), and supercomputers. Knowledge-intensive industries, somewhat loosely defined, are seen to be the largest source of foreign earnings in the future, and with this vision Japan, of all countries, continues to make the largest commitment to information technology.

12.2.2. Technological Capability

The striking feature of Japan's manufacturing capacity in information products is its breadth. There is growth and strength in almost every segment of the market— from integrated circuits to telecommunication equipment, facsimile devices, printers and other peripherals, and the full array of computers, from the very largest down to microcomputers and office automation products. As was the case in Chapter 9 for the U.S. industry, it is not possible here to document the full story, but a few representative tables and charts will illustrate the Japanese capability.

Chip technology lies behind not only the computer and telecommunication industries, but others as well. Consumer items such as cars or microwave ovens without microcomputer controls are obsolete. Hitachi, Fujitsu, and Nippon Electric Company (NEC) all mass-produce chips. Table 12.2 shows trends in the utilization of CPU chips. But Japan has only 1% of the global market share in CPU chips. The outstanding success has been in random-access memory (RAM) chips. After a breakthrough in the 16K RAM market, Japanese suppliers captured

TABLE 12.2 UTILIZATION TRENDS FOR CPU CHIPS IN JAPANESE PRODUCTS

	Number of Chips Used in:									Total Value
Year	Consumer Appliances	Business Machines	Industrial	Trans- portation	Testing/ Measuring	Communi- cations	Data Processing	Others	Total Number	(millions of yen)
1978	2,646,662	310,766	67,037	10,640	45,008	44,964	35,201	133,622	3,314,302	3,029
1979	4,039,665	387,155	162,972	25,310	82,587	78,190	52,163	416,973	5,265,015	4,921
1980	6,004,410	293,633	296,746	31,505	113,522	151,969	60,730	688,270	7,640,725	7,196

Source: Japan Electronics Almanac (Tokyo, Dempa Publications, 1981).

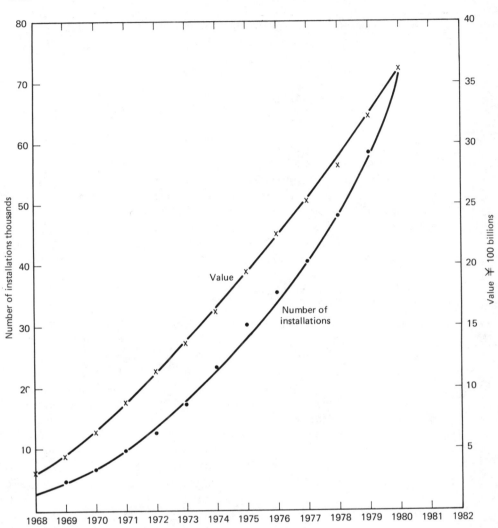

Figure 12.1 Growth of general-purpose computers in Japan (from *Japan Electronics Almanac* [Tokyo: Dempa Publications, 1983).

70 to 80% of the world market for 64K RAM chips in 1982, and took a dominant position for 256K and higher-density memory chips.

Figure 12.1 charts the growth of general-purpose computers in Japan. The recent sharp increase in the slope of the curve for number of installations, compared with the relatively constant slope for value, reflects a trend toward a large number of smaller computers. This is even more pronounced in the demand for minicomputers and office computers, for which the sales have been increasing at an annual rate of some 40% (Table 12.3).

TABLE 12.3 MINICOMPUTERS AND OFFICE COMPUTER SALES (INSTALLATIONS) IN JAPAN

	Year								
	1975	1976	1977	1978	1979	1980	1981	1982	1985 (Projected)
Minicomputers	2,966	3,850	4,640	7,459	8,800	9,931	10,900 (est.)	16,180 (est.)	
Office computers	6,966	7,614	9,607	12,668	20,828	32,831	50,073	68,000	125,000

Source: Japan Electronics Almanac, (Tokyo: Dempa Publications, 1983).

Table 12.4 shows the data processing revenues for the six major Japanese computer companies together with those for the principal U.S.-based companies. The revenues of Fujitsu exceeded those of IBM for the first time in 1980. All the Japanese companies market a complete range of computers, from large scale through medium range to minis, micros, and special machines for use in control applications. Especially noteworthy is the sharp rise in the number of companies producing microcomputers and office machines. There were over 50 of them in 1980, and by their very number they are beginning to challenge the orderly growth that MITI has hitherto been able to impose on the computer industry.

Table 12.5 shows data for production, exports, and imports of computer-related equipment to 1981. The value of exports for Japanese computer products continues to rise. These were $371 million in 1980 and $844 million in 1981, and there are signs that eventually Japan could challenge the United States in exports

TABLE 12.4 DATA PROCESSING REVENUES OF JAPANESE COMPUTER COMPANIES

Company	DP Revenues (millions of dollars) in:		DP Export Revenues (% of total) In:	
	1981	1980	1981	1980
Fujitsu	2063	1730	12	10
IBM	1950	1538	25	20
NEC	1489	1160	11	6
Hitachi	1309	1138	10	7
Toshiba	432	347	8	6
Oki	425	358	14	8
Nippon UNIVAC	413	357	2	2
Mitsubishi	332	282	10	8
Burroughs	260	230	2	2
NCR	225	219	4	5

Source: Datamation, 29, no. 1 (January 1983).

TABLE 12.5 PRODUCTION, EXPORTS, AND IMPORTS OF COMPUTER-RELATED EQUIPMENT, JAPAN

Year	Production	Exports (millions of yen)[a]	Imports (millions of yen)
1970	310,463	5,786	95,795
1971	346,349	9,009	93,436
1972	420,688	11,351	89,089
1973	472,396	12,293	107,494
1974	589,034	18,816	144,833
1975	541,246	21,552	130,660
1976	618,897	39,279	132,621
1977	720,113	41,000	146,471
1978	910,240	69,686	111,000
1979	1,123,360	80,885	154,279
1980	1,292,556	121,697	215,805
1981	1,478,094	193,628	208,168

[a]In 1983 U.S. $1 was approximately 220 yen.

Source: Japan Electronics Almanac, (Tokyo: Dempa Publications, 1983), based on data from MITI, Ministry of Finance.

of computer products.* An important aspect of the Japanese approach is the readiness of companies such as Fujitsu, NEC, and IBM Japan to tie in with foreign competitors. This is in contrast to the OEM (original equipment manufacture) companies, where the Japanese have traditionally pursued a more independent path.

The strongest evidence of Japanese capabilities with respect to computers is the manner in which the industry has progressed from imitation to innovation, especially as seen in the major government-funded research programs. The Pattern Information Processing Project (PIPS) was an 8-year effort, ending about 1980, with special emphasis on voice recognition and output. The results are just beginning to appear as commercial products, which initially have limited vocabularies and applicability but are expected to become more versatile. The VLSI project, involving all the major producers as well as two government electronics research laboratories, was budgeted at $350 million (of which approximately 40% was from government sources) and scheduled for completion 1984–1986. In 1981, MITI, through its Agency of Industrial Technology, launched an $85 million project to develop a 10,000-MIPS computer for scientific purposes. In 1983, Hitachi announced for sale a 1000-MIPS machine, faster than the U.S.-produced CDC and Cray supercomputers. Another ambitious, $80 million project is the development of an optical computer, based on galium arsenide devices which process light pulses rather than electrical signals, intended for the telecommunications industry. The Japanese project that has captured the most attention interna-

*Estimates as high as $2.5 billion exports by 1986 have been made [*Datamation,* 29, no. 1 (January 1983)].

tionally is the "fifth-generation computer." This is intended to result in a family of machines based on VLSI with a density of 1 million transistors per chip, with data flow architecture, very different than that of conventional von Neumann computers. The computers that emerge are to accept continuous voice input, understand natural language, and have embedded knowledge-type data bases which would allow it to behave like an expert in many situations (see Feigenbaum and McCorduck, 1983). For the first time Japan invited American and European participation in this project, but the United States decided that defense implications required it to pursue independent development of any computer with such capabilities, and the United Kingdom, after much public discussion, undertook limited cooperation. The project is so ambitious, and depends so much on results from basic research which has yet to be done, that many doubt whether it can be achieved in the 10 years allotted for it. Also, there are recognized shortcomings in the Japanese ability to produce software, and Japanese computer companies have sought to forge links with software houses in the United States and the United Kingdom in order to develop expertise. A special organization, the Institute of New Generations Computers (ICOT), where the core of the research is being done, has been set up in Tokyo. MITI has allocated $540 million to the project, but contributions from industry are expected to double or triple that amount. Even a partial success toward fifth-generation machines would give Japanese firms a very large range of new products to sell the rest of the world during the 1990s.

Other factors to be noted about the Japanese computer industry are the numerous links with other sectors of the economy and the basic strength of the infrastructure. In robotics Japan is the undisputed world leader, with some 100,000 in use in 1982, nearly 70% of the world's total. Robot sales were estimated as $90 million in 1977, $125 million in 1978, and $210 million in 1980, with projected annual growth rates of 40 to 50% and exports equal to 20% of production. The export success of the Japanese telecommunication equipment manufacturing companies is built on an enormous expansion of the home market and a very high degree of integration of the computer and communications technologies. The key actor is NTT, Nippon Telegraph and Telephone, the national PTT. After NTT fulfilled two major goals in 1980, the elimination of telephone demand backlog and the installation of nationwide dialing, it set about to modernize services. Central offices were upgraded by adding electronic switching; packet-switched data communication networks were put into operation for banking, airline, hospital, and information retrieval applications; and broadband transmission systems based on fiber optics were placed in commercial service. NTT's $20 billion (1982) revenues and $3 billion equipment market make it a bulwark of the telecommunications industry, but its giant size and bureaucratic structure have meant that the same type of forces that are exerted on Euopean PTTs (and that acted on AT&T) are being exercised on it. Aggressive customers look for more interconnection, value-added services, and greater competition, as do companies outside Japan seeking a share of the local telecommunications market. In partial response NTT has set about on a modernization program which includes installation of an Information Network System and has on its own initiative encouraged decentralization.*

Parallel with telecommunications there is an active program for space technology in Japan. This includes the launching of test satellites (much of it in cooperation with U.S. firms), and a special effort directed toward developing and marketing ground stations for satellite control and applications in communications, meteorology, and remote sensing.

Behind these thrusts into high technology in Japan lies a highly competitive educational system in which prime emphasis is placed on scientific and mathematical skills. Just as pervasive is a widespread program in which the public is being constantly reminded of the importance of knowledge-based industries to Japan's future, through newspapers and through such activities as the National Computer Week, held annually. Japan's commitment toward achieving excellence in information technology is clear. More than any other country it has embraced this as a national goal, formulated policies toward achieving the goal, and progressed deliberately and effectively toward implementing the plans. For many countries Japan's policies for computers and communications have been a model to be emulated.

12.3. EUROPE

Of the countries in Europe, the United Kingdom and France have had the longest involvement with information technology. Using somewhat different approaches, each has had limited success in establishing an industrial presence. Since the 1970s especially, other member countries of the European Economic Community have seen the need to compete with the United States and Japan in information products as a matter of urgent priority, and individually and collectively they have tried to establish policies that would achieve this.

12.3.1. The United Kingdom

British participation in the very first researches on electronic computers, such as those involving EDSAC at Cambridge University, and ACE at the National Physical Laboratory, was followed by the early entry of British companies into manufacturing—Ferranti, British Tabulating Machines, Elliott Automation, English Electric, and others. As far back as 1948 the National Research Development Council (NRDC) encouraged companies to do research on computers and to take out patents. But through the 1950s and 1960s even the combined home and export markets were not enough to sustain the many companies. After a sequence of mergers, International Computers Limited (ICL) was formed in 1968, with the government holding 35% interest, to become the flagship British entry in the

*See *Business Week,* August 9, 1982, and *The New York Times,* January 8, 1984.

computer mainframe industry. ICL continues to market a wide range of computer products, from peripherals and micros to the very largest systems. It is often given preference in orders placed by national and local governments, sometimes over the objections of its Common Market partners. In spite of the advantages, ICL sales have been consistently less than those of IBM, U.K. (e.g., £700 million in 1981 versus £1020 million for IBM); after some profitable years between 1976 and 1978 it suffered a loss of £133 million in 1981 but again showed a profit in 1983; it is chronically short of capital and has undergone several reorganizations.

However, the U.K. government presence in the computer industry goes far beyond participation in ICL. In 1965 the National Computer Centre (NCC) was established and its activities in portable software, programming standards, users' forums, job classification and training schemes have done much for the software industry. Many other high-level agencies have been involved, issuing reports, generating legislation, and launching programs with varying degrees of success, and the pace quickened appreciably after a 1978 BBC documentary film about the job implications of computer technology, *Now the Chips Are Down,* attracted nationwide attention and strong government interest. In 1981 NRDC and the National Enterprise Board (NEB), a state holding company formed to expand into promising areas of manufacture, merged to become the British Technology Group. The 1979 and 1980 NEB funding levels were $765 million and $625 million, respectively. Other important agencies are the National Economic Development Council (NEDC), the Prime Minister's Advisory Committee (ACARD), the National Defence Industries Council (NDIC), and the Universities Grants Committees. The principal legislative umbrellas are the Science and Technology Act of 1965 and the Industry Act (1972, 1975, amended 1976), according to which there are grants and tax incentives for expansion into regions where jobs are needed, covering capital investments, research and development, training, and even licensing and marketing costs. The principal ministries are the Department of Industry (DoI) and since 1980, the Ministry of Information Technology. Table 12.6 is a partial list of the numerous initiatives, programs, and schemes which illustrate the active partnership between British government and industry in information technology.

The forms of government intervention underwent an important shift with the election of the Thatcher government in 1979, which like the Reagan administration in the United States, looked to the private sector to become the principal investor. An initial period during which the government divested itself of interests acquired earlier, and reconstructed many of the instruments already in place, was soon followed by one where the government was again active, but always so as to involve the private sector. Typical are the deregulation and privatization efforts centered on the communications industry. First, a long-contemplated move to separate communications from the British Post Office was taken, and a separate entity, British Telecommunications (BT), was set up. Also, BT's monopoly over telecommunications was ended with the licensing of Mercury, a private company which soon became a serious competitor. BT has labored to modernize Britain's

TABLE 12.6 GOVERNMENT SUPPORT OF INFORMATION TECHNOLOGY IN THE
UNITED KINGDOM

Date	Program	Description
1973	Requirement Boards	R&D expenditures of DoI; $139 million (total) in 1980–1981
	Software Products Scheme	Contributes up to 50% of *cost* for developing or marketing new softwares; $10 million spent in 1983, $20 million additional authorized
1977	INSAC	Wholly owned government corporation, under NEB, with holdings in software companies (Systems Designer, Logica, Systine, Nexus, etc.); sold in 1981
	Product and Process Development Scheme (PPDS)	Grants of up to 25% for design, development of new products (e.g., robots, computerized book ordering)
1978	INMOS	Semiconductor production; research facility in U.S.; production in U.S. and Japan; $120 million initially, later participation reduced
	Microelectronics Industry Support Program (MISP)	$160 million initially—preproduction orders of equipment (e.g., integrated circuits)
	Microprocessor Applications Project (MAP)	Diffusion of microprocessing in industry (training, demonstrations); initial budget £55 million, augmented by £30 million in 1983
1979	PRESTEL (commercial operation)	Videotex (electronic database) service for home and business developed by British Post Office; approx. £25 million in 1980
1981	Joint Appraisal Scheme	Cooperative venture between NRDC and banks to raise additional capital for MAP-funded projects
	Optoelectronics Support Scheme	R&D support for joint ventures relating to fiber optics; $55 million initially
	Microelectronics Education Program (MEP)	Acquisition of microcomputers for secondary schools; 50% contribution
1982	British Information Technology Export Organization	To promote sales of British software in the U.S.

antiquated communications network and to satisfy the backlog of orders for telephones and data communications. To this end it developed System X, a digital electronic switching system, ordered equipment from suppliers other than those in the United Kingdom, introduced new switched and nonswitched services, entered into cross-licensing agreements with Japan, and participated actively in the communication satellite programs of the European Space Agency. Still, services remain poor compared to those in the United States, Japan, France, or Canada, and the government, committed to selling a majority interest in BT to allow the private sector to do better, achieved this in 1984.

The British policy on information technology, like that of the United States, is decentralized, but it has behind it a long history of research activity, industrial entrepreneurship, and government presence, as well as a recent history of public awareness and concern.* With the creation of the Ministry of Information Technology in 1979 there was some focusing, as witnessed by the direct information technology support, which increased from £50 million in 1979 to £200 million in 1983, a sharp contrast from the trend in other sections of government. The main government thrust was to foster a favorable economic climate by reducing inflation and improving the efficiency of markets rather than adopting an interventional policy of designating sectors needing special support. But if funds are taken as a measure of commitment to a national information technology program, levels in Britain are very low compared to those in the United States, Japan, or France. Investment capital is scarce both in the public and private sectors. Of BT's capital expenditures, 80 to 90% have to be financed from revenues. Although, after much debate, the government accepted a report of the Alvey Commission to participate in Japan's fifth-generation computer project, the 5-year funding was set at £350 million, rather than the recommended £500 million. If other criteria are applied to measure the success of information policies, the same mixture of results is to be seen. There are repeated criticisms that for all the exhortations of MAP and similar programs, British management and labor have been slow to move into the new technologies.† The growth in output for the information technology sector in the United Kingdom is illustrated in Fig. 12.2, but the "combined turnover of the six biggest British-owned information technology companies was about equal to that of Siemens of West Germany, which itself was sixth in the world league.‡ Growth in output has not been enough to offset an increasing deficit in the balance of trade for information on products¶ or to prevent decreases of employment levels in the information technology industries (Fig. 12.3).

Despite calls from industry and editorials in trade publications that Britain must have an integrated national policy for information technology, including a blueprint of goals and a schedule for achieving them, adoption of such a plan would be contrary to history and to the approach of a Conservative government, although not, of course, to a Labor government. It is likely that there will continue to be many special programs and that any government will continue to assign a high priority to information technology. But like most other industrialized countries, Britain is finding it difficult to carve itself out a niche in the global information economy.

12.3.2. France

In its policy of "dirigisme" (planning) the French government, next to Japan, is the most interventionist of the free market nations. Dirigisme gained the ascendancy

---

*This awareness was very much heightened because of the educational and demonstration programs that took place in 1982 as part of Information Technology Year 82.

†*Financial Times,* March 25, 1982; *Computing,* November 25, 1982.

‡Quotation from Kenneth Baker, Minister of Information Technology, *Financial Times,* March 24, 1982.

¶For details, see the *Mackintosh Yearbooks of West European Electronics Data.*

Information Technology UK Output (£billion)

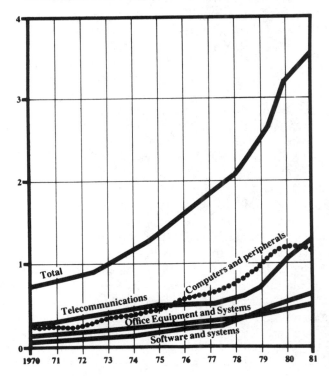

Figure 12.2   Information technology UK output (from *Computing,* January 13, 1983, with permission).

when De Gaulle set out to make France independent in high-technology areas such as nuclear energy, aeronautical and space engineering, and informatique (computers). The principal instruments are a program of massive subsidies in the form of development grants, guaranteed purchases to domestic industries ready to work with government, and the support of large government research facilities. With the Mitterand government, complete nationalization of major industries was undertaken. For computers there have been a sequence of state-directed blueprints called Les Plan Calculs, the fourth of which spanned the period 1979–1982, and since 1982 there has been a special Action Plan on Electronics (Filière électronique).

France, like Japan and the United Kingdom, has its flagship company in the computer industry, Bull S.A. (formerly CII-HB, Compagnie Internationale pour l'Informatique-Honeywell Bull). Like ICL, Bull S.A. is the result of a long sequence of mergers in which the government played an active part. It markets some 60 mainframe computer systems, and with annual sales exceeding $1 billion since 1978 and over 20,000 employees, it is the largest computer company in the world outside of those in the United States and Japan. With its share of 25 to 30%

Information Technology UK Employment (Thousands)

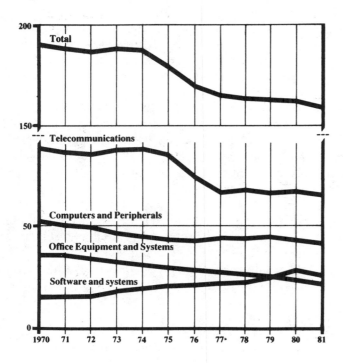

Figure 12.3 Information technology UK employment (thousands) (from *Computing,* January 13, 1983, with permission).

of the market in France and 10 to 20% in Europe, Bull S.A. outsells U.S. companies in Europe. Its export volume of more than half a billion dollars to over 60 countries (1982) is a principal reason why France is the only country other than the United States which has a favorable balance of trade with regard to computers. The government stake in Bull S.A., always important, became a controlling share under Mitterand's nationalization program, and led to Honeywell's dissociating itself from the company when state control became too direct.

France set itself high targets for sales of information technology products and penetration of foreign markets, and toward this end, computer and telecommunication companies formed numerous joint ventures with foreign firms. Thomson-CSF, the largest electronics company (also nationalized), aligned itself with Motorola and Fortune Systems in the United States for VLSI technology and microcomputers, respectively. CIT-Alcatel, a subsidiary of the multibillion-dollar Compagnie Générale d'Électricité (CGE*), with government approval entered into an agreement with AES Data, Canada, as part of its thrust in office

*Not affiliated with GE in the United States.

automation. Matra S.A. contracted with Harris and Intel for chip production, and with Tandy for the production of TRS-80 microcomputers. St. Gobain linked with National Semiconductors for chip manufacture, and the French oil company Schlumberger acquired Fairchild Camera and Instrument in the United States.

The export drive is based on a home market for telecommunication products which has shown very high rates of growth since the middle 1970s. Between 1977 and 1983 the number of telephone subscribers in France increased from 6 to 16 million.* Later expansion has focused on packet-switched networks (TRANS-PAC), digital exchanges, fiber optics, and cable television services. A much publicized effort was the experiment to provide 250,000 customers in Ille-et-Vilaine with video terminals instead of telephone directories. The mass-produced terminals, supposed to cost about $100, were of interest to the distributors of the Source data base in the United States. But the history of the project is also illustrative of the difference between achievement and promise. It was much delayed and had to be modified when subscribers insisted on having the choice of terminals *or* conventional telephone books, but eventually the project did achieve momentum. By 1984 175,000 videotex had been installed in France, with 3 million predicted for 1986. The French capability in information technology products is real and broadly based. Software companies and service bureaus are large (CAP-SOGETI is Europe's largest software house, with over 3000 employees) and are active throughout Europe, generating substantial export revenues. The peripheral components industry is vigorous. Areas of weakness, such as chip production, are given special attention by Le Plan Calcul.

Supporting this capability there is a network of cognate industries, research organizations, and educational institutions. France has been an avid proponent of a defense posture independent from that of the United States and even from its European allies, and stemming from this has strong national programs for nuclear and space technologies. In its aerospace program France cooperates with the European Space Agency, works with Germany in mounting direct broadcast TV satellites, and with its Ariane series of launch vehicles competes with the United States in offering delivery of commercial communication satellites. Each technological area has well-funded government R&D centers, Centre National D'Études Spatiales (CNES) for aerospace, Centre National d'Études Techniques (CNET) for communications, and Institut National de Recherche en Informatique (INRIA) for computers.

If anything, the governments that followed De Gaulle have been even stronger in their commitment to informatique and télématique. Giscard D'Estaing commissioned the celebrated Nora–Minc Report (1978), which mobilized French will to become a leader in information technology. In 1979 a highly publicized event, La Semaine Informatique, was held to increase public and media awareness of the implications for society. Mitterand repeatedly went on record with his conviction that in the application of information technology lay the solutions to bettering the

---

*But still leaving the per capita number substantially less than in other major industrialized countries.

French economy and society and to helping developing countries. Among his earliest actions on taking power was a dramatic increase of 66% in research funding for data processing and computers, the nationalization of major computer companies so as to provide more capital and promote a greater entrepreneurial spirit, and the creation of a new international institute, the World Center for Informatics and Development of Human Resources, intended to help developing countries use microcomputers, in which other countries were invited to participate. Beneath these highly visible actions of the various French governments there has been a very complex structure of advisory and planning committees, such as the Direction des Industries Électroniques et de l'Informatique, which took over the functions of the earlier Délégation à l'Informatique for Le Plan Calcul; the Mission à l'Informatique, which harmonizes government procurement policy in the public and private sectors; CEESI, created in 1978 to develop management information systems for French administrations; and Comité Consultatif de la Recherche en Informatique, for coordinating data processing research. The strongest form of government presence is in the trend toward nationalization and government-directed restructuring of the industries, to the extent that about half of the French electronics industry is under direct government control. This trend continued in the decision to merge the two largest telecommunications manufacturers, CIT-Alcatel and Thomson CSF, into a single company, CIT-Thomson Télécommunications (CTT).

In spite of the existence of such a highly focused and clearly articulated policy with respect to information technology in France, and definite signs of success in home and European markets, there have been serious expressions of doubt about the ultimate success. The principal criticism is that the planning process in France is so strongly directed from the top down, and the French bureaucracy is so restrictive, the innovation at the working levels of industry is invariably stifled. The need of Honeywell to withdraw from CII-Honeywell Bull has already been noted. De Vos (1983) documents the workings of the government committees that support industrial research projects in some detail. There is, for example, an unusual provision whereby some companies are required to repay a government grant if a project *fails* but not if it succeeds. Such a practice inevitably leads companies to propose low-risk ventures. It is true that government support of these may release internal funds for more risky projects, but such rules (which also have their political side because the government wants to be seen as backing successes) run counter to the usual ones for government funding. Also, France's traditional protectionist stance compromises its ability to arrive at good working relationships with multinational companies for the transfer of technology and the sharing of markets. This stance is seen in many ways, for example in an insistence on separate standards, which makes it difficult for foreign equipment to be sold in France, in a highly discriminatory rate structure for U.S. telecommunication services, in an unwillingness to open up a modest 10% of its domestic communications market to European-wide bidding, and in a procurement policy for computers and peripherals which strongly favors national champions such as Bull S.A.,

Thomson-CSF and CIT-Alcatel, even though such policies are forbidden by terms of the EEC agreement, and meet with vigorous protest from other member countries. Finally, it has to be noted that the bitter conflicts often seen between left-wing and right-wing factions in French politics, and between employees and employers, preclude the creation of a Japanese-style consensus among government, industry, and labor.

The U.S. and Japanese experience in information technology shows the importance of creating a strong domestic market, and in this respect France has been one of the small number of countries with a respectable showing. The three-decade commitment to planning and government expenditures has also resulted in an industry which has shown the ability to generate exports in Europe. But as has been emphasized in the preceding two chapters, the continuing high costs of research, and the ubiquitous presence of American and Japanese firms, make it necessary for information technology industries to operate in a global environment, and above all to be continually responsive to the emergence of new products and new markets. Against these criteria the success of the French télématique policies has yet to be measured.

12.3.3. Other European Countries

Table 12.7 shows the 1982 data processing revenues for the 25 largest computer companies in Europe. Twelve of these have their parent company in the United States, four in West Germany, three in the United Kingdom, three in France, and one in each of the Netherlands, Sweden, and Italy (none in Japan). In a general way this reflects the information technology capabilities of the European countries. Of the European countries, the greatest strength in production as well as exports for electronic products is in West Germany (Table 12.8).

The approach of the Federal German Republic to information technology, like that of Japan and France, is highly interventionist, even though there is not quite the same master plan in place. The principal government agencies are the Ministry for Research and Technology (BMFT) and the Ministry of Economic Affairs (BMWI). The support programs are massive, broadly based, and, what is particularly important, have long planning horizons, so that results are cumulative and research is given the opportunity of turning into industrial capability.* Starting about 1973 there was a shift from taxation-based incentives (e.g., write-offs for research) to direct financial aid allocated for specific projects in key technologies such as optics, chemicals, electronic components, data processing, space research, and telecommunications. The thrust is to future-oriented, expensive research which would not be undertaken without government aid. In practice this means that most of the funds go to large companies (with Siemens taking on the role played by Fujitsu in Japan, ICL in the United Kingdom, and Bull S.A. in France), but there are also special programs directed to medium-sized and small firms.

*See de Vos (1978, Chap. 5) for details.

TABLE 12.7 REVENUES OF EUROPEAN DATA PROCESSING COMPANIES, 1982

Company	Location of Parent Company Headquarters	Revenues (millions of dollars)		
		DP, European	DP, Worldwide	Total, Worldwide
IBM[a,b]	U.S.	9,747	34,364	34,364
Olivetti	Italy	1,310	1,616	2,469
Siemens	W. Germany	1,270	1,270	16,980
Bull S. A.	France	1,200	1,238	1,238
Digital Equipment	U.S.	1,041	3,880	3,880
ICL	U.K.	994	1,304	1,304
Burroughs[c]	U.S.	970	3,848	4,186
Sperry	U.S.	813	2,800	5,571
Nixdorf	W. Germany	796	942	942
Control Data	U.S.	794	3,302	4,292
Philips[a]	Netherlands	787	1,047	16,104
NCR	U.S.	702	3,173	3,526
Hewlett-Packard	U.S.	694	2,212	4,254
CIT Alcatel	France	517	554	1,894
Honeywell	U.S.	478	1,684	5,490
Thompson-CSF[d]	France	299	320	4,139
Ericsson Information Systems	Sweden	287	387	387
Wang	U.S.	282	1,159	1,159
Kienzle	W. Germany	247	276	396
ITT	U.S.	220	600	15,958
Rank Xerox[a]	U.S.	211	n.a.[e]	8,450
Triumph Adler	W. Germany	204	443	809
Plessey[a]	U.K.	204	296	1,838
Ferranti	U.K.	197	218	589
Data General	U.S.	155	806	806

[a]Estimate.

[b]DP revenues include all activities.

[c]Figures for Europe include African revenues.

[d]DP revenues include photocopiers.

[e]Not available.

Source: "Europe's Leading Lights," *Datamation,* 29, no. 9 (September 1983), 185–87, with permission.

Perhaps the strongest feature of the West German approach is the way in which the many different institutions, industry sectors, and levels of government are all involved in the coordination process, which in this respect is much closer to the Japanese model than to the French. Thus in 1979 the total R&D budget was made up of $6.4 billion from the federal government, $3.7 billion from the Lander (state) and municipal governments, and $10.2 billion from the private sector. Subsidies to employ R&D personnel in industry came to $192 million from BMFT and $191 million from BMWI. Research funds are for pure science, conducted in a network of regionally coordinated centers, including universities and applied science institutes, which carry out R&D through contracts. The emphasis on electronics, microelectronics, and telecommunications is clear. Computers have been the

TABLE 12.8 ELECTRONIC PRODUCTION OF EUROPEAN COUNTRIES, 1980 (MILLIONS OF DOLLARS)

Country	Computer Systems	Control and Instrumentation	Communications and Telecommunications	Consumer	Components	Total
West Germany	2,641	3,347	3,896	3,937	5,355	19,176
France	1,988	1,017	8,042	1,017	1,912	13,976
United Kingdom	1,997	1,445	3,359	942	2,228	9,971
Italy	978	281	2,132	687	764	4,842
Netherlands	269	637	1,073	240	927	3,146
Belgium	410	200	1,114	499	529	2,752
Sweden	365	300	1,310	177	276	2,428

Source: Data from *Mackintosh Yearbook of West European Electronics Data* (London: Mackintosh Publications Ltd., 1980).

object of successive plans, with allocations for fundamental and applied research, hardware, applications, and training (387 million DM for 1967–1970, 2410 million DM for 1971–1975, and 1575 million DM for 1976–1979).* An Electronic Components Program (1974–1978) focused on integrated circuits and semiconductors, with the result that in 1981, among semiconductor industries in Europe, that of Germany was rated as having the best chance of survival.† At the same time there is strong support for field trials and pilot projects involving the *application* of information technology, as evidenced by Germany's presence in the European Space Agency (especially the joint ventures with France in the Symphonie and Telecom satellites) and the very extensive tests of Bildschirmtext, a videotex system patterned after the British Prestel, involving some 70,000 subscribers. Trade unions are influential in Germany, and the various levels of governments have responded to this by encouraging unions to become knowledgeable about computers and by studies and legislation concerning their social impact. The German government under Helmut Kohl increased its commitment to information technology. In May 1983 it announced plans to spend DM 3 billion over the next four years, an amount considerably greater than that of any other European country. Much of the research and development to be undertaken is along the lines of fifth-generation project in Japan, and the Alvey project in the United Kingdom. In summary, the technological and production capabilities for computer hardware, software, and telecommunications are consistent with Germany's position as the strongest economy in Europe. These capabilities derive from a long-term financial commitment to the information technologies, and there is a clear recognition of the crucial importance of the technologies to future industrial strategy.

Report Concerning the Developments in the Data Processing Sector in the Community ...tion *to the World Situation*, Vol. III, (Brussels: Commission of the European Community, 1979).

†G. Dosi, *Technical Change and Survival: Europe's Semiconductor Industry*, Sus European Research Centre, University of Sussex, 1981, p. 36.

With differences in scale appropriate to the size of the economy, and differences in emphasis that reflect the national tradition, the other countries in Europe have addressed the problem of maintaining industrial competitiveness by encouraging and adapting innovations based on microcomputers and information technology. The long-standing policy in the Netherlands has been to create a favorable *climate* for industry by promoting stable labor relations, the creation of a well-educated work force, and by aiding research indirectly through quasi-governmental agencies. But after planning studies on innovation, there has been a shift toward more direct support of targeted areas such as microelectronics, and "picking winners" where venture capital is needed. The importance of multinational companies to the Dutch economy has precluded the general adoption of protectionist measures such as local procurement, and of course the giant Philips company, with its multiple strengths in electronics, occupies a special place. In Sweden until even the late 1970s the vast preponderance of government funding went to declining industries such as steel, textiles, shipbuilding, and forest products. But a report of the influential Swedish Board for Technical Development, *Technology for the Futures: Perspectives 1979,* focused on the need to integrate electronics into industrial process control, communications, and engineering in general, and a subsequent report from the Commission on Computers and Electronics led to earmarked funds for computer-aided design and industrial robots. The Swedish multinational champion is L.M. Ericsson, which expanded from its base in telecommunications into terminals, minis, micros, office automation, and software, often in conjunction with companies abroad. Sweden has a solid engineering-based infrastructure, but research spending has been low and fragmented, and the government has become soberly aware of the need for innovation, strategic planning, and effective coordination of the public and private sectors in the face of international technological competition.

Accompanying all these national programs concentrating on information technology there have been persistent attempts to bring about coordinated efforts by common market countries. The stark choice of capitalizing on the potential of information technology or stagnating economically is put forward recurrently; the Fifth Parliament of the Council of Europe, held in 1981 at Helsinki, took Information/Communications Technologies and the Microelectronics Revolution as its theme. Much of the action has been directed at limiting the penetration of IBM, which as can be seen from Table 12.7, holds the dominant position in Europe as it does in other countries. The EEC pursued an antitrust suit against IBM for 10 years, trying to get IBM to release details about interfaces with peripherals so that plug-compatible manufacturers could compete more fairly.* Standards are another tool for isolating the European market, as seen in the European adoption of the Open Systems Interconnections (OSI) for communication protocols as opposed to IBM's System Network Architecture (SNA).† Most difficult to achieve

---

*Interestingly enough, the complaint was initiated by U.S. companies.

†Such technical barriers, however, are eventually overcome by building systems that can accept either protocol.

have been joint research programs. Although the EEC commissioner responsible for industrial affairs has had cooperative programs on information technology approved, funding and actual start on the work has been slow to materialize. The European Strategic Research Programme in Information Technology (ESPRIT), approved in 1983, is intended as a 10-year project, with the first 5-year phase costing about $1.3 billion, for which half the funds would come from industry and the other half from a tax levied on EEC members. But the record of cooperation between European countries on information technology has not been good; for example, a joint undertaking between CII-HB and Philips was short lived. Each country has tended to support its national champion and been reluctant to see integration with European competitors, even though special ventures with U.S. or Japanese companies for sharing technology and markets are not uncommon.

The sense of urgency, in all the major European countries, of the need to establish control over the information technology industries is very strong. In the larger countries, such as Germany, France, and the United Kingdom, the planning has extended over many years and the investments have been enormous. But individually, and even collectively, the European countries are waging an uphill struggle against the United States and Japan in their attempts to obtain a share of the global market or even to maintain a major presence in their own respective markets.*

12.4. THE GLOBAL VIEW

It would be possible to list, at length, reports about the importance of information technology from almost every industrialized country and would-be-industrialized country in the world. But it will be sufficient here to cite only a few other national studies in addition to those which have already been referenced. In Canada the principal agencies are the Department of Communications, the Science Council of Canada, the Canadian Radio and Telecommunications Commission, and the Ministry of Science and Technology. There are dozens of reports dating from the 1960s; three recent ones, *Telecommunications and Canada* (1979), *The Information Revolution and Its Implication for Canada* (Serafini and Andrieu, 1980), and *Planning Now for an Information Society—Tomorrow Is Too Late* (1982), reflect the sense of crisis.† The 1983 federal budget responded to this sense with C$828 million allocated for information technology developments. The closest approach to a national champion in Canada is Northern Telecom, a subsidiary of Bell Enterprises, which has expanded from its base product line of electronic exchanges to become a global company, marketing a wide variety of telecommunication and computer equipment. In Australia an increase in the value of computer imports

---

*For additional details on budgetary allocations of European countries to information technology, see Gassman (1984).

†See also Zeman et al. (1983) for a report published by the Province of Quebec.

from A\$64 million to A\$291 million between 1973 and 1979 spurred the call for an Australian information technology industry (see Caelli, 1980). In Brazil the Commission for the Coordination of Electronic Data Processing (CAPRE) took an aggressive role in promoting the use of computers and in building a national industry, with special emphasis on producing minicomputers for export to Latin American countries (see *Brazilian Computing Resources*, 1977). CAPRE's successor organization, Secretaria Especial de Informática (SEI) has been strongly influenced by the French Nora-Minc report.

Brazil is one of the developing countries that has aspirations to become a producer of at least selected products in information technology, as well as a consumer. After concentrating on the production of small computers, with some success, it has turned its attention to software. Other examples are countries in Southeast Asia (Malaysia, Taiwan, Korea), where there are plants for manufacturing chips and electronic products. The focus in developing countries, generally, has been on the *application* of computer technology to improve the quality of government administration and the productivity of industry. Toward this end, *The Application of Computer Technology for Development,* the very first report on computers for developing countries, published by the United Nations in 1971, emphasized education, training, and technology transfer, and this has been a theme of subsequent reports (see Bennett and Kalman, 1981). However, in the matter of transborder data flows and telecommunications, the developing countries have been more aggressive, as evidenced by the positions taken at UNESCO on the New World Information Order and at the SPIN conferences of the Intergovernmental Bureau for Information (see Section 11.2.1 and Jussawalla and Lamberton, 1982). With respect to telecommunications, at meetings of the International Telecommunication Union (ITU) developing countries insist on their right of *access,* by which is meant the right to space in the electromagnetic spectrum, and to have reserved places for geostationary orbiting satellites, even though few are ready to use the allotments. Several countries (e.g., India) see software as the most promising market sector to develop.

The pattern for industrialized nations throughout the world, and for would-be-industrialized nations as well, with respect to information technology is clear.

- National studies on innovation, technology transfer, and industrial strategy without fail identify microcomputers and telecommunications as pivotal industries of the future.
- In almost all countries there are calls for much greater support of these industries; in many these calls take the form of an appeal to create a national policy for information technology.
- Only in Japan and France are there seen to be in place policies that address the overall situation.
- Only in Japan is there a feeling that the technological capability of the country has been growing at a satisfactory rate, and confidence in the future competitive position.

TABLE 12.9 ELECTRONIC PRODUCTION (INDUSTRIAL, CONSUMER, COMPONENTS) OF MAJOR COUNTRIES

| | 1965 | | 1980 | |
	Revenues (millions of U.S. dollars)	Percent	Revenues (millions of U.S. dollars)	Percent
United States	17,552	69.4	104,326	58.1
West Germany	2,062	8.2	12,798	7.1
Japan	1,830	7.2	38,137	21.2
Total of three next largest countries	3,848	15.2	24,226	13.6
Total, six major countries	25,262	100.0	179,487	100.0

Source: Ministry of International Trade and Industry, Japan.

The driving force that has brought this pattern about is illustrated in its most elementary form by Table 12.9, which shows the change that has taken place in the worldwide production of electronic products (industrial, consumer, and components) between 1965 and 1980. Of course, electronic products are only part of the total range of information products, which include software, printed and electronically recorded data, communication and telecommunication devices, and much more, but they play a key role in the industries built around these other products. Table 12.9 suggests a trend to a duopoly, where two countries, the United States and Japan, dominate the industries which many believe will be the controlling ones from the 1990s and into the twenty-first century. It is difficult to believe that this will be allowed to happen, for it would represent a major realignment in the relative economic strengths of the free market nations. In spite of the great importance that countries have attached to information technology plans during the last 10 years, we can only expect that the emphasis will increase in the decade ahead.

BIBLIOGRAPHY

BENNETT, J. M., and R. E. KALMAN, *Computers in Developing Nations.* Amsterdam: North-Holland, 1981.

Brazilian Computing Resources, Special Edition. Brasilia: CAPRE, 1977 (see also *Technical Bulletins,* 1977–1979).

CAELLI, W. J., "Arguments for an Australian Information Technology Industry," in *Technological Change—Impact of Information Technology 1980,* ed. A. Goldsworthy. Canberra: Information Technology Council, 1980.

DIEBOLD, J., *The Information Technology Industries as a Case Example of International Trade Policy Issues in High Technology in the 1980's.* Institute for International Economics, 1982.

DE VOS, D., *Government and Microelectronics—The European Experience.* Hull, Quebec: Science Council of Canada, Canadian Government Publishing Centre, 1983.

EDELSTEIN, A. S., J. E. BOWES, and S. M. HARSEL, *Information Societies: Comparing the Japanese and American Experiences.* International Communication Centre, 1978.

FEIGENBAUM, E., and P. MCCORDUCK, *The Fifth Generation.* Reading, Mass.: Addison-Wesley, 1983.

GASSMAN, H. P., "Information Technology Policy in Europe and Japan", in *The Information Economy: Its Implication for Canada's Industrial Strategy,* C. C. Gotlieb, (ed.), Proceedings of a conference held at the University of Toronto, May 30–June 1, 1984, Ottawa, Royal Society of Canada (to appear).

GOLDSWORTHY, A., ed., *Technological Change—Impact of Information Technology 1980.* Canberra: Information Technology Council, 1980.

GOTLIEB, C. C., and Z. P. ZEMAN, *Towards a National Computer and Communications Policy: Seven National Approaches.* (Toronto: The Institute for Research on Public Policy, 1980).

HAZEWINDS, N., and J. TOOKER, *The U.S. Microelectronics Industry.* Elmsford, N.Y.: Pergamon Press, 1982.

Japan Electronics Almanac. Tokyo: Dempa Publications, 1980.

JUSSAWALLA, M., and D. M. LAMBERTON, eds., *Communications, Economics and Development.* Elmsford, N.Y.: Pergamon Press, 1982.

Long-Range Goals in International Telecommunications and Information—An Outline for United States Policy, Report of the National Telecommunications and Information Administration. Washington, D.C.: U.S. Government Printing Office, 1983.

NORA, S., and A. MINC, *The Computerization of Society: A Report to the President of France.* Cambridge, Mass.: MIT Press, 1980. Originally published as *L'Informatisation de la Société* Paris: La Documentation Francaise, 1978.

Planning Now for an Information Society—Tomorrow Is Too Late, Hull, Quebec, Canada: Science Council of Canada, Report 33, Canadian Government Publishing Centre, 1982.

SCHILLER, D., *Telematics and Government.* Norwood, N.J.: Ablex, 1982.

SERAFINI, S., and M. ANDRIEU, *The Information Revolution and Its Implications for Canada,* Communications Economics Branch, Department of Communications, 1980.

Telecommunications and Canada, Report of the Consultative Committee on the Implications for Canadian Sovereignty. Hull, Quebec: Canadian Government Publishing Centre, 1979.

The Foundation of United States Information Policy. Washington, D.C.: National Telecommunications and Information Administration, U.S. Department of Commerce, 1980.

ZEMAN, Z. P., C. C. GOTLIEB, R. A. RUSSELL, K. HANCOCK, and U. DOMB, *Les Stratégies de communication dans quatre pays.* Quebec: Ministère des Communications du Québec, 1983.

Index

DATE DUE